The Crucible of Desegregation

The Chicago Series in Law and Society
Edited by John M. Conley, Charles Epp, and Lynn Mather

ALSO IN THE SERIES:

Cooperation without Submission: Indigenous Jurisdictions in Native Nation-US Engagements
by Justin B. Richland

BigLaw: Money and Meaning in the Modern Law Firm
by Mitt Regan and Lisa H. Rohrer

Union by Law: Filipino American Labor Activists, Rights Radicalism, and Racial Capitalism
by Michael W. McCann with George I. Lovell

Speaking for the Dying: Life-and-Death Decisions in Intensive Care
by Susan P. Shapiro

Just Words, Third Edition: Law, Language and Power
by John M. Conley, William M. O'Barr, and Robin Conley Riner

Islands of Sovereignty: Haitian Migration and the Borders of Empire
by Jeffrey S. Kahn

Building the Prison State: Race and the Politics of Mass Incarceration
by Heather Schoenfeld

Navigating Conflict: How Youth Handle Trouble in a High-Poverty School
by Calvin Morrill and Michael Musheno

The Sit-Ins: Protest and Legal Change in the Civil Rights Era
by Christopher W. Schmidt

Working Law: Courts, Corporations, and Symbolic Civil Rights
by Lauren B. Edelman

The Myth of the Litigious Society: Why We Don't Sue
by David M. Engel

Policing Immigrants: Local Law Enforcement on the Front Lines
by Doris Marie Provine, Monica W. Varsanyi, Paul G. Lewis, and Scott H. Decker

The Seductions of Quantification: Measuring Human Rights, Gender Violence, and Sex Trafficking
by Sally Engle Merry

Invitation to Law and Society: An Introduction to the Study of Real Law, Second Edition
by Kitty Calavita

Pulled Over: How Police Stops Define Race and Citizenship
by Charles R. Epp, Steven Maynard-Moody, and Donald Haider-Markel

The Three and a Half Minute Transaction: Boilerplate and the Limits of Contract Design
by Mitu Gulati and Robert E. Scott

Additional series titles follow index.

The Crucible of Desegregation

The Uncertain Search for Educational Equality

R. SHEP MELNICK

The University of Chicago Press
Chicago and London

The University of Chicago Press, Chicago 60637
The University of Chicago Press, Ltd., London
© 2023 by The University of Chicago
All rights reserved. No part of this book may be used or reproduced in any manner whatsoever without written permission, except in the case of brief quotations in critical articles and reviews. For more information, contact the University of Chicago Press, 1427 E. 60th St., Chicago, IL 60637.
Published 2023
Printed and bound by CPI Group (UK) Ltd, Croydon, CR0 4YY

32 31 30 29 28 27 26 25 24 23   1 2 3 4 5

ISBN-13: 978-0-226-82471-0 (cloth)
ISBN-13: 978-0-226-82552-6 (paper)
ISBN-13: 978-0-226-82551-9 (e-book)
DOI: https://doi.org/10.7208/chicago/9780226825519.001.0001

Library of Congress Cataloging-in-Publication Data

Names: Melnick, R. Shep, 1951– author.
Title: The crucible of desegregation : the uncertain search for educational equality / R. Shep Melnick.
Other titles: Uncertain search for educational equality | Chicago series in law and society.
Description: Chicago : The University of Chicago Press, 2023. | Series: Chicago series in law and society | Includes bibliographical references and index.
Identifiers: LCCN 2022047673 | ISBN 9780226824710 (cloth) | ISBN 9780226825526 (paperback) | ISBN 9780226825519 (e-book)
Subjects: LCSH: School integration—Law and legislation—United States. | Segregation in education—Law and legislation—United States. | School integration—United States—History. | Education and state—United States.
Classification: LCC KF4155.M45 2023 | DDC 344.73/0798—dc23/eng/20221201
LC record available at https://lccn.loc.gov/2022047673

♾ This paper meets the requirements of ANSI/NISO Z39.48-1992 (Permanence of Paper).

To my children

Contents

Preface ix

1 Why Desegregation Still Matters 1
2 The Great Debate 26
3 Critical Junctures 62
4 Breakthrough: The Reconstruction of Southern Education 82
5 Supreme Abdication 107
6 Left Adrift: Desegregation in the Lower Courts 145
7 Varieties of Desegregation Experiences 164
8 Termination without End 181
9 Looking Beyond Courts: ESEA and Title VI 209
10 What Have We Learned? 248

Notes 271
Index 303

Preface

Between 1965 and 1980 the federal government undertook an ambitious and controversial effort to desegregate American public schools. This project produced both spectacular successes and tragic failures. Since the key events occurred over half a century ago, to most people—including, no doubt, the majority of readers of this book—school desegregation is but a distant memory. Nor is there a shortage of books and articles exploring the topic from a variety of points of view. Why revisit the issue now?

This book began its life as one chapter in a book on the American "civil rights state," by which I mean the extensive regulatory apparatus developed since 1964 to prohibit discrimination on the basis of race, sex, language, disability, age, and other factors. School desegregation was a defining moment in the creation of this civil rights state. Here was the first appearance of the court-agency alliance that has characterized many other forms of regulation. Here the courts invented the "structural injunction," an enforcement tool used by courts not just to restructure school systems, but also to reform prison, police forces, institutions for the mentally ill and developmentally disabled, public housing authorities, and state welfare offices. And here interpretation of civil rights statutes and the Fourteenth Amendment shifted from color-blindness to an emphasis on achieving racial proportionality. In desegregation cases, judges for the first time confronted difficult questions about the education of English learners and students with disabilities. Their rulings on these and related topics stimulated further action by Congress and the executive branch, substantially expanding the scope of the civil rights state. In short, school desegregation was a crucial component of what political scientists and historians call "institution building." Tracing its origins helps us understand the peculiar nature of our expansive civil rights state.

William Faulkner's famous lines—"The past is never dead. It's not even past"—apply particularly well to school desegregation. Not only are some of the desegregation orders issued in the 1960s and 1970s still in effect, but the issues at the center of those controversies remain as important as ever. The academic achievement gap between white and black students remains disturbingly large. As the proportion of white students in the school-age population declines, more black and Hispanic students attend predominantly minority schools, a trend often misleadingly labeled "resegregation." For a variety of reasons (these issues are rarely simple), black and Hispanic students receive more out-of-school punishments and fewer slots in gifted and talented programs than their white and Asian peers. School districts across the country are experimenting with methods for creating more racial diversity within their elementary and secondary schools and improving the quality of education offered to minority students. The Obama and Biden administrations have interpreted Title VI of the Civil Rights Act to prohibit practices such as out-of-school punishments that have a "disparate impact" on minority students and contribute to the "school to prison pipeline." Thus, a second reason to study school desegregation: coming to a better understanding of the causes of racial disparities in education, what has worked in the past, what has not, and how we can do better.

One cannot seriously address these perennial questions about race and education without asking a more basic one: What does it mean for desegregation to "work"? A central theme of this book is that the Supreme Court and the federal judiciary as a whole have been grossly negligent in failing to provide a full and forthright answer to this pivotal question. Decades of ambiguous, meandering, inconsistent, and at times disingenuous rulings by the Supreme Court—documented in chapters 2, 5, and 8—left lower courts adrift amid a sea of competing claims by self-proclaimed desegregation experts, rapidly changing demographics, volatile politics, and excruciating policy choices (the topic of chapters 6 and 7). In public policy as in ordinary life, if you don't know where you are going, you probably won't get there. Thus, a third reason for revisiting the desegregation saga: it forces us to think harder about what we mean by desegregation and integration, why we want them, how best to achieve them, and the relative ability of various government institutions to move us in that direction.

A final reason for studying desegregation is to help us reach a more adequate understanding of how the American political regime has dealt with the country's original sin of racial oppression. According to one commonly held view, school desegregation was working until it ran headlong into northern racism—and then stopped dead in its tracks. In other words, the civil rights revolution of the 1960s and the great statutes it produced did not put an end to racism, but merely led it to take more subtle forms. A leading proponent of this point of view is Nikole Hannah-Jones, the prime mover behind the *New York Times*'s "1619 Project." That ambitious project asserts that the true founding of the United States occurred when the first slaves were brought to this country, rather than in 1776 when we announced the "self-evident truth" that "all men are created equal"; or in 1789 when we created a new Constitution to "promote the general Welfare" and "secure the Blessings of Liberty"; or at the end of the Civil War, which Lincoln saw as the moment of a "rebirth of freedom"; or with the enactment of the seminal civil rights statutes of 1964–65. According to this view, we have never moved far beyond slavery and Jim Crow. White supremacy remains intact; Jim Crow 2.0 is simply a more sophisticated and disguised form of its predecessor.

According to an alternative point of view, desegregation succeeded admirably when it targeted de jure segregation in the South. The problem came when the effort abandoned a color-blind understanding of the Equal Protection clause and the 1964 Civil Rights Act in order to overcome the consequences of residential segregation and to eliminate what came to be known as "racial isolation." Pursuing racial balance became an end in itself, leading to "white flight" and the deteriorating condition of public education in urban areas. This reorientation betrayed the guiding principle behind the initial desegregation effort, namely that government should never categorize, reward, or punish people on the basis of their race. The eventual result, according to this viewpoint, is the emergence of a new form of racism that hides behind the slogan of "diversity." The solution is to return to the "color-blind" interpretation of equal protection endorsed by those who argued for and decided *Brown v. Board of Education* and those who wrote and voted for the 1964 Civil Rights Act.

A principal argument of this book is that neither of these commonly held positions is adequate for understanding either the history of school desegregation or the challenges currently confronting public education. The claim that desegregation was "working" until halted by racist opposition is hard to sustain when one looks in detail at the diverse educational experiments taking place in cities throughout the country. Desegregation orders were both diverse and experimental because the Supreme Court never explained what lower court judges were expected to achieve. Racist opposition to busing there clearly was. Not to be overlooked, though, was the extent to which many desegregation orders not only failed to produce the promised educational revolution, but reduced the quality of education provided to students of all races and ethnicities in some of the school districts subject to desegregation orders. Improving the quality of education provided to black and Hispanic students requires far more than having them attend schools with white children. Nothing brings this lesson home as much as a close look at the history of school desegregation in cities throughout the nation.

The principal shortcoming of the alternative, color-blind approach to desegregation is that it proved far too easy to evade. Years of resistance, dissimulation, and administrative manipulation by southern school officials convinced federal judges and administrators that they needed statistical evidence to ensure that school districts were making good-faith efforts not just to undo legal segregation, but to address its subtle, long-lasting effects. That, in a nutshell, is the story of chapter 4. Within a few years the numerical guidelines first employed by the Department of Health, Education, and Welfare and the Fifth Circuit Court of Appeals had been transformed into de facto quotas that district court judges were expected to meet regardless of educational consequences—a classic example of what in the sociological literature is known as "goal displacement." The eventual misuse of statistics to achieve racial proportionality should not, though, blind us to the inadequacy of a color-blind approach for uprooting the racial caste system of the South and addressing subtle forms of discrimination throughout the country.

After two centuries of slavery and many decades of Jim Crow, in the 1950s and 1960s the United States finally made a major effort to address racial inequality. The initial efforts to desegregate southern schools were far too weak; the subsequent efforts to reduce racial isolation throughout the country were often counterproductive. Neither of the simple stories we have constructed to make sense of school desegregation captures the rich complexity of this multi-decade experience.

Overcoming the legacy of centuries of slavery, segregation, and discrimination requires far more than good intentions and emotionally freighted slogans. Unfortunately, it frequently requires more knowledge about human behavior than we have so far been able to muster. That is particularly true of education, the focus of this book. A political system that for decades provided the legal framework for the subordination of African Americans cannot escape responsibility for addressing the deeply rooted consequences of that subordination. As President Johnson explained in his famous 1965 address at Howard University,

> You do not wipe away the scars of centuries by saying: Now you are free to go where you want, and do as you desire, and choose the leaders you please. You do not take a person who, for years, has been hobbled by chains and liberate him, bring him up to the starting line of a race and then say, "you are free to

compete with all the others," and still justly believe that you have been completely fair.[1]

In the United States, we have long expected public education to level the playing field, helping those who grow up in disadvantaged families and neighborhoods to compete with their more fortunate peers. But we also know that with each year of schooling, the achievement gap between affluent students and poor students and between white students and black students often grows wider rather than narrower. Large-scale answers to this monumental problem still elude us.

One of the key lessons of the desegregation saga is that no silver bullet shot from above—whether it be by Congress, the federal courts, or even state governments—is likely to ensure equal educational opportunity. In the long run, *how* education policies are carried out at the local level is more important than the details of policy pronouncements issued from above. As Frederick Hess puts it, "What matters in schooling is what actually happens to 50 million kids in 100,000 schools. That's *all* implementation." Policies announced from Washington, state capitals, or the federal bench, he emphasizes, "can make people do things, but it can't make them do them well."[2] School culture is more important than rules or even money—but far more difficult to alter in a beneficial direction. If the history of desegregation reminds us of the difficulty of the task of providing greater educational opportunity, it should also remind us of the importance of that endeavor.

This book does not culminate in a grand plan to promote racial equality. It is content to offer a detailed analysis of how our political and legal institutions have dealt with these problems in the past, how their diverse efforts have fared, and the competing visions of antidiscrimination policy that continue to roil our political community. Although it does not provide a framework for action, my hope is that it will provide a useful political and legal education for those involved in the crucial yet frustratingly difficult job of education reform.

My greatest debt is to the scholars whose works have helped me understand not just school desegregation, but the larger effort to address racial inequality through government action. Some of these people I know well; others I have never met. Ideologically and methodologically, they are a motley crew. In fact, I suspect that some of them would not want to be in the same room as the others. Yet I have learned from them all. At the top of this list are David Kirp, whose writings on desegregation are unparalleled, and the late Hugh Davis Graham, whose work has guided me through the thicket of civil rights law and policy. Close behind are Joshua Dunn, John Skrentny, Stephan

Halpern, Gary Orfield, Gareth Davis, Owen Fiss, David Armor, Kevin McMahon, Max Eden, Abigail and Stephen Thernstrom, and, as always, Peter Schuck. Josh Dunn and Martin West started me down this road many years ago when they asked me to contribute an essay to their volume *From Schoolhouse to Courthouse: The Judiciary's Role in American Education*. Josh has offered me comments on the manuscript, as have Paul Peterson, Chester Finn, Michael Hanson, Mike Petrilli, Adam White, my Boston College colleague Michael Hartney, and two anonymous but extraordinarily helpful reviewers. Sam Hayes and Nathan Davies helped whip the footnotes into shape. For years my wife, Joanne Linden, carefully listened to and skillfully challenged my evolving arguments on the topic. My wonderful colleagues in the Boston College Political Science Department created the perfect intellectual environment for the long, slow development of this book. My thanks also to the editors at the University of Chicago Press who helped me turn an unwieldy manuscript into a shorter and, I hope, more readable book.

1

Why Desegregation Still Matters

In the summer of 2019, the issue of busing to achieve racial integration of public schools suddenly emerged as a salient and divisive issue in the battle for the Democratic presidential nomination. Then-Senator Kamala Harris criticized Joe Biden for bragging about his ability to work with segregationist senators in the 1970s, adding, "Not only that, but you also worked with them to oppose busing." What drew media attention to Harris's charge was her personal story: "And, you know, there was a little girl in California who was part of the second class to integrate her public schools, and she was bused to school every day. And that little girl was me." "Do you agree today," she asked the former vice-president, "that you were wrong to oppose busing in America then?"

Biden tried to defuse the issue by claiming that he only opposed busing imposed by the federal government, not the form of voluntary busing adopted by the Berkeley, California, school district attended by young Kamala Harris. While it is true that Biden had focused his effort on limiting the authority of federal courts and agencies to mandate busing, he was highly critical of all efforts to create racially balanced schools by transporting students far beyond their neighborhoods. "I oppose busing," he stated in a lengthy 1975 TV interview:

> It's an asinine concept, the utility of which has never been proven to me.... The new integration plans being offered are really just quota-systems to assure a certain number of blacks, Chicanos, or whatever in each school. That, to me is the most racist concept you can come up with. What it says is, in order for your child with curly black hair, brown eyes, and dark skin to be able to learn anything, he needs to sit next to my blond-haired, blue-eyed son. That's racist!

Who the hell do we think we are, that the only way a black man or woman can learn is if they rub shoulders with my white child?[1]

Opposition to court-imposed busing was not a momentary concern for Senator Biden. Throughout the 1970s and early 1980s, he supported most (but not all) of the antibusing legislation that came to the Senate floor. In 1981, he reported that "no issue has consumed more of my time and energy."[2] He took this position in part because the extensive busing plan mandated for Wilmington, Delaware, by the federal courts was highly unpopular in his state. But it is also clear that Biden thought that such desegregation orders were a huge mistake, both politically and educationally.

During the 1970s, the busing issue nearly tore the Democratic Party apart. Antibusing furor helped the arch-segregationist George Wallace win the Democratic primaries not just in Florida, Maryland, North Carolina, and Tennessee, but also in traditionally liberal Michigan. In the 1972 primaries, nearly as many Democrats voted for Wallace as for the eventual nominee, George McGovern. In the years that followed, many northern liberal Senators and members of the House joined Biden in supporting legislation to limit the authority of federal courts and agencies to order transportation of students beyond the nearest or next nearest schools. Only use of the Senate filibuster—previously the preferred tool of southern segregationists—by other Senate Democrats (including Senator McGovern) prevented most of these restrictions from becoming law.

A frequently cited 1973 Gallup poll found that only 5 percent of the public supported mandatory busing to achieve racial balance.[3] Other polls in the 1970s (and later in the 1990s) found support for busing in the 15–20 percent range, with 75–80 percent of the public consistently opposed.[4] Desegregation orders that required students to travel far beyond their neighborhoods seldom garnered support from Hispanic and Asian families and community leaders. By the mid-1980s, support for busing among African Americans fell below 50 percent—in part because their children often had the longest bus rides and in part because the educational benefits of desegregation plans frequently proved disappointing.[5] In short, not since Prohibition had a federal policy provoked such strong opposition. Republicans—including President Nixon—realized that this was a wedge issue they could use to pull voters away from the Democratic Party. Most Democratic elected officials were understandably relieved when the issue slowly faded from view. Democrats who could remember the 1970s were in no hurry to repeat the experience.

Although Senator Harris had hoped to use the busing issue to strengthen her support among African American voters, it soon became apparent that she did not want to pull the Party back into the busing maelstrom. A few days after the July debate, she indicated that she and Biden differed little on the issue, explaining to reporters that "busing is a tool among many that should be considered" by local school districts. Under current circumstances, she maintained, there is no need for federal mandates.[6] Thus muted, the summer kerfuffle did not prevent Biden from choosing Harris as his running mate. Nor did it damage Biden's standing among African American leaders and voters. Indeed, it was their strong support for his candidacy that resurrected his campaign in the spring of 2020.

The Return—and Reconfiguration—of the Desegregation Debate

As much as President Biden and most other Democrats would like to avoid a return to the harsh desegregation debates of the 1970s, there are a number of reasons to believe the issue will return to center stage in coming years. The long-standing rift within the Democratic Party and among civil rights advocates—between those who believed that busing had been a tragic mistake and those who insisted that opposition to busing was based on nothing but racism—has been papered over, but not resolved. This schism was apparent in the many media stories commenting on the Biden-Harris exchange. For example, Sherrilyn Ifill, president of the National Association for the Advancement of Colored People (NAACP) Legal Defense and Education Fund, Inc., wrote in *Slate* that the Democratic debate

> reignited the most resilient and pernicious myths about busing and school desegregation, myths that continue to thwart this country's efforts to fully achieve the goal of school desegregation. That busing has long been presented as an independent evil worthy of bipartisan resistance in both white and black communities represents the triumph of a false narrative package to excuse one of the ugliest and most destabilizing realities of American society: the extent to which raw racial prejudice and the protection of white supremacy have divided the nation since its founding through today.

Busing, she maintained, worked. Only racial animus led to its demise. To bring home the point, she cited a 1972 report by her organization "provocatively titled 'It's not the distance, "It's the Niggers."'" Half a century later, racial prejudice hiding behind opposition to "forced busing," Ifill argued, threatens to prevent the country from addressing the "resegregation" of our public schools.[7]

This argument was presented in greater depth a week later by Nikole Hannah-Jones, the *New York Times* writer, Pulitzer Prize winner, and guiding force behind the *Times's 1619 Project*. The title of her July 2019 article announced its central theme: "It Was Never About Busing: Court-Ordered Desegregation Worked. But White Racism Made It Hard to Accept."[8] Court orders mandating racial balance in urban schools, she claimed, provided substantial benefits to black students without harming whites. Opposition from politicians such as Biden was based entirely on their willingness to kowtow to racist voters. Since such policies "worked," they should be reinstated. Long-time busing advocate and UCLA professor Gary Orfield reiterated this position, as did Dartmouth professor Matthew Delmont, who argued in a 2019 *Atlantic* article that "the successes of school desegregation have been drowned out by a chorus of voices insisting busing was an inconvenient, unfair, and failed experiment."[9] In another *Atlantic* article spurred by the Biden-Harris debate, Will Stancil wrote that "scholars have used the moment to chip away at resilient myths about busing," and to point out that "as a method of producing school integration, court-ordered busing was generally effective."[10] Journalists, academics, and activists routinely claim not only that our schools are "resegregating," but that opposition to busing by politicians like Joe Biden was responsible for the failure of integration efforts. "Antiracism," they suggest, requires us to embrace the policies that provoked so much opposition decades ago.

Four factors have reignited and reshaped the desegregation debate. Most obvious is the renewed attention to questions of racial equality spurred by the mass protests of 2020. If, as many people (including President Biden) claim, the United States is characterized by "systemic racism," then the country's educational system is a key component of that unjust system. Decades of research indicate that the concentration of low-income minority students in urban schools contributes to the racial achievement gap, which has remained stubbornly large since the late 1980s. Given the extent to which the student population in many large cities has become overwhelmingly black and Hispanic, addressing this problem might well require us to take a fresh look at some of the student assignment policies rejected in the 1970s—especially those that cross municipal lines.

A second key factor is the troubling combination of the persistence of the racial achievement gap and economic changes that have put a premium on education. From 1970, when desegregation finally took hold in the South, through the mid-1980s, the racial achievement gap measured by the National Assessment of Educational Progress test narrowed significantly, declining in both math and reading for all age groups. For some age groups, the gap was cut nearly in half. Then progress stalled. Although there has been some improvement since 2000, the gap has been depressingly persistent for several decades.[11] Education reforms promoted by the Clinton, Bush, and Obama administrations and a variety of state governors have highlighted the problem, instituted innovative programs, and sometimes met with mild success. Meanwhile, though, the economic consequences of these educational disparities have grown more dire.

As a result of technological change, globalization, and immigration, over the past half century education has become far more important for economic success. Since 1970, the wages of those with a high school degree or less have not just stagnated but declined. Meanwhile, the income of those with a college degree has increased substantially. The result is increasing inequality and reduced mobility. African American and Hispanic workers are not the only ones to feel the sting of these developments, but they make up a disproportionate share of those left behind in the new economy.[12] Without substantial improvement in public education, these trends will continue.

The third key factor is demographic change. During the "civil rights revolution" of the 1960s, school desegregation could be seen in simple black-and-white terms. The overriding goal was dismantling the Jim Crow system in the South. Today the picture is much more complicated. By 2017, white students constituted less than half the public-school population, twenty-four million out of the nearly fifty-one million enrolled in public elementary and secondary schools. Since 2000 the percentage of African American students has declined slightly to 15 percent of the total, while Hispanics have risen to 28 percent, Asian Americans to about 5 percent, and those reporting "two or more races" to 5 percent.[13] Over the next decade the proportion of Anglos in public schools is expected to decline to 45 percent, and Hispanics to grow to 29 percent. In the West, Hispanics already outnumber Anglos 42 percent to 38 percent. Even in the South (including Texas), Hispanics have overtaken African Americans, 25 percent to 23 percent.[14] During the first decade of the twenty-first century, the student body of the twenty largest school systems in the country was made up of 20 percent Anglos, 38 percent Hispanics, 32 percent African Americans, and 9 percent Asians. In 2017 the percentage of white students was 7 percent in Los Angeles and Miami-Dade County; 5 percent in Dallas; 8 percent in Houston; 2 percent in Detroit; 12 percent in Chicago; 14 percent in San Francisco and Philadelphia; 15 percent in Boston; and 16 percent in New York City.[15] In the largest school systems, only those in the South (primarily Florida) enrolled a majority of Anglo students.[16]

The most obvious consequence of this demographic shift is a substantial increase in the number of schools that are predominantly "minority"—a term that is rapidly losing its meaning. Today almost half of black and Hispanic students attend schools with very few whites. This forces us to confront the question of what we mean by the crucial term "desegregation." Does desegregation depend on the number of whites in a school or classroom, the number of whites and Asians, the percentage of students who are black or Hispanic, or just the percentage of African Americans? Given that many people consider themselves both Hispanic and white, how do we determine who counts as "white" or "minority"? In the 1960s and 1970s, the implicit goal of desegregation plans was to make virtually all schools majority white. But today, making schools majority white is out of the question in many parts of the country, and may at times conflict with the goal of promoting racial and ethnic diversity.

We frequently hear that in recent years our schools have been "resegregated." If this description means that the number of white students in schools attended by the average black and Hispanic students has decreased, then it is true. If it suggests that the average white student is going to school with more white children, it is false: in fact, the average white student now goes to school with more non-white students than in years past. Indeed, a 2019 analysis conducted by the *Washington Post* found that "the number of children attending U.S. public schools with students of other races has nearly doubled over the past quarter-century, a little-noted surge that reflects the nation's shifting demographics."[17]

In the 1970s, the debate over busing centered on the question of whether minority students in the inner cities would be transported to schools in the predominantly white suburbs and white students from the suburbs would be assigned to schools in the predominantly minority urban core. Today that picture has been altered significantly. As Brookings demographer William Frey has pointed out,

> The black city/white suburb paradigm has almost completely broken down. Only in slowly growing northern parts of the country does this stereotype partially hold, and even there changes are afoot as newly arrived Hispanics and Asians contribute to population gains. . . . The old path of white flight to the suburbs is now followed by Hispanics, Asians, and, to a greater extent than ever before, blacks—all aspiring to achieve the suburban American Dream.[18]

If some minority students have become more isolated in urban schools, others have become more integrated with white students in suburban schools. Such demographic changes help explain why the percentage of white students attending predominantly white schools has markedly declined.

On the one hand, these demographic shifts have made the case for addressing the inadequacies of predominantly minority schools more compelling. On the other hand, they have also made the meaning of "integration" more obscure. Simply reassigning the decreasing number of white students in metropolitan areas is unlikely to significantly improve the quality of education for black and Hispanic students. Old problems remain, but the old remedies do not fit the new demographic reality.

Nowhere are the implication of these new demographics more evident than in the current debate over selective "exam schools." In Boston, New York, San Francisco, Virginia's Loudoun County, and elsewhere, these schools have come under attack for enrolling too few African American and Hispanic students. To address this problem, some school districts have reduced (or eliminated) the weight placed on entrance exams and grades, and increased the weight put on race-related factors. The biggest losers in this shift have not been white students, but Asian Americans, who have often vigorously opposed the demotion of exams.

A final factor contributing to the renewed debate over desegregation is the changing roles of the courts and local school officials. From the late 1960s through the 1980s, the federal courts were the driving force behind desegregation—in fact virtually the only source of governmental support for busing. They frequently (but not always) faced recalcitrant state and local officials. Today, in contrast, the courts have become a major *obstacle* to race-based student assignment plans adopted by local school districts. In its 2007 *Parents Involved* decision, a divided Supreme Court struck down plans in Seattle, Washington, and Louisville, Kentucky, that based school assignments in part on race.[19] The Court held that the use of racial classifications is constitutional only if it serves a "compelling state interest" and is "narrowly tailored" to meet that goal. Exactly how and when schools can use racial assignments to enhance educational opportunity and diversity remains unclear, in part because the deciding vote in the case was cast by Justice Kennedy, whose concurring opinion was characteristically enigmatic. Once again, the Supreme Court put some of the hardest questions off to another day.

The Louisville and Seattle examples indicate the extent to which many school boards, school superintendents, and other local officials are searching for ways to reduce the concentration of poor minority students in city schools. A 2020 study by the Century Foundation identified 140 public school districts and charter networks that voluntarily—that is, without being subject to a desegregation order or other legal agreement—"consider race and/or socioeconomic status in their student assignment or admissions policies." These policies include redrawing attendance zone boundaries to increase racial and socioeconomic diversity; magnet schools that consider race and socioeconomic status (SES) for assignments; transfer policies designed to increase diversity; and "controlled choice" plans that take racial and SES diversity into account when considering which students will be given their top choice of schools.[20] No doubt this trend will continue as school leaders pledge to combat "systemic racism."

How many of these plans to promote racial and SES diversity will survive judicial review is one of the biggest questions in desegregation law. The Court's decision in *Parents Involved* did not limit school districts' authority to seek more socioeconomic diversity in their schools. Unlike race, SES is not a "suspect classification" subject to the restrictions noted above. But given the close relationship between race and SES in the United States and the emphasis many school leaders have placed on racial diversity, the outcome of the extensive litigation to come will depend on the details of schools' plans, the justifications offered by school officials, and the decisions of a federal judiciary stocked with many Bush and Trump appointees.

Presidential administrations continue to influence desegregation policy not just through judicial appointments, but also through federal agencies' rules and guidance documents. During the Obama Administration, the Department of Education issued guidelines suggesting how school districts could increase racial diversity within the confines of Justice Kennedy's concurring opinion in *Parents Involved*. It also issued controversial rules on racial disparities in school discipline and allocation of school resources. (These administrative actions are described in chapter 9.) Although the Trump administration withdrew the school-discipline guidelines, those guidelines will likely be reinstated in some form by the Biden Departments of Education and Justice. These reinstatements, too, will become the target of judicial challenges.

Learning from the Past

As a new chapter in the desegregation controversy begins, we have an opportunity to reflect on the lessons of the long first round of policymaking. Many of the hundreds of desegregation orders first imposed in the 1960s and 1970s remained in place through the turn of the millennium. By 2010, though, most of the nearly 1,200 school districts previously under court order had been declared "unitary" and released from judicial supervision. These "unitary" findings put an end to the pathbreaking busing plans for Charlotte, North Carolina; the long-standing and controversial plans for Detroit, Denver, Cleveland, Kansas City, St. Louis, Columbus, and Dayton; and the urban/suburban busing plan for Indianapolis and Senator Biden's Delaware. As we transition from one stage of desegregation to another, now is the time to step back and look at what we have learned over the past half century.

This book offers a detailed examination of the evolution of federal desegregation policy from *Brown* in 1954 through the termination of desegregation decrees in the first decades of the twenty-first century, with an emphasis on the interaction between federal judges and administrators. What has a half century of desegregation taught us? The length of this book indicates that there is no simple answer to this question. With policy questions of this magnitude, there seldom are. Nonetheless, this book develops three key themes that can inform the coming debate.

The first is the continuing ambiguity of the key term "desegregation." Remarkable as it may seem, the courts have never offered a clear definition of the central goal, laid out the rationale for competing understandings, or explained how we would know that a school system has attained "unitary status." One lesson we should learn from the past is the importance of being clear about what we are trying to achieve and why.

The second theme is the importance of institutions: the inherent difficulty of changing the practices of educational institutions combined with the fragmented nature of American political institutions. Here the principal lesson is the difficulty of trying to implement major educational change from the center—especially when the effort has little political support. With little guidance from the Supreme Court, federal district court judges developed desegregation plans on an ad hoc, city-by-city basis, with little effort to compare the effectiveness of competing approaches. Educational reformers of the 1960s and 1970s can be forgiven for believing that court-ordered desegregation could be the silver bullet that would transform the American educational system. Half a century later, there is no excuse for such wishful thinking.

The third theme is the key role desegregation played in the development of the American civil rights state. Since 1964 the US has built an extensive regulatory apparatus to address discrimination based on race, ethnicity, language, national origin, gender, sexual orientation, religion, disability, and age. As the first major initiative of the post-1964 era, the desegregation effort shaped the institutions of this civil rights state in many ways. The expansion of the civil rights state increased the capacity of the national government to address questions of racial justice. At the same time, though, it added to the federal government's agenda a variety of educational issues that compete— and at times even conflict—with desegregation objectives. The third lesson, then, is to understand how these new powers and new purposes have complicated the desegregation equation.

THEME I: WHAT DOES "DESEGREGATION" MEAN?

In his famous concurring opinion in the 1973 *Denver* case, Justice Lewis Powell wrote, "At the outset, one must try to identify the constitutional right which is being enforced. This is not easy, as the precedents have been far from explicit."[21] As we will see, that was an understatement. The Court's subsequent opinions did more to muddy than resolve this central question.

Chief Justice Warren's opinion for a unanimous Court in *Brown* made little attempt to define the constitutional rights of Linda Brown and her fellow students, or to explain what school systems must do to comply with the Court's interpretation of the Fourteenth Amendment. In its pivotal reinterpretation of *Brown* in *Green v. County School Board of New Kent County* (1968), the Court held that once a school system has been found guilty of segregation, it must take immediate action to achieve "unitary status." In Justice Brennan's memorable phrase, those school districts have a duty to "fashion steps which promise realistically to convert promptly to a system without a 'white' school and a 'Negro' school, but just schools."[22] Although achieving "unitary status" has for decades remained the key judicial test for whether a school district has successfully desegregated, lower court judges and Supreme Court justices have frequently admitted that they did not know what the term means. In 1992 Justice Kennedy conceded that "the term 'unitary' does not have fixed meaning or content."[23] A few years later, district court judge Sue Robinson wrote in the Delaware case, "Although the attainment of 'unitary status' has been the ostensible goal of this forty-plus-year litigation, the concept of 'unitariness' is a kaleidoscope of sometimes conflicting and certainly evolving principles reflecting the social, political, educational, and jurisprudential thought which has molded the school desegregation process since 1954."[24] Despite issuing nearly three dozen school desegregation decisions, the Supreme Court has never explained what "desegregation" means.

As chapter 2 explains in greater detail, the Court has for decades bounced between two competing understandings of that crucial term. One is based on the "color-blind" interpretation of the Equal Protection clause of the Fourteenth Amendment first enunciated in Justice Harlan's celebrated dissent in *Plessy v. Ferguson*: "Our Constitution is color-blind, and neither knows nor tolerates classes among citizens."[25] According to this understanding, states can use racial classifications only in the most unusual circumstances—when such classifications are "narrowly tailored" to achieve a "compelling state interest." Although Chief Justice Warren's opinion in *Brown I* did not invoke this argument, his brief opinion a year later in *Brown II* seemed to endorse it: school officials have a constitutional responsibility "to achieve a system of determining admission to the public schools *on a nonracial basis.*"[26]

This position was clearly shared by the NAACP lawyers who brought *Brown v. Board of Education*. When the case first came before the Court, they maintained that the "Fourteenth Amendment precludes a state from imposing distinctions or classifications based upon race or color alone." A year later their brief stated, "That the Constitution is color blind is our dedicated belief."[27] In oral argument, the NAACP's Robert Carter explained that the "one fundamental contention which we will seek to develop" is that "no State has any authority under the equal-protection clause of the Fourteenth Amendment to use race as a factor in affording educational opportunity among its citizens."[28] Thurgood Marshall assured the Court that "the only thing that we are asking for is that the state-impose racial segregation be taken off, and to leave the county school board, the county people, the district people, to work out their solutions of the problem to assign children on any reasonable basis they want to assign them on."[29] A colleague of Marshall described Justice Harlan's *Plessy* dissent as the "'Bible' to which he turned during his most depressed moments."[30]

As we will see in chapter 4, adhering to a strict color-blind, no-racial-assignments interpretation of *Brown* created nearly insuperable obstacles to the task of uprooting school segregation in the South. Instead of demanding that "admission to public schools" be determined "on a nonracial basis," judges *required* race-based assignments in order to achieve the racial balance that would indicate the school district had achieved "unitary status." Initially this practice was viewed as a necessary but temporary evil: once the "dual school system" had been dismantled, race-based remedies could be lifted and color-blind policies instituted. In most cities under court order, though, these "temporary" remedies remained in place for decades. That was because a much different interpretation of *Brown* and the Equal Protection clause came to dominate the thinking of most Supreme Court justices and lower court judges.

This alternative understanding was never laid out clearly in Supreme Court opinions. The closest approximation came in Justice Breyer's *Parents Involved* dissent—fully fifty-three years after *Brown* and nearly thirty years after *Green*. Instead, its most forthright exposition and explanation came in lower court opinions. At the heart of this understanding lies the conviction that the problem was never simply de jure segregation—the separation of the races by law—but what became known as "racial isolation"; that is, the relegation of African American students to schools that were overwhelmingly black (and later, black and Hispanic).

This position was stated first and most clearly in a 1967 report of the United States Commission on Civil Rights entitled *Racial Isolation in the Public Schools*. It confidently concluded that "Negro children suffer serious harm when their education takes place in public schools which are racially segregated, *whatever the source of such segregation may be*." Racial isolation restricts the aspiration of minority children, reduces their confidence, and makes them "more likely to fear, dislike, and avoid white Americans."[31]

This message was conveyed to federal judges by expert witnesses who testified in the trial phase of desegregation cases. At the beginning of the long-running Denver case, Judge William Doyle stated, "We cannot ignore the overwhelming evidence to the effect that isolation or segregation per se is a substantial factor in producing unequal educational outcomes."[32] A federal judge in San Francisco predicted that "integration of schools would improve the academic performance of black children," while having "little or no adverse effect on the academic performance of white children."[33] During the first round of the *Swann* litigation, Judge James MacMillan confidently asserted that "the experts all agree" not only that "a racial mix in which black students heavily predominate tends to retard the progress of the whole group" but also that "if students are mingled with a clear white majority such as a 70/30 ratio . . . the better students can hold their pace, with substantial improvement for the poorer students."[34]

As a Supreme Court justice, Thurgood Marshall rejected the color-blind approach he had favored years before as an NAACP attorney. "Actual desegregation," he wrote in his ringing 1974 dissent in *Milliken v. Bradley*, means that white and black children will "go to school together." Marshall warned that "unless our children begin to learn together, there is little hope that our people will ever learn to live together." Equal educational opportunity requires the elimination of "all-Negro schools," which constitute "the very evil that *Brown I* was aimed at." Without such "actual desegregation," black children will be denied their right to "an equal start in life and to an equal opportunity to reach their full potential."[35] Even extensive reassignment of students might not be enough to create schools that pass constitutional muster: "Indeed, the poor quality of a system's schools may be so severe that nothing short of a radical transformation of the schools within the system will suffice to achieve desegregation and eliminate all of its vestiges."[36]

In his 2007 *Parents Involved* dissent, Justice Breyer offered a more detailed explanation of this expansive understanding of desegregation. *Brown*, he argued, had "long ago promised" school children a "racially *integrated* education."[37] Achieving this integration means "eliminating school-by-school racial isolation and increasing the degree to which racial mixture characterizes each of the district's schools and each individual student's public school experience." "Research suggests," he claimed, "that black children from segregated educational environments significantly increase their achievement levels once they are placed in a more integrated setting." Moreover, integration will teach black and white children alike how "to engage in the kind of cooperation among Americans of all races that is necessary to make a land of three hundred million people one Nation."[38]

In short, according to the understanding implicit in several Supreme Court decisions and explicit in many lower court decisions, "desegregation" means not just ending "racial isolation" whatever its cause, but substantial improvement in the quality of education offered to minority students. According to Richard Matsch, who supervised the Denver desegregation order, a desegregated school system is one in which all students have "equal access to the opportunities for education" and "a chance to develop fully each individual's potential, without being restricted by an identification with any racial or ethnic groups."[39] This is what Justice Breyer called "the hope and the promise of *Brown*."

Did desegregation "work," as its many defenders claim? Or did it deepen racial animosities and accelerate white flight, as Senator Biden and others have argued? Given the ambiguity of the term, the different interpretations adopted by judges across the country, and the multiple metrics developed to measure each interpretation, there is no unambiguous way to answer this question. Thus the first lesson to be learned from the history of desegregation: the importance of being explicit about the goal of the enterprise—something so many judges, advocates, and commentators have refused to do. Most people who write on the topic insist that their definition of "desegregation" reflects the true meaning of *Brown*. This book, in contrast, places the ambiguity of that key term—and the courts' unwillingness to confront the question directly—at the heart of its analysis. If there is anything to be learned from the history of desegregation, it is the hazard of failing to acknowledge hard choices.

THEME II: WHY INSTITUTIONS AND IMPLEMENTATION MATTER

Understanding the desegregation saga requires an appreciation of the sheer enormity of the task at hand and the limited policy leverage of the federal government. Gary Orfield has rightfully described the first stage of desegregation as the "reconstruction of southern education."[40] If constructing effective educational institutions is hard, reconstructing them can be even harder.

School segregation was the keystone of the Jim Crow system in the South. The *Brown* decision was greeted by the "Southern Manifesto"—a declaration of determined opposition signed by almost all members of Congress from the South—and "massive resistance" at the state and local level. Governors stood in the schoolhouse door, pledging "segregation forever." They whipped up crowds to threaten schoolchildren brave enough to enter formerly white schools. Meanwhile, school officials crafted assignment plans designed to maintain the status quo without explicitly using racial classifications. "Nothing would be worse," Justice Felix Frankfurter noted during oral argument in *Brown v. Board*, than for the Court "to make an abstract declaration that segregation is bad and then have it evaded by tricks."[41] But, of course, that is exactly what happened in the deep South over the next decade. By 1963, less than one half of one percent of black children in the South went to school with any white children.

To overcome this stonewalling, federal judges had to delve into the details of school-assignment policy in hundreds of districts and, even more importantly, establish measurable standards for what constituted adequate progress toward full desegregation. The guidelines issued by the federal Department of Health, Education, and Welfare (HEW) in 1965 and 1966 provided an essential assist: they specified how many black students must be admitted to formerly white schools in the upcoming years. Such specification was a necessary step—but only a first step. Judges still needed to determine what constituted full desegregation, and how these rules would be applied in large cities with substantial residential segregation.

When the Supreme Court finally reentered the picture in 1968, it explained that eliminating the "racial identification" of schools must extend "not just to the composition of student bodies," but "to every facet of school operations—faculty, staff, transportation, extracurricular activities and facilities."[42] Faculty assignment was a particularly difficult issue since so many white parents objected to their children being taught by black teachers. Long underfunded black schools had to be substantially upgraded or replaced with new buildings. School assignment zones, feeder plans, transportation routes, disciplinary and tracking policies—all these matters commanded the attention of judges handling desegregation suits. Especially in school districts in Texas and the Southwest with many Hispanic students, questions about English-language training and related curricular issues rose to the fore. Judges regularly adjusted school-assignment rules and plans for new construction to maintain racial balance in the face of demographic change.

Once focus shifted from upending the Jim Crow system in the South to addressing racial isolation throughout the country, the challenge became even greater. The number of large school systems subject to desegregation plans increased substantially. Since school districts in the North and Midwest tend to be significantly geographically smaller than those in the South and West, creating majority-white schools there would require reconfiguring the political structure of education—replacing existing districts and school boards with mega-districts that stretch into the suburbs. Emphasis subtly shifted from undoing previous racial discrimination to improving the education provided to minority children. As the special master in the Boston case put it, "What the hell is the point in desegregation if there are no good schools?" Noting the "inferior education being meted out to those who were the victims of discrimination," the judge in the Cleveland case devised remedies to address "such educational policy concerns as educational testing, reading programs, counseling, extracurricular activities, and relations with universities, businesses and cultural institutions, as well as techniques of achieving a better racial mix."[43] Nowhere were these "second generation" desegregation issues more prominent than in Kansas City, Missouri, where the judge mandated a $2 billion overhaul of the entire school system, turning each city high school into a magnet school with a special theme, ranging from science and math to classical Greek, from visual and performing arts to agribusiness.[44]

Originally seen as an effort to stop the racial assignment of students in the South, school desegregation became a much more ambitious campaign to improve educational opportunity for minority students throughout the country. This effort by the national government took place against the backdrop of the incredibly decentralized nature of the American educational system. When *Brown* was announced, the US had over eighty thousand independent school districts. By the time desegregation began in earnest in the mid-1960s, there were still about twenty-five thousand districts, each with its own school board, superintendent, power structure, and policies.[45] Although the authority of state education agencies grew during the second half of the twentieth century, control over education practices remained lodged in these many local school districts. Most desegregation litigation proceeded on a district-by-district level, with little coordination among the cases.

An even bigger challenge to the national government's effort to change educational practices is the nature of schools as bureaucratic organizations. Schools are what James Q. Wilson has called "coping organizations."[46] We lack reliable measures of the productivity of the "street-level bureaucrats" who carry out the principal tasks of schools, i.e., teachers. While testing has become a key metric for judging the performance of schools over the past two decades, we recognize that reading and math tests do not measure everything we expect schools to do. We also know that how well students do on tests is a result of many factors other than the quality of teaching in their school.

A second defining feature of "coping organizations" is that it is difficult for supervisors to observe what these "street-level bureaucrats" do on a regular basis. Especially in the United States, teachers work within an "egg crate" model, each in their own separate classroom. Only occasionally does the principal or a mentor observe the classroom, and the presence of an outsider tends to change classroom dynamics. As a result, new policies announced from above are frequently modified or even ignored by the crucial actors at the bottom. As Frederick Hess has noted, this disconnect is particularly evident when successive school leaders announce new initiatives only to leave before they are put into action. The churning of reforms makes teachers reluctant to buy into new practices touted from above.[47] Changing what goes on in the classroom is even more difficult when directives come not from within the organization, but from without—whether from new state and federal laws or from court orders.

In addition, school leaders lack control over a key resource: the composition of their student body. Families move into or out of school districts in part on the basis of parents' perception of the quality of their schools. Parents also have the option of enrolling their children in private schools. Even before desegregation, those with resources were leaving urban centers for the suburbs. Such "white flight" accelerated in cities subject to busing plans. As a result, desegregation orders designed to promote integration can reduce the number of affluent white student in city schools—and, consequently, political support for school budgets. If federal courts had required extensive urban-suburban busing in the North (as they came within one Supreme Court vote of doing), families retained two options: private school and moving to more distant suburbs. Given the extent to which the goal of desegregation efforts often was to integrate higher-SES white students with lower-SES minority students, the response by parents of the former to desegregation plans was crucial to those plans' success.

Brown established the right to attend a desegregated school as a *national*, constitutional right. But how much control does the national government have over the decentralized education system described in the last few paragraphs? Before 1965 the federal government's role in elementary and secondary education was minimal. The Elementary and Secondary Education Act of 1965 put the issue on the national agenda. But federal funding seldom exceeded 10 percent of the total, and that law explicitly barred the federal government from becoming involved in curricular matters. The Department of Education was not created until 1980, and it remains the smallest federal department: it employs only about four thousand people—compared with the more than seven million employed by state and local school systems. In the second half of the 1960s, the Office for Civil Rights in the Department of Health, Education, and Welfare played an important role in southern school desegregation. But after 1970 its involvement was severely limited by both President Nixon and Congress. In effect, the federal judiciary was on its own.

Despite the attention lavished on the Supreme Court in the press and the academic literature, the federal judiciary is a highly decentralized institution. The Supreme Court decides only seventy-five to one hundred cases annually, a tiny slice of the four hundred thousand to five hundred thousand cases filed in federal court each year. The Supreme Court allows conflicts among the circuit courts of appeal to "percolate" for many years—and even then may offer only vague guidance on how to resolve those conflicts. The circuit courts issue more opinions—about fifty thousand per year—but generally defer to trial judges' evaluation of the evidence put before them. They are particularly reluctant to second-guess district court judges on what constitutes an "equitable remedy." Determining whether a school district without a history of de jure segregation had over the years taken steps that produced racially identifiable schools was considered a question of "fact" requiring trial judges to evaluate days of testimony and years of official records. Although circuit courts would not rubber stamp these determinations, they were reluctant to question trial judges' evaluation of the "totality of the evidence."

Once a school district was found guilty of "segregative acts," the trial judge had even more discretion in fashioning an appropriate remedy. The most important judicial innovation to emerge from desegregation litigation was the structural injunction. These are detailed, extensive, ongoing judicial orders that seek to reorder many features of school life. They were usually negotiated by those representing the plaintiffs, the defendant school district, other interested federal and state officials, and experts and special masters appointed by the court. Remaining in effect not just for years, but for decades, they were frequently revised to reflect experience and demographic change.

Yale Law professor Owen Fiss, the country's foremost authority on (and defender of) desegregation injunctions, has explained that the process of devising structural injunctions "should be seen as *concentrating* or *fusing* the decisional power of the judge; it represents the antithesis of separation of powers." It is both "decentralized" and "peculiarly personalized": "The power is not allocated to the judiciary as much as it is allocated to the multitude of individual trial judges." It "becomes an expression of a person, as much as it is an expression of an office . . . when we speak of the decisional authority of the injunctive process we often talk not of *the law* or even of *the court*, but of Judge Johnson or Judge Garrity."[48]

Chief Justice Warren Burger tried to spell out the authority of trial judges to establish "equitable remedies" in the famous Charlotte desegregation case. There he noted that "the scope of a district court's equitable powers to remedy past wrongs is broad, for breadth and flexibility are inherent in equitable remedies." Judges must have the power to adapt "each decree to the necessities of the particular case." Burger went so far as to say that in establishing "the limits on remedial power of courts in an area as sensitive as we deal with here, words are poor instruments to convey the sense of basic fairness inherent in equity."[49] But in truth "words" are the only instrument appellate courts have for guiding and constraining the behavior of lower court judges.

With Congress and the president largely silent on the subject and the role of federal administrators tightly constrained, desegregation proceeded on a city-by-city basis, with the key policy choices established in the less-than-transparent remedy phase of litigation. As David Kirp and Gary Babcock put it in their study of desegregation injunctions in several cities, "remedy-shaping is the centerpiece" of desegregation litigation. "The scope of the remedy is accordionlike": it can be limited to achieving racial balance or "expanded to encompass much of the ordinary business of the school district." In the end it falls to the district court judge "to describe the problem and to imagine a fit solution."[50]

One of the strangest consequences of this extraordinary form of policymaking was that years later we do not know how many school districts remain under court order. In 2012 Stanford education professor Sean Reardon and his associates wrote, "The number of U.S. school districts that were ever under court order is not clear."[51] After conducting an extensive two-year investigation of the status of desegregation decrees, ProPublica found that "officials in scores of school districts do not know the status of their desegregation orders, have never read them, or erroneously believe that orders have been ended." Moreover, "some federal courts don't even know how many desegregation orders still exist on their dockets."[52]

One possible advantage of this decentralization is that it allows for experimentation: we can compare results to see what works best. But with desegregation, few such comparisons were ever made. Trial judges, Kirp and Babcock found, seldom inquired about what other judges were doing.[53] Roger Levesque notes that "comprehensive research that would explain how desegregation could result in the most positive outcomes emerged only after research indicated that desegregation pervasively did not lead to the intended positive effects."[54] The effect of this phase of research on federal policy has been limited. Not only did it begin as federal supervision was waning, but it indicated that the most positive results came with voluntary rather than court-ordered desegregation.

The bottom line is that desegregation was not only a remarkably ambitious undertaking, but one pursued in an ad hoc fashion by a national government with limited leverage over a sprawling educational network. Far from a uniform national policy, desegregation was a collection of shifting educational experiments with little systematic effort to evaluate their effectiveness—or even to decide what "effectiveness" should mean. To offer a global assessment either that desegregation "worked" or that it "failed" is to ignore this fundamental feature of the enterprise.

THEME III: DESEGREGATION AND THE CIVIL RIGHTS STATE

The legacy of the desegregation effort extends far beyond race and schooling. It laid the foundation of the larger American civil rights state, that is, the institutions we have created since 1964 to interpret and enforce the vast array of statutes, court rulings, and administrative regulations that prohibit discrimination on the basis of race, ethnicity, gender, sexual orientation, disability, religion, and national origin. While the term "civil rights state" may sound jarring to some, it is designed to highlight the fact that "making rights real" (to adopt Charles Epp's useful phrase[55]) requires the assertion of governmental authority, indeed, one of the most aggressive and far-reaching assertions of the authority of the national government in our history. Defining and protecting civil rights is a form of government regulation—a fact that is easy to overlook but impossible to deny.

If anyone in the huge crowd that heard Martin Luther King's stirring 1963 "I Have a Dream" speech had thought to look around the nation's capital for evidence of a "civil rights state," they would have come up empty. Starting in 1964, it was built on the fly, without a clear institutional blueprint or coherent set of founders. Like its cousin the American welfare state, the civil rights state is fragmented, with enforcement authority lodged in a variety of agencies, some well-known, others quite obscure: the Equal Employment Opportunity Commission, the Civil Rights Division of the Justice Department, the Office of Federal Contract Compliance Programs in the Department of Labor, several fair housing offices in the Department of Housing and Urban Development, and separate civil rights offices in nearly every department and independent agency. These agencies share both interpretive power and enforcement authority with the federal courts.

That the civil rights state is a motley array of unfamiliar government units should not lead us to underestimate its reach or power. In comparison with other advanced industrial democracies, the US is usually considered a relatively "weak state" with less generous welfare programs and greater faith in the market. When it comes to civil rights, though, the usual transatlantic pattern is reversed: American government is more energetic and more efficacious than its European counterparts. In his comparison of race policy in the US,

Britain, and France, Robert Lieberman points out that despite the "resolutely color-blind laws" that formed the legal foundation of the civil rights regime in the United States, "the 'weak' American state ... not only produced more active and extensive enforcement of antidiscrimination law; it also managed to challenge the color-blind presumptions of its own law and to forge an extensive network of race-conscious policies and practices that have proven strikingly resilient in the face of political and legal challenges."[56] Abigail Saguy and Kathrin Zippel have demonstrated that American law deals much more harshly with sexual harassment than French, German, or EU law.[57] Eric Bleich has shown how heavily and consciously Britain borrowed from the US when it sought to strengthen its own civil rights laws in the 1970s.[58] Most comparative studies have found that a key explanation for the strength of this allegedly "weak state" is the pivotal role played by the judiciary in the US.[59]

Desegregation contributed to the construction of this civil rights state in at least three ways. First was the structural injunction. The development of this powerful and largely unconstrained remedial tool was in large part a response to years of resistance to school desegregation. As Paul Gewirtz has noted, it was southern determination to resist *Brown* "that required the courts to intrude with such coercion, with such detail, with such stubborn patience and courage, and with strategic and managerial preoccupations that strained the boundaries of the traditional judicial function."[60] Years of obstructionism and insubordination led to the imposition of extraordinary authority. The Supreme Court was reluctant to impose limits on the use of these "equitable remedies," lest it appear to undercut often-heroic efforts of lower court judges. Soon, structural injunctions were employed in many other contexts, ranging from reforming institutions for the mentally ill and developmentally disabled to attacking discrimination in housing and policing.

Second was the development of a new division of labor between courts and agencies, one in which agencies promulgated guidelines under civil rights statutes and courts supplied the enforcement muscle. This pattern first appeared in the desegregation of southern schools in the second half of the 1960s. HEW issued guidelines under Title VI of the Civil Rights Act. The Fifth Circuit then embraced these rules and issued injunctions to enforce them. A similar symbiotic relationship developed between courts and agencies on sex discrimination (under Title IX), education for English learners (under the "national origin" provision of Title VI), and employment discrimination (under Title VII). This division of labor in effect gave federal administrative agencies a role in defining constitutional rights, while relieving them of the politically dangerous task of using termination of federal funds to enforce nondiscrimination mandates. It also allowed courts and agencies to engage in a process of policy "leapfrogging," with each building upon the initiatives of the other while claiming to do nothing new.[61]

Third, desegregation litigation opened up new areas of federal regulation of education. In Texas desegregation cases, judges faced the issue of language training for Mexican American students with limited English proficiency. Their rulings contributed to the growing demand for bilingual education. A major desegregation case in the District of Columbia called attention to the number of minority children shunted off into understaffed special education classes. Similar litigation eventually led Congress to enact the Education for All Handicapped Children Act (later renamed the Individuals with Disabilities Education Act). Legal challenges to the tracking of students in California schools led to a finding that the tests used by school districts were racially biased. Efforts to challenge school-funding formulas on the basis that they denied students in property-poor districts the "equal educational opportunity" promised in *Brown* failed in federal court. But similar suits succeeded in dozens of state courts around the country. Because administrative guidelines issued under Title VI had played such a major role in southern desegregation, Congress used that section of the 1964 Civil Rights Act as a model for attacking gender discrimination when it passed Title IX of the Education Amendments of 1972. The policy waves produced by school desegregation spread out in many directions.

The expansion of the civil rights state has important implications for the coming chapters of the desegregation story. Most importantly, it points to the enhanced role of administrators, particularly in the Department of Education, and to the ways in which the interplay of courts and agencies can produce federal mandates that neither judges nor administrators would be willing to announce on their own. The Obama administration made aggressive use of "Dear Colleague" letters to address discrimination based on race, sex, and national origin. It is likely that the Biden administration will do the same. To what extent will the federal judiciary, stocked with many additional Republican appointees, build upon or limit these efforts by the executive branch? That is one of the most important questions about the direction of the American civil rights state.

Organization of the Book

This book offers a detailed policy history of desegregation policy from *Brown* through termination of many court orders in the first decades of the twenty-first century. It combines legal analysis with attention to institutional relations, especially the symbiotic relationship that developed between courts and agencies in early days, the inability of the nine members of the Supreme Court to give clear direction to the lower courts, the use of innovative judicial remedies, and the varied responses of lower courts to the complex challenges that confronted them. Looming over the entire six-decade story is the ambiguity of the stated goal—"desegregation"—coupled with the dogmatic insistence by nearly every party that its definition of that term was the only one consistent with the Constitution, *Brown*, and the goal of racial justice.

Chapter 2, "The Great Debate," examines competing interpretations of "desegregation" and the evidence on the effects of desegregation efforts. It describes the two most influential understandings, which I call the "color-blind/limited intervention" position and the "racial isolation/equal educational opportunity" position. Both approaches have significant appeal—and significant drawbacks. That is why few judges have been willing to embrace either in its entirety. The chapter also reviews the extensive social-science evidence on desegregation, explaining why "inconclusive" and "variable" are the words most often used to describe the results of research on the topic.

Chapter 3, "Critical Junctures," introduces the history of the federal desegregation effort by identifying the key events that shaped the several stages of policymaking: the *Brown* decision and the resulting "massive resistance" in the South; passage of the Civil Rights Act of 1964, which brought two federal departments to the aid of civil rights litigants; the Fifth Circuit's *Jefferson County* decisions in 1966–67, which jump-started desegregation in Dixie; the Supreme Court's flurry of desegregation decisions in the decade following *Green* in 1968; the proliferation of busing decisions that followed the pattern set by Judge MacMillan in Charlotte; the debate over termination of desegregation that began with the Supreme Court's decisions of the early 1990s; and Obama and Biden administrations' regulatory efforts to promote integration without support from the courts. This chapter is designed to provide a road map to the longer chapters that follow.

Chapter 4, "Breakthrough: The Reconstruction of Southern Education," explores how the Fifth Circuit worked with the Office of Civil Rights in HEW to break the back of southern resistance to desegregation in the second half of the 1960s. This achievement required significant institutional innovation. It also left a key issue unresolved: was the use of racial assignments and the demand for racial balance in schools limited to school districts found guilty of intentional, legal discrimination, or was some form of racial balance now required for almost all school districts? In other words, how widely would these new race-based remedies be applied? Only in the South? Only where there was indisputable evidence of intentional discrimination? Or wherever courts found racial "isolation"?

Chapter 5, "Supreme Abdication," looks at how the Supreme Court addressed these questions from 1968 through 1980. After more than a decade of ducking the issue, the Court issued twenty-five desegregation decisions in those years—more than twice as many as it had issued before or since. The combination of these decisions moved the Court toward the more ambitious "racial isolation/equal educational opportunity" position. But the justices never explained the rationale for this shift. Divisions within the court produced both a crucial constraint—no urban-suburban busing except in unusual circumstances—and uncertainty over how committed the majority would remain to this position. The central theme of this chapter is the Court's inability to establish, defend, or maintain a clear position on the meaning of "desegregation."

Chapter 6, "Left Adrift," describes the diverse circumstances facing the district court judges who heard desegregation cases, and the factors that shaped their interpretation of the Supreme Court's shifting and ambiguous commands. Chapter 7, "Varieties of Desegregation Experiences," describes the range of remedies applied by these trial judges and the evolution of these remedies over the years. Taken together, these two chapters emphasize the decentralization of judicial policymaking and the ad hoc nature of the desegregation process.

Chapter 8, "Termination without End," starts with a review of Supreme Court decisions issued in the early 1990s explaining when school systems can be deemed "unitary" and desegregation orders lifted. It then turns to the delayed response of the lower courts, and to the extent to which public schools have been "resegregated." Not surprisingly, that assessment depends on how one interprets "desegregation."

Chapter 9, "Looking Beyond Courts: ESEA and Title VI," reminds us that despite their prominence, judges have not been the only federal officials determined to equalize educational opportunities. The first part of the chapter examines congressional efforts to use money and mandates to improve education for poor and minority students, for English learners, for women and girls, and for students with disabilities. The second part traces the evolution of administrative interpretations of Title VI of the Civil Rights Act, which prohibits recipients of federal funding from discriminating on the basis of race or national origin. This section includes a review of the Obama administration's ambitious efforts to use Title VI guidelines to encourage racial integration, to address racial disparities in school discipline, and to increase the resources available to predominantly black and Hispanic schools.

Chapter 10, "What Have We Learned?," offers an extended discussion of the three themes briefly described above. It does not pretend to offer a precise set of policies to improve the quality of education provided to minority students. But it does try to provide a framework for addressing these issues in a more honest, realistic, and institutionally informed manner.

The Desegregation Paradox

School desegregation was the first and greatest challenge facing the American civil rights state, indeed the impetus for its creation. From this searing experience, judges, administrators, and civil rights advocates learned important lessons about how to build effective regulatory institutions as well as about the dangers of setting unrealistically ambitious goals. Almost all the educational initiatives that followed in the wake of school desegregation—from bilingual education for Hispanic and Asian students to special education for students with disabilities, from programs to combat gender discrimination to those addressing racial discrimination within the classroom—were shaped by the desegregation experience. In short, school desegregation was the crucible in which the institutions of the civil rights states were slowly forged, and the gateway through which the federal judiciary entered an arena filled with difficult questions about the meaning of "equal educational opportunity."

In some ways, though, school desegregation was an outlier. No other area of civil rights received so much political attention or generated such intense public opposition. No other area remained so fully grounded in constitutional law rather than in statutes passed by Congress. In no other area did federal courts stand so clearly at the center of the political storm or rely so heavily on detailed, multi-year injunctions. Nowhere else did the Supreme Court manage to issue so many decisions while doing so little to clarify the central objective. And nowhere else was it so hard to forge a political or judicial consensus.

The school desegregation story is thus a tangle of paradoxes. It was the civil rights movement's greatest victory, but also its most troubling defeat. *Brown* and its aftermath added immensely to the moral standing and political capital of the federal judiciary, but the controversy over busing sparked unprecedented attacks on the "imperial judiciary." The decades-long desegregation effort produced a new arsenal of remedial powers for federal judges, but at the same time demonstrated the limits of judicial power. What had originally appeared as a question of "simple justice" that could unite both Court and country eventually became a complex social-policy issue that divided the justices and the citizenry at large. To some people, school desegregation demonstrates America's capacity to live up to its ideals; to others it represents yet another example of American hypocrisy.

Unraveling all these competing strands is the task before us. It requires us to discard the simple morality tales so common to discussion of the topic. Desegregation was neither an utter failure nor a complete success: it encompassed far too many disparate parts to be reduced to such terms. To be sure, the story includes heroes and villains. But more numerous by far were ordinary, well-meaning judges, administrators, advocates, and school officials swimming in a sea of uncertainty and facing hard choices. Politics, Max Weber claimed, is the "strong and slow boring of hard boards." The combination of education policy with race in the American context presents us with the hardest wood of all.

2

The Great Debate

Few issues in American politics have been debated so long or so vehemently as school desegregation. Given the elevated status of *Brown v. Board of Education*, virtually everyone who takes part in this debate insists that their position is the only one consistent with *Brown*: those who take a contrary position, they charge, have betrayed the grand purposes of the most important Supreme Court decision of the past hundred years. At the same time, though, almost everyone acknowledges that the *Brown* opinions of 1954–55 were far from clear on what desegregation means, why segregation is unconstitutional, and what schools must do to come into compliance.

Over the years, two contrasting understandings of *Brown* gradually took shape. The purpose of this chapter is to lay out the central elements of these competing positions without endorsing or condemning either. On the one hand, this chapter argues, both understandings are consistent with some elements of the Court's short, ambiguous opinions in *Brown*. On the other hand, both encountered serious problems when put into practice. Understanding the byzantine history of desegregation requires an appreciation of the underlying rationales and the limitations of these competing interpretations of *Brown*.

I label these two sets of arguments the "color-blind/limited intervention" approach and the "racial isolation/equal educational opportunity" approach. Both approaches combine (1) an interpretation of the Equal Protection clause with (2) an assessment of the institutional capability of the federal judiciary and (3) an evaluation of the social-science evidence on the causes and effects of school segregation. Each has an Achilles heel: the former makes evasion too easy; the latter expects more from judges than they can ever hope to deliver. Consequently, proponents of each position have searched for a more realistic middle ground. As we will see in subsequent chapters, that search produced vague legal formulations rather than effective educational policies. Seven decades after *Brown*, the search for a workable middle ground continues.

Brown's Unanswered Questions

In writing his brief opinion in *Brown v. Board*, Chief Justice Warren understood that his chief challenge was not to provide the most convincing legal argument for invalidating state-sponsored segregation, but rather to produce a unanimous decision, to avoid inflaming the South, and to offer a morally compelling explanation for the Court's action, one that would resonate with the public at large. In other words, Warren sought an opinion that would unite the nation as well as the Court, one short enough to be reprinted in newspapers and clear enough to command public support. By postponing the question of remedies for another year—and then only requiring compliance "with all deliberate speed"—the Court hoped to defuse opposition in the South. The Court's even shorter opinion in *Brown II* did little to clarify what *Brown I* required.

Warren's 1954 opinion was more notable for what it did *not* say than what it clearly established. He argued that the "inconclusive" history of the Fourteenth Amendment offered no guidance as to the meaning of the Equal Protection clause: what a majority of those "in Congress and the state legislatures had in mind cannot be determined with any degree of certainty."[1] Determining the constitutionality of school segregation thus required the Court to "consider public education in the light of its full development and its present place in American life throughout the Nation." Warren refused to say that racial segregation is unconstitutional in all contexts: "We conclude that *in the field of public education* the doctrine of 'separate but equal' has no place." School segregation became unconstitutional, he argued, only when the role of public schools increased to the point where access to education determines students' opportunity "to succeed in life."[2]

Warren did not endorse—or even mention—Justice Harlan's famous dissent in *Plessey v. Ferguson* in which he declared "our Constitution is colorblind." Nor did he mention the obvious fact that "separate but equal" had always been a fraud, since resources and facilities were never distributed equally: the outcome of the legal challenges "cannot turn on merely a comparison of these tangible factors in the Negro and white schools." Most importantly, in neither opinion did the Court explain what measures schools must institute to come into compliance with the Constitution.

Instead of looking at the intent of those who ratified the Fourteenth Amendment in 1868 or those who maintained segregated schools in 1954,

Warren argued that "we must look instead to the *effect* of segregation itself on public education." In one of his most memorable lines, the chief justice wrote of primary and secondary school students, "To separate them from others of similar age and qualifications solely because of their race generates a feeling of inferiority as to their status in the community that may affect their hearts and minds in a way unlikely ever to be undone." Quoting one of the courts below, he explained,

> Segregation of white and colored children in public schools has a detrimental effect upon the colored children. The impact is greater when it has the sanction of the law, for the policy of separating the races is usually interpreted as denoting the inferiority of the negro group. A sense of inferiority affects the motivation of a child to learn. Segregation with the sanction of law, therefore, has a tendency to [retard] the educational and mental development of negro children and to deprive them of some of the benefits they would receive in a racial[ly] integrated school system.[3]

Consequently, "separate educational facilities are *inherently* unequal." By announcing the rule that racially segregated schools are always unconstitutional, *Brown* relieved litigants and lower court judges of the nearly impossible burden of determining in what circumstances "separate" was in fact "equal."

How did Warren know that segregation had such an effect on African American children? His answer incited years of controversy: "Whatever may have been the extent of psychological knowledge at the time of *Plessy v. Ferguson*, this finding is amply supported by modern authority."[4] At the end of this sentence Warren placed the famous footnote 11 that cited Kenneth and Mamie Clark's doll studies and Gunner Myrdal's *American Dilemma*—relatively weak reeds for supporting such a pivotal claim.

It is highly likely that the justices who signed onto Warren's opinion agreed with Justice Harlan's argument that the Fourteenth Amendment forbids the use of racial classifications in all but the most unusual circumstances. That was the argument long endorsed by Thurgood Marshall and the NAACP. In *Bolling v. Sharpe*, the companion case to *Brown* that struck down school segregation in the District of Columbia, Chief Justice Warren wrote that "classifications based solely upon race must be scrutinized with particular care, since they are contrary to our traditions, and hence constitutionally suspect."[5] *Brown II* required school districts "to achieve a system of determining admission to the public schools on a *nonracial* basis." Thurgood Marshall assured the justices that desegregation could be accomplished in only a few months because it required school officials simply to end race-based assignments and to redraw attendance lines so all children would go to the closest school.

Over the next two years the Court struck down legal segregation of public parks, golf courses, beaches, and transportation—without any explanation or effort to investigate the effects of segregation outside the educational context.[6] In 1963 the Court unanimously rejected a plan that allowed students to transfer from a school in which they were the minority to one in which they were the majority, explaining that racial classifications are "obviously irrelevant and invidious," and thus "invalid."[7] By the mid-1960s the Court would establish race as a "suspect classification" that could be used only when tightly connected to a "compelling state interest."[8]

At the same time, though, Warren alluded to a broader reading of the Equal Protection clause. "Today," he wrote, "education is perhaps the most important function of state and local governments." Not only is it "the very foundation of good citizenship," but "in these days, it is doubtful that any child may reasonably be expected to succeed in life if he is denied the opportunity of an education." Consequently, "such an opportunity, where the state has undertaken to provide it, is a right which must be made available to all on equal terms."[9] Warren's invocation of social-science evidence in footnote 11 opened the door to the possibility that subsequent research could show that many other educational practices deny minority children "equal educational opportunity." Although the "impact" of such patterns and practices might be greater when they have the explicit "sanction of the law," more subtle features of public-school systems could also deny students their constitutional right to equal educational opportunity.

For the next decade and a half, the Supreme Court did little to explain the meaning or implications of *Brown*. Meanwhile, southern political and school leaders engaged in "massive resistance." The lower federal courts were left with the difficult task of figuring out what *Brown* means and how they could bring thousands of school districts into compliance. Southern school desegregation did not begin in earnest until Congress enacted the Civil Rights Act of 1964. As the courts grappled with the harsh realities of desegregation, the two positions described below slowly emerged. As we will see in chapter 5, the Supreme Court issued a long series of muddled opinions that offered little guidance to the lower courts. Not until the Court's 2007 decision in *Parents Involved in Community Schools* did the justices openly explore the issues that had divided them for decades. And even then, they could not muster five votes for a single position.

The Color-Blind/Limited Intervention Approach

The "simple, yet fundamental, truth" announced in *Brown*, Justice Clarence Thomas claimed in 1995, is "the principle that the government must treat citizens as individuals, and not as members of racial, ethnic, or religious groups."[10] Echoing Martin Luther King Jr's dream that we be judged by the "content of our character" rather than the color of our skin, Thomas has consistently argued that it "demeans the dignity and worth of a person to be judged by ancestry instead of by his or her own merit and essential qualifications." Although Justice O'Connor occasionally disagreed with Thomas on the application of this principle, she emphasized that "distinctions between citizens solely because of their ancestry are by their very nature odious to a free people whose institutions are founded upon the doctrine of equality."[11] Consequently, Justice John Paul Stevens wrote, "racial classifications are simply too pernicious to permit any but the most exact connection between justification and classification."[12] This understanding of the Equal Protection clause creates a very strong—indeed nearly irrebuttable—presumption against the assignment of students to schools on the basis of race, even if the goal is to promote racial balance rather than to enforce segregation.

THE HAZARDS OF "BENIGN" USES OF RACE

The rationale for prohibiting the use of racial classification was easy to grasp in 1954, when state-sponsored segregation was used to keep African Americans in a subordinate position. But why should the same rules apply to the use of race for such "benign" purposes as integrating public schools and providing more jobs to minority men and women? To this crucial question, advocates of the color-blind approach have offered several answers.

First, regardless of its stated purpose, the use of racial classifications encourages us to think of others as representatives of a race rather than as individuals. "Reduction of an individual to an assigned racial identity for differential treatment is among the most pernicious actions our government can undertake," Justice Kennedy wrote in *Parents Involved*. "To be forced to live under a state-mandated racial label is inconsistent with the dignity of individuals in our society." Even "benign" use of race stigmatizes and patronizes the purported beneficiaries, and "reinforces the belief, held by too many for too much of our history, that individuals should be judged by the color of their skin."

Second, the use of racial classifications by government heightens racial competition and animosity. Race-based policy "lead[s] to corrosive discourse, where race serves not as an element of our diverse heritage but instead as a bargaining chip in the political process."[13] When the government classifies by race, Kennedy noted, "it must first define what is meant to be of a race. Who exactly is white and who is nonwhite?" It must then determine which racial (and ethnic) groups deserve what. According to Kennedy, "the allocation of governmental burdens and benefits, contentious under any circumstances, is even more divisive when allocations are made on the basis of individual racial classifications."[14] Too often the default position becomes crude proportionality: government benefits should be divided among these groups according to their proportion of the population, regardless of all other, nonracial factors—including the preferences of the alleged beneficiaries.

Once racial quotas are established, Justice O'Connor warned, there is "no logical stopping point."[15] Maintaining racially balanced schools, Justice Thomas claimed in *Parents Involved*, is a never-ending endeavor:

> Individual schools will fall in and out of balance in the natural course, and the appropriate balance will shift with the school district's changing demographics. Thus, racial balancing will have to take place on an infinite basis—a continuing process with no identifiable culpable party and no discernable end point.[16]

Like all benefits conveyed by government, those distributed on the basis of race are hard to retract. Extraordinary remedies soon become ordinary.

Third, deploying racial classifications to atone for previous discrimination places "unnecessary burdens on innocent third parties who bear no responsibility for whatever harm" the remedial program seeks to rectify.[17] "Every time the government uses racial criteria to 'bring the races together,' someone gets excluded, and the person excluded suffers an injury solely because of his or her race."[18] For example, desegregation plans that sought to counteract discrimination against African American students often required Asian and Hispanic children to be bused far beyond their neighborhood schools against the wishes of their parents—despite the fact that they were in no way responsible for the segregation discovered by the court. Such considerations led Chief Justice Roberts to conclude, "It is a sordid business, this divvying up by race."[19]

Finally, distinguishing between "benign" and invidious use of racial classifications is no easy task. In 2003 Justice Thomas warned against "the benighted notions that one can tell when racial discrimination benefits (rather than hurts) minority groups."[20] The segregationists who instituted Jim Crow in the South, he later noted, claimed this was good for blacks and whites alike. According to Justice O'Connor, the endorsement of "'benign racial classifications' suggests confidence in [courts'] ability to distinguish good from harmful governmental uses of racial criteria. History should teach greater humility."[21]

Although a few of the quotations in the preceding paragraphs came in school desegregation litigation, most appeared in Supreme Court affirmative action cases. When federal courts first began to mandate racial assignments of students to achieve racial balance in the 1960s, some of these themes were voiced in lower court decisions. But the Supreme Court did not address the issue head-on in desegregation cases for many decades. When it finally did so, both sides relied heavily on precedents established in post-*Bakke* affirmative action cases.

It is important to recognize that advocates of the "color-blind" interpretation of the Fourteenth Amendment and civil rights statutes do not claim that it will right all wrongs or wring all forms of discrimination out of our educational system. The Fourteenth Amendment and the Civil Rights Act, they insist, do not create a mandate for extensive, judicially led reform of public schools. Rather, they establish a clear *rule*—rather than an abstract goal or amorphous promise—that prevents public officials from employing a particularly dangerous tool. The role of the federal courts is to enforce this crucial rule rather than engage in an open-ended effort to restructure public education.

INSTITUTIONAL AUTHORITY AND CAPACITY

The "color-blind" interpretation of the Fourteenth Amendment and civil rights statutes thus went hand in hand with two key institutional arguments: respect for federalism, and doubts about the capacity of federal judges to improve the quality of public education. These concerns became prominent in the dissenting opinions of Justices Powell, Rehnquist, and Burger in the 1970s and in the Supreme Court's opinions on the termination of desegregation cases in the 1990s.

Chief Justice Burger emphasized the first theme in his opinion for the Court in *Milliken v. Bradley*: "No single tradition in public education is more deeply rooted than local control over the operation of schools; local autonomy has long been thought essential both to the maintenance of community concern and support for public schools and to quality of the educational system."[22] Nearly two decades later, Chief Justice Rehnquist argued that "local control over the education of children allows citizens to participate in decisionmaking, and allows innovation so that school programs can fit local need."[23]

This understanding of "local control" does not mean that localities should be free to run their schools however they see fit: both the Equal Protection clause and the Civil Rights Act place substantial limits on what subnational governments can do. *Brown*, after all, is the Supreme Court's most important effort to define those limits. According to the "limited intervention" approach, federal judicial intervention must be based on *specific violations* of federal law and limited to *temporary* measures designed to remedy those *particular* misdeeds. In a 1979 dissenting opinion, Justices Rehnquist and Powell argued that because system-wide desegregation orders constitute "as complete and dramatic a displacement of local authority by the federal judiciary as is possible in our federal system," the "violations of constitutional rights" that trigger such judicial intervention must be "carefully and clearly defined," and "the subsequent displacement of local authority" must be "limited to that necessary to correct the identified violation."[24] In other words, judicial incursions into state and local educational matters should be considered such an extraordinary departure from the operation of our constitutionally created governing institutions that they must be carefully limited in both time and scope.

Such willingness to defer to the authority of state and local officials was reinforced by skepticism about the capacity of the courts to assess evidence on educational matters and control the myriad factors that affect the lives of students and teachers. Proponents of the "color-blind/limited intervention" point of view repeatedly warned that actions can lead to deeply flawed outcomes even if taken with the best of intentions. In particular, system-wide desegregation orders could lead to "white flight," increasing the number of predominantly black schools and depriving the school system of political and financial support. Long bus rides to distant schools can reduce the amount of time and energy students devote to their schoolwork, and the extent to which their parents can be involved in school activities.

In 1973 Justice Powell warned that by requiring extensive busing "solely to maximize integration," courts "risk setting in motion unpredictable and unmanageable social consequences. No one can estimate the extent to which dismantling neighborhood education will hasten an exodus to private schools . . . [or] to suburbs . . . [or] the deterioration of community and parental support for public schools."[25] He later argued that experience during the 1970s

> has cast serious doubt upon the efficacy of far-reaching judicial remedies directed not against specific constitutional violations, but rather imposed on an entire school system on the fictional assumption that the existence of identifiable black or white schools is caused entirely by intentional segregative conduct, and is evidence of systemwide discrimination.

"Restructuring and overseeing the operation of major public school systems" constitutes "social engineering that hardly is appropriate for the federal judiciary."[26] In the end, the expectation that court orders can produce integrated schools is "an illusion." More than a decade later, Justice Kennedy argued that maintaining racial balance in the face of changing demographics "is beyond the authority and beyond the practical ability of federal courts."[27]

Even harder than maintaining a particular racial balance is guaranteeing that all students receive "equal educational opportunity." Judge Avern Cohn, who handled the final stages of the Detroit desegregation case, later told an audience at the University of Michigan,

> I'm not sure any of the judges had a particular goal in mind . . . I doubt any of us were very philosophical or had any long-range views. . . . Judges are frequently the last to know about the total environment in which a case exists. We only have, by and large, what the lawyers give us and generally in any particular case in court there is a much larger world surrounding it that we don't know very much about.[28]

As we will see in chapters 7 and 8, judges who initiated education reforms with high hopes often left frustrated by the complexity of the task, the extent of resistance from the school bureaucracy, and the paucity of measurable improvement.

Adherents to the "color-blind/limited intervention" position tended to be similarly skeptical of the claims of social science. Some members of the Supreme Court—like some members of the NAACP's litigation team in *Brown*—have been wary of relying on the sort of evidence cited in the decision's footnote 11.[29] In the *Parents Involved* case, Justice Thomas accused Justice Breyer and his fellow dissenters of "unquestioningly accepting the assertions of selected social scientists, while completely ignoring the fact that those assertions are the subject of fervent debate." The claim that "racially balanced schools improve educational outcomes for black children," Thomas argued, is "hotly disputed among social scientists." "In reality," he maintained, "it is far from apparent that coerced racial mixing has any educational benefits, much less that integration is necessary to black achievement."[30] Warning that the dissenters would "constitutionalize today's faddish social theories," he pointed out that a century before, scholars at reputable institutions invented pseudoscientific theories that justified Jim Crow. His bottom line: "Beware of elites bearing racial theories."[31]

SHORTCOMINGS AND MODIFICATIONS

The most serious problem with the "color-blind/limited intervention" understanding of *Brown* is the ease with which it can be circumvented. Such evasion was all too evident in the decade following the Supreme Court's 1954 decision. Substituting high-discretion "pupil placement plans" for laws that explicitly segregated students on the basis of race, southern school districts managed to maintain the segregation status quo. They later employed "freedom of choice" plans that combined informal intimidation with complex rules that limited opportunities for black children to move to formerly white schools. As we will see in chapter 4, without counting the number of black and white students in the schools within each district, it was impossible for federal judges and administrator to undo the effects of decades of segregation and discrimination. Some form of "racial body-count" was essential for uprooting Jim Crow. Such use of racial statistics soon morphed into a demand for racial "balance," initiating a long debate over what constituted the appropriate white/black ratio.

A somewhat different problem appeared in the North. There, years of decisions by school officials on where to place schools and how to draw attendance zones often combined with severe housing segregation to produce predominantly black and predominantly white schools despite the absence of de jure segregation. As southerners pointed out, in many cities it was hard to distinguish the South's de jure segregation from the North's government-abetted de facto segregation. Were courts powerless to address these troubling patterns because Boston or Detroit or Chicago had never publicly admitted what they were doing?

As members of the federal judiciary confronted these problems, they gradually shifted from the predominant "color-blind" interpretation of *Brown* to the "equal educational opportunity/racial isolation" understanding described in the following section. The Supreme Court justices quoted in the above paragraphs—Rehnquist, Burger, Powell, and later Kennedy, O'Connor, Roberts, and Thomas—accepted some features of this expanded desegregation jurisprudence. At the same time, they sought to erect barriers to this extension of judicial power. First in the mid-1970s and again in the early 1990s, they tried to

(1) tighten evidentiary rules for determining when school districts have engaged in unconstitutional action;
(2) limit courts' ability to create mega-districts to pull in white students from the suburbs;
(3) reduce federal judges' authority to require regular revision of their injunctions;
(4) allow school districts to be released from court orders after complying in good faith for many years; and
(5) limit school officials' authority to use racial assignments to achieve racial balance.

The Court's expansive holdings of the late 1960s and early 1970s, Justice Scalia argued in 1992, were based on presumptions "extraordinary in law but not unreasonable in fact." In other words, the Court's many departures from ordinary legal principles had been justified by the extraordinary difficulty of overcoming opposition to desegregation. But "it has become absurd to assume, without any further proof, that violations of the Constitution dating from the days when Lyndon Johnson was president, or earlier, continue to have an appreciable effect upon current operation of schools." He therefore urged the Court to "revert to the ordinary principles of our law, of our democratic heritage, and of our educational tradition."[32] Of course, what proponents of the "color-blind/limited intervention" understanding saw as a return to ordinary principles of law and democracy, their opponents saw as a repudiation of *Brown* and equal protection of the laws.

The Racial Isolation/Equal Educational Opportunity Approach

Before becoming a Yale law professor and the nation's leading expert on injunctions, Owen Fiss was a young attorney in the Department of Justice working on southern desegregation cases. Looking back at those heady days, he noted that "antidiscrimination laws are capable of two basic interpretations." One focuses on process, seeking "the purification of the decisional process" by forbidding the use of "certain forbidden criteria," most importantly race. The alternative "emphasizes the achievement of a certain result, improvement of the economic and social position of the protected group." Although "the possibility of a divergence between the process-oriented and the results-oriented approach to antidiscrimination laws was perceived by some commentators" at the time, that "insight did not play an important role" in the thinking of Fiss and his colleagues. They were "preoccupied with the problems of extending coverage and ending open defiance" and "believed or hoped that the divergence would never materialize."[33] By the early 1970s, though, that divergence clearly had materialized, forcing civil rights advocates to decide what sort of "results" they sought to achieve.

The immediate cause of the shift from process to results was the widespread use of "freedom of choice" plans by southern school districts. In the abstract, allowing students and their parents to choose which school to attend seemed entirely consistent with the Court's opinion in *Brown*. But how could federal officials know if the choices made by black students were truly free? The first wave of "freedom of choice" plans included a number of rules that ensured the continuation of nearly all-white and all-black schools in districts that had for years run legally segregated school systems. Federal judges and HEW officials struggled to rid these plans of elements designed to protect the racial status quo.

Even after the official process had been "purified," serious problems with "freedom of choice" plans remained. Often, black parents who dared send their children to formerly white schools faced intimidation—economic, social, and sometimes physical—by private parties. At oral argument in the 1968 *Green* case, Chief Justice Warren expressed doubt about whether in the South such choices could *ever* be free given the "social and cultural influences and the prejudices that have existed for centuries there."[34] The NAACP argued that "freedom of choice" plans not only required black parents and children to withstand fear and intimidation, "but to unshackle themselves from the psychological effects of imposed racial discrimination of the past." Under segregation African Americans had been "schooled in the ways of subservience"; therefore, "freedom of choice" plans would simply replicate the inequalities of the past.[35] In other words, the choice of black parents to keep their children in predominantly black schools could be ignored as the product of false consciousness. The "reconstruction of southern education" required changing whites' attitudes toward blacks, and blacks' attitudes toward whites.

The controversy over "freedom of choice" plans that raged in the 1960s was one manifestation of a broader debate over the limitation of constitutional formalities. In the conclusion of his Bancroft Prize–winning book, *From Jim Crow to Civil Rights*, Michael Klarman provides this important insight:

> Constitutional interpretation that is limited to form and is unwilling to delve into substance is vulnerable to nullification by determined resistance. Southern whites were so creative and persistent that they almost completely eliminated black suffrage despite the existence of a constitutional amendment that forbids disenfranchisement based on race. Much of this disenfranchisement resulted from extralegal methods—force and fraud. But some of it simply took advantage of the evasive opportunities afforded by constitutional formalism. So long as the justices refused to inquire into legislative motive or to closely examine the discriminatory exercise of administrative discretion, southern whites were able to disenfranchise blacks without violating the Constitution.

"Similar evasive techniques," he adds, sustained "enormous racial disparities in education funding despite clear substantive constitutional norms prohibiting such discrimination."[36] A long decade of evasion after *Brown* led federal judges and administrators to distrust southern officials and to search for ways to evaluate the *results* of their desegregation proposals.

FROM "ANTI-CLASSIFICATION" TO "ANTI-SUBORDINATION"

During the heyday of the Warren Court, a few of its members—most notably Justices Goldberg, Brennan, Douglas, and Fortas—began to formulate a more ambitious alternative to the color-blind interpretation of the Equal Protection clause. For them, state-sponsored racial discrimination was just the tip of a very large iceberg. Guaranteeing "equal protection of the law" implies not just equal treatment by government, but, in Justice Goldberg's phrase, the right "to be treated as equal members of the community." They argued that the postwar amendments "do not permit Negroes to be considered as second-class citizens in *any* aspect of our public life."[37]

In the 1960s this meant applying the prohibitions of the Civil War amendments to the behavior of private citizens, not just "state action."[38] According to Justice Brennan, constitutional rights can be "violated by widespread habitual practices or conventions regarded as prescribing norms for conduct, and supported by common consent, or official or unofficial community sanctions."[39] The objective was to dismantle *all* elements of what Justice Goldberg called the "caste system in the United States," whether public or private, legal or customary.[40] This goal could be achieved only by piercing the veil of legal forms to recognize and attack underlying social inequalities. The "hope and promise of Brown," Justice Breyer wrote in 2007, "is the promise of true racial equality—not as a matter of fine words on paper, but as a matter of everyday life in the Nation's cities and schools."

In legal circles this perspective eventually became known as the "anti-subordination" challenge to the "anti-classification" understanding of the Fourteenth Amendment and civil rights statutes. In the words of Yale law professor Reva Siegel, the "anti-subordination" understanding is based on "the conviction that it is wrong for the state to engage in practices that enforce the inferior social status of historically oppressed groups."[41] Siegel and her colleague Jack Balkin explained that "antisubordination theorists contend that guarantees of equal citizenship cannot be realized under conditions of pervasive social stratification and argue that law should reform institutions and practices that enforce the secondary social status of historically oppressed groups."[42]

This perspective shifts the focus of Equal Protection jurisprudence from *legal status* to a broader, more amorphous *social status*, and from the treatment of *individuals* to the treatment of *groups*. In effect it dissolves the distinction between public action and private action. And it places on both judges and federal administrators continuing responsibility for reforming "institutions and practices" that contribute to systemic inequality, with no clear end in sight.

The most obvious implication for school desegregation is the elimination of the distinction between de jure and de facto segregation. If the effect of segregation is to provide an inferior education to minority students and thus to perpetuate their inferior social status, then it makes little difference what causes this racial separation. Moreover, so-called de facto segregation is the product not just of school districts' siting and assignment decisions, but of residential segregation, which itself is in part the product of decades of government policies at the state, local, and national levels. Although the Supreme Court never explicitly abandoned the de jure/de facto distinction, many of its decisions on evidentiary matters made it easy to prove that de facto segregation had been the product of illegal government action.

Another implication of the anti-subordination perspective is that judicial scrutiny should not stop at the achievement of racial balance in public schools, but must proceed to evaluate the *quality* of the education offered to minority students. Simply achieving the right ratio of white and black students (whatever that ratio might be) does not ensure that minority students are treated fairly within the classroom. Nor does it provide the resources that might be necessary for addressing all the effects that poverty and racial discrimination can have on the development of young minds. Balkin and Siegel highlight these vast ambitions when they write: "The antisubordination principle sits in perpetual judgment of American civil rights law, condemning its formalism, compromises, and worldly limitations, and summoning it to more socially transformative ends."[43] Remaking public schools was but one part of the larger anti-subordination project.

TARGETING RACIAL ISOLATION

The lower court judges who succeeded in jump-starting southern school desegregation in the mid-1960s did not engage in extended debate over the anti-classification and anti-subordination approaches to equal protection. Instead they focused their attention on the seemingly intractable practical problem of inducing thousands of recalcitrant school districts (and those federal district court judges who aided and abetted them) to change their ways. This unprecedented challenge kept the Fifth Circuit, the appellate court with jurisdiction over many southern states, in emergency session for months. In a pivotal 1965 decision, that court announced that "the time has come for foot-dragging public school boards to move with celerity toward desegregation." It "urged school authority to grasp the nettle now."[44] A year later the

Fifth Circuit instructed school officials "to take affirmative action" to achieve "the conversion of a *de jure* segregated dual system into a unitary, nonracial (nondiscriminatory) system—lock, stock, and barrel: students, faculty, staff, facilities, programs, and activities." "The only school desegregation plan that meets constitutional standards," it declared, "is one that *works*."[45] The Supreme Court echoed this theme in its pivotal 1968 *Green* decision: "*The burden on a school board today is to come forward with a plan that promises realistically to work, and promises realistically to work now.*"[46]

To determine what "works," Fifth Circuit relied on HEW's guidelines on the number of black students attending formerly white schools. (The details of these guidelines are described in chapter 4.) Without such clear quantitative guidelines, the judges realized, it would be nearly impossible to bring about substantial change in four thousand southern school systems. Use of racial statistics was an example of what John Skrentny has called "administrative pragmatism," the urgent need for judicially manageable standards in complex and contentious desegregation cases.[47]

As we will see in chapters 4 and 5, this initial demand for rather modest enrollment of black students in formerly white schools eventually morphed into a demand that the number of white and black students in each school reflect the racial ratio of the school district as a whole. Only then could a "dual" system demonstrate that it had become "unitary." To defend so extensive a change in public education, though, it was not sufficient to rely solely on an "administrative pragmatism" argument. It was quickly supplemented with a more compelling argument about the harm of "racial isolation."

This position was first enunciated in a 1967 report of the United States Commission on Civil Rights entitled *Racial Isolation in the Public Schools*. Its conclusion summarized what soon became the conventional wisdom:

> The central truth which emerges from this report and from all of the Commission's investigations is simply this: Negro children suffer serious harm when their education takes place in public schools which are racially segregated, *whatever the source of such segregation may be*. Negro children who attend predominantly Negro schools do not achieve as well as other children, Negro and white. Their aspirations are more restricted than those of other children and they do not have as much confidence that they can influence their own futures. When they become adults, they are less likely to participate in the mainstream of American society, and more likely to fear, dislike, and avoid white Americans.[48]

The Commission did not expect the federal courts to embrace this understanding of desegregation. It looked instead to Congress to enact legislation specifying that in no public school should black enrollment exceed 50 percent.[49]

Contrary to the Commission's expectations, federal judges were more willing to adopt this understanding of desegregation than was Congress. The message was conveyed to federal judges by the expert witnesses who testified in the trial phase of desegregation cases. For example, during the first round of the Denver litigation, Judge William Doyle stated, "We cannot ignore the overwhelming evidence to the effect that isolation or segregation per se is a substantial factor in producing unequal educational outcomes." Consequently, "we must conclude that segregation, *regardless of its cause,* is a major factor in producing inferior schools and unequal educational opportunity."[50] Reflecting on the testimony he had heard about the harm done by racial isolation, the trial judge in the Detroit case found it "unfortunate that we cannot deal with public school segregation on a no-fault basis, for if racial segregation in our public schools is an evil, then it should make no difference whether we classify it as de jure or de facto." The court's goal was simply "to remedy a condition which we believe needs correction."[51]

Behind this "racial isolation" argument lay two fundamental assumptions. The first was that *Brown* promised not just the elimination of racial discrimination, but "equal educational opportunity." As Justice Marshall put it in his *Milliken* dissent, "We deal here with the right of all our children, whatever their race, to an equal start in life and to an equal opportunity to reach their full potential as citizens."[52]

The second assumption was that social science has demonstrated that schools that are overwhelming minority offer their students an inferior education. "Research suggests," Justice Breyer claimed, "that black children from segregated educational environments significantly increase their achievement levels once they are placed in more integrated settings." While conceding that "other studies reach different conclusions," he was convinced that taken as a whole "the studies have provided remarkably consistent results." Moreover, integration teaches black and white children alike how "to engage in the kind of cooperation among Americans of all races that is necessary to make a land of three hundred million people into one Nation."[53] Justice Marshall similarly warned that "unless our children begin to learn together, there is little hope that our people will ever learn to live together."[54]

Especially in the late 1960s and early 1970s, federal district court judges relied heavily on social-science evidence to justify their desegregation orders. For example, the district court judge who ordered the desegregation of San Francisco's schools in 1970 cited the Coleman report and the Civil Rights Commission's *Racial Isolation* study to conclude that "black students in identifiably black schools do not perform as well as they would perform in an integrated school.... While integration of schools would improve the academic performance of black children, it would have little or no adverse effect on the academic performance of white children."[55] Similarly, in the Charlotte-Mecklenburg case, Judge James McMillan wrote,

> One point on which the experts all agree (and the statistics tend to bear them out) is that a racial mix in which black students heavily predominate tends to retard the progress of the whole group, whereas if students are mingled with a clear white majority, such as a 70/30 ratio (approximately the ratio of white to black students in Mecklenburg County), the better students can hold their pace, with substantial improvement for the poorer students.[56]

Reviewing the forty-one days of testimony presented to the trial judge in the Detroit case, Eleanor Wolf found,

> Taken as a whole, the message of the testimony on education was that school resources could not be equalized, learning could not be effective, background disadvantages could not be overcome in the absence of racial (plaintiffs' emphasis) or race-class (defendants' emphasis) mixture in the classroom. Mandatory reassignment to create such a mixture would improve the academic achievement of blacks, would not harm (and probably would help) whites, would stimulate black aspirations, enhance black self-esteem, heighten teachers' expectations, and improve interracial relations in both schools and society.[57]

Trial judges throughout the country listened to the same expert witnesses, and most reached the same conclusion.

DEEPER AND DEEPER

The "racial isolation" argument initially focused on the racial composition of the student body. The aim was to create urban schools that were roughly 70 percent white and 30 percent black. Such schools would enroll enough higher SES white children to establish a healthy school culture and enough black children to make them feel comfortable in their new surroundings. When schools dip below 60 percent white, social scientists warned, they reached the tipping point for massive "white flight."

Although student ratios loomed large in the early rounds of litigation, they were never the entire story. Desegregation orders required the reassignment of teachers as well as students, sometimes requiring that white and black teachers be distributed equally among schools within the district. In *Green* the Court explained that its mandate for conversion of "dual" school systems to "unitary" ones extended "not just to the composition of student bodies" but "to every facet of school operations—faculty, staff, transportation, extracurricular activities and facilities."[58] These became known as the six "*Green* factors" to which lower courts must attend.

Nine years after *Green*, the Supreme Court recognized the broad authority of district court judges to mandate programs designed to "restore the victims of discriminatory conduct to the position they would have enjoyed" had public officials not acted unconstitutionally. The injunction approved by the Court required Detroit to establish new magnet and vocational schools as well as "in-service training for teachers and administrators, guidance and counseling programs, and revised testing procedures." The Court explained that judges should not "close their eyes" to the many inequalities "that flow from a longstanding segregated system."[59]

As we will see in chapter 7, judges were increasingly drawn into "second generation" desegregation controversies such as bilingual education, tracking, discipline, special education, and "multicultural" curricula. According to Judge Richard Matsch, who oversaw the latter stages of the Denver desegregation effort, a "unitary school system" is one in which all students "have equal access to the opportunities for education, with the publicly provided educational resources distributed equitably, and with the expectation that all students can acquire a community-defined level of knowledge and skills consistent with her individual efforts and abilities."[60] In short, the "equal educational opportunity" reading of *Brown* that Justices Marshall and Breyer championed and that lay behind judicial efforts to address "racial isolation" required ongoing judicial supervision of nearly every feature of schooling.

The sweeping implications of the "racial isolation/equal educational opportunity" approach was evident in the appendix to the NAACP's 1991 amicus brief in *Freeman v. Pitts*, a heavily footnoted statement signed by fifty-two prominent social scientists. They argued that the Court should not authorize the termination of desegregation suits even after years of good-faith compliance by school officials. The social scientists emphasized that "assigning minority and white students to the same school is no panacea for educational inequality. The creation of racially-mixed rather than racially-segregated schools is *just the beginning of the long-term process* of interracial schooling." They explained that "brief exposure to whites, in schools that do nothing else to produce equal opportunity, will not cure the harms created by a history of segregation." Court-ordered changes "in student assignment cannot be understood in isolation from changes in the curriculum, the adjustments of teachers and administrators, the reaction in the community, the changes in housing patterns, or the consequences of past segregation." Since "the way in which desegregated schools are structured is crucial," the social scientists offered numerous recommendations including the following: developing "cooperative learning groups" within the classroom; "utilizing multi-ethnic texts"; "avoiding unnecessary ability groupings"; creating disciplinary codes that recognize "cultural differences"; "changing symbols and customs of the school to put 'old' and 'new' on equal footing"; establishing "detailed, practical, timely and empathetic human relations programs for teachers and students"; "promoting community and parental involvement in the development of desegregation plans"; and substantially increasing the number of minority teachers and administrators.[61] Nearly two decades later another amicus brief, this one signed by 553 social scientists, made a similar point, distinguishing "desegregation"—which "generally describes the creation of schools containing substantial percentages of students from two or more racial and ethnic groups"—from "integration"— which "refers to the positive implementation of desegregation with equal status for all groups and respect for all cultures."[62] The latter requires far more than reaching the right balance of black and white students.

These statements indicate just how extensive were the responsibilities thrust upon judges by the "equal educational opportunity" interpretation of *Brown*. Justice Marshall suggested that in some instances this would require a "radical transformation of the schools within the system."[63] As David Kirp and Gary Babcock explain in their study of desegregation efforts in several cities, judges who adopted this understanding of *Brown* "undertook to accomplish no less than the remaking of a system of education and the social order in which that system was embedded. . . . No one knew at the outset what the task involved."[64]

Judicial Capacity and Social Science

Do judges have the institutional capacity to accomplish such extensive reform of public schools? While proponents of the "color-blind/limited intervention" position shouted "no!" the advocates of the "racial isolation/equal educational opportunity" position responded ". . . well, maybe." To meet this challenge, they created new judicial procedures and remedial tools—most notably the structural injunction. As we will see in chapter 4, the Fifth Circuit both revamped its methods for overseeing district court decisions and formed a productive alliance with the Office for Civil Rights in the Department of Health, Education, and Welfare. These innovations marked the beginning of a new form of federal court case, which Harvard law professor Abram Chayes called "public law litigation."[65]

Innovation was necessary, advocates of this position insisted, because the alternative—continuing to rely on state and local officials to provide equal educational opportunity—was simply unacceptable. Existing public schools had failed poor and minority children for generations and would continue to do so unless subject to strict federal scrutiny. Since adequate supervision would not be coming from Congress or the executive branch, it must be provided by the federal judiciary. "Local control" was the problem, not an acceptable default position.

The success of this extensive judicial enterprise rested in large part on judges' access to reliable social-science findings. Trial judges heard testimony and enlisted the help of experts on three topics. The issue to which they devoted most time—but which in the long run was probably least important—was the extent to which decisions by school officials contributed to the racial isolation (or, as the NAACP often put it, "containment") of minority students. Such testimony combined extensive discussion of local history and demographics with dubious conjectures about the causes of residential segregation. By the end of the 1970s, Supreme Court doctrine on what constitutes evidence of intentional segregation had made it unlikely that any major city could be found innocent.

More important—as the above quotes from district court judges indicate—was social-science evidence on the harm done by segregation and the beneficial effects of achieving racial balance in the 70/30 to 60/40 range. Judges were frequently assured that the substantial educational benefit of desegregation thus defined was a well-established fact. But, as we will see, that consensus soon evaporated.

A third form of expertise became important after a school district had been found guilty of unconstitutional segregation. As litigation transitioned from the liability phase to the remedial phase, judges needed to figure out what to do next. Drawing new attendance zones was the first order of business, but then came wave after wave of questions about teacher assignments, language training, discipline, curriculum, extracurricular activities, conditions of school buildings, leadership, new construction, and much more. Judges typically appointed special masters, receivers, and monitoring committees to help draft injunctions, modify them on a regular basis, and oversee their implementation over the years. Sometimes these appointed "experts" were educational administrators with long experience. At other times, though, they were education school professors with little experience in the classroom or in the principal's office. Busy judges had no choice but to lean heavily on these surrogates. As the years passed, judges left more and more matters to those they had installed as agents of the courts. First from choice and then from necessity, reliance on educational experts was central to the "racial isolation/equal educational opportunity" perspective.

MORE DATA, LESS AGREEMENT

From *Brown*'s footnote 11 to the appointment of two education school professors to oversee the $2 billion court-ordered reconstruction of Kansas City schools, the battle over school desegregation has long been intertwined with disputes over interpretation of social-science evidence. When judges turned to social scientists for support and advice, many were eager to oblige. Over the years, the focus of social-science research went through three phases. In the 1940s and 1950s, the central question was the psychological effects of de jure segregation on black students. A statement attached to the NAACP's brief in *Brown* signed by thirty-five prominent social scientists presented the consensus of those who studied the issue: segregation enforced by law harms minority students' confidence and self-esteem, and thus reduces their ability to learn. In the 1960s and 1970s, focus shifted to the social consequences of racial isolation. Another consensus developed, this one emphasizing the advantages of interracial contact and the educational benefits of going to school with higher SES peers. Starting in the 1980s, research slowly shifted from broad-brush efforts to demonstrate the harm of racial isolation and the benefits of integration to more nuanced investigation of what forms and mechanisms of desegregation work best.

As a rule, the strength of the scholarly consensus on desegregation issues has been inversely proportional to the amount of available evidence. With more real-world examples to examine, studies of the consequences of desegregation multiplied in the 1970s and 1980s. They offered little support either for early claims about self-esteem or subsequent predictions about the benefits of reducing racial isolation. In her comprehensive 1991 review of studies of race relations in schools that had undergone desegregation, Janet Ward Schofield noted that "the aura of optimism and consensus that had characterized social science in earlier years had dissipated by the early 1980s. . . . many voices in the social science community were raised to assert or acknowledge that desegregation accomplished less than many had hoped it would."[66] These disappointing results led many social scientists to change the research questions they asked and the nature of the advice they offered. Only then, as Roger Levesque has noted, did researchers begin to isolate those "contextual and process factors" that seemed to make the difference.[67]

THE EVAPORATING CONSENSUS I: SELF-ESTEEM

In *Brown*, Chief Justice Warren placed heavy emphasis on the claim that segregation stigmatizes black students, "generat[ing] a feeling of inferiority as to their status in the community that may affect their hearts and minds in a way unlikely ever to be undone." The "sense of inferiority affects the motivation of a child to learn," and thus retards "the educational and mental development" of African American students. This view was widely shared: in the late 1940s a survey of social scientists who studied race relations found that "90% expressed the opinion that enforced segregation had detrimental psychological effects on segregated groups, even if equal facilities were provided."[68] Over forty social scientists had offered testimony to that effect in the lower court cases leading up to *Brown*. Since the very purpose of Jim Crow was to stigmatize and subordinate African Americans, such expert opinions seemed to confirm the common-sense understanding of the rationale for and consequences of a racial caste system.

The most influential presentation of this argument came in the Social Science Statement written by Kenneth Clark and Stuart Cook, appended to the NAACP's brief, and relied upon by Chief Justice Warren. The NAACP legal team had been badly divided over whether to include social-science evidence—particularly Kenneth and Mamie Clark's doll studies—in its argument before the Supreme Court. William Coleman, who had previously clerked for the pivotal Justice Felix Frankfurter and years later became US Secretary of Transportation, reported, "Of all the debunkers, I was the most debunking. . . . Those damn dolls! I thought it was a joke."[69] One problem with the study was its small sample size. Another was that although black girls in segregated schools preferred white dolls to black dolls, black children in integrated schools in the North seemed to prefer white dolls even more frequently. And preschool black girls had a stronger preference for white dolls than those who had spent time in school. So it was hard to argue that school segregation by itself was the cause of the problem. Although these difficulties were known to the NAACP lawyers—they had been pointed out by a *Yale Law Journal* article in 1953—Thurgood Marshall decided to include the study because it offered the Court a ready hook on which to hang its constitutional argument.[70] It is doubtful that anyone on the NAACP team or on the Supreme Court found the social-science evidence dispositive—or believed that a contrary finding should lead to a reversal of *Brown*.

A number of more sophisticated studies of students' aspirations and self-esteem later came to the surprising conclusion that African American children usually have *higher* self-esteem than white children of the same age, and that attending schools with more white students can *lower* their self-esteem. According to Roger Levesque, studies consistently found that "the level of aspirations of segregated Blacks was as high or higher than that of segregated Whites." Indeed, "annual surveys reveal that African American adolescents have higher self-esteem than any other ethnic group in the United States." In sum, "the general findings were strikingly consistent and in the opposite direction of what likely was expected after *Brown* as well as even today."[71]

Stuart Cook, one of the authors of the 1954 Statement, responded to this emerging evidence by claiming that although the earlier studies had been correct, "in the mid-1960s, the picture regarding black self-esteem changed radically."[72] Black pride neutralized the stigmatizing effects of segregation. Whether the new findings reflected improved research methods or changing attitudes, they undercut the original social-science arguments for mandatory desegregation. They also highlighted the tentative nature of social-science claims.

THE EVAPORATING CONSENSUS II: RACIAL ISOLATION

In the late 1960s and early 1970s, James Coleman, the nation's leading authority on educational opportunity, testified on behalf of the plaintiffs in the Washington, DC, and Denver, Colorado, desegregation cases. He highlighted the advantages of bringing more high-SES students into predominantly black schools, but conceded that doing so "takes only a small step toward equality of educational opportunity." Given the powerful effect of family SES, he explained, "even if the school is integrated, the heterogeneity of backgrounds with which children enter school is largely preserved in the heterogeneity of their performance when they finish."[73]

By 1975 Coleman had reluctantly concluded that "white flight" had drained so many high SES students from school systems subject to busing orders that some desegregation plans had become not just ineffective, but counterproductive.[74] For this heresy he was subjected to scurrilous attacks by his fellow academics. The president of the American Sociological Association led an effort to censure him and subject him to an ethics investigation. Although that effort was ultimately unsuccessful, Coleman was subjected to shrill denunciations by Association members carrying signs with swastikas over his name. Coleman later wrote, "We should not forget how strong the consensus was at the time among social scientists that busing was an unalloyed benefit, and a policy not to be questioned."[75]

The social-science research that led many judges to embrace the "racial isolation" approach to desegregation had two strands. One was based on the "contact theory" developed by Harvard psychology professor Gordon Allport. It held that the more frequently members of racial and ethnic groups come in contact with one another, the weaker stereotypes and prejudices become, and the greater these groups' ability to work together. To this seemingly common-sensical notion, Allport added crucial preconditions: the parties must come together with equal status; they must engage in common projects; and the institutions within which they operate must support the effort. Whether these conditions would be met in desegregated schools was the big question, but not one that received much attention in the heady first decade of desegregation.

The more prominent strand was sometimes given the clunky title "lateral transmission of values," and at other times simply called the "Pettigrew thesis" after its most prolific advocate, Harvard social psychology professor Thomas Pettigrew. It maintained that increasing the SES of minority students' peers improves the school's culture, changing the aspirations and expectation of teachers and students alike. "Lateral transmission of values" was primarily an argument about the integration of high- and low-SES students—not simply black and white. In school desegregation cases, its proponents tended to assume that racial balance would substantially increase the average SES levels of schools attended by minority students. This was sometimes the case—but not always. Much depended on the desegregation plan negotiated by federal officials and the subsequent choices of white parents.

Proponents of this argument often relied on the 1966 Coleman report for support. That seminal report had found that most variation in student achievement is a result of the SES of students' *families*. But it also concluded that the SES of a student's *peers* has some effect on that student's achievement, though not nearly as much as the SES of the student's family. (It was for this reason that Coleman had testified in support of several ambitious desegregation plans.) But in a generally friendly review of the Coleman report, Nobel laureate James Heckman warned that even these limited findings about peer effects "did not hold up in subsequent reanalysis of his data."[76] Unfortunately, some judges failed to heed the crucial distinction between the effect of the SES of a student's family and the SES of a student's peers. Frequently they heard only from proponents of the peer-effects thesis, with little testimony from a growing number of critics.

Cracks in the social-science consensus that busing was an "unalloyed benefit" first appeared in 1972–73 when Harvard sociology professor David Armor engaged in a debate with his colleague Thomas Pettigrew in the pages of the *Public Interest*.[77] Reviewing some of the early studies on the effects of early desegregation plans, Armor claimed that black students did no better in predominantly white schools than otherwise similarly situated black students who remained in predominantly black schools. Nor did he find any improvement in race relations in desegregated schools; indeed, the experience may have soured minority students on integration.

Pettigrew and his coauthors challenged Armor's methodology, claiming that he ignored more encouraging studies. They also criticized him for ignoring "the critical distinction between desegregation and integration." The former "is achieved by simply ending segregation and bringing blacks and whites together." The latter is a "complex, dynamic process" that "improves the quality of the racial interaction" by encouraging "positive group contact, cross-racial acceptance, and equal dignity and access to resources for both groups." The Armor-Pettigrew debate raised methodological issues that would haunt the desegregation question for decades to come. It also raised the question of how judges could go beyond "desegregation" to achieve "integration," and how researchers could distinguish one from the other. If "integration" means "desegregation done well," then by definition it will always be successful.

Over the next decade, studies of the effects of desegregation plans proliferated. Roger Levesque offers this summary of their findings:

> The general conclusion that emerges from this area of research is that findings reveal weak and inconsistent effects and generally view desegregated schooling neither as a demonstrated success or a demonstrated failure. Indeed, some major literature reviews of the research on desegregation's effects find studies' methodological limitations to be so problematic as to question the studies' legitimacy and relative worth.[78]

This verdict of "inconclusive" applies to studies of both race relations and academic achievement.

Contact Theory

In an important 1975 review of the literature, Nancy St. John noted that the preconditions that Allport had established for successful reduction in prejudice seldom apply to schools undergoing desegregation, where "classroom contact is often short run, competitive, and between unequals, and, though formerly sanctioned, may be informally resented and bypassed by those in authority."[79] A decade and a half later, noted University of Pittsburgh psychology professor Janet Schofield published the most exhaustive review of the growing literature on desegregation and intergroup relations. She found:

> In general, the reviews of desegregation and intergroup relations were unable to come to any conclusions about what the probable effects of desegregation were.... Numerous studies found generally positive effects. At least as many found generally negative effects. A substantial number found mixed results, that is positive for one group and neutral or negative for other groups. Finally,

some found no effect. Thus virtually all of the reviewers determined that few, if any, firm conclusions about the impact of desegregation on intergroup relations could be drawn.

Although this muddle was in part the result of methodological problems, "one other very simple factor also contributed substantially—the probably inevitable failure of researchers in the field to agree on an operational definition of the concept of desegregation."[80]

Schofield and virtually everyone else who examined the issue emphasized that according to "contact theory," *how* desegregation is carried out is far more important than the proportion of black and white students in each school.[81] Much the same could be said about the extent to which desegregation contributes to civil engagement among students. Although attending an integrated school can in some instances improve students' ability and willingness to engage in civic activities in our diverse democracy, sometimes "schools with multiethnic student bodies can foster *less* civic-minded behavior."[82] As Robert Putnam has reluctantly concluded, increased racial and ethnic diversity often reduce social capital, leading people to "hunker down" rather than engage in civic affairs.[83]

Academic Achievement

From the thirty-thousand-foot level, the argument that school desegregation substantially reduced the racial achievement gap seems strong. Between 1970 and 1986, the gap between black and white students' math and reading scores on the National Evaluation of Academic Progress (NAEP) test was cut in half. That improvement coincided with a substantial decrease in the number of predominantly minority schools. When the extent of racial mixing—measured either by "evenness" or "exposure"—leveled off, so did progress in reducing the racial achievement gap.

The central methodological difficulty is isolating the effect of one set of changes—federally mandated efforts to end de jure segregation and to reduce racial isolation—from an array of other changes taking place at the same time. One was the seismic cultural shift that accompanied the civil rights revolution of the 1960s. Overt prejudice steadily declined. The themes of black power and black pride grew to prominence within the black community. Another was the growing political power of African Americans, especially in the large cities home to so many minority children. A third was the expansion of federal programs that provided more educational resources to underserved school districts and students, e.g., Head Start and Title I money. Yet another was change in educational finance at the state and local levels: more money was directed at schools with a high percentage of poor children. The health and nutrition of poor and minority families improved throughout these decades, in part as a result of the expansion of welfare-state programs.

Perhaps most important was the increased educational levels of the *parents* of the African American students who attended school in the 1970s and 1980s. The SES of a student's family is the most important determinant of their performance in school. In 1971, 41 percent of white seventh graders but only 21 percent of black seventh graders reported having a parent with post–high school education. By 1990, that twenty-point gap had shrunk to only a four-point one: 53 percent for whites, 49 percent for blacks.[84]

As Robert Putnam has shown in a recent book, the rates at which African Americans graduated from high school and completed college rose rapidly from 1940 through 1970. Hoping to save their allegedly "separate but equal" segregated school systems, southern states poured money into black schools: between 1940 and 1954, spending on black schools increased by nearly 300 percent and on white schools by less than 40 percent.[85] Putnam argues that in many ways educational opportunities for African Americans improved more before 1970 than after. Whether or not this is true, certainly the effects of earlier improvements rubbed off on the children of those who attended school in the 1950s and 1960s.

What policymakers—whether federal judges, federal administrators, state officials, or local school leaders—most needed to know was how the desegregation plans *they* could put into effect would improve student achievement. By the mid-1970s a number of studies had examined the initial consequences of the massive desegregation that took place in the preceding decade. Here, too, the results were highly variable, with the most optimistic finding only modest improvement in the academic performance of black students. Desegregation seemed to improve the scores of African American students in some subjects, some grades, some years, some school districts, and even some schools within a district. Larger trends were surprisingly hard to discern.

Examining 120 studies completed by 1975, Nancy St. John concluded that

> desegregation has not rapidly closed the black-white gap in academic achievement, though it has rarely lowered and sometimes raised the scores of black children. Improvement has been more often reported in the early grades, in arithmetic, and in schools over 50% white, but even here the gains have usually been mixed, intermittent, or non-significant. White achievement has been unaffected in schools that remained majority white but significantly lower in majority black schools. Biracial schooling is apparently not detrimental to the academic performance of black children, but it may have negative effects on

self-esteem. It is not merely academic self-concept in the face of higher standards that is threatened, but also general self-concept. In addition, desegregation apparently lowers educational and vocational aspirations.[86]

A subsequent meta-analysis conducted by Crain and Mahart was somewhat more encouraging. They found a small improvement in educational achievement in desegregated schools (slightly less than one tenth of a standard deviation). But since almost all these gains appeared in kindergarten and first grade, it was unclear whether this improvement was the result of changes in schooling or in changes taking place before children entered school.[87]

The most comprehensive meta-analysis of achievement studies was undertaken by a panel established by the National Institute of Education (NIE) and published in 1984. The panel could identify only nineteen studies suitable for making causal inferences, and some panel members found even these studies methodologically flawed. Thomas Cook, the expert on social-science methodology who chaired the panel, concluded that although desegregation did not improve math scores, it did increase mean reading levels: "The gain reliably differed from zero and was estimated to be between two to six weeks [of a school year] across the studies examined." Median gains, in contrast, "did not reliably differ from zero." Cook found "the *variability* in effect sizes more striking and less well understood than any measure of central tendencies."[88]

A decade later Janet Schofield reviewed 250 studies of academic achievement and came to a similar conclusion: "Desegregation has had some positive impact on the reading skills of African American youngsters. The effect is not large, nor does it occur in all situations, but a modest measurable effect does seem apparent." Mathematics skills, though, "seem generally unaffected by desegregation."[89]

Ten years after that, Duke economic professor Charles Clotfelter, a respected authority on (and supporter of) desegregation efforts, echoed the NIE panel's finding: "Studies that have sought to determine the effect of desegregation on the achievement of blacks have come up with a decidedly mixed set of results. In general, the research suggests no effect on mathematics achievement for blacks with some modest positive effect on reading for blacks."[90] In 2012, Stanford professor Sean Reardon and his coauthors wrote, "it remains unclear if, and to what extent, school racial segregation affects student achievement."[91]

Although most desegregation studies focused on the racial achievement gap in reading and math, some looked at graduation rates and college attendance. There is some evidence that black students who attend racially mixed schools graduate at a higher rate than those who attend racially isolated schools, especially schools located in poor neighborhoods. Such students may also be more likely to enter and graduate from college, and less likely to engage in crime.[92] At the same time, some studies have indicated that raising the SES of the student body might actually increase dropout rates among Hispanic students. Others suggest that desegregation may increase the suspension rate for black students.[93] Evaluating the long-term effects of desegregation is particularly difficult because it requires following students for many years after leaving school.

WHAT REALLY WORKS?

These disappointing findings did not lead social scientists who studied race and education to give up on the desegregation project: the fact that in 2006 hundreds of prominent researchers signed a brief touting the benefit of integrated schools shows that was far from the case. Research demonstrates, the 553 maintained, "that racially integrated schools tend to provide benefits that are not available in segregated schools." But they were far more cautious than the experts who had previously testified in desegregation cases. On academic achievement, they reported:

> Reviews of early desegregation research lead to the conclusion that school desegregation . . . appears to have a positive impact on reading achievement, but there appears to be little or no effect on math scores. The impact of desegregation on achievement varies by context, appearing somewhat stronger for younger students. It also appears that there are stronger achievement gains when segregation is voluntary.[94]

"Racially desegregated schools," they warned, "are not an educational or social panacea and the extent of benefits will depend on *how desegregation is structured and implemented.*" In other word, creating racially balanced schools is not enough. The success of "integration"—which they carefully distinguished from "desegregation"—requires much more attention to what happens on a day-to-day basis in the classroom, the hallways, the cafeterias, and the playing fields of public schools. Such expert testimony at first led judges to become more deeply involved in education policy, and later to question their ability to engineer school improvement.

In the first two decades of the twenty-first century, a few studies found greater benefit from reducing racial isolation than had earlier ones. Some of these studies made innovative use of large national data sets. Others looked at the consequences of the termination of decades-old desegregation orders in particular cities. (These post-termination studies are reviewed in chapter 8.)

Almost all found the socioeconomic composition of the student body more important than the racial mix. Like previous studies, they also found that voluntary programs produce better results than mandatory ones, and that the effects are greater for younger students than for older ones.[95]

Two important National Bureau of Economic Research (NBER) papers used longitudinal data on the educational attainment and income history of thousands of white and black students to examine the long-term effects of desegregation.[96] Both took advantage of the fact that the timing of desegregation orders was "driven largely by a number of chance factors, not systematic differences in families or neighborhood conditions that may have independently affected children's outcomes."[97] This feature of court orders provides an opportunity to compare the trajectory of students who attended desegregated schools with that of students who attended schools that were similar in other respects but not yet desegregated—an ingenious way to produce a de facto control group.

In his 2011 NBER paper and in *Children of the Dream*, the book based on that research, Rucker Johnson found a strong relationship between the number of years students spent in a desegregated school and (1) total years of education (up 30 percent for those attending a desegregated school for twelve years), (2) adult wages (also up 30 percent), (3) adult health status, (4) incarceration rates (down 25 percent), and poverty rates (also down 25 percent).[98] Johnson attributes these beneficial outcomes to two shifts accompanying desegregation: "sharp increases in per-pupil spending (by an average of 22.5%) and significant reductions in the average class sizes experienced by black children."[99] These changes were particularly important in the South, where for years black schools were underfunded. Johnson found that money mattered much more than black-white student exposure. Where resources increased significantly but exposure did not, students did well. Conversely, "in court-ordered desegregation districts in which school spending for black children did not appreciably change, however, although the children experienced greater classroom exposure to their white peers, they did not make a comparable improvement in their educational and socioeconomic trajectories."[100]

In 2022 Garrett Anstreicher, Jason Fletcher, and Owen Thompson used the same technique to analyze a far larger, less skewed sample. While Johnson's sample contained fewer than 4,500 black respondents, their working sample included more than five million individuals, including "60% of all Black students attending public US schools in 1968." They found that in the South the positive effects "were qualitatively quite large," though not quite as large as Johnson's: "full exposure [to desegregation] was estimated to have increased high school graduation rates by approximately 15 percentage points, increased employment rates by approximately 10 percentage points, and increased hourly wages by approximately 30%."[101] Surprisingly, though, they found "no substantive effects outside of the South." They suggest that this result reflected the fact that spending on schools with a large number of black students increased more rapidly in the South than in other parts of the country, and that class size in schools with a significant number of black students fell in the South but not elsewhere.[102]

Anstreicher, Fletcher, and Thompson emphasized that the "strong regional heterogeneity" revealed by the mining of their large national data sets "has important implications for evaluating both the historical record of court ordered desegregation and the potential effects of current and future desegregation initiatives." In particular,

> Our results suggest that the most impactful legacy of these policies lies in their systematic dismantling of the overtly segregated educational systems that prevailed in the Jim Crow South. The large estimated effects of concrete measurable outcomes like adult educational attainment and poverty rates strongly indicate that this effort was not merely symbolic in nature, but was rather a generational achievement that tangibly improved the long term well-being of southern African American children.[103]

The "distinct paucity of effects outside the South," in contrast, indicate "the limitations to the efficacy of legally imposed integration initiatives in certain settings." Since most areas outside the South had not imposed de jure segregation, there "court ordered integration was a less direct challenge to the status quo." Moreover, the smaller size of school districts outside the South made white flight easier. They conclude that their "null results for northern school districts" raise serious doubts about "whether ongoing or potential future integration initiatives are likely to be effective in settings where they are not part of a transformative change to local education systems or where effective paths to avoiding integrated schools are available to white families." This finding, they caution, should not lead us to ignore the fact that their study provides "compelling evidence that court ordered integration was extraordinarily effective in the context of the post Civil Rights era South."[104]

In 2014, after nearly a half century of research on desegregation, Sean Reardon and Ann Owens argued that while researchers "are generally motivated by a concern that segregation leads to racial and socioeconomic disparities in educational outcomes," the literature on the topic "appears to lack a detailed and comprehensive theoretical model (or models) of exactly how segregation might affect educational and social outcomes."[105] In other words, we do not yet have a handle on which of the many granular features of public education improve and retard the educational achievement and racial attitudes of a variety of types of students. Nor can we claim to understand how cultural, social, and economic changes outside the classroom interact with these features of public education. Adjusting the ratio of black, white, and Hispanic students within a school might be a useful—though not essential—first step for improving the educational opportunities of minority children. But what goes on within these schools—and in families and neighborhoods—is even more important. And on all those crucial matters, the influence of federal judges and administrators is sharply limited.

THE LIMITS OF SOCIAL SCIENCE

Why has social science been of such limited help to those engaged in the difficult job of desegregating American schools? Part of the problem is inherent in the study of major social phenomenon. It is devilishly difficult to separate the contribution of one factor—in this case mandates from federal (and occasionally state) officials—from the many other factors that affect educational outcomes. Seldom are appropriate control groups—that is, students who are otherwise nearly identical to students affected by desegregation orders—available. As Janet Schofield has explained, "It is always possible that in research without a control group, changes resulting from desegregation will be confounded with changes resulting from larger societal trends."[106] Cities subject to desegregation orders usually differ in important ways from those not ordered to desegregate. Children who participate in voluntary desegregation plans differ from those who fail to volunteer. Students from neighborhoods relatively close to mixed-race schools will probably differ in important ways from those further away.

Additional problems abound. Early studies of desegregation looked only at short-term results, and thus may have missed long-term effects and overemphasized the consequences of tumultuous transitions. Following students over a longer period of time is not only more expensive, but inevitably means losing track of some of the students in the initial sample. School districts favorably disposed to desegregation are more likely to welcome researchers than those who are hostile, creating serious selection bias. Efforts to assess intergroup relations usually rely on surveys, which might not adequately reflect students' behavior. Most studies of changes in academic achievement rely on the NAEP, which uses relatively consistent questions over time. But the NAEP was instituted in 1970, making comparisons with previous years more difficult. These are only a few of the practical and methodological problems that have bedeviled researchers and led to extended arguments about the reliability of various studies.

Compounding the difficulties that frequently confront social scientists is a central feature of desegregation policy: the ambiguity of the key term coupled with disagreement over how success should be measured. Since the Supreme Court never offered a clear definition of what "desegregation" means, desegregation plans differed enormously from city to city. As Janet Schofield has pointed out,

> the social situations that our society labels as "desegregated schools" vary to an extraordinary extent. For example, a suburban school that receives bused inner-city blacks . . . is called "desegregated" even though it is less than 5% black. In sharp contrast, in some urban settings a school would not be considered desegregated unless it were at least 40% or 50% minority. Hence in practice researchers have studied very different situations without always recognizing that the fact that a situation is legally or popularly dubbed as desegregated does not guarantee that it has a great deal in common with other similarly labeled situations.[107]

Failure to distinguish among markedly different forms of "desegregation" makes studies that combine them extremely difficult to interpret: "It could be that desegregation has an impact that is masked because of the tremendous variation caused by other uncontrolled variables. Alternatively, the positive impact of desegregation in some school's classrooms might be counterbalanced by the negative impact in others."[108]

Given the profound disagreements over the meaning and purposes of desegregation described in this chapter, reaching agreement for determining "what works" is particularly difficult. If the purpose is not simply to take a dangerous instrument out of the hands of state and local officials, is it then to increase the resources available to minority students? Improve their achievement on standardized tests? Increase the chances that black and Hispanic students will graduate from high school and enter college? Promote toleration and mutual understanding among racial groups? Not only are some of these criteria hard to measure, but sometimes there are painful trade-offs among them. For example, increasing the average SES of students at a school seems to reduce dropout rates among Asian Americans but increase dropout rates among Mexican Americans. Attending schools with higher proportions of white students appears to reduce the likelihood that a black student will end up in prison but increase the likelihood of being subjected to violence while in school. In general, Hispanic students seem to benefit academically from attending racially diverse schools, but "English-proficient immigrant students perform better in mathematics and science when they attend school with their coethnics."[109]

In evaluating the extensive and conflicting evidence on the consequences of desegregation, it is important to keep in mind the central finding of the Coleman report, namely, that families and neighborhoods have more influence on children than do schools. "The inability of desegregation alone to effect dramatic change," Roger Levesque emphasizes, reflects the fact that

> multiple socializing institutions, both formal and informal, influence youth development. As a result, altering one critical factor in children's schooling may not enhance their self-esteem, improve intergroup relationships, or raise their academic achievement. These outcomes are highly influenced by families, communities, and general societal forces such as economic conditions and opportunities.[110]

Those who design desegregation plans have even less control over these environmental factors than over the day-to-day practices of school teachers and principals. Many judges, litigants, expert witnesses, and school officials initially saw desegregation as a silver bullet that would remake public education and society at large. Bitter experience—bolstered by social-science evidence—led them to lower their expectations.

Conclusion: The Price of Ambiguity

The main theme of this chapter is that over many decades, two competing, fervently held understandings of *Brown v. Board* slowly developed. Neither was ever fully endorsed or rejected by the Supreme Court. Both could find some support in the Court's ambiguous 1954 opinion. Each combined an interpretation of the Equal Protection clause with an assessment of the institutional capacity of the courts and the reliability of social-science findings. And each had a serious shortcoming: the "color-blind/limited intervention" approach could too easily be evaded; the "racial isolation/equal educational opportunity" approach asked more of federal judges and administrators than they could deliver.

A second theme is that social science proved to be a less reliable source of guidance for policymakers than they had originally expected. The results of desegregation studies have routinely been described as "variable" and "inconclusive." By 2006 even those social scientists who most strongly supported desegregation concluded that "the extent of benefits will depend on how desegregation is structured and implemented." Many of the most important factors—the availability of high SES peers, the attitudes and skills of school personnel, the extent to which desegregation is voluntary—are beyond the control of federal (and often state) officials. As we will see in chapters 6–8, the judges' experience with particular school districts combined with the social-science evidence described above led them to revise their expectations, which at first were often wildly optimistic. That is one reason why in recent years the major legal issue has shifted from what schools *must* do to comply with *Brown*, to what they *can* do to promote integration.

Although invocation of social science has occasionally been mere window-dressing in court decisions—as seems to have been the case with the evidence cited in *Brown*'s footnote 11—at other times, it has been more consequential. The evidence presented to lower court judges in the 1960s and 1970s on the detrimental effects of racial isolation and the benefits of racial integration proved to be particularly significant. Equally important (but less often noted) has been the effect of court decisions on social-science research. The failure of the courts to explain what "desegregation" means led researchers to deal equally cavalierly with this central issue. As Janet Schofield put it, "the fact that a situation is legally or popularly dubbed as desegregated does not guarantee that it has a great deal in common with other similarly labeled situations." Just as judges were reluctant to explain the intended outcome of desegregation cases, social-science researchers failed to confront the question of how one should measure success.

This chapter was written with the advantage of nearly seventy years of hindsight. As we will see in subsequent chapters, it took decades for judges, administrators, school officials, and commentators to develop the relatively coherent positions described here and to absorb some of the complicated finding of social scientists. For the most part they focused on the practical problems immediately before them: how to overcome southern resistance to *Brown*, how to counteract the effects of long years of racial segregation, how (and whether) to distinguish between de jure and de facto segregation, what items to include in desegregation decrees, how often to revise those injunctions, and when to release school districts from judicial supervision—to name but a few. District court judges had the best handle on the complicated facts on the ground, but little time to ponder the larger issues. The Supreme Court was responsible for exploring these overarching questions but found it easier to resolve disputes by issuing ambiguous and shifting guidance.

The legal debate over desegregation illustrates the hazards of excessive abstraction. The terms that dominated debate in the courts—"desegregation," "unitary school system," "segregative effect," "resegregation"—were a world apart from the educational practices that affect the lives of teachers and students. Only gradually did district court judges on the firing line learn that the most important factors were often beyond their control. Seldom did this insight percolate up to the Supreme Court.

The chapters that follow trace the serpentine development of federal policy on desegregation in the courts, the executive branch, and, to a lesser degree, Congress. They explain how the ideas, debates, and evidence introduced in this chapter were influenced by the structure of those institutions and, just as importantly, by their cooperation and competition. While we should not condemn those who struggled with these issues for failing to see what we (with hindsight) can, neither should we ignore their failure to confront central questions and dilemmas and to understand the enormous difficulty of improving the educational opportunities of minority children.

3
Critical Junctures

Brown v. Board of Education initially came before the Supreme Court in the waning days of the Truman administration. School desegregation did not begin in the South until the Johnson administration. The effort moved north during the Nixon, Ford, and Carter administrations. Most of the desegregation orders established in the 1960s and 1970s remained in place until the late 1990s. Although many were gradually terminated during the administrations of Bill Clinton, George W. Bush, and Barack Obama, others survived through the presidencies of Donald Trump and Joe Biden. During these decades the country went through thirteen presidents and five chief justices. The desegregation story thus spans a period of enormous change in American politics.

Over these many years the meaning and objectives of desegregation shifted substantially, moving first from destroying the keystone of the Jim Crow system in the South to ending the racial isolation of African American students throughout the country, and then to improving the educational opportunities of all minority children, including the rapidly growing number of Hispanic students. Since the Supreme Court remained frustratingly ambiguous on the purpose of desegregation, the job of specifying appropriate remedies—and, in effect, defining the meaning of desegregation—fell to the lower federal courts. Facing a vast array of educational and demographic situations, the decentralized federal judiciary adopted a wide variety of remedial policies, revising them repeatedly over the years.

As a result, desegregation is a complex story, with significant changes over time and major variations from region to region, from city to city. Much of the writing on desegregation tries to reduce this long history to simple morality tales: desegregation worked until progress was halted by racism operating under the banner of opposition to busing; desegregation worked until the Supreme Court rejected a color-blind interpretation of the Fourteenth Amendment and embraced racial balance as its goal; desegregation demonstrates the power of "an idea whose time has come"; white Americans celebrated racial integration in the abstract but rejected it in practice; courts are incapable of carrying out profound social change; desegregation illustrates the excesses of the "imperial judiciary." Although each of these claims contains a grain of truth, each is seriously incomplete. Learning from this seventy-year history requires us to confront its complexity.

Box 3.1 offers a road map for the chapters that follow by breaking the serpentine story into seven parts. This chapter reviews the key choices and events that shaped each of these distinctive periods.

BOX 3.1 The Phases and Faces of Desegregation, 1954–2022

1. The First Decade: "More Deliberation than Speed"
   - *Brown I* and *II* produce rapid desegregation in some border states, but "massive resistance," obstructionism, and tokenism in most of the South.
   - The Supreme Court largely withdraws from the field for over a decade.
   - Lower courts accept "freedom of choice" plans submitted by southern school districts.
   - By 1964 almost no black students in the states of the Confederacy attend public school with *any* white students.

2. Watershed: The Legislation of 1964–65
   - Fruits of the longest debate: Title IV of the 1964 Civil Rights Act authorizes the attorney general to initiate desegregation cases; Title VI prohibits HEW from distributing federal education funds to schools that engage in racial discrimination.
   - The 1964 act specifies that desegregation "shall not mean the assignment of students to public schools in order to overcome racial imbalance."
   - The Elementary and Secondary Education Act of 1965 establishes a larger role for the federal government in education; by offering federal aid contingent on desegregation, it gives federal administrators leverage against recalcitrant school districts.
   - Passage of the two laws reflects a major change in power within Congress, reducing the power of the "conservative coalition" and increasing the influence of entrepreneurial northern and western liberal Democrats.

Box 3.1 continued

3. **The Fifth Circuit and HEW Desegregate Southern Schools (chapter 4)**
   - HEW issues guidelines in 1965 and 1966 establishing minimum steps school districts must take to qualify for federal funding, including numerical targets for the number of black students enrolled in previously white schools.
   - The Fifth Circuit holds in *Jefferson County* (1966) that "freedom of choice" plans are acceptable only if they "work" to produce schools that cannot be identified as either white or black.
     ▷ The Fifth Circuit not only endorses HEW's guidelines, but also promises to follow future guidelines.
     ▷ That court substantially expands its oversight of district courts, writing model desegregation orders district courts are expected to put into effect immediately.
   - By 1972 over 90 percent of black students in the South are attending schools with whites.

4. **The Supreme Court Returns, 1968–80 (chapter 5)**
   - In *Green* (1968), the Supreme Court tacitly endorses the ruling in *Jefferson County*, adopts its language on "unitary" school systems, and suggests that "dual" systems must be reconstructed to ensure that each school reflects the racial composition of the district as a whole.
   - When the Nixon Administration tries to slow down desegregation, the Supreme Court responds by demanding *immediate* desegregation.
   - In *Swann* (1971), the Supreme Court endorses a busing plan for Charlotte, North Carolina, that uses extensive busing to create a 70–30 white-black ratio in most schools.
   - Outside the Court, emphasis shifts from uprooting Jim Crow to combating racial isolation in big cities in the North and West; racial unrest in northern cities gives special urgency to the demand for improving the lot of minority youths.
   - In *Keyes* (1973), the Supreme Court makes it easier to prove that school districts outside the South have engaged in racial discrimination sufficient to justify metropolitan-wide desegregation plans.
   - Busing orders in many northern and western cities create a political uproar, leading to strong opposition to court-ordered busing in Congress and the White House.
   - In *Milliken v. Bradley* (1974), a narrowly divided Court holds that judges cannot require busing between cities and suburbs unless the suburbs or the state government have engaged in intentional discrimination.

Box 3.1 continued

- After *Milliken*, many northern and western cities continue to be subject to desegregation orders, but only a handful of these orders involve urban-suburban busing.
- The Supreme Court starts to back away from *Swann* and *Keyes* in 1976–77, only to reverse direction again in 1979–80.

5. **Lower Courts in Limbo (chapters 6–7)**
   - Over the next decade the Supreme Court issues no major desegregation decisions, leaving the lower courts on their own.
   - Initially, lower courts focus on the racial balance of schools within school districts, with significant differences in how much between-school variation they allow.
   - Over the years, courts increasingly focus on magnet schools, "controlled choice," and other programs to boost the educational achievement of minority students.
   - Most desegregation decrees established in the 1960s and 1970s remain in effect through the 1990s, occasionally modified to reflect changing demographic patterns.

6. **Termination without End (chapter 8)**
   - Between 1991 and 1995 the Supreme Court issues three decisions that make it easier for school districts to prove they have achieved "unitary" status, and for district court judges to end long-running desegregation suits.
   - These decisions have little effect until 1999, when the number of terminations begins to increase.
   - Terminations spark debate over the extent and causes of "resegregation."
   - In *Parents Involved in Community Schools* (2007), the Supreme Court for the first time engages in open debate over the purpose of "desegregation"; a divided Court limits use of race-based assignments in school districts deemed "unitary."

7. **The Focus Shifts to Congress and the Executive (chapter 9)**
   - Attention to desegregation fades as political, educational, and civil rights leaders develop the "standards and accountability" framework exemplified by No Child Left Behind.
   - The Obama administration announces Title VI guidelines on affirmative action, use of race in school assignments, discriminatory distribution of school resources, and discrimination in school discipline.
   - The Trump administration rescinds those guidelines; the Biden administration considers reinstating them.

The First Decade: More Deliberation than Speed

Brown v. Board was the culmination of a decades-long litigation campaign by the NAACP. The NAACP's patient, sophisticated, justly celebrated, and frequently imitated strategy chipped away at the Supreme Court's 1896 endorsement of "separate but equal" in *Plessy v. Ferguson*. The first round of oral arguments in the case came in 1953, when Chief Justice Fred Vinson presided over a Court badly divided on the issue. Struggling to reach a consensus, the Court held the case over for reargument in 1954. By then Vinson was dead, replaced by former California governor Earl Warren. Warren excelled at bringing the justices together on controversial topics, and at explaining the outcome in terms accessible to non-lawyers.

The crucial ambiguities of *Brown I and II* were examined in detail in the previous chapter. Some of the justices recognized the difficult situation in which these decisions placed lower court judges. The chief justice thought that "to let them flounder" with only such vague guidance would be "rather cruel." Frankfurter feared that to "unload responsibility upon lower courts most subject to community pressure without any guidance for them except our decision of unconstitutionality" would lead to "drawn-out, indefinite delay without even colorable compliance."[1] Yet the justices could not agree on any further details. Frankfurter's prediction proved correct.

In a subsequent series of unexplained per curiam decisions, the Court quickly applied its no-racial-segregation rule to all other public facilities. Yet it made no effort to refine its command on school desegregation. Border states quickly ended de jure segregation, requiring most students to attend their neighborhood schools. The deep South, though, responded with "massive resistance" and transparent obstructionism. When Arkansas governor Orval Faubus whipped up an angry mob to oppose even token desegregation in Little Rock, the Court met in emergency session to reiterate that "these constitutional principles cannot be allowed to yield simply because of disagreement with them."[2] President Eisenhower reluctantly backed these judicial words with paratroopers.

Unfortunately, the Court made no effort to address more-subtle forms of resistance. Later in 1958 it issued a brief opinion upholding an Alabama "pupil placement law" that not only gave school officials nearly complete discretion over assigning students to schools, but even allowed parents to veto their children's assignment to a school previously used by the other race.[3] With such huge loopholes readily available, virtually no desegregation took place in the deep South. By 1962, less than one half of one percent of black children in the region went to school with *any* white children.[4] In fact, as the

Thernstroms report, eight years after *Brown* "not a single black pupil attended a white public school anywhere in Mississippi, Alabama, or South Carolina."[5]

As the nation's attention turned to civil rights in 1963–64, the Supreme Court seemed to be running out of patience. In 1963 a unanimous Court struck down "minority to majority" transfers—the common practice that allowed white students to transfer from majority-black to majority-white schools. Justice Clark explained that racial classifications had been "held to be invalid" in *Brown* and were "no less unconstitutional" in this form.[6] The next year the Court took the bolder step of preventing Prince Edward County in rural Virginia from completely shutting down its public school system to avoid desegregation. Justice Black declared that during the previous decade "there has been entirely too much deliberation and not enough speed."[7] While these decisions ruled some dilatory measures out of bounds, the Court gave no indication what school districts must do to comply with *Brown* or what standards lower courts should apply to evaluate their actions. On the eve of passage of the Civil Rights Act, the lower courts remained pretty much on their own.

Watershed: The Legislation of 1964–65

In the ten months between July 1964 and April 1965, Congress passed two of the most important pieces of legislation in American history: the Civil Rights Act (CRA) of 1964 and the Elementary and Secondary Education Act (ESEA) of 1965. Together they provided a powerful impetus for school desegregation. The first gave federal judges and administrators an imposing stick, the second an attractive carrot.

The prolonged debate over the Civil Rights Act not only produced that landmark law, but also marked the beginning of the end of southern Democrats' control over Congress and broke the stalemate over federal aid to education. Southern Democrats lost their ability to block civil rights legislation: in 1965 Congress enacted the Voting Rights Act; in 1968 it passed the Fair Housing Act; and in subsequent years these statutes were renewed and strengthened. Passage of ESEA ended the debate over whether the federal government had a legitimate role in supporting public schools. Federal spending, strings, and mandates grew steadily over the next decade and a half.

Two provisions in the CRA augmented the federal government's power to force school districts to desegregate. The first was Title IV, which authorized the Department of Justice to file desegregation suits. Previously, civil rights organizations—primarily the NAACP—bore the burden of litigating desegregation cases. Now the resources and the prestige of the Justice Department were brought to bear on the problem. Title IV also offered a definition of the key term:

> "Desegregation" means the assignment of students to public schools and within such schools without regard to their race, color, religion, or national origin, but "desegregation" shall not mean the assignment of students to public schools in order to overcome racial imbalance.

As the controversy over busing heated up in the early 1970s, Congress also specified that "no court, department, or agency of the United States" shall

> order the implementation of a plan that would require the transportation of any student to a school other than the school closest or next closest to his place of residence which provides the appropriate grade level and type of education for such student.[8]

On the one hand, Congress clearly indicated that it favored the color-blind interpretation of *Brown*. On the other hand, it had no authority to overturn the Court's interpretation of the Fourteenth Amendment, which was moving in a much different direction.

Title VI of the 1964 Civil Rights Act established the principle that "no person in the United States shall on the ground of race, color, or national origin, be excluded from participation in, be denied the benefits of, or be subject to discrimination under any program or activity receiving Federal financial assistance." It also directed federal agencies to issue "rules, regulations, or orders of general applicability" to carry out this provision, and to terminate funding for any "particular program" that failed to comply. Both Title II of the CRA (which banned discrimination in public accommodations) and Title VII (which banned employment discrimination) were extremely controversial, primarily because they applied nondiscrimination rules to private parties. In contrast, as Hugh Davis Graham has noted, "almost no attention was paid to Title VI," which applied mainly to the use of federal funds by state and local government and which seemed merely to establish a new procedure for enforcing existing constitutional rights. It was, Graham convincingly argues, "the sleeper that would become by far the most powerful weapon of them all."[9]

The Johnson administration and Department of Justice officials maintained that since agencies enforcing Title VI would follow the courts' interpretation of the Fourteenth Amendment, there was little need to explain what constitutes "discrimination." Consequently, congressional debate on Title VI focused exclusively on the extent of the powers granted to federal agencies. The House and the Senate imposed several constraints on their authority:

rules issued under Title VI must be approved by the president himself; federal agencies must give Congress thirty days' advance warning before terminating funds; state and local governments are entitled to public hearings prior to termination of funds and to judicial review after the fact; and such terminations apply only to the particular program found guilty of discrimination, not to the entire institution receiving funding. Having delegated substantial power to federal administrators, members of Congress wanted to make sure those administrators did not wield it precipitously, arbitrarily, or without giving Congress a heads-up. Congress later prohibited agencies from using "deferrals" to evade these restrictions.

It did not take long for administrators in the Department of Health, Education, and Welfare (HEW) to realize that termination of funding for state and local governments is neither politically palatable nor administratively attractive in ordinary times. In the mid-1960s HEW frequently threatened to cut off funds to small school districts in the South, but it seldom pulled the trigger. Before long, it became clear to everyone that in all but the most extreme cases the threat was an empty one. In the long run, Title VI was significant not because it provided a mechanism for administrative enforcement of judicial rules (the initial understanding), but because federal judges were willing to enforce (through private rights of action) the rules announced by federal administrators. This unexpected but effective reversal of institutional roles emerged soon after passage of the CRA in the furious battle to end segregation in the deep South.

Jefferson County: The Fifth Circuit and HEW "Grasp the Nettle"

Much of the burden of enforcing *Brown* in the South fell to the Fifth Circuit Court of Appeals, whose jurisdiction at the time extended to Mississippi, Alabama, Louisiana, Florida, Georgia, and Texas—the heart of Dixie intransigence. For many years the judges on this appellate court had battled with a significant number of district court judges within the circuit who had little interest in altering the educational status quo. Judges on the circuit court were acutely aware of the absence of measurable judicial standards for evaluating the constitutionality of the hundreds of pupil-placement and "freedom of choice" plans proposed by southern school districts. "The courts acting alone," Judge John Minor Wisdom wrote in his seminal 1966 opinion in *U.S. v. Jefferson County Board of Education*, "have failed."[10]

To rescue the court from "the bog on which it has been trapped for years," Wisdom and his colleagues sought help from HEW's "experts in education and school administration," whose guidelines "present the best system available for uniform application, and the best aid to the courts in evaluating the validity of a school desegregation plan and the progress made under that plan."[11] This institutional alliance produced dramatic change. By 1972, over 90 percent of black students in the South were going to school with whites. This was indeed the "reconstruction of southern education."[12]

The Fifth Circuit's *Jefferson County* decision marked a turning point in the history of desegregation. Previously, reviewing judges had focused on the nearly metaphysical question of whether the "freedom of choice" plans offered by school districts offered a genuinely free choice to black students and their parents. Judge Wisdom's opinion rejected that subjective approach, replacing "freedom of choice" with the duty "to take affirmative action" to achieve "the conversion of a *de jure* segregated dual system into a unitary, nonracial (nondiscriminatory) system—lock, stock, and barrel: students, faculty, staff, facilities, programs, and activities."[13] Focusing so intently on the rights of *individuals*, he claimed, had led judges to "overlook the fact that Negroes *collectively* are harmed when the state, by law or custom, operates segregated schools." As a result, the "right of the individual plaintiff must yield to the overriding right of Negroes as a class to a completely *integrated* public education."[14]

How could a judge know when the formerly "dual" school system had been converted into a "unitary" school system? Here Judge Wisdom and the Fifth Circuit leaned on HEW. The circuit court expected school districts not only to meet the milestones announced in HEW's 1966 guidelines, but to comply with all future administrative requirements. HEW reciprocated by endorsing the Fifth Circuit's interpretation of *Brown*.

With judges and administrators working on what education commissioner Francis Keppel called "parallel tracks," school districts had little alternative but reluctantly to comply. If they resisted, they might lose federal funds only to be subject to a court order soon thereafter. This unusual division of labor—with administrators providing the quantitative standards and judges the enforcement muscle—produced rapid and profound change. That collaboration is the central story of chapter 4.

This powerful alliance was by no means a foregone conclusion. In 1965 the fledgling civil rights office in HEW's Office of Education employed only fifteen people. According to Wilbur Cohen, the wily legislative strategist who served as undersecretary and secretary of HEW during those years, it was filled with "a bunch of amateurs with real good ideas" but no management strategy or "battle plan."[15] What the office did have, though, was the power to issue guidelines specifying what school districts must do to comply with Title VI and thus qualify for federal funding. In 1965 and 1966 it issued controversial guidance documents designed to shift federal regulation "from negotiation to performance." To convince federal administrators that a "freedom of choice" plan "is actually working," a school district must demonstrate that black students "have *in fact transferred from segregated schools*."[16] The guidelines provided specific percentage targets to allow regulators to determine whether the number of black students moving to formerly white schools was sufficient. This provision not only simplified administrators' review of thousands of desegregation plans, but also provided the courts with a method for determining which plans were "actually working."

The Fifth Circuit combined this doctrinal innovation with important structural changes. It took the unusual step of creating five standing three-judge panels to review desegregation cases. Each panel would remain on a case until it was resolved. This practice allowed appellate judges to become familiar with the facts and the history of each case, and thus to exercise much more control over district court judges. As a result, desegregation litigation "was now capable of mass production."[17]

How much of this judicial innovation was a temporary expedient to break the back of southern intransigence, and how much would prove to be a lasting change in judicial procedure and the meaning of *Brown*? Expedited appellate review did not last long, but the structural injunctions developed in southern desegregation cases became a standard judicial remedy.

On the crucial question of whether desegregation required some form of racial balance, the Fifth Circuit waffled. On the one hand, it took the crucial step of judging the adequacy of desegregation plans by how many black students had transferred to previously white schools. It emphasized that "freedom of choice is not a goal in itself," but merely "one of the tools available" for converting a dual system into a unitary one. On the other hand, the model decree designed by the court with HEW's assistance focused on standardizing the operation of "freedom of choice" plans, preventing school officials from pressuring black students to stay in their former schools and equalizing the resources available to formerly black and formerly white schools. Moreover, HEW's 1966 guidelines only required that 20 percent of students attending formerly black schools be allowed to attend formerly white schools—a far cry from racial balance in every school. In 1968 HEW issued additional guidelines explaining that desegregation plans "do not require the correction of racial imbalance resulting from private patterns."[18] Was "freedom of choice" to be purified—as the model decree and HEW required—or repudiated—as the court's *Jefferson County* opinions seemed to indicate? That was the question the Supreme Court faced in 1968—but failed to resolve.

The Supreme Court Returns

From 1955 to 1967, the Supreme Court said very little about what "desegregation" means. During the 1980s it again lapsed into silence. In the years between, though, it issued twenty-five decisions that shaped desegregation orders throughout the country. (These decisions are listed in table 5.1 and discussed at length in chapter 5.) Despite this flurry of activity, the Court failed to produce a coherent desegregation jurisprudence. Its decisions were often ambiguous and sometimes internally contradictory. In the end the Court tacitly fastened on an odd compromise, requiring any school district found responsible for committing "segregative acts"—which potentially included most large districts in the country—to produce racially balanced schools. But it took away the only remedial measure that could ensure that these schools would not become predominantly black or Hispanic: cross-district busing. This combination of commands and constraints put many district court judges in the awkward position of having to impose controversial desegregation orders that had little hope of reducing racial isolation or improving the educational opportunities of minority students.

Three factors contributed to the odd evolution of Supreme Court doctrine. One was the drama occurring outside the courtroom. The Court heard oral arguments in *Green* on April 3, 1968. The next day Martin Luther King was assassinated. By the time the justices issued their opinion, almost a hundred American cities had experienced the riots that followed King's murder. Immediate, decisive action seemed essential. Later that year Richard Nixon was elected president. Soon after taking office, his administration asked the Court to postpone desegregation deadlines for a number of southern school districts. The administration's call for delay had the unintended effect of strengthening the Court's resolve to require immediate action. A few years later, intense public opposition to busing clearly weighed on the justices' minds as they wrestled with northern desegregation cases.

The second factor was the changing composition of the Supreme Court. Shortly after the Court handed down its *Green* decision, Chief Justice Warren announced his resignation. Nixon eventually had the chance to nominate his successor, Warren Burger, as well as associate justices Harry Blackmun, Lewis Powell, and William Rehnquist. For a few years the Court was able to paper over its growing divisions by writing opinions that left key matters unresolved. By 1973, though, the Court could no longer present a united front. In many instances the Court was closely divided, with the swing votes tipping the balance first in one direction, then another. Dissenters one year became majority-opinion writers the next (see table 5.2).

Third, the cases coming before the Court grew steadily harder. The 1968 *Green* case involved a rural district with little residential segregation that had practiced de jure segregation and for years done little to comply with *Brown*. Busing was not an issue. The 1971 *Swann* case also involved a school system that had been segregated by law. Unlike Virginia's New Kent County, Charlotte, North Carolina was a huge, urban school system with substantial residential segregation. Here the district court judge had ordered extensive transportation of students in order to produce racially balanced schools. In the 1973 *Keyes* case, desegregation moved north. The question in this Denver case was what constituted evidence of "segregative intent" in cities that had not imposed segregation by law. And in the next year's *Milliken v. Bradley* decision, the Court addressed the explosive issue of whether federal courts could mandate the transportation of students across municipal lines in order to promote racial balance. As the issues became more difficult, the justices' divergent interpretations of *Brown* became ever more apparent.

In the first three decisions, *Green*, *Swann*, and *Keyes*, the Court moved decisively (though not explicitly) to embrace the "racial isolation" understanding described in chapter 2. A school district that had engaged in any "segregative acts" in the past—whether or not they had imposed de jure segregation—must take extensive action to transform its "dual" system into a "unitary" one. A "unitary" system is one without racially identifiable schools—which, the Court implied, meant that almost all schools in the district must approximate the racial balance of the school district as a whole. The Court approved an ambitious and controversial busing plan for Charlotte (which had a long history of de jure segregation), and then required an equally extensive plan for Denver (which did not). Remedies expanded, and the amount of evidence required to prove segregative intent diminished. Below the surface of these opinions lay the conviction enunciated by the Civil Rights Commission in 1967, that racial isolation deprived minority children of equal educational opportunity *"whatever the source of such segregation may be."*

From 1974 to 1977, the Court seemed to draw back from this interpretation of *Brown*, limiting desegregation orders to remedying specific discriminatory actions taken by public officials. Most importantly, in *Milliken v. Bradley* a closely divided court rejected a lower court order consolidating the Detroit school district with fifty-three surrounding suburban districts and requiring the reassignment of students to eliminate majority-black schools. Chief Justice Burger's majority opinion stressed that "the scope of the remedy is determined by the nature and extent of the constitutional violation": the constitutional right of black children in Detroit "is to attend a unitary school system *in that district*." The dissenters' claim that black children in Detroit have a constitutional right to attend school alongside white children from the suburbs "can be supported only by a drastic expansion of the constitutional right itself, an expansion without any support in either constitutional principle or precedent."[19] Of course, the foundations for such a "dramatic expansion" had in fact been laid by the Supreme Court in its *Green*, *Swann*, and *Keyes* decisions, but had never been explicitly announced or defended. Now, apparently, that expansive interpretation had been abandoned.[20]

But not for long. In 1979, the Court returned to the logic of the *Green-Swann-Keyes* trilogy. In two decisions involving Ohio cities, the Court held that if a school system had in 1954 contained schools that were "racially identifiable"—that is, predominantly black—it constituted a "dual school system" even if segregation had never been legally required and even if some of the city's schools were integrated at the time. In other words, virtually all urban school systems with a significant number of black students in 1954 were susceptible to being deemed "dual systems" a quarter century later. Consequently, they had an affirmative duty to transform their "dual" systems into "unitary" ones. To do so, they needed to avoid any actions that would have the "anticipated and foreseeable consequence" of maintaining predominantly minority schools, and to take all feasible steps to minimize racial isolation. In short, the 1979 decisions made it difficult for any large city to avoid a "systemic" desegregation order—albeit one not extending to the suburbs.

The Lower Courts Attack Racial Isolation

While the Supreme Court was going through these doctrinal gyrations, the lower courts faced the unenviable task of resolving complex litigation in a wide variety of contexts. On the one hand the Supreme Court had instructed them to take immediate action to transform "dual" school systems into "unitary" ones, and had strongly suggested that a school system could not be considered "unitary" until the racial balance of all its schools reflected the racial composition of the district as a whole. On the other hand, the Court denied that racial balance should be considered an end in itself, and had pretty much shut the door on urban-suburban desegregation plans that were often the only way to prevent many urban school systems from becoming predominantly minority.

In *Brown II*, Chief Justice Warren had emphasized that "full implementation of these constitutional principles" would "require solution of varied local school problems." Given "their proximity to local conditions," federal district court judges would bear primary responsibility for "fashioning and effectuating" desegregation decrees. Over the next three decades, these "local conditions" became even more varied. Some school districts had experienced de jure segregation; others had not. Some (especially in the South and West) were geographically large, including both urban centers and suburbs. Others (especially in the Northeast and Midwest) were tiny, with predominantly black cities surrounded by multiple, predominantly white suburbs. Some had few Hispanic and Asian students, others many more. Some urban school systems, especially in the Rust Belt, saw their enrollments shrink and their financial situations badly deteriorate. Others, especially in the Sun Belt, continued to grow. Some district court judges were eager to address what they saw as savage educational inequalities, others reluctant. Some of the latter changed their tune after hearing evidence presented by the NAACP and the Department of Justice. Conversely, some of the former became more cautious as they discovered the obstacles to educational reform.

In a 1979 dissent, Justice Rehnquist warned that the Court's "Delphic" desegregation opinions created "the disturbing prospect of very different remedies being imposed on similar school systems because of the predilections of individual judges and their good-faith but incongruent efforts to make sense of this Court's confused pronouncements today."[21] He expected that this warning would force the Court to reexamine the issue. His first prediction proved correct; the second not. Chapters 6 and 7 describe some of the ways lower courts responded to the Court's "Delphic" pronouncements.

In the early 1970s, most district court judges placed greatest emphasis on creating a racially balanced student body in each school. Establishing this balance usually required busing. Although courts differed in the degree of allowable variation among schools, they agreed on the importance of eliminating schools that were overwhelmingly minority. The model here was Judge McMillan's desegregation order for Charlotte-Mecklenburg County, upheld with much fanfare in the Supreme Court's *Swann* decision.

Over the course of the decade, the focus of desegregation orders slowly shifted from maintaining racial balance to improving the quality of education in urban school systems. In part this revised focus was a response to demographic change. As the proportion of white students in these school districts shrank and the proportion of Hispanic and Asian students grew, "racial balance" became ever harder to define. Moreover, in many cities it was becoming apparent that merely shifting students and teachers from one school to another would not guarantee educational equality. Judges and the special masters they appointed began to pay more attention to what happens *inside* schools. Tracking, discipline, professional training, curriculum, bilingual education, special education, AP and gifted programs, guidance and counseling programs—all became subject to judicial scrutiny. At the extreme (most notably Kansas City), a few judges tried to remake entire school systems. Others concluded that improving school quality was not a subject within the institutional capacity of judges. Many of the cases initiated in the 1960s and 1970s remained inactive for years. Seldom, though, were they formally terminated. Structural injunctions, it seemed, never die; they just fade away—sometimes without anyone knowing that technically they remain in effect.

Termination Begins

After a decade of silence, the Supreme Court again reentered the picture, this time to address the question of when the lower courts can terminate years-old desegregation orders. It was not possible to provide a clear answer to this question without addressing the long-evaded issue of the underlying meaning and purpose of desegregation. The divisions in the Court that had first become evident in the 1970s reappeared, never to be resolved. Once again, the Supreme Court left the key choices to district court judges. It took almost another decade for the termination of court orders to proceed in earnest.

When district court judges issued desegregation orders in the 1960s and 1970s, they gave little thought to how long those orders would remain in effect or how they would end. The task immediately before them was hard enough. Moreover, the structural injunction was an experiment borne of necessity, not a well-defined judicial tool. In most cities, initial court orders were followed by occasional adjustments and lengthy periods of judicial inaction. Only a few judges closed their desegregation cases in the 1980s, and even in those instances the status of their injunctions remained unclear. Toward the end of that decade, the circuit courts began to consider when a school system can be declared "unitary." They could not agree on the answer.

Between 1991 and 1995 the Supreme Court handed down three opinions designed to resolve conflicts among the circuits: *Board of Education of Oklahoma City v. Dowell* (1991), *Freeman v. Pitts* (1992), and *Missouri v. Jenkins* (1995). While acknowledging that the lower courts disagreed on what constituted a "unitary" school system, the justices made little effort to explain how a "dual" school system could achieve "unitary" status. Although school boards and the lower courts were "entitled to a rather precise statement of its obligations under a desegregation decree," Chief Justice Rehnquist merely indicated that district courts had substantial discretion to determine when school districts have adequately complied with court order "in good faith."[22]

In these termination cases, the justices' competing understandings of the desegregation project quickly became apparent. If the purpose of the enterprise was to rectify discrete instances of segregation and discrimination perpetrated by government officials, then many years of good-faith compliance with court orders should be sufficient to cure the problem. In *Freeman v. Pitts*, Justice Kennedy insisted that racial balance "is not to be achieved for its own sake," but pursued only "when racial imbalance has been caused by a constitutional violation." School districts are "under no duty to remedy imbalance that is caused by demographic factors." Moreover, judicial supervision of schools was originally "intended to be a temporary measure," and "returning schools to the control of local authorities at the earliest practical date is essential to restore their true accountability in our governmental system."[23]

In his dissent in *Board of Education of Oklahoma City v. Dowell* (his final desegregation opinion), Justice Marshall laid out a much broader understanding of desegregation and the responsibilities of the courts. The "vestiges" of segregation include not just features of the education system directly related to specific acts of discrimination but extend "to *any condition* that is likely to convey the message of inferiority." It is not enough that a district had long ago stopped discriminating: "Our school desegregation jurisprudence establishes that the *effects* of past discrimination remain chargeable to the school district regardless of its lack of continued enforcement of segregation, and that the remedial decree is required until those effects have been finally eliminated." Appropriate remedies include "remedial education programs and other measures to redress the substandard communications skills of Afro-American students formerly placed in segregated schools." Since "predominantly minority public schools typically receive fewer resources than other schools in the same district," courts must continue to monitor the distribution of teachers and money. Before terminating desegregation cases, judges must be convinced that "the stigmatic harm identified in *Brown* will not recur upon lifting the decree. Any doubt on the issue ... should be resolved in favor of the Afro-American children affected by this litigation."[24]

Despite fears that the Court decisions of 1991–95 would lead to "resegregation" of schools previously under court order, they had little immediate effect. Of the 480 southern school systems under court order for which the DOJ had records, thirty-two had been released in the 1970s, seventeen in the 1980s, and twenty-two in the 1990s.[25] The most important consequence of the decisions was to reduce the authority of circuit courts to stop district court judges from terminating desegregation cases. But during the 1990s few district courts tried to do so, in part because few school boards asked them to. They saw little reason to reopen old wounds.

Termination picked up substantially in the last two years of the Clinton administration and during the George W. Bush administration. A number of factors contributed to this increase. The Justice Department showed more interest in closing out cases that had remained inactive for years. By the turn of the century, many judges were "exhausted from the decades-long effort and anxious to terminate their jurisdiction."[26] Financial crises in some cities, especially those in the Midwest, led to comprehensive reform packages that combined more resources for urban schools with the ending of desegregation orders. In other cities, most notably Charlotte, suits by white parents challenged racial quotas in magnet schools and surviving busing orders. Sometimes black parents objected to their children's long bus rides, and to the practice of allowing "white" seats in magnet schools to sit empty while hundreds of black children remained on waiting lists.[27] African American mayors in Denver, Minneapolis, and Cleveland supported efforts to have their schools declared unitary.[28] By the second decade of the twenty-first century, the number of surviving desegregation orders had shrunk to a few hundred—though no one knows for sure what the exact number is.

The Focus Shifts to Congress and the Executive

By the late 1980s court-ordered desegregation had fallen to the bottom of the agenda of civil rights organizations and education reformers. The federal government was in the midst of a transition from the "equity regime" for education to a "standards and accountability regime." The former focused on inputs—above all, money—and on the federal government's responsibility to improve the opportunities offered to disadvantaged groups, especially racial minorities, English learners, and students with disabilities. The latter, in contrast, focused on outputs—primarily test scores and graduation rates—and on ensuring that all students leave high school "college and career ready." The leading exemplars of the "standards and accountability regime" were No Child Left Behind (NCLB)—a joint venture of President George W. Bush and congressional Democrats—and the Obama administration's "Race to the Top."

Whatever their shortcomings (of which there were many), both NCLB and the Obama administration's education initiatives sought to use federal funding to highlight and improve educational opportunities for disadvantaged children. For this reason, the Leadership Conference on Civil Rights declared in 2008 that "NCLB is a civil rights law, and that some of the requirements of NCLB constitute, in essence, the rights of children to obtain a quality education."[29] This version of education reform started with an insight that many judges had reached after struggling with desegregation cases for years: far more important than the race of students in a school is the quality of education they receive there.

While the Obama Administration was pushing its Race to the Top, the Common Core, charter schools, and new efforts to restructure failing schools, its Department of Education was also using guidelines issued under Title VI of the Civil Rights Act to address discriminatory educational practices and to promote integration. In 2010 Secretary of Education Arne Duncan told a crowd in Selma, Alabama, "The hard truth is that, in the last decade, the Office for Civil Rights has not been as vigilant as it should have been in combating gender and racial discrimination and protecting the rights of individuals with disabilities. But that is about to change."[30] Not since the Johnson administration had Title VI guidelines achieved such importance.

Between 2010 and 2016 the Department of Education released eleven guidance documents under Title VI. In 2013 it joined with the Justice Department to issue "Guidance on the Voluntary Use of Race to Achieve Diversity and Avoid Racial Isolation in Elementary and Secondary School." Its purpose was to show how schools could continue to promote racial diversity within the confines of the Supreme Court's 2007 decision in *Parents Involved*. It offered the Department's first defense of the "racial isolation" argument that had been so central to the courts' desegregation jurisprudence in the 1960s and 1970s:

> Where schools lack a diverse student body or are racially isolated (i.e. are composed overwhelmingly of students of one race), they may fail to provide the full panoply of benefits that K-12 schools can offer. The academic achievement of students at racially isolated schools often lags behind that of their peers at more diverse schools. Racially isolated schools often have fewer effective teachers, higher teacher turnover rates, less rigorous curricular resources (e.g. college preparatory courses,), and inferior facilities and other educational resources.[31]

With the Supreme Court limiting school officials' authority to use race-based criteria, the Obama administration used Title VI guidelines to indicate how much autonomy they retained.

Two additional Title VI "Dear Colleague" letters (DCLs) addressed issues that had arisen in desegregation cases. Its "Guidance to Ensure All Students Have Equal Access to Educational Resources" announced that "facially neutral policies that are not intended to discriminate" still violate Title VI if they "have an unjustified, adverse disparate impact on students based on race, color, or national origin."[32] Once federal officials determine that the distribution of *any* educational resource disadvantages a protected minority, schools must not only "demonstrate that the policy or practice is *necessary* to meet an *important* educational goal," but also show that there is no "comparably effective alternative policy or practice that would meet the school district's stated educational goal with less of a discriminatory effect." Equal per-pupil spending is not enough; comparative spending levels should reflect the "extra costs often associated with educating low-income children, English language learners, and students with disabilities." This DCL seemed to give the Department wide-ranging authority to determine how school districts distribute resources. But lacking help from the courts and unwilling to cut off funding to school districts, the Department made little effort to enforce it. By the time the Trump Administration withdrew the DCL in 2018, it had produced more paperwork than redistribution of resources.

The Department's 2014 DCL on "Nondiscriminatory Administration of School Discipline" left a greater imprint on schools' policies. Here the Department relied on disparate-impact analysis to address the "school to prison pipeline" by reducing out-of-school punishments. According to the DCL, schools violate Title VI when they "evenhandedly implement facially neutral policies and practices" if those practices "nonetheless have an *unjustified effect* of discriminating on the basis of race."[33] Once it has been established that minority students as a group have been punished more frequently or more severely than white students, the burden shifts to the school system to demonstrate that its policies are "*necessary* to meet an important educational goal" and that no "comparably effective alternative policies" would meet the school's educational goals with fewer adverse consequences for minority students. This burden of proof was virtually impossible to meet, since the Department listed a number of alternatives it considered effective.

The Department's school-discipline guidelines proved highly controversial. They raised complex evidentiary and enforcement issues: To what extent are racial differences in discipline the result of differences in student behavior rather than discriminatory application of school rules? Would reducing out-of-school punishments create more disorder in schools, thus reducing the quality of education provided to disadvantaged children? To what extent would teachers and principals actually comply with the agreements school districts signed with federal regulators? Would the courts stand behind the Department's assertion of authority under Title VI? These issues became moot when the Trump administration withdrew the DCL in 2018. But it is likely that the guidance will be reissued in some form by the Biden administration. At that point, all these issues will reemerge.

New Patterns, Old Issues

As this overview indicates, institutional patterns shifted significantly during the seven-decade debate over desegregation. Initially the Supreme Court took the lead, with the lower courts and Congress dragging their feet. Later, the lower courts and federal administrators jump-started southern school desegregation. In the 1970s the Supreme Court pushed the lower courts to address racial isolation; by the 1990s it was encouraging them to end judicial supervision. Presidents Clinton, Bush, and Obama, rather than the courts, took the lead in promoting efforts to address the racial achievement gap. The Obama administration's use of Title VI regulation was the most aggressive in nearly half a century.

Yet most of the underlying issues remained the same. What determines educational opportunity—the racial composition of the student body? money? teacher quality? schools' disciplinary and tracking practices? their curriculum? their leadership and ethos? Just as importantly, how do we know when minority students have received equal opportunity—when the racial achievement gap disappears? when racial animosity disappears? when economic inequalities disappear? For that matter, what constitutes a discriminatory practice—one that uses racial classifications? one based on bad motives? one that has a disproportionate impact on minority students? Despite years of debate and study, seldom has a consensus developed on any of these matters. The following chapters describe the many institutional forms policymaking on these issues has taken since the 1950s.

4

Breakthrough:
The Reconstruction of Southern Education

> HEW Guidelines offer new hope to Negro school children long denied their constitutional rights. A national effort, bringing together Congress, the executive, and the judiciary may be able to make meaningful the right of Negro children to equal educational opportunities. The courts acting alone have failed.
>
> JUDGE JOHN MINOR WISDOM, *U.S. v. Jefferson County*, 1966

> There are so few Supreme Court decisions on school desegregation that inferior courts must improvise in dealing with de facto segregated schools, faculty integration, site selection of schools, and many other problems. To this extent, the Fifth Circuit is forced into a policy-making position as to decisions only tangentially dependent on the Supreme Court.
>
> JUDGE WISDOM, *Southwestern Law Journal*, 1967

A decade after *Brown*, little had changed in the deep South. In 1962 not a single black student attended a white school anywhere in Mississippi, Alabama, or South Carolina. When Congress finally passed the Civil Rights Act, barely 1 percent of black students went to school with whites in the eleven states of the old Confederacy.[1] In 1964 the Supreme Court stated the obvious: over the past decade there had been "entirely too much deliberation and not enough speed." The "time for mere 'deliberate speed,'" it announced, "has run out."[2] But on the crucial question of *how* federal judges should overcome pervasive southern obstructionism, the Court remained silent.

Over the next several years change did indeed come—and with striking rapidity. As table 4.1 shows, between 1966 and 1972 de jure segregation in the South finally came to an end. In these years the percentage of black students in the South attending 90–100 percent minority schools dropped from 78 percent to 25 percent. By this measure the South went from the most segregated region in the US to the least segregated.[3] Gary Orfield exaggerated only slightly when he described the desegregation of southern schools from 1965 to 1968 as "a social transmutation more profound and more rapid than any other in peacetime American history."[4]

What caused this transformation? The most obvious factor was enactment of the 1964 Civil Rights Act. That law not only expressed the nation's commitment to racial equality, but empowered the Department of Justice to file suit to enforce *Brown* and gave the Department of Health, Education, and

TABLE 4.1. Percentage of southern black children attending schools with some white students

School year	Percentage
1954–55	0.001
1960–61	0.16
1962–63	0.45
1963–64	1.2
1964–65	2.3
1965–66	6.1
1966–67	16.9
1968–69	32.0
1970–71	85.9
1972–73	91.3

Source: Gerald N. Rosenberg, *The Hollow Hope* (Chicago: University of Chicago Press, 1991), 50.

Welfare (HEW) authority to cut off federal funds to school systems that failed to desegregate. In 1965 Congress offered a new pot of federal money to school districts, increasing the incentives to comply with HEW guidelines.

Administrative action was an important part of the story. Recognizing the enormity of the task before them, judges on the Fifth Circuit welcomed the assistance of the federal bureaucracy. Guidelines issued by HEW in 1965 and 1966 played a key role in southern school desegregation. But the frequently repeated "bureaucrats to the rescue" story seriously exaggerates the authority and capacity of HEW's fledgling Office for Civil Rights (OCR). In practice, the funding cutoff proved to be an administratively cumbersome and politically perilous enforcement tool. The small office charged with enforcing Title VI was staffed with dedicated but inexperienced, overwhelmed, and often politically naïve administrators.

The pivotal moment in southern school desegregation came in 1966–67, when the Fifth Circuit Court of Appeals endorsed HEW's guidelines and adopted aggressive measures to enforce them. At the time, the jurisdiction of that court covered much of the deep South. Judge Wisdom and his colleagues recognized that success hinged upon their developing a working alliance with the Department of Justice and HEW. This chapter explains how the symbiosis between courts and agencies jump-started the desegregation of southern schools while the Supreme Court remained on the sidelines.

Weak Agency, Influential Guidelines

According to many accounts, school desegregation did not take off until the federal bureaucracy replaced judges as the principal engine of reform.

Armed with the power to deprive school districts of an expanding pot of federal money, and free from the necessity of engaging in ponderous litigation, administrators in HEW's Office for Civil Rights could finally bring real change to southern school districts. There is an important element of truth in this version of the story. Desegregation did begin in earnest shortly after OCR entered the picture. Federal administrators provided the first numerical milestones for evaluating schools' efforts. Once the Fifth Circuit had endorsed those standards, administrators drew up desegregation plans for hundreds of school districts and monitored their compliance.

The primary shortcoming of this account is that it overlooks the profound weakness of the civil rights agency and the extent to which administrators depended upon the cooperation of federal judges for enforcing their guidelines. To put it baldly, OCR became a serviceable adjunct to the federal courts. The nature of its influence can be understood only by examining the symbiotic relationship it developed with the federal judiciary—a relationship that soon appeared in several other policy arenas.[5]

CALLOW YOUTH

In the late 1960s southern politicians often portrayed OCR as a group of storm troopers hell-bent on punishing the South and creating racially balanced schools. But in the years immediately following passage of 1964 Civil Rights Act, they looked much more like Keystone Kops. The Office of Education (OE)—the section of HEW in which the civil rights bureau was originally located—had never been an influential organization. According to Hugh Davis Graham, the office "existed for a century as a kind of bastard child, an object of bureaucratic ridicule in Washington, a skeleton staffed by third-rate 'educationalists' who compiled obscure statistical reports that gathered dust."[6] OE had played no role in crafting Title VI. In fact, people in the office were stunned to learn of their new responsibility. Assistant Secretary James Quigley, a former member of Congress who was initially given responsibility for civil rights policy within HEW, told an interviewer that he "couldn't believe my eyes" when he learned that the administration had included Title VI in the 1964 act.[7]

In 1965 this "third-rate" organization was handed yet another massive new job, distributing money under the landmark Elementary and Secondary Education Act (ESEA). Most of OE's career staff wanted to focus on ESEA, not become enmeshed in a heated political battle over desegregation. According to Gary Orfield, "both the leaders of the major education grant programs and the HEW legal staff were hostile to the fund-withholding idea. Relationships with state officials were seen as a precious asset of the various programs, not to be jeopardized for any extraneous purpose."[8] Career OE staff also feared that southern school districts would simply turn their backs on federal aid rather than desegregate. Nor could HEW secretary Anthony Celebrezze muster any enthusiasm for enforcing Title VI. He refused to sign the controversial 1965 Title VI guidelines proposed by OE. In short, as Allan Wolk has put it, the new law placed "legal responsibility for public school desegregation into the hands of a staff that was few in number, lacking in experience, and philosophically unsuited for this type of program."[9]

Title VI enforcement did have two strong supporters within the Office of Education: Commissioner Francis Keppel and his successor, Harold Howe II. OCR began its life as a small, temporary office created by Keppel. It was headed by David Seeley, who only a few years before had been Keppel's graduate student at the Harvard School of Education. Seeley later conceded that he was "too inexperienced for the job," and that within his fledgling office there was a "general lack of appreciation of the monstrousness of the task before us."[10] Wilbur Cohen, who served as undersecretary and secretary of HEW during those years, described Seeley as a "gung-ho" fellow with "no political knowledge" and "no real administrative ability." According to Cohen, the young lawyers surrounding him "had good ideas, but their concept of enforcement and administration was juvenile." They were "just a bunch of amateurs ... wandering around in the desert of Sinai."[11] Sharing Cohen's disdain for the new unit, the Department of Justice (DOJ) wrote the first set of Title VI regulations by itself.

The civil rights office reinforced its reputation for political naiveté when it announced that the first Title VI funding cutoff would target not a recalcitrant school district in Mississippi, but rather the city of Chicago, home of the most powerful Democratic boss in the country, Richard J. Daley. The Johnson White House forced OE to reverse its position and required all future funding terminations to be pre-cleared by the White House. What is commonly referred to as "the Chicago fiasco" led to Keppel's being "kicked upstairs" and to a major shake-up in the civil rights office.

One of the strangest manifestations of the young organization's seat-of-the-pants policymaking was the publication of the pivotal 1965 desegregation guidelines. They appeared not in the *Federal Register*, the usual venue for announcing federal rules, but in an article in the popular magazine *Saturday Review of Literature*. Commissioner Keppel and his advisors were desperate to give school districts guidance on the type of desegregation plans HEW would consider adequate. But Secretary Celebrezze refused to approve them. In response, Keppel authorized one of OE's legal consultants to write an article explaining what the office would accept, and he arranged to have copies mailed to school districts throughout the country. To say the least, this manner of announcing administrative policy was quite a departure from the procedures laid out in Title VI, which requires rules issued under it to be approved by the president of the United States, not the managing editor of the *Saturday Review of Literature*.

In 1965–66 the office charged with reviewing desegregation plans in more than four thousand southern school districts had only fifteen permanent staff members. Its most important work was performed by ten law professors who served as part-time consultants. During the summer of 1966 it also relied on untrained and largely unsupervised law-student interns to negotiate desegregation plans with southern officials. In early 1967 the civil rights unit was taken out of OE and lodged in the Secretary's office. A new, more politically astute director took the helm. By 1968 it had more than three hundred employees, a figure that rose to six hundred in 1972 and more than a thousand by 1977.[12]

ADMINISTRATIVE CONSTRAINTS

Two vexing problems continued to face the rapidly growing civil rights agency. Both left a lasting imprint on its methods for handling school desegregation. The first was defining its relationship with federal courts. The Department of Justice insisted that the Office of Education could not deny funding to any school system that was operating under a judicial desegregation order, even if OCR had grave doubts about whether the district was actually complying with it. DOJ officials considered this stipulation an integral part of the deal they had negotiated with Senator Humphrey during the lengthy debate over the 1964 law. Moreover, they did not want to create a confrontation between OE and the courts over the meaning of the Equal Protection clause. In such a confrontation, they feared, the executive branch would lose, seriously compromising its authority.[13] Commissioner Keppel agreed, arguing that the executive and judicial branches should remain "on parallel tracks running at about the same speed" because "if the Executive Branch had different standards than the courts there would be loss of confidence . . . in the minds of the people."[14]

In the short run, the assumption that federal administrators could not stray from judicial doctrine meant that southern school districts could qualify for federal funding merely by showing that they were subject to judicial orders. In the long run, this legal orientation meant that OCR and DOJ attorneys would take their lead from their understanding of "where the cases were going," reading case law in the light of "the spirit of the most recent Supreme Court decisions," and trying to stay "a hop, skip, and a jump ahead of them."[15] In the agency's early years, law professors rose to prominence because they were the only ones who could credibly "extrapolate from court decisions to the specific issue under discussion." As Orfield puts it, "there was a widely shared assumption that Title VI was designed to enforce the Constitution as interpreted by the courts, and no one else in the Office had any idea about a source of desegregation standards to rely on."[16]

A subtler consequence of OCR's deference to the courts was that it could concentrate its effort on rural areas and small cities in the South, not that region's largest cities. Since most of those cities were subject to court orders, OCR could leave the most complicated problems to the judiciary. When OCR did venture to establish desegregation plans for Raleigh, North Carolina, Columbia, South Carolina, and the huge suburban district of Prince George's County, Maryland, negotiations dragged on until private litigants filed suit in federal court. Thus it was federal judges, not administrators, who first faced the question of how to handle large school districts with substantial residential segregation.[17]

The second perennial problem confronting OCR was that the threat of funding cutoffs generated intense opposition in Congress and the White House. When Congress enacted Title VI, it included provisions to protect recipients of federal funds from arbitrary administrative action, most notably the right to pre-termination hearings and to judicial review of termination decisions. It also required the agency to notify Congress sixty days before any planned funding cutoff—thus giving the local member of Congress time to object. At first OCR tried to get around these restrictions by "deferring" rather than terminating funding. An irritated Congress responded by passing an amendment to Title VI prohibiting administrators from deferring funds for more than ninety days without going through the statutory termination procedures.[18]

The funding cutoff, federal officials soon learned, was a blunderbuss, not a rifle—and one with substantial political kickback. Statistics provided by Beryl Radin vividly demonstrate the weakness of this sanction. Between 1964 and 1970, the period in which OCR was most aggressive and most successful in attacking southern school segregation, it initiated administrative proceedings against six hundred of the more than four thousand school districts in the South. Federal funding was "terminated in 200; in all but four of these 200 districts, federal aid was subsequently restored, often without a change in local procedures."[19] The most recalcitrant rural districts were willing to forgo federal funds rather than desegregate.[20] At that point, litigation was the only option.

Even when it avoided termination of funding, OCR faced congressional attacks on its authority. Most of the hostile legislative proposals were eventually killed, some only after the department's defenders relied on the traditional tool of segregationists, the Senate filibuster. Committees without legislative jurisdiction over HEW regularly threatened it with investigations and budget cuts. The head of OCR testified before Congress twenty times during the first eight months of 1966. As a result, he reported, congressional criticism was "always in the back of our minds."[21] Administrators discovered that even strong supporters of the Civil Rights Act could turn into critics when schools in their district came under attack. OCR's troubled relationship with Congress, coupled with the problems inherent in cutting off funding for programs central to the department's mission, made the agency all the more dependent on judicial enforcement.

HEW'S PIVOTAL GUIDELINES

Those who have studied the early years of OCR agree that its most important—and most controversial—contribution to school desegregation was the guidance issued in 1965 and 1966. These guidelines established timetables and percentage targets for black enrollment in formerly white schools. (See tables 4.2 and 4.3) Both sets of guidelines were quickly endorsed by the Fifth Circuit. Once it became clear that the courts would use their authority to enforce these standards, OCR could take a tough enforcement stance against southern school districts. It knew that in the vast majority of cases either voluntary compliance or court action would occur before it would face the question of whether to cut off federal funds.

The initial set of Title VI rules announced by HEW and the Justice Department in 1964 were far too general to offer much guidance on what constituted an adequate desegregation plan. While a few political executives in HEW preferred to negotiate with southern school districts on an ad hoc basis, Commissioner Keppel and his advisors recognized that unless school districts had a clear idea what was expected of them, the entire regulatory undertaking would collapse. As Beryl Radin put it, they "wanted to be able to tell state and local school officials that they were applying known standards" in their review of desegregation plans.[22] It was this bureaucratic imperative that led Keppel to authorize the magazine article that laid out four key demands:

(1) to qualify for federal funds, districts with a history of de jure segregation must submit either a final court order together with a legally binding promise to

> **BOX 4.1**
>
> Major requirements of April 1965 guidelines
> - Prior to the beginning of the 1965–66 school year, districts with a history of de jure segregation must either—
>   ▷ Submit a final court order along with a statement of their willingness to comply with it and a report on their progress in meeting its requirements, or
>   ▷ Submit a desegregation plan approved by the Commissioner of Education
> - "Freedom of choice" plans, geographic attendance zones drawn on a nonracial basis, or a combination of the two are all acceptable.
> - "Freedom of choice" plans must allow students to select any school; schools must use simple, standardized forms; forms must be mailed to all parents; admission to oversubscribed schools must be based on proximity, not on which school the student formerly attended.
> - Schools must demonstrate good faith by desegregating at least four grades in the fall of 1965: the first grades of elementary school, junior high school, and high school; and the last grade of high school.
> - All school activities and programs must be desegregated.
> - Schools must prepare plans for desegregation of faculty.

comply with it, or a desegregation plan approved by the Commissioner of Education;

(2) districts must at a minimum desegregate four grades during the 1965–66 school year;

(3) they must desegregate all school activities and programs, not just classrooms; and

(4) they must make plans for desegregating faculty and staff in the near future.

These rules explicitly condoned the use of "freedom of choice" plans, but mandated procedures designed to prevent school officials from placing obstacles in the way of black students who wished to attend formerly white schools.

After much prodding from federal officials, during the summer of 1965 almost all the South's four thousand school districts submitted desegregation plans in order to qualify for ESEA money. As a result, federal administrators were "inundated with piles of paper forms." But, as Beryl Radin noted, federal administrators had real problems determining whether schools were really desegregating. The paper assurances and plans gave little guide to such an evaluation. And the guidelines issued by OE did not help a staff member—even one who visited the site to evaluate performance—decide whether the system was making substantial progress toward desegregation and not simply leap-frogging around the requirement.[23]

Most districts employed "freedom of choice" plans that delegated substantial discretion to local officials. Gary Orfield pointed out that "in administrative terms, there was simply no conceivable way in which a tiny staff in Washington could accurately assess the subtleties of local resistance used to subvert free-choice plans."[24] To make matters worse, some school districts were purposely using paper compliance with OE standards to delay desegregation litigation in federal court. OE temporarily denied funding to a small group of intransigent districts (mainly in Mississippi, Alabama, and Louisiana) that had refused to submit any plans at all. But it did not terminate funds to a single district that had filled out the required paperwork.[25]

In 1966 these persistent difficulties led OCR and the new Commissioner of Education, Harold Howe II, to issue additional guidelines to cover the 1966–67 school year. These guidelines were among the most important rules ever issued by a civil rights agency. When embraced by the Fifth Circuit later that year, they fundamentally altered the course of school desegregation. Their basic purpose, as Howe told a congressional committee, was to shift regulation "from negotiation to performance." "Negotiating desegregation plans for individual school districts," he explained, had "proved to be a truly monumental task" that had failed to induce southern school districts to make "any real efforts" to devise effective desegregation plans.[26] According to the guidelines' key sentence, "The single most substantial indication as to whether a free-choice plan is actually working is the extent to which Negro and other minority group students have, *in fact, transferred from segregated schools.*"[27] They provided specific percentage targets to allow regulators to judge whether schools' plans were "actually working":

- schools with 8–9 percent of minority students in formerly white schools in 1965–66 were expected to double those percentages in 1966–67;
- schools with 4–5 percent of minority students in formerly white schools were expected to triple those percentages;
- and schools with less than 4 percent were expected to more than triple that percentage over the next year.

> **BOX 4.2**
>
> Major requirements of March 1966 guidelines
> - The focus of the regulations shifted "from negotiation to performance."
> - "The single most substantial indication as to whether a free-choice plan is *actually* working is the extent to which Negro and other minority group students have, in fact, transferred from segregated schools." To determine whether a desegregation is "actually working," the guidelines established the following expectations:
>   - Schools with 8-9 percent of minority students in formerly white schools in 1965-66 must *double* those percentages (to 16-18 percent) in 1966-67;
>   - Schools with 4-5 percent of minority students in formerly white schools in 1965-66 must *triple* those percentages (to 12-15 percent) in 1966-67;
>   - Schools with less than 4 percent of minority students in formerly white schools must *more than triple* that percentage in 1966-67;
>   - Schools that remained completely segregated must make "a very substantial start" enabling them "to catch up as quickly as possible with systems which started earlier."
> - Desegregation of faculty and staff must begin during the 1966-67 school year.
> - The guidelines included ten attachments providing model forms for informing parents of the choices available to their children for transfers, etc. Such detail made the 1966 guidelines five times as long as the 1965 guidelines.

The 1966 guidelines also demanded that faculty integration begin later that year, and they placed more procedural restrictions on "freedom of choice" plans.

These specific performance standards enabled OCR's small staff to move beyond paper compliance. They also gave school officials a clear idea of what was expected of them. Behind the guidelines lay not an ideological commitment to racially balanced schools but a desperate effort to get a handle on an administrative task that until then had proven intractable. The 1966 guidelines were, as Orfield put it, "more a response to bureaucratic need for certainty and predictability than to any civil rights impulse within the Office."[28]

The guidelines did not constitute a demand for racial balance: they did not require that more than 20 percent of minority students attend formerly white schools. Just as importantly, the guidelines said nothing about eliminating all-black schools. Secretary of HEW John Gardner emphasized that the percentages should be considered an "administrative guide" rather than a binding requirement.[29]

Opponents of the guidelines could nonetheless see that a Rubicon was being crossed, and they strenuously objected. Southern school officials and members of Congress argued that the guidelines violated the Civil Rights Act's prohibition of "racial balance" requirements and ignored the circuit courts' approval of "freedom of choice" plans. The House passed an appropriations rider prohibiting HEW from enforcing its desegregation rules, and it came close to approving legislation stripping HEW of all power to issue rules under Title VI. The House Rules Committee grilled Commissioner Howe at hearings on the guidelines. Civil rights groups failed to come to Howe's defense. Instead, they attacked him for moving too slowly. The Senate blocked the House efforts to reduce the authority of federal administrators. But Gardner, Howe, and OCR leaders knew they were skating on thin ice.[30]

The big question was whether the courts would support or repudiate the 1966 guidelines. During the previous year the Fifth Circuit had given "great weight" to the 1965 guidelines. In *Singleton v. Jackson Municipal School District*, Judge Wisdom wrote that there should be a "close correlation" between the standards applied by the judicial and executive branches. "Absent legal questions, the United States Office of Education is better qualified than the courts and is the most appropriate federal body to weigh administrative difficulties inherent in school desegregation plans."[31] Another panel of the Fifth Circuit welcomed this "long overdue" executive contribution, and ordered district courts to adopt its requirement that schools desegregate at least four grades during the 1965–66 school year.[32] But the 1966 guidelines would be a much harder sell since they could be interpreted as challenging the logic of "freedom of choice" plans and raising the specter of racial quotas.

The 1966 guidelines were one small step for a beleaguered agency, but a giant leap for school desegregation. Without measurable performance standards, federal officials could never know the extent to which informal pressure and administrative trickery had infected the "freedom of choice" plans used throughout the South. Nor could they provide the courts with the assistance judges increasingly craved. To be sure, the percentages required by the guidelines were not especially demanding. But for that reason, it was hard to claim that any school district that had failed to meet these standards a dozen years after *Brown* was acting in good faith.

The 1966 guidelines constitute a prime example of what John Skrentny has described as "administrative pragmatism": a defense of quantitative racial targets that rests on administrators' determination to produce measurable results and thus avoid "presid[ing] over a demonstrably failing agency."[33] At the same time, the guidelines were a critical first step toward a new understanding of "desegregation," one that culminated in the Supreme Court's description of a "unitary school system." The bridge between HEW's pragmatic guidelines and the Supreme Court's expansive redefinition of "desegregation" was the Fifth Circuit's opinion in *U.S. v. Jefferson County Board of Education*.

The Transformation of *Jefferson County*

With jurisdiction over much of the recalcitrant South, the Court of Appeals for the Fifth Circuit had long been at the center of the school-desegregation storm. By 1964 many judges on the court had grown frustrated and impatient with the pace of desegregation. Unlike Supreme Court justices who could ignore the issue for long periods, lower court judges in the South had for years "gone to bed and woken up with school desegregation problems on their mind."[34]

After 1964 the Fifth Circuit's school-desegregation docket grew by leaps and bounds. In 1961 the NAACP's Legal Defense Fund handled forty-six school cases; four years later it was litigating 185. Most of these new suits targeted the South's largest cities.[35] In the months after passage of the Civil Rights Act, the Department of Justice had focused its attention on voting rights. But in June 1965, Attorney General Katzenbach pledged a "full scale campaign against segregated schools."[36] During the preceding fiscal year DOJ had initiated seven school suits. Over the next twelve months it filed forty-four. By the end of fiscal year 1967 it was handling 132 desegregation cases.[37] These statistics only begin to tell the story: many of these suits consolidated cases against a number of school districts; one covered all one hundred school districts in the state of Alabama. DOJ lawyers had long argued that the best way to enforce HEW's guidelines was through court action rather than termination of federal funds. Now they were putting their prestige and resources behind that strategy, placing great strain on judges in the Fourth and Fifth circuits.

Those judges were a varied lot. Some district court judges within these circuits were notorious for their lack of zeal for desegregation, not surprising since they had been selected by segregationist Senators in the 1940s and 1950s.[38] But this group also included such fervent and innovative supporters of desegregation as Frank Johnson of Alabama and J. Skelly Wright of Louisiana (at least until President Kennedy appointed him to the DC Circuit to get him out of New Orleans, where he had become a social pariah). On the Fifth Circuit sat Elbert Tuttle, John Minor Wisdom, John Brown, and Richard Rives, known as "The Four" for their aggressive attack on school segregation. During the 1960s these judges were joined by future US Attorney General Griffin Bell, Lyndon Johnson's unsuccessful Supreme Court nominee Homer Thornberry, former Mississippi governor James Coleman, and seven other LBJ appointees. Circuit court judge Ben Cameron became their increasingly bitter and implacable foe.[39] In the late 1960s and early 1970s the Supreme Court almost always let decisions of the Fifth Circuit stand while reviewing—and overturning—decisions of the more conservative Fourth Circuit, which had jurisdiction over Virginia, North Carolina, and South Carolina.

The extraordinary burden placed on the Fifth Circuit by desegregation was a result not only of the number of school districts being sued, but the intransigence of some district court judges. Pro-segregation judges such as Frank Scarlett of Georgia and William Cox of Mississippi engaged in rank insubordination. Some cases went back and forth between district and circuit courts as many as ten times within a few years. Under Chief Judges Tuttle and Brown, the Fifth Circuit responded by requiring expedited review of civil rights cases. As a result, during the mid-1960s the court was perpetually in emergency session. The circuit court also took the unusual step of issuing its own injunctions, both to stay orders of district court judges and to issue direct commands to them. But the judges on the circuit court learned that such unusual procedures alone would not suffice. "As the Fifth Circuit found itself caught in an increasing maelstrom of school desegregation appeals," Frank Read and Lucy McGough write, "it desperately searched for uniform standards of enforcement."[40]

WISDOM'S WISDOM

In *Singleton I*, the first in a series of important decisions issued by the Fifth Circuit in the wake of HEW's 1965 guidelines, Judge Wisdom expressed hope that those rules would provide the uniform standards the court had long sought. Announcing that "the time has come for foot-dragging public school boards to move with celerity toward desegregation," he "urged school authority to grasp the nettle now."[41] The court attached "great weight" to the 1965 guidelines and ordered the school districts before it to follow HEW's mandate to desegregate four grades in the coming fall. He warned that "if judicial standards are lower than H.E.W. standards, recalcitrant school boards in effect will receive a premium for recalcitrance; the more intransigence, the bigger the bonus." In short, the only way out of the seemingly endless morass was for the federal government to speak with a single voice and to establish specific deadlines for school officials.

A year later, Judge Wisdom and the Fifth Circuit went several steps further, endorsing HEW's second set of guidelines, calling into question the adequacy of most "freedom of choice" plans, equating "desegregation" with "integration," and exerting unprecedented appellate court control over judicial remedies. The 1966 decision of the three-judge panel in *U.S. v. Jefferson County (Jefferson I)* was upheld by the full Fifth Circuit a few months later when it heard the case en banc (*Jefferson II*).[42] The importance of these decisions, Frank Read notes, "cannot be overemphasized."[43]

Reflecting the court's determination to establish general rules rather than deal with each school district on an individual basis, *Jefferson County* was a consolidation of seven desegregation cases from Alabama and Louisiana. Judge Wisdom announced that the court's patience had finally run out. Of the sixty thousand black students in the districts named in *Jefferson*, only one hundred had managed to escape segregated schools. In the twelve years since *Brown*, district courts within the circuit had heard 128 cases and issued 513 orders. The appeals court had heard forty-two cases, half of them twice, and several of them four or five times. Extricating the court from this morass, Judge Wisdom determined, required jettisoning the long-standing but misguided embraced of "freedom of choice" plans. Echoing HEW's guidelines—and presaging the words of the Supreme Court in *Green v. County School Board*—the court announced that "the only school desegregation plan that meets constitutional standards is one that *works*."[44] As the dissenters noted in *Jefferson II*, between the lines of his opinion Judge Wisdom offered a novel understanding of what it means for a desegregation plan "to work."

The centerpiece of Judge Wisdom's opinion was a frontal assault on the "*Briggs* doctrine" announced by the Fourth Circuit in 1955 and accepted by most federal courts in the years that followed. *Briggs* held that the Constitution "does not require integration," but "merely forbids segregation."[45] If students are allowed to choose their schools and if those choices are not infected by intimidation or manipulation by school officials, then it does not matter how many black students go to school with white students. HEW, too, had adopted this position. Like many judges, federal administrators frequently questioned the *genuineness* of the choices offered by southern schools, but they did not challenge "freedom of choice" in the abstract.

In words that would reverberate throughout desegregation case law, Judge Wisdom replaced "freedom of choice" with the duty "to take affirmative action" to achieve "the conversion of a *de jure* segregated dual system into a unitary, nonracial (nondiscriminatory) system—lock, stock, and barrel: students, faculty, staff, facilities, programs, and activities."[46] Creating such a "unitary" school system required elimination of all racially identifiable schools. The question of what constitutes a "racially identifiable school" and a "unitary system" thus moved to the center of desegregation litigation.

To dispel the "mystique" of the *Briggs* doctrine, Wisdom insisted upon using the terms *integration* and *desegregation* "interchangeably." Here he took an important step beyond HEW's guidelines, which had insisted that racial body counts were only a rule of thumb to determine whether school officials were implementing "freedom of choice" plans in good faith. Wisdom, in contrast, offered a controversial redefinition of the right established by *Brown*. In *Briggs*, he argued, the court had focused solely on the rights of *individuals*, "overlook[ing] the fact that Negroes *collectively* are harmed when the state, by law or custom, operates segregated schools." Indeed, "the unmalleable fact *transcending in importance the harm done to individual Negro children* is that the separate school system is an integral part of the Southern States' program to restrain Negroes *as a class* from participating in the life of the community."[47] Since segregation is a "group phenomenon," its destruction requires examining the condition of African Americans as a group. As a result, the "right of the individual plaintiff must yield to the overriding right of Negroes as a class to a completely *integrated* public education." As we will see, the Supreme Court followed the logic of Wisdom's argument, but it was never so candid about its redefinition of the underlying right.

The major implication of Wisdom's argument was that individual minority students and their parents cannot be allowed to exercise choices that run counter to the collective interest of African Americans. He did not linger on the awkward question of how a few white judges could discern the collective interest of a racial group. Rather, he quickly moved to more pragmatic arguments: having for years denied "equal educational opportunity" to black students, southern schools now had an obligation "to undo the effects of past discrimination." Doing so might mean creating compensatory educational programs. It certainly meant that schools attended by black students could not receive fewer resources—including quality teachers—than those attended by whites. Wisdom hinted that merely by being predominantly black, schools might be considered inferior because they stigmatize and demoralize their students. If segregated schools generate a feeling of inferiority among minority students (as *Brown* stated), then to exercise "free choice"—even choice free of intimidation and manipulation—might reflect this long-reinforced myth of black inferiority.

Integrating dual school systems required not just redefining the pivotal constitutional right but revising institutional practices. By 1966 it was clear to everyone that *Brown II*'s strategy of giving district court judges vast discretion to fashion desegregation decrees had been a miserable failure. "Leaving school officials with a broad area of uncontrolled discretion" supervised only by local judges, Judge Wisdom complained, too often produced only "paper compliance with the duty to desegregate."

Departing from the ordinary practice of leaving remedies in the hand of trial-court judges, the Fifth Circuit created a lengthy model decree that it expected all judges in the circuit to employ. This decree was based almost entirely on HEW's guidelines. Centralization of authority within the judicial branch was thus fused with judicial deference to administrative authority. According to the Fifth Circuit, this combination offered, "for the first time, the prospect that the transition from a *de jure* segregated dual school system to a unitary integrated system may be carried out effectively, promptly, and in an orderly manner." "Prepared in detail by experts in education and school administration," the guidelines were "intended by Congress and the executive to be part of a coordinated national program." Consequently, they "present the best system available for uniform application, and the best aid to the courts in evaluating the validity of a school desegregation plan and the progress made under that plan."[48] To "encourag[e] the maximum legally permissible correlation between judicial standards for school desegregation and HEW Guidelines," the Fifth Circuit would regularly update its requirements to match those of HEW.

Judge Wisdom presented his deference to HEW as deference to Congress, and thus an exercise in judicial modesty: "When Congress declares national policy, the duty the other two coordinate branches owe to the Nation requires that, within the law, the judge and the executive respect and carry out that policy." Congress, he stressed through unusual capitalization, "speaks as the Voice of the Nation." Given how often Congress had insisted that desegregation does *not* mean assigning students to schools on the basis of race in order to achieve racial balance, the argument that the court was listening to the "Voice of the Nation" was less than convincing.

More persuasive was Judge Wisdom's pragmatic argument that if judicial standards were more lenient than administrative standards, school districts would refuse to negotiate with HEW and take their chances in court—a particularly unappealing outcome for a court desperate to shrink its desegregation docket. As Judge Griffin Bell noted, "The general theme of the majority is that HEW has the carrot in the form of federal funds but no stick. A stick is needed in those situations where school boards may not take federal funds. The aim is to make a stick out of the federal courts." While agreeing that courts should cooperate with HEW, Judge Bell questioned whether they should be willing to wield "any stick that HEW may formulate" in the future.

CRUCIAL AMBIGUITIES

Jefferson County did make a formidable "stick out of the federal courts." But to what end? The answer to that question remained elusive. A fundamental tension permeated the Fifth Circuit's two opinions in the case, a tension that haunted the federal judiciary's jurisprudence on school desegregation for years to come. On the one hand, the central thrust of Judge Wisdom's opinion in *Jefferson County* was the rejection of the "mystique" of the "*Briggs* doctrine," the discrediting of "freedom of choice" plans, the recognition of the rights of black children "as a class," and the insistence that schools begin immediately to create a "unitary school system." On the other hand, the elaborate model decree designed by the court with HEW's assistance focused above all on standardizing the operation of "freedom of choice" plans, preventing school officials from pressuring black students to stay in their former schools, and equalizing the resources available to formerly black and formerly white schools. Was "freedom of choice" to be purified—as the decree required—or repudiated—as Judge Wisdom's opinion announced?

This tension was particularly evident in the en banc court's brief (six-paragraph) per curiam opinion. It followed Judge Wisdom's longer opinion in establishing public schools' duty to create "an integrated, unitary school system in which there are no Negro schools and no white schools—just schools." The full court was even more explicit than the three-judge panel in explaining that "freedom of choice is not a goal in itself," but merely "one of the tools available" for converting a dual system into a unitary one. "It is not enough," the court held in *Jefferson II*, "to offer Negro children the opportunity to attend formerly all-white schools.... [O]vercoming the effects of the dual school system in this circuit requires integration of faculties, facilities, and activities, as well as students."[49] The ultimate "objective of this conversion is educational opportunities on equal terms to all." By so broadening the purpose of desegregation, the court seemed to make the practical problem of evaluating compliance more difficult than ever.

One judge who voted with the majority in the en banc proceeding wrote a concurring opinion explaining that he did not read the per curiam opinion as directing "that there shall be a specified percentage of the various races in any particular public school or that there shall be proportional representation of the races brought about by arbitrary order." Under the en banc ruling and its lengthy decree, Judge Coleman claimed, "the District Courts are left free to consider all the evidence, including racial attendance percentages, in determining whether the children of any particular school district have been offered a reality [of choice] instead of a shadow." He voted with the majority because after examining the decree, he did "not understand that this Court has abandoned freedom of choice, if that choice is real instead of illusory." In other words, what the court had *ordered* did not jive with what it had *said*. Coleman "anticipated that the bridge will later have to be crossed when we come face to face with a situation wherein there can be no doubt of the freedom but the results are displeasing and are attacked solely for that reason."[50]

The three dissenters in *Jefferson County II* raised several additional issues that would define the desegregation debate for years. The first was the status of HEW's guidelines. Judge Gerwin noted that "the guidelines were not approved by the President as required by the Civil Rights Act." Nor had they ever been subjected to a public hearing or any other form of public input: "It is unthinkable that matters that so vitally affect this phase of the national welfare should be decided in such summary fashion." Judge Griffin Bell described the process by which the guidelines were adopted as "a shocking departure from even rudimentary due process." Even worse, according to the dissenters, was the fact that the circuit court had commanded lower courts to show great deference to *future* administrative guidelines. In an effort to launch a coordinated assault on school segregation, they charged, the court had delegated to HEW the job of interpreting the Fourteenth Amendment, and thus "seriously erode[d] the doctrine of separation of powers as between the Executive and the Judiciary."[51]

Second, the dissenters expressed their unease with appellate courts depriving trial judges of discretion to adapt remedies to local circumstances. Gerwin complained that the circuit court had given "no consideration" to differences among school systems: "Urban schools, rural ones, small schools, large ones, areas where racial imbalance is large or small, the relative number of Negro and white children in any particular area, or any of the other myriad problems which are known to every school administrator, are not taken into account." Under the new regime "all things must yield to speed, uniformity, percentages and proportional representation." The only functions remaining for the district court, Gerwin claimed, were "to order the enforcement of the detailed, uniform, stereotyped formal decree, to supervise compliance with its detailed provisions . . . and to receive periodic reports much in the same fashion as reports are received by an ordinary clerk in a large business establishment."[52] No doubt Judge Wisdom and his allies in the majority hoped this would in fact be the case!

Finally, the dissenters suggested that the logic of demanding the establishment of "unitary" school systems could not stop at the Mason-Dixon line. If predominantly black schools were unconstitutional in Mississippi and Alabama, why should they be tolerated in in Chicago and Detroit? Judge Bell noted that "all children everywhere in the nation are protected by the Constitution, and treatment which violates their constitutional rights in one area of the country, also violates such constitutional rights in another area."[53] "If equal educational opportunity includes the right to a racially-mixed education," Judge Godbold pointed out, "it is not clear why the class stops at district lines" that are merely "convenient device[s] for administration . . . wholly irrelevant to the quantum of constitutional entitlements."[54] As early as 1967, it was evident that creating a "unitary system" might require busing between predominantly-black inner cities and white suburbs in the North as well as in the South.

Sensitive to the possibility that he might be placing the court on a steep and slippery slope, Judge Wisdom had tried in his initial opinion to draw a bright line between the de jure segregation found in the South and the de facto segregation of the North. The similarity between what he oddly termed "pseudo *de facto* segregation in the South" and "actual *de facto* segregation in the North" is "more apparent than real." In the South

> school boards, utilizing the dual zoning system, assigned Negro teachers to Negro schools and selected Negro neighborhoods as suitable areas in which to locate Negro schools. Of course the concentration of Negroes increased in the neighborhood of the school. Cause and effect came together. In this circuit, therefore, the location of Negro schools with Negro faculties in Negro neighborhoods and white schools in white neighborhoods cannot be described as an unfortunate fortuity: It came into existence as state action and continues to exist as racial gerrymandering, made possible by the dual system. Segregation resulting from racially motivated gerrymandering is properly characterized as 'de jure' segregation.[55]

The NAACP would soon make precisely this argument in one northern city after another. It is hard to believe that Judge Wisdom and others on the Fifth Circuit did not foresee that possibility. Maintaining the strained distinction between "pseudo *de facto* segregation" and "actual *de facto* segregation" allowed them to assure northerners that their schools were not threatened by this redefinition of desegregation. Nonetheless, in *Jefferson County* the court was inching toward a policy that would require major changes in schools throughout the country.

THE COURTS' BIG "STICK"

Although Judge Wisdom's attack on "freedom of choice" plans, his endorsement of "integration" and group rights, and his embrace of HEW's guidelines were the best-known features of the *Jefferson County* decision, Judge J. Harvie Wilkinson has argued that "the most remarkable aspect of *Jefferson* was the remedial decree." "By any measure," Wilkinson writes, "the *Jefferson* decree was an extraordinary step" that "foretold a level of judicial involvement in local education unimaginable at the time of *Brown*."[56]

The Fifth Circuit's procedural innovations provide a good example of how efforts to dismantle the Jim Crow system spurred institutional change. Based on interviews with Chief Judge John R. Brown, Frank Read reports that Brown and the other members of his court "came to a tacit agreement that no further *en banc* hearings would be held and opinion writing by three-judge panels would be avoided where possible." Judge Brown told Read that he had "preached over and over to his judges, 'All that can be said about school cases has been said; there is no point in writing further words.'"[57] Under these new procedures, district court decisions could be affirmed or reversed without an explanation, and often without a hearing. The Fifth Circuit created five standing three-judge panels to review desegregation cases. Each panel would remain on a case until it was resolved. This practice allowed appellate judges to become familiar with the facts and the history of each case, and thus to exercise much more control over district court judges. At times the standing panels even met with the parties to speed up negotiations over the details of remedial decrees. Since en banc reconsideration was no longer tolerated, the panels tried to ensure uniformity by circulating their rulings to all judges on the full court.[58]

Because *Jefferson County* had made it so easy for litigants to impose the Fifth Circuit's uniform decree on districts that had failed to meet HEW's rules of thumb, that court's caseload ballooned. Appointed attorney general the same month the Fifth Circuit announced its per curiam decision, Ramsey Clark spurred the Department of Justice to file more desegregation suits, including some against northern cities.[59] The new legal-services offices created as part of the War on Poverty began to file desegregation suits as well. The NAACP reopened desegregation cases throughout the Circuit with what became known as "*Jefferson* motions"—twenty cases in Alabama, twenty-seven in Florida, six in Georgia, thirty-three in Louisiana, thirty in Mississippi, and five in Texas.[60]

Desegregation litigation "was now capable of mass production. Cases could now be brought and disposed of wholesale"—forty-four at one time in a 1968 Fifth Circuit decision, thirty-eight in one 1969 case and twenty-five in another.[61] The Fifth Circuit's 1967 ruling in *Lee County* covered every school district in the state of Alabama.[62] Between December of 1969 and September of 1970, these panels issued 166 "opinion orders" on desegregation. These streamlined procedures produced "another quantum leap in school desegregation activities."[63]

At the district court level an even more significant and long-lasting change in judicial process was taking place: the development of the structural injunction. In his seminal textbook on injunctions, Owen Fiss uses Judge Frank Johnson's long series of orders in the Montgomery, Alabama, desegregation case to illustrate the extent to which decrees grew longer and more detailed as judges were drawn deeper and deeper into educational issues.[64] As the "tricks and evasions" Justice Frankfurter had warned about multiplied, so too did the length and intrusiveness of judicial orders.[65]

Southern resistance was not the only reason for the expanding reach and specificity of structural injunctions. Common sense dictated that judges pay attention to the many factors other than school-assignment rules that could affect the long-term success of desegregation. Desegregating schools meant reassigning teachers as well as students; that was Judge Johnson's primary concern in the Montgomery case. School siting decisions can have a big impact on the future composition of individual schools. It made little sense to integrate school buildings, and then allow administrators to resegregate classrooms through their decisions on tracking. Were too many minority students being assigned to special-education classes? Were they receiving harsher punishments and more frequent suspensions? Given the track record of southern schools, there seemed little reason for judges to rely on the good faith of school officials.

Chapter 6 explains how the structural injunction concentrates authority in the hands of district court judges. On how they should exercise this vast discretion, the Supreme Court remained mum. As Judge William Fletcher has noted, the Supreme Court has remained "generally uninterested in procedural and tactical details in school cases," failing to "set out principles to govern the use of experts, masters, or supervisory committees" or to clarify the crucial issues of "intervention and participation, or of permissible strategies of inducing settlement."[66] In the first decade after *Brown*, the Court's broad grant of discretion to trial judges led to endless foot-dragging. In the decade and a half following *Jefferson County*, that same delegation of authority contributed to a remarkable expansion of judicial supervision of public schools.

Parallel Tracks

HEW secretary John Gardner immediately described *Jefferson County I* as a "very very constructive decision" that went "right down the line" in supporting the department's guidelines. It should, he asserted, "lay to rest" any doubts about the guidelines' legality.[67] Buoyed by the court's endorsement, the department initiated hundreds of termination hearings over the next few months. Secretary Gardner then announced a new set of guidelines requiring more faculty desegregation during the next school year.

The combination of the 1965–66 guidelines and the *Jefferson County* decisions produced the symbiotic relationship between federal courts and agencies that Judge Wisdom had sought. As Beryl Radin put it, "the hand-in-glove relationship between the substantive requirements of the guidelines and the most current Fifth Circuit standards" produced "an interchange of evidence and justification and continual interaction between the administrative and judicial ends." This interdependence, Stephen Halpern has emphasized, demonstrates "the synergistic power of the bench and bureaucracy's working together."[68]

In part, this partnership worked because each branch could provide the other with additional legitimacy and political cover. HEW's claim to base its guidelines on the courts' interpretation of the Constitution, Halpern notes, gave them "the imprimatur of legality, adding badly needed legitimacy, credibility, and authority to HEW's fledgling effort to enforce Title VI." When confronted with complaints from southern officials, federal administrators could accurately claim that they had no choice but to follow the courts' interpretation of the Constitution. OCR "realized that federal courts were a good ally, and the agency had few allies in beginning the politically touchy task of enforcing Title VI."[69] Conversely, the Fifth Circuit relied on HEW's educational "expertise"—despite the fact that those who wrote the guidelines had little contact with education bureaucracy. In short, each could pass the buck to the other, and both could claim that they were deferring to Congress and following the Constitution rather than making public policy.

Just as important were the practical administrative benefits of this evolving division of labor. The Fifth Circuit needed help getting control over the district courts within its jurisdiction. Its model decree, which was designed to reduce the discretion available to this often-obstreperous group, was based almost entirely on HEW's guidelines. Having taken the extraordinary step of seizing control over the fashioning of remedial decrees, the Fifth Circuit also needed a way to learn what was actually going on within the school districts subject to their control. The growing staff at OCR provided circuit-court judges with eyes and ears "on the ground." As a perceptive student note in the 1967 *Yale Law Journal* explained, finding itself "unable to rely completely on the lower courts," the Fifth Circuit recognized that "it must relinquish efforts to function as a normal appellate court and instead act more like an administrative agency." "Having found it necessary to impose standards from above," the Fifth Circuit "quite naturally looked for guidance to another centralized government body which had already evolved ways to handle very similar administrative problems."[70]

OCR could demand plans from school districts. It could help them draw attendance zones and estimate their effect on the racial composition of individual schools. It could threaten districts with financial sanctions by initiating termination proceedings. What it would almost never do was pull the trigger and cut off federal funding. And what it definitely could not do was order schools to take specific actions to correct their desegregation plans, especially when those plans were subject to a court order.

With the streamlining of the judicial enforcement process achieved by the Fifth Circuit, resort to administrative termination hearings became superfluous. Once the courts' remedial process had been expedited, there was "no comparison with the speed with which a court may grant a temporary injunction or move to enforce its own order if not complied with."[71] Even more importantly, the courts could demand "specific performance"; that is, they could require school officials to take specified actions immediately. Those who balked could be held in contempt of court and personally subject to serious sanctions. Since a great many southern districts were already operating under court orders, administrators could combine the threat of court action with the promise of federal money: cooperate and you will not face any loss of federal funds; remain recalcitrant and you will be forced to comply by the court and lose federal money in the process. It was an offer few school districts could afford to refuse.

This division of labor proved most effective when judges and administrators remained "on parallel tracks"; that is, when they agreed on the purposes and standards of the enterprise. In the years immediately following *Jefferson County*, reaching such agreement was seldom a problem. Judges and administrators could agree that school systems should follow OCR's new procedures for the operation of "freedom of choice" plans and should quickly move 10–20 percent of the black student population into formerly white schools.

What's Next?

As desegregation progressed at an unprecedented rate, the key question became: At what point does "a good start" become full compliance? In March of 1968, HEW published what Radin describes as a "tersely written statement of general policy" announcing that the department's desegregation rules "do *not* require the correction of racial imbalance resulting from private patterns."[72]

What "racial balance" ultimately means and when it would be required was never directly confronted by either the Fifth Circuit or HEW. Nor did the Supreme Court settle the matter in 1968 when it handed down its reinterpretation of *Brown* in *Green v. County School Board of New Kent County*.

In *Green*, the Supreme Court incorporated many of Judge Wisdom's arguments, as well as some of his best aphorisms. Over the next year and a half, though, the Supreme Court twice took the odd step of reprimanding the Fifth Circuit for not moving quickly enough. The Fifth Circuit's response was to further expedite its review of desegregation plans and to place even more emphasis on racial body counts. Judges in the circuit drew school-attendance lines to minimize the number of predominantly white and black schools. They made frequent use of "pairing"—dividing grades between two adjacent schools—and "clustering"—a similar practice involving three or more schools. They closed schools in predominantly black neighborhoods and created biracial committees to make decisions about the siting of new schools.

Judges in the Fifth Circuit could not agree on what should be done when all these measures fail to eliminate predominantly black schools in residentially segregated urban areas. Some insisted that the Supreme Court did not require the elimination of one-race schools. For example, the standing panel on which Judge Griffin Bell sat approved a desegregation plan for Tampa that reduced "the number of Negro students attending all or virtually all Negro schools" from 60 percent to 21 percent. Further than this it would not go.[73] In a case involving the Florida county that includes Orlando, Bell's panel argued that a combination of neighborhood schools, gerrymandering of assignment zones to increase racial mixing, and a majority-to-minority transfer option would be enough to satisfy *Green*.[74] The panel did not order busing to eliminate the remaining all-black schools.

Another standing panel reached a much different conclusion in the Houston case. It held that that "the continued existence of all-black or virtually all-black schools is unacceptable where reasonable alternatives exist," and that busing constituted such a "reasonable alternative."[75] A third panel agreed, explaining that "the Supreme Court has made it clear that school boards cannot avoid their responsibility to create a unitary system simply by resorting to nondiscriminatory, geographical zoning where such zoning would be ineffective."[76] The panel on which Judge Wisdom sat rejected the Bell panel's approach, and required busing in Clarksdale, Mississippi.[77] For these panels, creating a "unitary" system meant eliminating all schools in which African Americans remained in the majority. With the Fifth Circuit divided against itself, where would the Supreme Court stand?

New Means, Uncertain Ends

Two sets of changes brought about the "reformation of southern education" in the late 1960s and early 1970s. One was doctrinal: racial balance became the test of whether a school district that had previously engaged in de jure segregation had complied with *Brown*. Here two questions remained unresolved. First, what does "racial balance" mean in practice? An even distribution of races among schools in a district? No predominantly black schools? All majority-white schools? Second, was racial balance a temporary administrative expedient to force action by obstreperous school districts? Or was racial balance constitutionally required for other reasons? If the latter, should this standard be applied in school districts not guilty of de jure segregation? The questions raised by *Jefferson County* continued to roil desegregation cases for decades.

The other change was institutional: the division of labor that developed between the Fifth Circuit and OCR; the expedited appellate review instituted by that court; and the development of the structural injunction. Each began as an extraordinary measure designed to overcome years of southern resistance to desegregation. Expedited review by the Fifth Circuit did, in fact, prove temporary. The structural injunction, in contrast, was soon applied in many other contexts.

By 1970, the court-agency alliance that had proved so effective over the previous half-decade had fallen apart. President Nixon made it clear that he did not want his administration to be blamed for pushing southern school desegregation, and he fired OCR director Leon Panetta when Panetta failed to fall in line. (The consequences of that pivotal event are discussed in chapter 9.) After that, the federal courts were forced largely to go it alone on school desegregation. But the alliance reappeared elsewhere, most notably on bilingual education and Title IX. Southern school desegregation had offered powerful evidence of its effectiveness.

5

Supreme Abdication

> At the outset, one must try to identify the constitutional right which is being enforced. This is not easy, as the precedents have been far from explicit.
> JUSTICE LEWIS POWELL, *Keyes v. School District #1, Denver*, 1973

While the Fifth Circuit and the Office of Civil Rights were jump-starting school desegregation in the South, the Supreme Court remained silent. The lower courts took the lead both in defining what constitutes unconstitutional segregation and in designing appropriate remedies. Beginning in the spring of 1968 and continuing for a little more than a decade, the Supreme Court issued a flurry of decisions purporting to give the lower courts more specific instructions on these fundamental questions. (See table 5.1 for a chronological list of these rulings.) Several of these decisions—especially *Green v. County School Board* (1968), *Swann v. Charlotte-Mecklenburg Board of Education* (1971), *Keyes v. School District #1, Denver* (1973), and *Milliken v. Bradley* (1974)—became central components of its desegregation jurisprudence.

What these decisions did *not* do, though, was offer a clear explanation of the meaning and purpose of desegregation. Sometimes the Court used inspiring but ambiguous phrases to hide disagreements among its members (especially *Green*). Sometimes these disagreements produced opinions with glaring internal contradictions (especially *Swann*). Sometimes the Court used technical arguments to hide the implications of its rulings (especially *Keyes*). Sometimes its decisions seemed to undermine the rationale of earlier rulings (especially *Milliken*). And sometimes the Court simply changed direction without admitting it (compare *Dayton I* with *Dayton II*). Seldom has a constitutional issue of this importance been handled in such an ambiguous, convoluted, even duplicitous manner. By the end of the 1970s the Court's instructions to the lower courts were hardly clearer than they had been a decade before.

To some extent this indecision reflected growing divisions within the Court. For nearly two decades, the Court had struggled to produce unanimous opinions in desegregation cases. By 1971 the norm of unanimity could no longer hide serious disagreements among the justices: of Chief Justice Burger's hopelessly muddled opinion in *Swann*, Judge Griffin Bell observed, "It's almost as if there were two sets of views laid side by side."[1] As box 5.1 shows, after *Swann*, few of the Court's desegregation rulings were unanimous. Dissenting opinions became the norm. Justice Brennan's opinion in *Keyes* could command only five votes. The same was true of Chief Justice Burger's opinion the next year in *Milliken v. Bradley*. Even brief per curiams and decisions on granting *cert.* elicited dissents

The two justices Nixon appointed in 1971, Rehnquist and Powell, became the Court's most consistent defenders of the "color-blind/limited intervention" approach described in chapter 2. Meanwhile, Justices Brennan and Marshall nudged the Court toward the competing "racial isolation/equal educational opportunity" approach. The outcome of each case depended on the four swing voters, two veterans of the Warren Court (White and Stewart) and two recent Republican appointees (Blackmun and Stevens). Chief Justice Burger usually seemed to agree with Powell and Rehnquist on the merits but engaged in gamesmanship that only he could fathom. By the late 1970s, Stevens and Blackmun were more likely to side with Brennan and Marshall than with Powell and Rehnquist, leaving White and Stewart as the key swing votes.

Two additional factors influenced the outcome of desegregation cases over these dozen years. First was the fevered political environment. As noted above, shortly before the Court handed down its decision in *Green*, Martin Luther King was assassinated in Memphis; cities around the country erupted in violence. Many observers warned that only major policy change would prevent further unrest. The Nixon administration's efforts to delay southern school desegregation buttressed the justices' resolve to resist the new president's "southern strategy." A few years later, intense political opposition to school busing probably influenced the Court's decision not to mandate city-to-suburb busing in the 1974 Detroit case.

The second factor was the changing nature of the cases that came before the Court: they grew harder and harder. *Green* came from the rural South, *Swann* from the urban South, *Keyes* from the urban North, and *Milliken* from a northern city that was becoming predominantly black. The early cases did not force the justices to decide which understanding of desegregation they endorsed. The later cases did. It became more difficult for justices to sit on the fence; the side on which the swing votes landed often depended on the peculiar features of each case. Guiding principles remained elusive.

TABLE 5.1. Supreme Court decisions on school segregation

1954	Brown v. Board of Education I, 347 U.S. 483
1955	Brown v. Board of Education II, 349 U.S. 294
1958	Cooper v. Aaron, 358 U.S. 1
	Shuttlesworth v. Birmingham Board of Education, 358 U.S. 101
1963	McNeese v. Board of Education, 373 U.S. 668
	Goss v. Board of Education, 373 U.S. 683
1964	Griffin v. School Board, 377 U.S. 218
1968	Green v. County School Board, 391 U.S. 430
	Raney v. Board of Education, 391 U.S. 443
	Monroe v. Board of Commissioners, 391 U.S. 450
1969	U.S. v. Montgomery Board of Education, 395 U.S. 225
	Alexander v. Holmes County Board of Education, 396 U.S. 19
1970	Carter v. West Feliciano School Board, 396 U.S. 290
	Northcross v. Board of Education, 397 U.S. 232
1971	Swann v. Charlotte-Mecklenburg Board of Education, 402 U.S. 1
	Davis v. Bd. of School Commissioners of Mobile County, 402 U.S. 33
1972	Wright v. Council of City of Emporia, 407 U.S. 451
	U.S. v. Scotland Neck Board of Education, 407 U.S. 484
1973	Bradley v. School Board of City of Richmond, 412 U.S. 92
	Keyes v. School District No. 1, Denver, 413 U.S. 189
1974	Milliken v. Bradley, 418 U.S. 717
1975	Buchanan v. Evans, 423 U.S. 963
1976	Pasadena City Board of Education v. Spangler, 427 U.S. 434
	Austin Independent School District v. US, 429 U.S. 990
1977	Dayton Board of Education v. Brinkman I, 433 U.S. 406
	Milliken v. Bradley II, 433 U.S. 267
	Brennan v. Armstrong, 433 U.S. 672
	School District of Omaha v. U.S., 433 U.S. 667
1979	Dayton Board of Education v. Brinkman II, 443 U.S. 526
	Columbus Board of Education v. Penick, 443 U.S. 449
1980	Estes v. Metropolitan Branch, Dallas NAACP, 444 U.S. 437
1990	Missouri v. Jenkins II, 495 U.S. 33
1991	Bd. of Education of Oklahoma City v. Dowell, 498 U.S. 231
1992	Freeman v. Pitts, 503 U.S. 469
1995	Missouri v. Jenkins III, 515 U.S. 70
2007	Parents Involved in Community Schools v. Seattle, 551 U.S. 701

Note: Table 5.1 does not include three minor desegregation decisions and three cases only tangentially related to school desegregation. The former are *Dowell v. Board of Education*, 396 U.S. 269 (1969), a brief per curiam that carried out the Court's directive in *Alexander*; *Board of Education v. Swann*, a companion to the Swann case discussed in detail below; and *McDaniel v. Barresi*, 402 U.S. 39 (1971), a reversal of a Georgia Supreme Court decision that applied *Green* in a relatively straightforward manner. The latter three are *Board of Education, NYC v. Harris*, 444 U.S. 130 (1979), an interpretation of the Emergency School Aid bill; *Washington v. Seattle School District #1*, 458 U.S. 457 (1982), which involved a Washington State referendum overturning a voluntary integration plan instituted by the city of Seattle; and *Missouri v. Jenkins I*, 491 U.S. 274 (1989), on attorneys' fees.

BOX 5.1 Supreme Court voting patterns, 1968–1980

1968 * *Green v. County School Board*
      <u>Brennan</u> for unanimous Court
      * *Raney v. Board of Education*
      <u>Brennan</u> for unanimous Court
      * *Monroe v. Board of Commissioners*
      <u>Brennan</u> for unanimous Court

Burger replaces Warren as chief justice

1969 * *U.S. v. Montgomery Board of Education*
      <u>Black</u> for unanimous Court
      * *Alexander v. Holmes County Board of Education*
      Per curiam
1970 * *Carter v. West Feliciano School Board*, per curiam
      Harlan, <u>Burger</u>, White, and Steward concur
      * *Northcross v. Board of Education*
      Per curiam
      <u>Burger</u> concurs in judgment
      Marshall does not participate

Blackmun replaces Fortas

1971 **Swann v. Charlotte-Mecklenburg Board of Education*
      <u>Burger</u> for unanimous Court
      **Davis v. Bd. of School Commissioners of Mobile County*
      <u>Burger</u> for unanimous Court

Powell and Rehnquist replace Black and Harlan

1972 **U.S. v. Scotland Neck Board of Education*, unanimous
      <u>Stewart</u> for Douglas, Brennan, White, and Marshall
      <u>Burger</u> concurs with Blackmun, Powell, and Rehnquist
      **Wright v. Council of City of Emporia*, 5–4
      Majority = <u>Stewart</u>, Douglas, Brennan, White, and Marshal
      Dissent = <u>Burger</u>, Blackmun, Powell, and Rehnquist
1973 **Bradley v. School Board of City of Richmond*,
      Equally divided, 4–4; vote not disclosed
      Powell did not participate
      **Keyes v. School District No. 1, Denver*, 6–2
      Majority = <u>Brennan</u>, Douglas, Stewart, Marshall, and Blackmun
      <u>Burger</u> concurs in the judgment
      Dissent = <u>Powell</u> and <u>Rehnquist</u>
      White did not participate
1974 **Milliken v. Bradley*, 5–4
      Majority = <u>Burger</u>, Stewart, Blackmun, Rehnquist, and Powell
      Concurring opinion by <u>Stewart</u>
      Dissent = <u>Douglas</u>, <u>White</u>, <u>Marshall</u>, and Brennan

Box 5.1 continued

1975 *Buchanan v. Evans, 6–3, affirmed without opinion
Dissent = <u>Rehnquist</u>, Powell, and Burger
Stevens replaces Douglas
1976 *Pasadena City Board of Education v. Spangler, 7–2
Majority = <u>Rehnquist</u>, Burger, Stewart, Blackmun, Powell, White, and Stevens
Dissent = <u>Marshall</u> and Brennan
*Austin Independent School District v. U.S.
Per curiam
<u>Powell</u>, Rehnquist, and Burger concur
Brennan and Marshall dissent without opinion
1977 *Dayton Board of Education v. Brinkman I
Majority= <u>Rehnquist</u>, Burger, Stevens, White, Blackmun, Powell, and Stewart
<u>Brennan</u> and <u>Stevens</u> concur in judgment only
Marshall did not participate
*Milliken v. Bradley II
<u>Burger</u> for unanimous Court
Concurring opinion by <u>Marshall</u>
<u>Powell</u> concurs in judgment only
*Brennan v. Armstrong
Per curiam
Dissent = <u>Stevens</u>, Brennan, and Marshall
*School District of Omaha v. U.S., per curiam
Dissent = <u>Brennan,</u> Marshall, and Stevens
1979 *Dayton Board of Education v. Brinkman II, 5–4
Majority = <u>White</u>, Brennan, Marshall, Stevens, and Blackmun
Dissent = <u>Stewart</u>, <u>Rehnquist</u>, <u>Powell</u>, and Burger
*Columbus Board of Education v. Penick, 7–2
Majority = <u>White</u>, Brennan, Marshall, Blackmun, and Stevens
<u>Stewart</u> and Burger concur in judgment only
Dissent = <u>Powell</u> and <u>Rehnquist</u>
1980 *Estes v. Metropolitan Branches, Dallas NAACP
per curiam
Dissent = <u>Powell</u>, Rehnquist, and Stewart
Marshall did not participate
*Delaware State Board of Education v. Evans
Cert. denied without opinion
Dissent = <u>Rehnquist</u>, Powell, and Stewart
Stevens did not participate

Note: Underlining indicates that the justice wrote an opinion.

Green's New Deal

Seldom has context been more important for understanding a Supreme Court opinion than in *Green v. County School Board of New Kent County*. This was true in three senses. First, the extraordinary national context: not only the assassination of Martin Luther King, but also the Kerner Commission's warning that "Our nation is moving toward two societies, one black, one white—separate and unequal."

The second contextual element was the nature of the school district in question. New Kent County was a small school district in rural Virginia that had for years maintained segregated schools and refused to comply with *Brown*. Since it had only two schools and little residential segregation, *Green* raised none of the difficult student-assignment questions that inevitably arose in large metropolitan school districts. Under the "freedom of choice" plan that the school district had established with approval from the Department of Health, Education, and Welfare (HEW), 115 black students attended the formerly white school along with all the district's 550 white students, leaving 625 black students and no white students in the formerly black school. The Fourth Circuit held that a "freedom of choice" plan was acceptable if students and their parents "annually exercise an uninhibited choice," free from "economic or other pressures in the community." Judge Haynsworth (later nominated by President Nixon for the Supreme Court but rejected by the Senate) distinguished New Kent County's acceptable "freedom of choice" plan from one in which "the initial assignments are both involuntary and dictated by racial criteria," thus creating "an illusion and an oppression which is constitutionally impermissible."[2]

The third contextual element was conflict among the circuit courts. As the number of desegregation cases multiplied, so did disagreements in the lower courts. The Fourth Circuit and the Sixth Circuit remained receptive to the "freedom of choice" plans rejected by the Fifth Circuit in *Jefferson County*. The Eighth Circuit issued decisions on both sides of the divide.[3] By choosing to review the Fourth Circuit's ruling in *Green v. County School Board* rather than the Fifth Circuit's seminal decision in *Jefferson County*, the Court sidestepped the controversial issues raised by the Fifth Circuit's more comprehensive analysis.

The Fourth Circuit's decision in *Green* offered a stark contrast to *Jefferson County*. It approved a "freedom of choice" plan that did not come close to producing racially balanced schools or eliminating all-black schools: "As long as each pupil, each year, attends the school of his choice, the Constitution does not require that he be deprived of his choice unless its exercise is not free." The

Fourth Circuit had not raised such contentious issues as the validity of HEW's guidelines, the meaning of "integration," or whether desegregation involves group rights rather than individual rights. Since the court below had not issued a remedial decree, the Supreme Court could simply remand the case without explaining what would constitute an appropriate remedy. These features of the Fourth Circuit's opinion allowed Justice Brennan to write an opinion for a unanimous Court that adroitly signaled its agreement with the Fifth Circuit's position—especially by appropriating Judge Wisdom's most memorable language—while barely mentioning the controversial elements of his opinion.

As Owen Fiss (a great admirer of Justice Brennan) once noted, "Despite the captivating quality of these phrases, they do not indicate the basis for invalidating the [freedom of] choice plan."[4] In *Green* the Supreme Court did *not* hold that "'freedom of choice' plans can have no place" in an acceptable desegregation remedy. Indeed, Justice Brennan insisted that "there is no universal answer to complex problems of desegregation"; each plan "must be assessed in light of the circumstances present and the options available in each instance."[5] Why, then, was New Kent County's plan unacceptable? With only passing reference to either *Brown I* or *Jefferson County*, Justice Brennan explained that "freedom of choice" is merely "a means to a constitutionally required end—abolition of the system of segregation and its effects," and that "the general experience under 'freedom of choice' to date has been such as to indicate its ineffectiveness as a tool of desegregation."[6] Despite the presence of black students in the formerly white school, "the school system remains a dual system."

With *Green*, the distinction between a "dual" and a "unitary" school system became the crux of desegregation jurisprudence. In the years that followed, the memorable lines in Justice Brennan's opinion were repeated in virtually every lower court decision. Most importantly—

- "*The burden on a school board today is to come forward with a plan that promises realistically to work, and promises realistically to work now*."[7]
- School boards previously "operating state-compelled dual systems" are "clearly charged with the affirmative duty to take whatever steps might be necessary to convert to a unitary system in which racial discrimination will be eliminated root and branch."[8]
- The "racial identification" of "dual school systems" extends "not just to the composition of student bodies" but "to every facet of school operations—faculty, staff, transportation, extracurricular activities and facilities."[9]
- School boards have a duty to "fashion steps which promise realistically to convert promptly to *a system without a 'white' school and a 'Negro' school, but just schools.*"[10]

This language sent a clear message to school districts and lower court judges: the Supreme Court expected rapid change in previously segregated schools. Don't just stand there, *do* something!

But do what, exactly? How does one know when a plan "works" and a district has become "unitary"? Justice Brennan's opinion in *Green* raised this fundamental question but failed to answer it. Does a plan "work" when all the children in the district have a genuine choice about which school to attend? Or when a significant number of black children—say, 20 percent, the target set by HEW's guidelines—attend formerly white schools? Or when there are no predominantly black schools? Or when the racial balance in each school reflects the balance of the district as a whole? Or when all schools are predominantly white? The Court's opinion only hinted at answers, and these hints appeared in enigmatic footnotes.

One footnote in *Green* quoted at length from a Commission on Civil Rights report on the many factors that can inhibit black children and parents from choosing to attend formerly white schools. Brennan coyly added that "we neither adopt nor refuse to adopt" those views.[11] At oral argument, Chief Justice Warren expressed doubt about whether in the South such choices could *ever* be free. The system in New Kent County, Warren claimed, was "booby trapped" by "social and cultural influences and the prejudices that have existed for centuries there."[12] The NAACP argued that "freedom of choice" plans not only required black parents and children to withstand the fear and intimidation, but also "to unshackle themselves from the psychological effects of imposed racial discrimination of the past." Since under segregation African Americans had been "schooled in the ways of subservience," "freedom of choice" plans would simply replicate the inequalities of the past.[13] To the extent that the justices accepted this critique, not only were "freedom of choice" plans doomed, but the views of black parents could safely be ignored as the product of false consciousness.

In another lengthy footnote Justice Brennan suggested two simple ways New Kent County could transition to a unitary system. The first was to convert one of its two buildings into a 1-7 elementary school and the other into an 8-12 high school. The district's small size made this proposal feasible. The second was "by means of geographic zoning—simply by assigning students living in the eastern half of the county to the [formerly white] New Kent School and those living in the western half of the county to the [formerly black] Watkins School."[14] The latter option received support from the lawyers arguing the case for the United States. They contrasted the cumbersome "freedom of choice" plans with the "old-fashioned, traditional system of neighborhood schools."[15] Brennan explained that although the neighborhood school approach might not be "universally appropriate," it made sense in areas such as New Kent County "where there is no residential segregation." His intimation that geographic assignment might *not* be sufficient in systems with significant residential segregation seemed to suggest that a "unitary" school system was one that exhibited some form of racial balance. But once one gets drawn into the game of drawing inferences from cryptic statements in footnotes, it should be evident that the Supreme Court had not adequately addressed the issue.

Brennan's failure to be more forthcoming in *Green* was in part a result of the justices' commitment to producing unanimous decisions in desegregation cases. Brennan had initially tied his opinion more closely to *Brown* by citing its language on the sense of inferiority generated by state-sponsored segregation. According to his first draft,

> So long as the racial identify ingrained, as in New Kent County, by years of discrimination remains in the system, the stigma of inferiority likewise remains. Only by reorganizing the system—extending to pupils, teachers, staff, facilities, school transportation systems, and other school-related activities—can the State redress the wrong of depriving Negro children of some of the benefits they would have received in a racially integrated school system.[16]

Brennan dropped this language when Justices White and Harlan argued that it put too much weight on *Brown*'s much-criticized social-science evidence. Brennan's "stigma" argument later resurfaced in the opinions of Justice Marshall, who converted it into an attack on all forms of racial isolation.

On the surface, *Green* seemed more modest than Judge Wisdom's opinion in *Jefferson County*. There was no sustained attack on "freedom of choice" plans, no mention of group rights, no discussion of HEW's authority, and no model decrees. But in at least three ways *Green* was more expansive—or at least more expandable—than the decision of the Fifth Circuit. First, while the Fifth Circuit's en banc opinion and model decree placed great weight on procedures designed to purge "freedom of choice" plans of imperfections, the Supreme Court declared that the acceptability of desegregation plans depended on whether they produced racially non-identifiable schools. The gap between the Supreme Court and the Fifth Circuit on the status of "freedom of choice" plans would grow over the next few years.

Second, since the Supreme Court did not discuss HEW's guidelines, it did not limit itself to the modest percentages laid out by administrators in 1966. Looming behind *Green*'s abstractions was the assumption that the percentage of black and white students in each school must approximate the percentages in the district as a whole—a much more ambitious goal than that embodied in HEW's rules. In fact, the simple math of *Green* indicated that the Court was not content with the standards being set by HEW and the Fifth Circuit. In 1965–66 almost 16 percent of black students in New Kent County (115 of 740) were going to school with whites—well within the parameters established by HEW in its 1965 and 1966 guidelines and better than many desegregation plans approved by the Fifth Circuit. As a result, the Fifth Circuit had to revise many of its desegregation orders to comply with *Green*.[17]

Third, the Supreme Court did not say, as Judge Wisdom had, that these rules apply only in the South. Once the Court had extended its understanding of a "dual" school system to include many in the North and West, they too bore the burden of proving they had been converted into "unitary" systems "lock, stock, and barrel." In short, by saying so little, *Green* provided the Supreme Court with plenty of room to maneuver in the future.

A comparison of *Green* and *Jefferson County* reveals an important difference between the Supreme Court and federal courts of appeal. The latter cannot pick and choose among the cases they review. When a circuit court relies on a vague standard to resolve a difficult case, that case often returns to its docket—as the Fifth Circuit had learned from bitter experience. That is why the Fifth Circuit was so intent upon establishing clear desegregation criteria. The Supreme Court, in contrast, has more incentives and more opportunities to use ambiguity to paper over internal disagreements. The appeal of ambiguity was particularly true for desegregation, where the justices put a premium on unanimity. The Court not only chose relatively simple cases but remained maddeningly vague on remedies. Circuit and district court judges live in a world where litigants demand specific answers to real legal controversies. When it came to desegregation, the justices lived in a world of easily manipulated legal abstractions.

The Nixon Paradox

Less than a month after the Court handed down *Green*, Chief Justice Warren announced his retirement. He expected his announcement would give President Johnson and the Democratic Senate sufficient time to appoint his successor. Of course, he was wrong. Senate Republicans filibustered Johnson's nomination of Justice Abe Fortas to become chief. Soon after Richard Nixon won the 1968 election, Fortas became embroiled in a scandal that led to his resignation. As a result, Nixon could fill two vacancies—with two more to come within two years. Through his appointments to the Court and key positions in HEW and the Department of Justice, Nixon had the opportunity to influence the timing and direction of desegregation. Like Nixon himself, that legacy was complicated, with significant gaps between what he said and what he did.

During the 1968 campaign Nixon had adopted a then-unorthodox "southern strategy" that seemed to leave him in debt to segregationists such as South Carolina's Senator Strom Thurmond. He had also campaigned against the Warren Court, promising to appoint "strict constructionists" rather than liberal activists such as Chief Justice Warren. Two actions early in his administration seemed to confirm fears that Nixon was intent upon sabotaging desegregation. The first was the Justice Department's 1969 request for a four-month delay in the Fifth Circuit's desegregation order for thirty-three Mississippi school districts. The second was the 1970 firing of Leon Panetta, director of the Office for Civil Rights (OCR). Panetta had ignored White House instructions to go slow on desegregation in the South. His successor, Stanley Pottinger, subsequently pulled back on school desegregation, prudently opting "to look for other problems to solve."[18]

The Nixon administration failed to slow the pace of southern school desegregation. Federal judges took umbrage at what they saw as the administration's assault on civil rights and the rule of law. This was most apparent in the fall of 1969, when a unanimous Supreme Court—including the recently appointed chief justice—called for immediate desegregation of those thirty-three Mississippi districts. A few years later, federal judges in the District of Columbia in effect placed the Office for Civil Rights in receivership, establishing the agency's priorities under Title VI, laying down new procedures, and excoriating it for allowing politics to affect the enforcement of civil rights laws. As the district court judge who handled that case for many years put it, executive branch officials "have no discretion to negate the purpose and intent of the [Civil Rights Act] statute by a policy described in another context as one of 'benign neglect.'"[19] "Benign neglect," of course, was the term commonly associated with the Nixon administration's cautious approach on racial issues.

Just as important was the fact that Nixon was even more cynical than his critics at the time realized. Recent scholarship based on newly released documents suggests that Nixon had no real interest in stopping or even slowing down southern school desegregation. He simply wanted to resolve the issue as soon as possible, and to make sure that no one in the South could blame *him* for what was happening. Nixon feared that if he seemed to obstruct desegregation, he would lose support in the North. But if he appeared eager to move the process along, he would lose support in the South. If the dispute dragged on into 1972, it would add worrisome uncertainty to his reelection campaign. Consequently, Nixon's strategy was to deflect responsibility away from the executive branch and onto the courts. As Kevin McMahon has shown in his detailed study, "Nixon wanted to display his willingness—but certainly not his eagerness—to enforce desegregation orders in the South." But "he didn't want this administration to take the lead on desegregation; his instructions to members of his administration focused on obeying the law but doing nothing more." Nixon "was willing to move forward on implementation as long as the blame lay somewhere else"—meaning the courts.[20] At the time, the journalists Evans and Novak noted that Attorney General John Mitchell "wanted the onus of school desegregation shifted from the federal bureaucracy (controlled by Nixon) to the federal courts (not controlled by Nixon), so that Nixon could tell the South: It's not our fault."[21]

Mitchell was remarkably candid about this, telling reporters, "You'd be better informed if instead of listening to what we say you watch what we do." What his Department of Justice did was file a number of desegregation suits, including one against all 195 school districts in the state of Georgia. Nor did OCR immediately fade into the woodwork. In the summer of 1969, it announced new funding terminations in Florida, Georgia, and South Carolina.[22] The administration shifted emphasis from the threat of funding cutoffs to litigation, but this had always been the preferred strategy of career litigators in DOJ and many civil rights lawyers. The new case-management procedures instituted by the Fifth Circuit in 1970 made litigation more attractive than ever, further reducing the importance of termination proceedings.

We now know that the Supreme Court's decision in *Alexander* (discussed below) set off a fierce debate within the White House on how the president should respond. Vice President Agnew and presidential advisor Pat Buchanan urged Nixon to adopt a defiant stance, attacking the courts and "forced integration." Counseling the president to steal the thunder of George Wallace and Lester Maddox, the ax-wielding governor of Georgia, Buchanan wrote (in glee, not sorrow) that "the second era of Reconstruction is over; the ship of integration is going down . . . and we ought not to be aboard."[23] But Nixon instead took the advice of Leonard Garment and Pat Moynihan, who advised him to take the "high road" of enforcing the law rather than engaging in the sort of "hysterical demagoguery" promoted by Agnew and Buchanan. Nixon concluded that any political advantage he might gain in the South through defiance would be more than offset by losses elsewhere. He told John Ehrlichman, "I'm a firm believer that the law should and must be carried out. It is in our political interest to put the issue behind us now. If there are to be confrontations let's have them in 1970, not 1972."[24] While Nixon's commitment to obeying the law is open to serious doubt, clearly he saw his political interest in letting the Supreme Court determine the pace and scope of desegregation. Gareth Davies has convincingly argued that Nixon was one of the few people at the time not to see the desegregation issue in moral terms or even to care very much about the outcome. He wanted the courts to resolve the issue quickly and to remove it from the political agenda because that served his political self-interest.[25]

Of Pace and Purpose

For nearly two decades the Supreme Court had been timid about enforcing *Brown*. It preferred to let the Fifth Circuit take the heat and the lead. But in 1969 and 1970 the Burger Court issued three decisions upbraiding the Fifth Circuit for not moving aggressively enough to uproot "dual" school systems. If the meaning of "unitary" remained obscure, it was clear that for the Court "now" meant immediately. The issue of pace predominated, pushing the issue of purpose into the background.

The first of these three decisions, *U.S. v. Montgomery County Board of Education*, raised the thorny issue of desegregation of teaching staff. Judge Frank Johnson, one of the heroes of southern school desegregation, had issued a sweeping desegregation plan for Montgomery, Alabama. Among many other things, it required the district to ensure that "in each school the ratio of white to Negro faculty members is substantially the same as it is throughout the system." The Fifth Circuit upheld most of the decree but found such a "fixed mathematical ratio" too rigid.[26]

The Supreme Court disagreed, possibly indicating that it would find nothing objectionable about "fixed mathematical ratios" for students as well. To be sure, faculty assignments differ from assignment of students in several significant respects: there is no tradition of geographic assignment; faculty assignment unavoidably involves administrative discretion; and in 1960s Alabama, white students were extremely unlikely to enroll in a school with a majority of black teachers. Nonetheless, the *Montgomery* decision represented the Court's first endorsement of hard-and-fast numerical goals in a desegregation case, and it demonstrated the Court's willingness to move beyond the Fifth Circuit.

What was striking about the Court's unanimous decision in *Montgomery* was not just that it was written by Justice Black—who merely a year before had threatened to dissent in *Green*—but that it was devoted primarily to praising Black's fellow Alabaman, Judge Johnson, rather than justifying the use of hiring quotas. According to Black, Johnson's "patience and wisdom are written for all to see and read on the pages of the five-year record before us."

Black concluded in an unusually upbeat and personal way: "It is good to be able to decide a case with the feelings we have about this one."[27] The decision revealed a subtle feature of Supreme Court review of desegregation orders: the justices' reluctance to overturn the decisions of district court judges who had courageously confronted recalcitrant school districts. "Stand behind the best troops on the front line" became one of the imperatives of the long desegregation war. It became particularly important in the Court's pivotal decision in the Charlotte-Mecklenburg case.

Green had encouraged NAACP and DOJ lawyers to ask federal judges to revise desegregation orders originally based on "freedom of choice." In one such case, the Fifth Circuit had required three dozen Mississippi school districts to make substantial changes in school assignments for the 1969–70 school year, then just two months away. When the Nixon administration asked the Fifth Circuit to give the districts until December to comply, that court agreed to extend the deadline.[28]

This four-month extension not only generated a firestorm of criticism from civil rights groups and careerists in the DOJ and HEW but drew a strong rebuke from the Supreme Court. Acting with unaccustomed speed, the Court heard the case at the beginning of its October term, overturned the Fifth Circuit's decision, and ordered the schools to "begin immediately to operate as unitary school systems."[29] Since this directive would speed up the process by two or three weeks at most, it is hard to see what legal or practical issue led the Court to reverse the usually reliable Fifth Circuit.

For the justices, it seems, this ruling was above all an opportunity to show the Nixon administration that they would not tolerate backsliding. In their inside look at the Supreme Court, Bob Woodward and Scott Armstrong report that in conference Justice Black insisted that five weeks "was not the issue. It was symbolic." To Black the issue was more political than legal:

> Any willingness on the part of the Court to grant a delay, no matter how slight, would be perceived as a signal. All those district court judges with hundreds of similar cases in their courts, all those Southern politicians, and the Nixon Administration itself, were waiting for the Court to show any sign of weakening in its resolve. To appear to waiver, even for a second, would be a betrayal. Black attacked Nixon and his administration bitterly. They were allowing the South hope of further evasion.[30]

According to Woodward and Armstrong, Justice Marshall had initially adopted a more conciliatory stance. He eventually decided that Black's "insistence on 'now' might be unreasonable, but it was quite likely the Court's best posture. It might be best to send a shock-wave message. An impractical order directing desegregation 'now' might underscore the Court's seriousness."[31] Several justices harbored doubts about the practicality of ordering desegregation in the middle of the school year but went along in order to present a united front.[32] This cohort included the new chief justice, who was intent upon demonstrating that he was not Nixon's stooge but a leader capable of unifying the Court.

At first the Fifth Circuit did not take the Supreme Court's command literally. When it met en banc the next month, it consolidated sixteen cases from multiple states and developed a strategy for further expediting the desegregation process. Making that court's job particularly difficult was the fact that some of the Mississippi school districts did not yet have the HEW-approved plans that the Supreme Court had ordered the court to enforce. On December 1, 1969, the en banc court voted unanimously to require that all the school districts currently before it implement plans for desegregating faculty, staff, transportation, services, and extracurricular activities by the following February, and to institute new student-assignment plans at the beginning of the *next* school year. The latter was necessary because "many students must transfer. Buildings must be put to new use . . . School bus routes must be reconstituted."[33] Even Judge Wisdom and the other members of the "Fifth Circuit Four" believed immediate changes in student assignments would constitute too much disruption in the middle of the school year.

In *Carter v. West Feliciano School Board*, the Supreme Court again acted quickly to reprimand the Fifth Circuit. In January 1970, it issued a per curiam stating that "insofar as the Court of Appeals authorized deferral of student desegregation beyond February 1, 1970, that court misconstrued our holding in *Alexander*." Four of the eight members then sitting on the Court—Black, Douglas, Brennan, and Marshall—adamantly refused to "retreat from our holding in *Alexander*" that dual school systems must be terminated "at once."[34] Justices Harlan and White preferred to give the lower courts another eight weeks to review the plans generated by HEW. But they were willing to bend in order to create a majority. Only Justice Stewart and the chief justice objected to summary reversal of the Fifth Circuit. But they, too, eventually relented. As Frank Read has noted, "the Fifth Circuit—which had been the most diligent court in America in desegregating public school facilities—was wrist-slapped for delaying massive student desegregation . . . to avoid disruption in the midst of an on-going school year."[35] If *Alexander* was a reprimand and warning to the Nixon administration, *Carter* was a signal to appellate court and school officials throughout the South: let's get it over with *now*.

The Fifth Circuit's initial response to *Carter* was perfunctory: it issued a one-paragraph per curiam opinion stating that the Supreme Court's holding on the timing of student desegregation "is made the judgment of this court" and that all other provisions of its previous order remained in effect. In other words, district courts should follow the Supreme Court's command. Exactly how they should do so was their problem, not the circuit court's. This opinion led two Fifth Circuit judges to dissent, lamenting that "the continuing failure of this Court to provide a lighthouse in the new storm which is upon us." Neither the Supreme Court nor the Fifth Circuit, the dissenters argued, had ever "described or defined what constitutes a dual system" or "the meaning of a 'unitary' system." How, Judge Colman asked, "are the struggling school authorities to know at what point they shall have succeeded in dismantling a dual system and setting up a unitary system?" He predicted that the demand for speed would drive judges to rely solely on statistics on the racial composition of each school, despite the fact that the Supreme Court "has never arbitrarily commanded that there must be racial balance in the student body of any school purely for the sake of racial balance."[36]

Given the opportunity to explain the underlying purpose of the desegregation enterprise, the Supreme Court responded not with alacrity but with obfuscation. In late 1969 the Sixth Circuit upheld a geographic-assignment plan for Memphis, Tennessee, that left many schools overwhelmingly black. Since white students were in a minority in Memphis and residential segregation severe, without busing this outcome was impossible to avoid. The NAACP challenged the court's plan, arguing that no school should diverge more than 10 percent from the racial balance of the district as a whole, which at the time was 55 percent black and 45 percent white. The Sixth Circuit disagreed, insisting that the Supreme Court had "not announced that such a formula is the only way to accomplish a 'unitary system.'" Quoting *Alexander*, the appeals court held that it was "satisfied" that Memphis had "converted its pre-*Brown* dual system into a unitary system 'within which no person is to be effectively excluded because of race.'"[37]

In a brief per curiam opinion, the Supreme Court held that the Sixth Circuit had erred in finding the Memphis system "unitary." It provided no explanation of what Memphis needed to do to become "unitary." The implication seemed to be either that no significant departures from racial proportionality would be allowed or that all predominantly black schools must be eliminated. Chief Justice Burger's brief concurring opinion suggested that "as soon as possible" the Court should "resolve some of the basic practical problems," including whether "any particular racial balance must be achieved in the schools," to what extent school district lines and attendance zones "may or must be altered as a constitutional matter," and "to what extent transportation may or must be provided to achieve the ends sought by prior holdings of the Court." Burger conceded that in *Green* and *Alexander* the Court had spoken "perhaps too cryptically." "The time has come," he declared, "to clear up what seems to be a confusion, genuine or simulated, concerning this Court's prior mandates."[38] Unfortunately, when the chief justice tried to provide such a clarification a year later, he succeeded only in making matters worse.

What Does *Green* Mean? The Many Contradictions of *Swann*

In 1970, desegregation policy stood at a crossroads. In the South the old Jim Crow system was being dismantled with remarkable speed. In rural areas and small cities, the long battle was all but over. In district after district, "freedom of choice" plans had been replaced by a combination of geographic assignment, affirmative racial gerrymandering, pairing, and clustering that produced "racially non-identifiable" public schools. But it remained unclear the extent to which racial balance would be required in southern cities with substantial residential segregation, whether similar mandates would be imposed on northern cities, and what "balance" would mean in school districts that had become majority black. These issues are usually subsumed under the single word "busing." But busing is only a means, and the underlying debate was over ends.

One crucial question was whether the tools used to end delay and evasion in the formerly Jim Crow South would be extended to an attack on racial isolation throughout the country. If the Supreme Court were to embrace the more ambitious "racial isolation/equal educational opportunity" framework described in chapter 2, it needed to take three steps. The first was to define the amount of racial mixing constitutionally required. Must white and black students be evenly distributed across all the schools within a district? Or is it sufficient to ensure that no schools are predominantly black? Where do Hispanics and Asians fit into these equations? The second was to find a way to apply this standard in states that had never imposed legal segregation or had long ago abandoned it. In other words, the Court would need to end the distinction between de jure and de facto segregation. Third, the justices would need to redraw school-district lines to pull into urban districts enough white students to end racial isolation, however defined.

The Supreme Court addressed the first issue in *Swann* (1971) and the second in its *Keyes* (1973). It began to confront the third issue in two lesser known 1972 decisions, *Wright v. Emporia* and *U.S. v. Scotland Neck*, before shutting the door on most urban-suburban busing in *Milliken* (1974). This combination of rulings left lower courts in an ill-defined no-man's-land between the "intentional discrimination" and "racial isolation" understandings of desegregation. The Court drifted back and forth between the two until it gave up and all but abandoned the field in 1980.

If *Green* was a particularly good case for illustrating the problems with "freedom of choice" plans, *Swann v. Charlotte-Mecklenburg Board of Education* was an ideal case for highlighting the virtues and the practicality of a judicial attack on racial isolation. Although the school district had for decades engaged in de jure segregation, Charlotte was by no means a redneck town. Rather, it was a booming city, an icon of the "New South" in which school leaders were eager to avoid the sins of the past. It was also a huge school district covering 550 square miles (almost half the size of the entire state of Rhode Island), with eighty-four thousand students and over one hundred schools. That meant that Charlotte's suburbs were located within the larger school district. The county's white/black student ratio was 71 percent to 29 percent—by lucky coincidence almost exactly the balance recommended by integration advocates such as Pettigrew and Coleman. Thus, the prospects of successful integration were better in Charlotte than in most cities, and in fact desegregation fared comparatively well there. For supporters of a frontal assault on racial isolation, it was fortuitous that Charlotte was the first case in which the Court confronted the busing issue.

Swann provided the Supreme Court with the opportunity to address the "racial isolation" issue directly. That is because the district court judge, James MacMillan, had relied so explicitly on the testimony of the key proponents of the racial isolation argument. "The experts all agree," he claimed, that predominantly black schools "retard the progress of the whole group." But when students "are mingled with a clear white majority, such as a 70/30 ratio (approximately the ratio of white to black students in Mecklenburg County), the better students can hold their pace, with substantial improvement for the poorer students."[39] As noted in chapter 2, MacMillan was only one of many district court judges to embrace this understanding. The Supreme Court, though, completely ignored MacMillan's explanation for his controversial desegregation plan.

The Supreme Court's *Swann* opinion is best known for two things. First, it approved unanimously and *in toto* Judge MacMillan's use of busing to eliminate predominantly black schools and to ensure that most schools in the district approached the 71–29 ratio. The plan approved by the Court required bus rides of up to half an hour for elementary school children, the most controversial feature of MacMillan's order. *Swann* was a particularly satisfying victory for advocates of vigorous integration because it was written by Nixon appointee Warren Burger. It could not be dismissed as the work of Warren Court holdovers.

Second, the chief justice's opinion was one of the most confused and confusing ever produced by the Court. At the time, the *New Republic* described it as "a negotiated document looking in more than one direction."[40] That was right: detailed investigation of the Court's internal negotiations by Bernard Schwartz and by Woodward and Armstrong show that *Swann* was the product of a long, torturous, even comical effort to extract a unanimous ruling from a deeply divided court.[41] In the end Burger seemed not to understand the message his opinion sent to the public and to lower court judges. A few months later, acting in his capacity as supervising justice for the Fourth Circuit, he mailed to every lower court judge in the country an eleven-page opinion that seemed to contradict much of what he had just said in *Swann*. Even Lino Graglia, who shared Burger's criticism of busing, described his behavior as "surely one of the strangest performances in the history of the Court." The chief justice, Graglia noted, "sought to nullify on his own the busing requirement that he . . . had greatly assisted the Court in imposing."[42]

At the outset, two members of the Supreme Court, Black and Burger, were inclined to overturn Judge MacMillan's plan for relying too heavily on busing. They viewed the modified neighborhood plans recently approved by the Fifth Circuit for Tampa and Orlando as constitutionally sufficient. Five members of the court, Douglas, Brennan, Marshall, White, and (surprisingly) Harlan, firmly supported the district court judge. That left Stewart and the newly appointed Justice Blackmun in the middle. Stewart was reluctant to adopt a broad reading of *Green*, but loath to reverse a courageous district court judge such as MacMillan.[43] Burger apparently voted with the majority in order to assign himself the job of writing the all-important opinion, a stratagem some justices considered unethical. His initial draft underwent so many revisions that it ended up looking nothing like the original. As in *Alexander*, all the justices were as interested in the symbolism of the case—whether they were seen as supporting or undercutting MacMillan—as they were in the formal doctrines they announced.

In *Swann*, the Court promised to define "in more precise terms" the "duty of school authorities and district courts" to "eliminate dual systems and establish unitary systems at once." Unfortunately, it would be hard to find a Supreme Court opinion *less* precise than *Swann*. It addressed the issue only indirectly, focusing instead on the *remedies* a district court can employ to turn a dual system into a unitary one. Burger's opinion emphasized the extensive authority granted to district courts to assess the peculiar factors in each case:

> The scope of a district court's equitable powers to remedy past wrongs is broad, for breadth and flexibility are inherent in equitable remedies. The essence of

equity jurisdiction has been the power of the Chancellor to do equity and to mould each decree to the necessities of the particular case. Flexibility, rather than rigidity, has distinguished it.[44]

In desegregation cases, Burger claimed, "we must of necessity rely to a large extent, as this Court has for more than 16 years, on the informed judgment of the district courts in the first instance and on courts of appeals."[45]

In his quest to unite the Court, Burger kept revising his opinion to delegate more power to district court judges and make their duties more ambiguous. On the pivotal question of the use of "racial balance or racial quotas," the resulting opinion was inscrutable. On the one hand, the opinion seemed to reject racial balance as the standard for judging desegregation plans:

> If we were to read the holding of the District Court to require, as a matter of substantive constitutional right, any particular degree of racial balancing or mixing, that approach would be *disapproved* and we would be obliged to reverse. The constitutional command to desegregate schools does *not* mean that every school in every community must always reflect the racial composition of the school system as a whole.[46]

On the other hand, "awareness of the racial composition of the whole school system is likely to be a useful starting point in shaping a remedy to correct past constitutional violations." The use of "mathematical ratios" is acceptable so long as it remains a "starting point . . . rather than an inflexible requirement."[47]

Burger found that Judge MacMillan had aimed at the 71–29 ratio "so that there will be no basis for contending that one school is racially different from the others" and that "no school should be operated with an all-black or predominantly black student body." But MacMillan had not succeeded in achieving these goals; reaching them fully "would appear to be impossible." Such "very limited use made of mathematical ratios was within the equitable remedial discretion of the District Court."[48] In other words, it is OK to rely almost exclusively on these ratios as long as one calls them a "starting point" and one does not attain them with precision—stunningly easy hurdles to overcome. Burger rejected racial balance as the "norm," but offers no alternative definition of the norms that should guide district court judges. In the process, he ignored the rationale for racial mixing that MacMillan had in fact offered.

The advice the Court offered on the other issues was similarly worthy of Polonius. On the one hand, "the existence of some small number of one-race, or virtually one-race, schools within a district is not, in and of itself, the mark of a system that still practices segregation by law." On the other hand, district court judges should "be concerned with the elimination of one-race schools," because in school districts with a history of segregation, there is "a presumption against schools that are substantially disproportionate in their racial composition." In case the lower courts were under the mistaken impression that these ambiguous sentences constituted some sort of guidance from above, the chief justice added, "No per se rule can adequately embrace all the difficulties of reconciling the competing interests involved." When it came to drawing attendance zones, "no fixed or even substantially fixed guidelines can be established as to how far a court can go, but it must be recognized that there are limits."[49]

On the most politically volatile issue, the extent of busing, the Court all but threw up its hands. Noting that "the scope of permissible transportation of students . . . has never been defined by this Court," Burger immediately conceded that "by the very nature of the problem it cannot be defined with precision." District court judges should keep in mind that "the time or distance of travel" should not be "so great as to either risk the health of the children or significantly impinge on the educational process." They should take into account the "age of the students" being bused. But again, "no rigid guidelines" can adequately address "the infinite variety of problems presented in thousands of situations." While recognizing that the "reconciliation of competing values in a desegregation case is, of course a difficult task with many sensitive facets," the Court soothingly (but mistakenly) concluded that it is "fundamentally no more so than remedial measures courts of equity have traditionally employed."[50]

In short, the chief justice insisted that there were limits on the court's authority to bus young children and to require numerically balanced schools, but the Supreme Court could not say what they were. He concluded with a remarkable admission of appellate impotence:

> In seeking to define the scope of remedial power or the limits on remedial power of courts in an area as sensitive as we deal with here, words are poor instruments to convey the sense of basic fairness inherent in equity. Substance, not semantics, must govern.

Words, though, are the *only* instruments that an appellate court that hears fewer than one hundred cases per year has at its disposal to control the direction of hundreds of lower court judges. Certainly the words of Chief Justice Burger in *Swann* proved to be a "poor instrument" for imposing any limits on the lower courts. Although Burger clearly found the *Swann* injunction excessive and distasteful, he was "unable to conclude that the order of the District Court is not reasonable, feasible and workable."[51]

If *Swann* sent the message to lower court judges that they had vast authority to take aggressive steps to combat racial isolation, its less well-known companion case, *Davis vs. Board of School Commissioners of Mobile County*, demonstrated that judges who failed to adopt such measures risked being reversed by the Supreme Court. In this case the Court refused to approve a desegregation plan adopted by a panel of the Fifth Circuit that had used geographic zoning to reduce administrative mischief, mild gerrymandering to increase racial mixing, and optional majority-to-minority transfers to reduce but not eliminate one-race schools. This plan, the Supreme Court announced, was not enough. According to the Court's brief opinion, once a judge has found a constitutional violation, he must "make every effort to achieve the greatest possible degree of actual desegregation, taking into account the practicalities of the situation." In this case "inadequate consideration was given to the possible use of bus transportation and split zoning."[52] It is hard to see how a district court judge could interpret this ruling as anything other than a command to use all available measures to achieve the "mathematical ratios" that Burger had described as a "starting point" but not a binding "norm" in *Swann*. The author of *Davis*? Chief Justice Burger.[53]

Swann had an immediate effect, if not the one imagined by the chief justice. Within months, Orfield writes, "there were more than forty court decisions embodying its principles. Federal courts in the South rapidly updated old desegregation plans to conform to their interpretation of the new requirement."[54] Judges on the Fifth Circuit were frustrated by *Swann*'s lack of specificity but understood that the combination of *Swann* and *Davis* put a premium on achieving racial balance in all schools. After all, the circuit court had been overturned in *Davis* for tolerating too many one-race schools but had never been reversed for demanding too much busing. Busing orders were soon issued for Little Rock, Arkansas; Jacksonville and Tampa, Florida; Columbus and Savannah, Georgia; Louisville, Kentucky; Prince George's County, Maryland; Oklahoma City, Oklahoma; Memphis and Nashville, Tennessee; Dallas, Fort Worth, and Waco, Texas; and Norfolk, Virginia. *Swann* seemed to give the Supreme Court's imprimatur to the view that the purpose of desegregation was to end racial isolation regardless of its cause.[55]

Moving North: Heavy Burden on the Burden of Proof

In 1967 the Commission on Civil Rights doubted that the Supreme Court would ever declare racial isolation in the North unconstitutional. Over the next few years the Department of Justice launched an attack on a few northern school systems, arguing that they had engaged in a variety of activities—especially siting school buildings and drawing attendance zones—that amplified the effects of residential segregation. Not until 1973 did the Supreme Court address the question of whether school districts that had never imposed overt, legal segregation could be found guilty of running a "dual" school. Once again, the Court addressed the issue obliquely, arguing at length about the relevance of various forms of evidence and the appropriate burden of proof rather than the rationale behind its expanding understanding of desegregation.

The Court's next step toward embracing the racial-isolation framework came in *Keyes v. School District No. 1, Denver.* Denver was one of the first major cities outside the South to face a desegregation suit. Judge William Doyle initially found that in one section of the city, Park Hill, school officials had manipulated attendance zones and sited new schools to keep Anglo students separate from black and Hispanic students. (One of the most important new elements in this case was the tripartite division of students into black, Hispanic, and Anglo.) Judge Doyle also found that the predominantly black and Hispanic schools were inferior to those attended by whites. His desegregation plan combined busing of students in the Park Hill section with compensatory education programs—English as a second language, bilingual education, and classes on "Negro and Hispanic culture and history"—at all schools with a substantial number of minority students. The Tenth Circuit upheld the trial judge on the reassignment of Park Hill students but rejected its compensatory education programs for schools that had not been directly affected by intentional discrimination.[56]

The Supreme Court not only overruled the Tenth Circuit, but required the district court to go further in its effort to desegregate Denver's schools. The imperative to stand by judges on the front line yielded to the majority's determination to extend the desegregation effort to the North. Justice Brennan's lengthy opinion for six members of the Court focused solely on the nature of proof required to determine whether an entire school system remained "dual." The heart of Brennan's argument was that once a court finds that a school district has engaged in segregative acts in one part of town, it must assume that the entire school system has been unconstitutionally segregated. Since in Denver there was evidence "that the school authorities have carried out a systematic program of segregation" in some areas, "it is only common sense to conclude" that the district had engaged in similar illegal activity elsewhere. "Proof of state-imposed segregation in a substantial portion of the district will suffice to support a finding by the trial court" that the entire district is "a dual system."[57]

School officials would have an opportunity to rebut this presumption of guilt. But to meet the burden of proof established by the Court, it would not be enough for school authorities "to rely upon some allegedly logical, racially neutral explanation for their actions." Rather, they must "adduce proof sufficient to support a finding that segregative intent was *not* among the factors that motivated their actions."[58] But if offering "logical, racially neutral explanations" is not enough to rebut the assumption of discrimination, it was hard to see how school districts could ever meet their burden of proof. In practice, the presumption of system-wide violation was irrebuttable. Brennan's rules of evidence virtually guaranteed that almost all urban areas would be subjected to the extensive remedies approved by the Court two years earlier in *Swann*.

Although newspaper reporters did not grasp the significance of *Keyes* at the time (the *New York Times* failed to mention the decision), its far-reaching consequence did not escape the notice of Justices Powell and Rehnquist. Powell, the former chairman of the Richmond, Virginia, school board, wrote a lengthy "concurring and dissenting" essay arguing that the de facto/de jure distinction had "outlived its time," and that the Court should "formulate constitutional principles of national rather than merely regional application." Powell explained how *Green*, *Swann*, and *Keyes* had fundamentally altered the holding in *Brown*, creating "the constitutional obligation of public authorities in the school districts *throughout our country* to operate *integrated* school systems."[59] He accepted this revised understanding of *Brown*, but argued that the obligation to integrate should be balanced against "other, equally important educational interests which a community may legitimately assert." He warned against the "overzealousness" that he saw in the Charlotte case:

> Courts in requiring so far-reaching a remedy as student transportation solely to maximize integration, risk setting in motion unpredictable and unmanageable social consequences. No one can estimate the extent to which dismantling neighborhood education will hasten an exodus to private schools, leaving public school systems the preserve of the disadvantaged of both races. Or guess how much impetus such dismantlement gives the movement from inner city to suburb, and the further geographical separation of the races. Nor do we know to what degree this remedy may cause deterioration of community and parental support of public schools, or divert attention from the paramount goal of quality in education to a perennially divisive debate over who is to be transported where.[60]

As prescient as these comments might seem, Powell gave no indication how *courts* could hope to weigh all these factors to provide "the best possible educational opportunity for all children." Should they extend their review to cover all features of education rather than focusing so heavily on the assignment of students to racially balanced schools? Or should they withdraw, and leave to school officials the difficult job of balancing these competing concerns? Powell offered no alternative guidelines, nor did he indicate what should be done in Denver. He offered a commentary on the problem, not a solution.

Rehnquist's dissent was more confrontational. He charged that the Supreme Court had declared the Denver school system segregated by "judicial fiat." *Keyes* moved well beyond *Green*, which itself represented a "drastic extension" of *Brown*. It took "a long leap," he charged, to equate Denver's gerrymandering of attendance zones in one part of the city with the rigid legal segregation of the Jim Crow South. The Court had moved from insisting that "the assignment of a child to a particular school is not made to depend on his race" to requiring "that school boards affirmatively undertake to achieve racial mixing in schools where no such mixing is achieved in sufficient degree by neutrally drawn boundary lines."[61] In *Keyes*, Rehnquist wrote alone. The ever-inscrutable Chief Justice Burger voted with the majority. That would soon change.

The Supreme Court's decision in *Keyes* gave an immediate boost to the desegregation cases against northern and western cities. Among those subject to desegregation orders after *Keyes* were Indianapolis, Indiana; Boston, Massachusetts; Wilmington, Delaware; Detroit, Grand Rapids, and Kalamazoo, Michigan; Minneapolis, Minnesota; Omaha, Nebraska; Dayton, Columbus, Cleveland, and Cincinnati, Ohio; St. Louis and Kansas City, Missouri; Milwaukee, Wisconsin; San Jose, San Diego, Stockton, Oxnard, and San Bernardino, California; Des Moines, Iowa; and Las Vegas, Nevada. Other cities, most notably Los Angeles, were subject to desegregation orders issued by state courts. Southern politicians who had long complained that their region had been subject to a double standard took delight in seeing unpopular desegregation mandates applied outside Dixie.

The move North and West brought new educational challenges—and the erosion of political support. Many of these cities had significant Hispanic populations. How would they be handled in a debate that had long been viewed in black-white terms? Moreover, most northern school districts follow city, not county lines, and thus are smaller than their southern counterparts and less likely to include suburban areas. Both these issues loomed large in subsequent litigation.

Drawing the Line

Keyes makes sense only if one assumes that racial isolation rather than intentional discrimination is the evil to be combated, and that eliminating predominantly black and Hispanic schools promises to reduce the racial achievement gap. For this strategy to work, there must be an adequate supply of (presumably middle-class) white students to mix with (presumably lower socioeconomic status) minority students. Since an adequate supply was not available in many urban areas or in some rural counties in the South, attacking racial isolation required redrawing school-district lines. The Court would eventually confront the question of school-district boundaries in its controversial 1974 *Milliken v. Bradley* decision. But in two prior rulings it had seemed to inch toward evaluating revision of district lines by the consequences for addressing racial isolation.

Those two 1972 cases, *U.S. v. Scotland Neck City Board of Education* and *Wright v. Council of City of Emporia*, were mirror images of the Richmond and Detroit cases that later came before the Court. In those large cities, district court judges had ordered white suburban districts to be consolidated with predominantly black urban districts. Scotland Neck and Emporia, in contrast, were towns with a roughly 50/50 racial balance that wished to secede from predominantly black counties. The Court prohibited them from doing so, explaining that proper legal analysis "focused upon the *effect*—not the purpose or motivation—of a school board's action.[62] Boundary changes that worsen the black/white ratio for most students are impermissible even if they improve that ratio for some.

Scotland Neck was the easier of the two cases because there was some evidence that the town sought to leave the Halifax County school system to lessen the impact of desegregation. Yet the effect of secession was not easy to categorize. Allowing Scotland Neck to run its own education system would create a new district that was 57 percent white and 43 percent black—an integrated school by most standards. Meanwhile the proportion of black students in the rest of the county would rise from 77 percent to 80 percent—a difference few students would notice. The Court agreed with the district court, which had found that the special legislation separating the two systems "was enacted with the effect of creating a refuge for white students of the Halifax County School system."[63] But it is hard to see how a school with a 57–43 ratio constitutes a forbidden "refuge" for whites rather than the type of majority-white school favored by busing proponents. Nevertheless, the Court's decision was unanimous, no doubt reflecting continuing skepticism as to the motivation of southern school districts.

Wright v. Council of City of Emporia, in contrast, drew a dissent joined by all four Nixon appointees. Here, both sides seemed to agree, the city had sought to establish its own schools for economic reasons. If the city were allowed to secede, the number of white and black students in its schools would be close to equal, though with a slight black majority. The percentage of black students in the rest of the county would rise from 66 percent to 72 percent. The dissenters emphasized that there was no evidence of intentional discrimination, that the Emporia school would not become a "white island in an otherwise black county," and that the racial composition of county schools would change only slightly.[64] Therefore, they argued, federal courts should defer to the political process.

Justice Stewart's opinion for the majority, in contrast, announced that "the existence of a permissible purpose cannot sustain an action that has an impermissible effect." In itself a 6 percent increase in the percentage of black students in county schools was not enough to condemn the plan. But the trial court was justified in concluding that the withdrawal of a large number of white children from county schools might send the wrong message to black schoolchildren, causing the same "adverse psychological effect" on minority students that the Supreme Court had described in *Brown*. Once again, the Court threw a contentious issue back to district court judges: the judgment of whether secession "would actually impede the process of dismantling the existing dual system" was deemed "primarily the responsibility of the district judge" who must consider "the totality of the circumstances."[65]

To Chief Justice Burger, *City of Emporia* demonstrated the Court's preoccupation with mathematical ratios, a focus he thought he had put to rest in *Swann*:

> Obsession with such minor statistical differences reflects the gravely mistaken view that a plan providing more consistent racial ratios is somehow more unitary than one which tolerates a lack of racial balance. Since the goal is to dismantle dual school systems rather than to reproduce in each classroom a microcosmic reflection of the racial proportions of a given geographical area, there is no basis for saying that a plan providing a uniform racial balance is more effective or constitutionally preferred.[66]

Lurking behind this narrow debate over racial ratios was the question of how judges would deal with racial isolation in northern cities. The Sixth Circuit later cited *Scotland Neck* and *City of Emporia* to support its contention that existing school-district lines are "artificial barriers" which courts can disregard "for the limited purpose of providing an effective desegregation plan." It reasoned that "if school boundary lines cannot be changed for an unconstitutional purpose, it follows logically that existing boundary lines *cannot be frozen* for an unconstitutional purpose."[67] Little-noticed precedents established in cases involving small southern towns were about to have major consequences for big northern cities.

City Limits

Between 1968 and 1973 the Court slowly moved toward the position that majority-black schools are unacceptable whatever their cause, and that federal judges should take all steps necessary to eliminate them. Yet it had never enunciated the constitutional basis for this understanding. As more northern cases came before the Court and as the remedies devised by district court judges became more extensive, the tension between the Court's legal framework—which presented the creation of "unitary" school systems as a remedy for intentional state-mandated segregation—and its underlying purpose—eliminating racial isolation in order to provide equal educational opportunity to minority students—could no longer be ignored.

In 1973 the Court faced a case that presented the underlying choice in stark terms. District court judge Robert Merhige had instituted a desegregation plan for Richmond, Virginia, that consolidated the city school district (which was by then two-thirds black) with two predominantly white, suburban districts. He did so with the support of the Richmond school board and with the expectation that his metropolitan busing plan would curb white flight and improve the academic performance of inner-city children. Unlike *Scotland Neck* and *City of Emporia*, the implications of this case were enormous for Richmond and for northern cities. The Fourth Circuit overruled Judge Merhige, concluding that a federal judge cannot "compel one of the States of the Union to restructure its internal government for the purpose of achieving racial balance in the assignment of pupils to the public schools."[68]

The Supreme Court finally had a chance to explain what it meant by a "unitary" school system—and blew it. After Justice Powell recused himself, the Court split 4–4, upholding without explanation the ruling of the Fourth Circuit.[69] It would confront the issue a year later in the Detroit case.

From the beginning the litigation in Detroit was designed to drive a final nail into the coffin of the intentional-segregation framework. The NAACP decided to support a case against the Detroit school board not because that board had resisted integration, but because the board had done everything in its power to *promote* it. If the NAACP could convince a judge to find Detroit "segregated," then the burden of proof for demonstrating intentional discrimination would be so low as to allow litigators to prevail in virtually every major city.

The district court judge in the case, Stephen Roth, held over forty days of hearings on the extent and causes of residential segregation, the racial composition of Detroit schools, and the effects of racial isolation on student achievement. While praising the school district for taking so many steps to encourage integration, he nevertheless found the school system unconstitutionally segregated, largely as a consequence of residential patterns. Residential segregation was the product of many years and many forms of government-sponsored discrimination. It was not necessary to determine that such school segregation was the result of "any evil intent or motive." "Motive, ill-will, and bad faith," he (incorrectly) claimed, had "long ago been rejected as a requirement" for finding a constitutional violation. Reflecting the conventional wisdom on the harm done by racial isolation, Roth found it "unfortunate that we cannot deal with public school segregation on a no-fault basis, for if racial segregation in our public schools is an evil, then it should make no difference whether we classify it as de jure or de facto."[70]

Soon after ruling that the school system had not done enough to counteract the effects of residual segregation, he found that there was nothing that the city *could* have done to remedy the situation. He then began to consider a desegregation plan that included the surrounding suburbs. Seeing such an order coming, suburban communities asked to intervene. Judge Roth denied the suburbs' request to present evidence rebutting the evidence presented at trial. That meant that the real adversary, the suburban school districts, were barred from participating in the liability phase of what had essentially become collusive litigation.

Judge Roth's remedial order created a consolidated school district that incorporated fifty-three suburban districts, enrolled over half a million students, and covered an area nearly as big as the state of Delaware. While more than two-thirds of the children in Detroit's schools were black, 75 percent of the students in the new super-district would be white. Under Roth's plan most schools in the new district would be between 20 and 30 percent black, a balance consistent with the extensive social-science evidence presented at the trial. About 40 percent of the students in the district would be bused. The Sixth Circuit upheld almost all of Judge Roth's remedy. The busing plan created a political furor, propelling George Wallace to victory in the 1972 Democratic presidential primary in the normally liberal state of Michigan.

In *Milliken*, the Court's internal divisions could no longer be papered over. Taking his lead from the brief written by US solicitor general Robert Bork, Chief Justice Burger's majority opinion stressed that "the scope of the remedy is determined by the nature and extent of the constitutional violation." No one claimed that Detroit's boundaries had been drawn in order to increase school segregation. Rather, the evidence at the trial focused on the way in which government action had contributed to residential segregation *within* Detroit, and the Detroit school district's failure to mitigate the consequences of that residential segregation. Following the letter of the Court's holdings in *Green* and *Swann*, Burger wrote that "the constitutional right of the Negro respondents residing in Detroit is to attend a unitary school system *in that district*."[71] The dissenters' claim that black children in Detroit have a constitutional right to attend school alongside white children from the suburbs "can be supported only by a drastic expansion of the constitutional right itself, an expansion without any support in either constitutional principle or precedent."[72] On the first claim—that the dissenters proposed a significant expansion of the constitutional right—Burger was clearly right. On his second claim, that such expansion had no support in precedent, he was wrong.

Writing in dissent allowed Justice Marshall to be more candid than his ally Justice Brennan had been in either *Green* or *Keyes*. He repeatedly described the goal as "actual desegregation" and eliminating "segregation in fact," which he contrasted to the legalistic understanding of desegregation endorsed by the Court. "Actual desegregation" means that white and black children will "in fact go to school together." Without urban-suburban busing, "Negro children will continue to attend all-Negro schools." Such single-race schools were "the very evil that *Brown I* was aimed at."[73] Without "actual desegregation" black children will be denied the right "to an equal start in life and to an equal opportunity to reach their full potential as citizens." Marshall warned that "unless our children begin to learn together, there is little hope that our people will ever learn to live together."[74] His dissenting opinion was as close as any member of the Court had yet come to saying that the central problem was racial isolation, not intentional discrimination.

In providing the critical fifth vote, Justice Steward explained that he would have upheld the district court if it had found that the state of Michigan had "contributed to the separation of the races" by (among other things) "racially discriminatory use of state housing or zoning laws."[75] As Marshall pointed out, the trial judge in fact *had* pointed to evidence implicating the state in creating discriminatory housing patterns within Detroit. Stewart seemed to want to block Judge Roth's massive busing plan but leave open the possibility of urban-suburban busing in other cities. Once again Stewart (and by implication the Court as a whole) allowed the basic meaning of "desegregation" to rest on district court judges' evaluation of the peculiar facts of each case.

Back and Forth—Then Silence

Over the next few years, it seemed possible that the Court would rethink the entire line of post-*Green* decisions, drawing the federal judiciary back to its original focus on intentional, state-sponsored segregation. In 1976 and 1977 the Court issued two opinions written by Justice Rehnquist that appeared to place further restrictions on the remedies available to district court judges. But in 1979 the Court issued two more decisions that reversed that short-lived trend. They established evidentiary rules requiring "systemic" remedies—extensive busing to achieve racial balance and to eliminate predominantly black schools—in most large northern and western cities. After 1979 the Court avoided saying anything at all on the topic for more than a decade. In effect, it continued to pass the buck to lower court judges to make sense of its meandering jurisprudence.

THE SHORT-LIVED RETREAT

In *Pasadena v. Spangler*, Justice Rehnquist wrote his first majority opinion in a desegregation case. The Court held that once a city had instituted a court-approved busing plan, it could not be required to adjust the plan annually in response to demographic change. The 1970 decision in the Pasadena case had stated that "there shall be no school in the District, elementary or junior high or senior high school, with a majority of any minority student."[76] The plan approved by the district court made no mention of annual adjustments. The trial judge, Manuel Real, later told the litigants that his order "meant to me that at least during my lifetime there would be no majority of any minority in any school in Pasadena."[77] Such an ongoing mandate to maintain majority-white schools, the Supreme Court ruled, went well beyond *Swann*. In *Swann* the Court had explicitly stated that annual readjustment is not constitutionally required, and it had insisted that racial quotas are a "starting place" rather than binding norms. Having "once implemented a racially neutral attendance pattern in order to remedy the perceived constitutional violation," Rehnquist argued, the district court "had fully performed its function of providing the appropriate remedy for previous racially discriminatory attendance patterns."[78] The objective was not to eliminate all majority-minority schools, but to impose a one-shot remedy designed to undo the effects of previous discriminatory actions.

The next year the Court took a more significant step to cabin *Keyes*. The district court had found Dayton, Ohio, guilty of some segregative acts, but had attributed most of the racial imbalance in that city's schools to residential patterns not traceable to government action. The judge therefore ordered changes only in those schools affected by identifiable discriminatory government action. He refused to institute a citywide desegregation plan that would eliminate (at least temporarily) most majority-black schools. The Sixth Circuit reprimanded the district court for failing to take more aggressive action to eliminate "all vestiges of state-imposed school segregation." Under *Keyes*, the appeals court argued, any failure to maximize integration creates a strong presumption of unconstitutional behavior by the school district, thus triggering a system-side plan to eliminate racially identifiable schools. The district court reluctantly ordered the busing of fifteen thousand Dayton students.[79]

The Supreme Court disagreed, finding the Sixth Circuit's remedy "entirely out of proportion to the constitutional violation found by the district court." Rehnquist's opinion held that the circuit court had mistakenly "viewed the present structure of the Dayton school system as a sort of 'fruit of the poisonous tree,' since some of the racial imbalance that presently obtains may have resulted in some part from the three instances of segregative action found by the District Court." "Instead of tailoring a remedy commensurate to the three specific violations," the Sixth Circuit had "imposed a systemwide remedy going beyond their scope."[80] Gone was the assumption so prominent in *Keyes* that a violation in one part of the district created a presumption that the whole system was "dual." According to *Dayton I*, a court can demand a "systemwide remedy" only when it can show that intentional discrimination has had "a systemwide impact." If a district court finds that a city has engaged in purposeful discrimination, it must "determine how much *incremental segregative effect* these violations have on the racial distribution" of the student body, which requires it to compare the present distribution with "what it would have been in the absence of such constitutional violation."[81] In short, *Dayton I* required judges to match their remedies with the specific constitutional violations they had uncovered.

Dayton I reflected a shift in the Court's interpretation of the Equal Protection clause that had been announced in *Washington v. Davis* (1976) and *Arlington Heights v. Metropolitan Housing Corp.* (1977). According to Justice White's majority opinion in *Washington v. Davis*, "our cases have not embraced the proposition that a law or other official act, without regard to whether it reflects a racially discriminatory purpose, is unconstitutional solely because it has a racially disproportionate impact." Playing fast and loose with some of the Court's desegregation precedents, White claimed that they had "adhered to the basic equal protection principle that the invidious quality of a law claimed to be racially discriminatory must ultimately be traced to a racially discriminatory purpose." The existence of "predominantly black and predominantly white schools in a community is not alone" enough to establish a constitutional violation.[82] Similarly, Justice Powell's majority opinion in *Arlington Heights* argued that the Court had "made it clear that official action will not be held unconstitutional solely because it results in a racially disproportionate impact."[83]

The renewed emphasis on discriminatory purpose called into question many of the desegregation orders issued in wake of *Keyes*. In 1976 the Court issued brief per curiam decisions requiring judges in Omaha and Milwaukee to reconsider their system-wide desegregation plans in light of *Dayton I*, *Washington v. Davis*, and *Arlington Heights*.[84] In both cases Justices Marshall and Brennan offered vigorous dissents, arguing that under the standards established in *Keyes* the lower court judges had uncovered sufficient evidence of systemic violations. They were joined by the newest member of the Court, Justice Stevens, who soon became their reliable ally.

REVERSING THE RETREAT

This trend proved remarkably short-lived—in fact, by 1979 it had completely disappeared. In two cases from Ohio, *Columbus Board of Education v. Penick* and *Dayton II*, the Court not only ignored the restrictions announced in *Dayton I*, but went beyond what it had said in *Keyes* about the duty of district court judges to impose system-wide remedies. In both cases, Justices White and Blackmun switched sides to form a majority with Brennan, Marshall, and Stevens. The same coalition later blocked Supreme Court review of busing plans for northern Delaware and Dallas.

Justice White's majority opinions in the two Ohio cases followed the Sixth Circuit on two key points, virtually eliminating the de jure/de facto distinction. First, if a school system had in 1954 contained schools that were "racially identifiable"—that is, predominantly black—it constituted a "dual school system" even if segregation had never been legally required and even if some of the city's schools were integrated at the time. As a result, almost every urban school system that had enrolled a significant number of black students in 1954 must now be considered "dual." Second, school districts have an affirmative duty to transform such "dual" systems into "unitary" ones. To achieve this goal, school officials must not only forego any actions that have the "foreseeable and anticipated consequence" of maintaining predominantly minority schools, but also take all feasible steps to minimize racial isolation. Having turned *Dayton I*'s "intent" standard into a "foreseeable effects" standard, the Court ignored what it had said two years earlier about limiting remedies to "incremental segregative effects." White's brief opinions were devoted entirely to evidentiary issues, offering no explanation for the emphasis on eliminating majority-minority schools. The 1979 decisions made it difficult for any large city to avoid a "systemic" desegregation order.

An important difference between the two Ohio cases was the initial ruling of the trial judges. The district court judge in Dayton, Carl Rubin, had been reluctant to require wide-scale busing. His limited remedies had twice been overturned by the Sixth Circuit. The judge in Columbus, Robert Duncan, acted much more aggressively and had been upheld by the appellate court. The Supreme Court accepted the judgment of the trial judge in Columbus but rejected the findings of the judge in Dayton. This contrast led Justice Stewart, the Court's leading proponent of deferring to the assessments of judges familiar with local circumstances, to dissent in the Dayton case but vote with the majority on Columbus.

Writing in dissent, Justices Powell and Rehnquist charged that the Court had not only "endowed prior precedents with new and wondrous meanings," but had subjected cities to busing plans that were doomed to fail. According to Powell, these "profoundly disturbing" decisions appeared "to endorse a wholly new constitutional concept."[85] He accused the majority of "stringing together of a chain of 'presumptions,' not one of which is close enough to reality to be reasonable." That led the Court "inexorably to the remarkable conclusion that the absence of integration found to exist in a high percentage of the 241 schools in Columbus and Dayton was caused entirely by intentional violations of the Fourteenth Amendment by the school boards of these two cities."[86] At the same time, the Court assumed "that the same school boards—under court supervision—will be capable of bringing about and maintaining the desired racial balance in each of these schools." "The experience in city after city," he warned, "demonstrates that this is an illusion."[87] The bulk of Powell's dissent was devoted to his claim that such desegregation orders would lead to white flight and a decline in educational quality.

Rehnquist complained that the Court had instituted a "radical new approach to desegregation" without either admitting it or explaining why. A judge must now impose a citywide desegregation order if he finds "some evidence of discriminatory purpose prior to 1954, without any inquiry into the causal relationship between those pre-1954 violations and current segregation in the school system."[88] This interpretation, Rehnquist claimed, made "school desegregation litigation a 'loaded game board,' but one at which a school board could never win." A school system's "only hope of avoiding a judicial receivership would be a voluntary dismantling of its neighborhood school program."[89] In short, *Columbus* and *Dayton II* created a strong presumption that district court judges should mandate racial balance in all major cities.

AVOIDANCE—WITH ONE EXCEPTION

The Supreme Court did not issue another desegregation opinion for a dozen years. The Court's refusal to address the difficult issues with which the lower courts were struggling elicited further dissents from Justices Powell and Rehnquist in 1980. Powell was particularly distressed by the Court's refusal to grant *cert.* in the Dallas case. The Court's inconsistency and failure "to give more than general instructions," he claimed, has produced "confusion in the lower courts." The resulting citywide busing orders were "self-defeating":

> The pursuit of racial balance at any cost—the unintended legacy of *Green*—is without constitutional or social justification. Out of zeal to remedy one evil, courts may encourage or set the stage for other evils. By acting against one-race schools, courts may produce one-race school systems.... A desegregation plan without community support, typically one with objectionable transportation requirements and continuing judicial oversight, accelerates the exodus to the suburbs of families able to move. The children of families remaining in the area affected by the court's decree are denied the opportunity to be part of an ethnically diverse student body.... When the more economically advantaged citizens leave the city, the tax base shrinks and all city services suffer.[90]

The district court judge in Dallas had warned of these unintended consequences, only to be reversed by the Fifth Circuit. For that reason, Powell saw the case as a particularly good opportunity to revisit the issue. But he could not muster the four votes needed to grant *cert.*

The second case the Court declined to review was an unusual one. Several years earlier the federal courts had established a busing plan for Wilmington, Delaware, and its surrounding suburbs. This was the only two-way mandatory busing plan in the country to cross city lines. *Milliken* had required a finding that the state government had contributed to cross-boundary segregation before such a plan could be imposed. No such determination had been made in this case. Why a majority of members of the Court refused to review a decision so inconsistent with *Milliken* remains a mystery. A few justices continued to believe that *Milliken* had been wrongly decided. Justice Blackmun may have regretted his vote in that case. Others might have viewed the Delaware case as a useful experiment. In any event, the complicated jurisdictional issues raised by the case offered a pretext for dodging it.

Justice Rehnquist (joined by Powell and Stewart) argued that the lower court in the Delaware case had not just deviated from the central holding of *Milliken* but violated basic constitutional principles. By merging the Wilmington school district with eleven suburban districts, the court had "abolish[ed] the county's system of education and disenfranchise[d] the voters who formerly retained popular control of education." This it had done "even though no court has found that these local school boards have engaged in any purposeful discrimination since 1954." *Milliken* had allowed judges to merge urban and suburban districts only upon "the most exacting showing of necessity." Here the lower court had "treated a series of independent school districts much as if they were a 'railroad in reorganization,' without any attempt to comply with the requirements of *Milliken* and *Dayton*." Nothing warranted such "total substitution of judicial for popular control of local education."[91] For want of a fourth vote for granting *cert.*, the Delaware anomaly survived.

On one desegregation issue, at least, the Court managed to present a united front. In the second round of the Detroit litigation, it provided some relief—both literally and metaphorically—to district court judges dealing with school systems that were hemorrhaging white students. *Milliken II* (1977) held that the district court could require Detroit to establish—and the state of Michigan to help pay for—new magnet and vocational schools as well as "in-service training for teachers and administrators, guidance and counseling programs, and revised testing procedures." The Court deferred to the lower court's judgment that such educational matters were "needed to remedy effects of past segregation to assure successful desegregation effort, and to minimize the possibility of resegregation." Taken as a whole, Chief Justice Burger claimed in his opinion for the Court, the mandated programs would "restore the victims of discriminatory conduct to the position they would have enjoyed" had public officials not acted unconstitutionally. Judges should not "close their eyes to inequalities ... which flow from a longstanding segregated system."[92] As we will see in the next chapter, faced with the prospect of spreading around a diminishing number of white students, few of whom could be described as high SES, district courts found compensatory education to be an appealing alternative.

Institutional Failure

If any theme emerges from this chapter, it is the failure of the Supreme Court to explain what the Constitution prohibits and what it requires in school districts serving children of different races and ethnicities. Incredible as it may seem, nearly seventy years after *Brown* the Supreme Court has yet to explain with precision what "desegregation" means. The Court has remained silent on the issue for years at a time. When it did speak, it frequently issued decisions that somehow managed to be both vague and contradictory. Starting with *Green* in 1968, it pushed lower courts to require racially balanced schools throughout the country without explaining the rationale for this ambitious reinterpretation of *Brown*. In *Milliken* the Court backed away from a full-scale assault on racial isolation, leaving the lower courts to contend with a serious mismatch between their constitutional responsibilities and their legal authority. For half a century, no issue before the Court has been more important or more controversial than school desegregation. The Court has insisted that it—not Congress, not the president—must determine what the Constitution requires. But the Warren, Burger, and Rehnquist Courts all failed to do so.

The major cause of this institutional failure has been the inability of the justices to agree on the underlying nature of the enterprise. They have papered over their disagreements by combining abstract formulations (*Brown I, Brown II, Green*, and the termination cases discussed in chapter 8) with two-handed advice (especially *Swann*) and seemingly technical rulings on evidence and remedies (*Keyes, Milliken, Spangler, Dayton I and II*, and *Columbus*). The Court frequently avoided contentious issues by handing them over to district court judges, who were told to devise the best policy in light of the "totality of local circumstances."

The pressure to evade hard choices was greatest when the justices were committed to producing unanimous decisions. Unanimity came at a high price: decades of uncertainty over the meaning of key precedents. Even as the norm of unanimity eroded, the Court's opinions remained murky and shifting. Some of the justices (most notably Stewart, O'Connor, and Kennedy) tried to stake out an ill-defined middle ground. Others seemed unsure where they stood. (Blackmun shifted slowly over time; White oscillated from case to case.) Warren Burger tried to use his position as chief justice to reduce the role of the federal courts but showed little ability either to create a consensus or to establish a coherent position of his own. Burger was repeatedly outfoxed by Justice Brennan, who was adept at using seemingly narrow and innocuous doctrinal innovations to effect substantial policy change. Given the coalition-building burdens placed on justices writing for Court majorities, it is not surprising that the most memorable opinions have been dissents and concurrences in which the author speaks only for himself (for example, Justice Marshall in *Milliken* and Justice Powell in *Keyes*).

Central institutional features of the Supreme Court contributed to this pattern of ambiguity, inconsistency, incoherence, and avoidance. Most obviously, since the docket of the Court has become almost completely discretionary, the justices can ignore difficult issues for years. The justices refer to this practice as allowing legal issues to "percolate." Meanwhile, to continue the metaphor, lower court judges are left in hot water. Moreover, since the justices take so few cases, the peculiar facts of those it reviews will often affect the development of legal doctrine. If the Court had granted *cert*. in *Jefferson County*—a truly important case with a provocative majority opinion and probing dissents—rather than the simpler *Green v. County School Board*, it might have been forced to depart from its mellifluous generalities. Had its first busing case come from anywhere but Charlotte—with its huge areas and ideal 71–29 racial mix—the issue might have looked different and the long negotiations within the Court taken a different turn. If the Wilmington case had come to the Court before Detroit, it is quite possible that urban-suburban busing would have commanded a fifth or even sixth vote. The justices simply did not examine enough cases to get a sense of the variety of issues facing lower court judges or the idiosyncrasies of the cases before them.

Just as importantly, the modern Supreme Court does not really "decide" cases at all. It can choose to address some of the issues presented by a case and ignore all the others. It usually offers a few words of wisdom, and then remands the case to the court below "for further proceedings not inconsistent with this opinion." Having offered such sound parental advice, it then turns to other matters. On a regular basis one of the justices insists "this is an issue we must soon confront." But in most instances the Court never does. As we will see in the next chapter, this kind of procrastination is a luxury not available to district and circuit court judges.

6

Left Adrift:
Desegregation in the Lower Courts

> Today the Court affirms the Court of Appeals ... in opinions so Delphic that lower courts will be hard pressed to fathom their implications for school desegregation litigation.... [The Court's approach] holds out the disturbing prospect of very different remedies being imposed on similar school systems because of the predilections of individual judges and their good-faith but incongruent efforts to make sense of this Court's confused pronouncements today.
> JUSTICE REHNQUIST, *Columbus Board of Education v. Penick*, 1979

The Supreme Court's desegregation decisions placed a huge responsibility on lower court judges but offered little consistent guidance on how to carry out this complex and controversial task. From 1954 to 1967 the Supreme Court directed the lower federal courts to desegregate southern schools "with all deliberate speed," but said nothing about what such "desegregation" requires. In a flurry of opinions issued between 1968 and 1974, it insisted that federal judges take immediate action to create "unitary" school systems and suggested that a school system could not be considered "unitary" until the racial balance of each of its schools reflects the racial composition of the district as a whole. Later Court decisions made it nearly impossible for any large school district in the country to prove that it had *not* engaged in unconstitutional segregation. At the same time, the Court denied that racial balance should be considered an end in itself and shut the door on the urban-suburban desegregation plans that might prevent urban school systems from becoming predominantly minority. The Court implicitly endorsed the "racial isolation/equal educational opportunity" understanding of desegregation, but then took away the most important tools for creating majority-white schools.

Lower court judges could not help but notice that while the Supreme Court demanded that they immediately produce "unitary" school systems, it had never explained the meaning of that crucial term. When Judge James McMillan approved a 1974 revision of the desegregation plan for the Charlotte-Mecklenburg school district, he explained that he had a duty to create a "unitary" system, adding "whatever that is."[1] A quarter century later the district court judge who finally ended judicial supervision of that school district complained that "the term 'unitary status' has no fixed meaning."[2] Looking back over the long history of the Wilmington, Delaware, school litigation, district court judge Sue Robinson described "unitariness" as "a kaleidoscope of sometimes conflicting and certainly evolving principles reflecting the social, political, educational, and jurisprudential thought which has molded the school desegregation process since 1954."[3]

In 1979 Justice Rehnquist had warned that "the Court cannot, for long, like Pilate, wash its hands of disparate results in cases throughout the country." His prediction that the Court would soon be forced to reenter the picture proved incorrect: for over a decade it remained silent on the topic. Meanwhile, two factors shaped the lower courts' response to the Supreme Court's muddled desegregation jurisprudence. The first was a crucial judicial innovation produced by desegregation litigation: the structural injunction. The remedial decree allowed judges to tailor their remedies to the idiosyncrasies of school districts and to modify their mandates over time. These injunctions concentrated enormous power in the judges and the masters and experts they appointed to carry them out. The second factor was diversity: the school districts subject to desegregation litigation differed enormously one from the other. Northern, southern; urban, rural; large, small; led by cooperative and hostile school officials; largely white, predominantly black, increasingly Hispanic—the variations were endless. The first section of this chapter examines the development of the structural injunction. The second describes the diversity of circumstances judges faced in desegregation cases. Together they lay the foundation for chapter 7's exploration of desegregation orders in a variety of American cities.

Extraordinary Remedies

Of all the legal and institutional innovations wrought by the civil rights revolution, none were more important than the structural injunction, which was developed by the lower courts in response to the heavy and often conflicting demands placed on them by the Supreme Court's desegregation decisions. The tools district courts used to address school desegregation were soon applied to institutions for the mentally ill and developmentally disabled, jails and prisons, police departments, and welfare agencies. The Supreme Court made only sporadic efforts to define or constrain the remedial power of the lower courts.

Yale Law professor Owen Fiss, the leading academic expert on the civil rights injunction and one of its most enthusiastic champions, has emphasized that when school desegregation litigation began to gather steam in the early 1960s, the injunction remained a "disfavored practice," one "to be used only if all else fails."[4] For progressives, it still carried the stench of the anti-labor injunction used by conservative judges to stifle the labor movement. To be sure, judges did issue what Fiss calls "preventative injunctions," that is, judicial orders that "seek to prohibit some discrete act or series of acts from occurring in the future."[5] Far less common were "reparative injunctions" that compel defendants "to engage in a course of action that seeks to correct the effects of a past wrong." Initially judges hearing desegregation cases in the South simply ordered school districts to stop classifying students by race. But as evasions multiplied and the Supreme Court required the dismantling of the entire dual school system, court orders became more detailed, more extensive, and more demanding—less "preventative" and more "reparative."

Eventually—and without much acknowledgement of the extent of change—the "reparative" injunction morphed into the structural injunction, which "seeks to effectuate the reorganization of an ongoing social institution."[6] As David Kirp and Gary Babcock note in their study of the use of court-appointed masters in desegregation cases, when courts "undertook to accomplish no less than the remaking of a system of education and the social order in which that system was embedded," they were "plowing new ground. No one knew at the outset what the task involved."[7]

The result was a concentration of authority seldom seen in American politics. The "underlying reality" of the structural injunction, Fiss has explained, is "the centrality of the judge in the injunctive process." By "*concentrating* or *fusing* the decisional power of the judge," it "represents the antithesis of separation of powers." But this concentrated or fused power is also "decentralized" and "peculiarly personalized": "When we speak of the decisional authority of the injunctive process we often talk not of *the law* or even of *the court*, but of Judge Johnson or Judge Garrity."[8] The desegregation injunction was virtually unlimited in both time and scope; few features of school life were exempt from coverage. The judicial orders remained in place—subject to frequent revision—not just for years, but for decades. These lengthy decrees were developed in negotiations supervised either by the presiding judge or the special master appointed by him, typically without a public hearing or a written explanation. Ex parte communications, usually with the defendant school districts, were frequent. After examining six desegregation cases in detail, David Kirp and Gary Babcock found that "the nature and scope of this type of litigation remains ad hoc and case-specific."[9] To a large extent, the process is insulated from appellate review.

One of the most peculiar features of desegregation in the lower courts was the sharp division between the liability and remedy phases of litigation, and the disproportionate attention paid to the former. In northern and western cities without a history of de jure segregation, the liability phase usually involved many days of trial, extensive testimony by school officials and expert witnesses, volumes of discovery, long judicial opinions, and multiple rounds of appeals. The main charge against school districts was that they had sited school buildings and drawn attendance zones in ways that reinforced—or failed to counteract—the effects of housing segregation, which itself was in part the result of government action. Seldom did these extensive examinations of decades of school districts' practices include any discussion of appropriate remedies. That came only after the district had been found guilty of operating a "dual" school system. By then the court was legally and morally obliged to right the wrongs perpetrated by the district.

Although the Supreme Court frequently reminded judges that remedies must be linked to specific constitutional violations, the nature of the infractions recognized by the Court became so amorphous and so lost in the distant past that tying remedies to infractions became nearly impossible. Trial judges were required "to perform awesome mental experiments, imagining what the school district would be like if no illegal segregation had occurred."[10] And they had to do so without authority to change housing patterns or require busing between city and suburbs. Kirp and Babcock note that because the "proof of official wrongdoing" in many northern desegregation cases was so weak, the remedies ordered by federal judges are "better characterized as ad hoc efforts to better the situation of black students than derivations from the recital of wrongs."[11]

If remedies were not derived from the nature of the constitutional violation, how did district court judges construct their lengthy and detailed structural injunctions? They almost always began by asking the defendant school district to offer a proposal, without providing them with much guidance on what would be considered acceptable. Oddly, the victorious plaintiffs seldom played a major role in the remedy phase, in part because they knew less about the details of student and teacher assignments, and in part because the NAACP was far more interested in winning cases than in figuring out what to do next.[12] In most cases the judge would then appoint experts either to compose a new plan (when the district had been uncooperative) or to tweak the one submitted by cooperative school officials. Initially judges focused on student assignments, establishing an acceptable range of black and white students for each school building. Many eventually concluded that "complete relief required a review not just of race-specific matters, but also of curriculum, vocational programs, counseling, and teacher training; practically everything that a school system did was perceived as affecting, and being affected by, the racial issue."[13]

To work out the details, ensure that schools carried them out, and make the adjustments that would subsequently become necessary, judges appointed special masters and monitoring committees. Who received these appointments was a matter of great consequence, but remained entirely in the hands of the district court judge. For example, Professor John Finger, who frequently provided expert testimony in desegregation cases, was sitting at the plaintiffs' table during the remedy phase of the Denver case when Judge Doyle unexpectedly announced that he would be the judge's chief consultant: "So I moved from the table with my friends at the [NAACP] L[egal] D[efense] F[und] and went to sit with his law clerks."[14] In the long-running Kansas City case, Judge Clark chose as his experts two University of Missouri-Kansas City education professors who had testified before him, giving them broad authority to formulate and implement his $2 billion school-reform project.

The Federal Rules of Civil Procedure authorize judges to appoint special masters to engage in fact-finding in "exceptional" circumstances. The Rules spell out the procedures masters are expected to follow, as well as how their findings shall be reviewed by the judge. But in desegregation cases masters seldom served as fact finders or followed the procedures laid out in the Federal Rules.[15] Rather, as Kirp and Babcock show, they served as politicians negotiating agreements among a variety of government agencies and interest groups; educational, budgetary, and management experts helping the judge reshape school systems from top to bottom; monitors reporting back to the judge on the school district's progress; and administrators charged with putting into effect the plans envisioned by the judge.

One of the most dramatic examples of the latter came in Cleveland, where the judge appointed "an administrator of desegregation." This court-appointed "super-superintendent" had "authority over the entire Cleveland school system and report[ed] only to the judge." He immediately brought in a number of consultants and advisors, and "in the first 3 weeks on the job issued twenty-three detailed and specific orders to the superintendent, all with the purpose of securing compliance with the court's remedial orders." According to Kirp and Babcock, it was only a slight exaggeration to say that the judge, master, and administrator were "running Cleveland's schools."[16]

Most of these desegregation orders remained in place for years, requiring substantial revision as circumstances changed. Even judges who initially limited their orders to student and teacher assignments were drawn into disputes over what happens inside school buildings. How long should such oversight last? When could desegregation cases finally be closed? As the judges supervising these orders grew weary of the task—and in several cases died before they came to an end—these questions became harder to ignore. In a series of rulings in the early 1990s the Supreme Court provided a bit of guidance on the issue, while still leaving much to the discretion of the lower courts. (This is the topic of chapter 8.)

On matters involving the nature of structural injunctions and the role of special masters, the Supreme Court remained silent. As William A. Fletcher has noted, in desegregation cases "the Court has been willing to disregard to a remarkable degree . . . the normal constraints on the judiciary." It "has not set out principles to govern the use of experts, masters, or supervisory committees; nor has it discussed issues of intervention and participation, or of permissible strategies of inducing settlement." As a result, "the lower courts have been left largely on their own to encourage by informal means the achievement of school desegregation, and even school integration."[17] Although circuit courts carefully scrutinized district court decisions on liability, they, too, offered little guidance on remedies or the use of special masters and experts.

Nor did district court judges grappling with desegregation cases compare notes with their peers. Kirp and Babcock discovered that the judges they interviewed for their study "knew little about the use of masters elsewhere." Federal judges, they note, "are remarkably isolated from one another."[18] Faced with a massive but poorly defined task and given broad authority to employ novel forms of relief, they engaged in a variety of educational experiments—but made no effort to evaluate or compare their results.

Diversity on the Ground

In cases ranging from *Brown II* in 1955 to *Swann* in 1971 and *Columbus* in 1979, justices on the Supreme Court recognized that school districts are complex institutions that differ enormously from one another. Since the cases consolidated in *Brown I* "arose under different local conditions and their disposition will involve a variety of local problems," the Court asked for further consideration of appropriate remedies. "Full implementation of these constitutional principles," Chief Justice Warren explained in *Brown II*, would "require solution of varied local school problems." Warren emphasized that "traditionally, equity has been characterized by a practical flexibility in shaping its remedies and by a facility for adjusting and reconciling public and private needs." Given "their proximity to local conditions," federal district court judges would bear primary responsibility for "fashioning and effectuating" desegregation decrees. In doing so they might "consider problems related to administration, arising from the physical condition of the school plant, the school transportation system, personnel, revision of school districts and attendance areas into compact units to achieve a system of determining admission to the public schools on a nonracial basis."[19] Despite the checkered performance of district court judges in the South, in *Swann* the court again emphasized that "of necessity" it must rely on "the informed judgment of the district courts in the first instance."[20] By 1971 the strongest advocates for delegation of discretion to trial-court judges were not proponents of "massive resistance," but rather the Court's most liberal members.

What factors should judges take into account in desegregation cases? Certainly not local opposition to desegregation. As Warren emphasized, "it should go without saying that the vitality of these constitutional principles cannot be allowed to yield simply because of disagreement with them." During the Little Rock crisis, the Court remained resolute on this key point: angry mobs threatening violence could not be allowed to derail school desegregation. But what if opposition to desegregation took the form of white flight by parents who moved to the suburbs or enrolled their children in private schools? In this case, as Justice Powell warned, desegregation orders might prove counterproductive, leaving school systems almost entirely black. Should trial judges take that into account? If judges should discount the views of whites, how about the views of black, Hispanic, and Asian parents who prefer neighborhood schools? How should judges determine who speaks for those whose rights have been violated?

Another consideration that would always seem out of bounds is the private beliefs of judges. Judges who had long supported segregation were expected to follow Supreme Court commands. A few did, but too many others did not. As we saw in chapter 4, that stubborn fact led the Fifth Circuit to exert unprecedented control over district court judges under its jurisdiction. To expect judges to set aside entirely their political views on such a controversial matter while wielding wide discretion was unrealistic. Not only did district court judges differ significantly in their approaches to desegregation, but court of appeals decisions differed from circuit to circuit and even among the randomly assigned panels within the circuits.

The following pages examine factors that (properly or not) affected the remedies devised and implemented by federal judges. This review provides the context for chapter 7's discussion of particular cities and helps us understand why remedial measures exhibited such variation.

GEOGRAPHY AND DEMOGRAPHY

At the heart of most discussions of desegregation lie two distinctions: black and white; North and South. Both are obviously important. Each is more complicated than it might at first seem.

Legal, de jure segregation was practiced throughout the South and the border states but was rare in the rest of the country. All school districts in states that had a history of de jure segregation were required to demonstrate that they had transitioned to a "unitary" school system. Outside the South, plaintiffs (usually either the NAACP or the Department of Justice) were required to prove that the district had engaged in segregative acts—a labor-intensive, time-consuming task. Less obvious was another key geographic difference: school districts in the South and West tend to cover a much larger area than those in the Northeast and Midwest. The Charlotte-Mecklenburg school district covers 525 square miles. Oklahoma City and Houston are even larger, about 600 square miles. Many school districts in the Sunbelt, mountain West, and California run to about 300 square miles. In contrast, Boston's school district covers only 48 square miles; Cleveland's, 78; and Cincinnati's, 89. Given the Supreme Court's ruling that busing must stop at the district line, combatting racial isolation was particularly difficult in these compact cities. To make matters worse, many northeastern and midwestern cities were losing population, with higher socioeconomic status (SES) white families being the first to leave.

Another demographic difference between regions became increasingly significant: the percentage of Hispanic and Asian American students. In the early 1970s the judge in *Keyes* learned that Hispanic students outnumbered African Americans in Denver schools, and that their parents generally opposed busing. The judge in San Francisco faced an even more diverse population: the desegregation order for that city took into consideration nine different racial and ethnic categories. There, Chinese American parents were particularly committed to neighborhood schools. For Hispanic and Asian parents, helping English learners was more important than achieving racial balance. Should desegregation orders try to create majority-white schools (the implicit goal of southern desegregation decisions), or racially and ethnically diverse schools? If the former, then the effort would quickly become futile; if the latter, then desegregation would still be likely to produce many schools filled with poor black and Hispanic kids.

It is impossible to ignore the extent to which demographic change recast the desegregation debate. Between 2000 and 2010 the number of white children under age eighteen fell by 4.3 million, and the number of black children decreased slightly (by 250,000). Meanwhile, the number of Hispanic children rose by 4.8 million, the number of Asian children by 760,000, and those describing themselves as mixed race by almost nine hundred thousand.[21] Of course, these numbers are far from uniform across the country. By 2010, African American, Hispanic, and Asian school-age children already outnumbered white Anglos in ten states in the South and West.[22]

Over the next decade, white children ceased to constitute a majority of public school students. In the fall of 2020, 46 percent of those attending public elementary and secondary schools were white, 28 percent Hispanic, 15 percent black, 5 percent Asian, and 5 percent "two or more races."[23] If one defines a school system as "segregated" when most of its schools are predominantly black or Hispanic, then "desegregation" is out of the question in many parts of the country. This trend forced lower court judges to rethink their definition of that crucial term.

INTEREST GROUPS AND THEIR POLITICS

A defining feature of the "public interest litigation" epitomized by *Brown* is its polycentric (many-sided) nature.[24] In traditional "bipolar" cases, the identity and the interests of the plaintiffs and the defendants are clearly defined, and we can usually be confident that their lawyers are accurately defending those interests. Not so in desegregation cases. Nominal plaintiffs rarely do more than add their name to the case; the lawyers who handle the litigation are the ones who define the interests of the wider class they represent. School superintendents frequently see things differently from school boards, the nominal defendants. In some cities, desegregation litigation was collusive: defendant school boards saw litigation as a tool for extracting more money from state governments and more high-SES white students from the suburbs. The interests of other affected parties—Hispanics, Asians, teachers, suburbs, state governments, taxpayers—were often heard late in the process, if at all.

Brown v. Board was a class-action suit: the NAACP's lawyers spoke for all the African American students in four states. In 1966 the Federal Rules of Civil Procedure were amended to make it easier for federal judges to certify such classes. Although most desegregation cases took the form of class actions, judges seldom investigated the extent to which African Americans agreed among themselves about the interest of their children or accepted the position of the lawyers speaking on their behalf. Often judges did not even to bother certify a class at all.

Although it is difficult to speak with confidence on this matter, it seems safe to say that until the late 1960s there was broad support for *Brown* and the desegregation efforts of the NAACP among the African American community. By 1967 or 1968, though, that consensus began to fade for several reasons. First, in a number of cities, including Detroit, Atlanta, and Wilmington, Delaware, black leaders were gaining control over city government and school boards. Some of these newly empowered city leaders opposed metropolitan desegregation plans that threatened to take control of the schools out of their hands. In Detroit, African American leaders such as future mayor Coleman

Young advocated decentralization, favoring "community control" over control by a distant bureaucracy (or a federal judge).[25] In Atlanta, local civil rights leaders and the local chapter of the NAACP broke with the national NAACP to support a second "Atlanta Compromise" that limited busing while giving the black community more control over city schools.[26]

Second, the NAACP's litigational strategy sometimes put the organization at odds even with local leaders who vigorously supported school integration. Its lawyers were preoccupied with winning cases on the liability issue and developing precedents that would make that task easier in the future. In the pivotal Detroit litigation, for example, they shied away from endorsing a metropolitan remedy, insisting that simply redistributing the few white students remaining in the Detroit system would provide substantial educational benefits to black students. According to Paul Dimond, an attorney for the NAACP LDF in many of these cases, "insofar as possible, we continued to avoid taking any position on metropolitan relief." In fact, "as to appropriate remedies, neither [chief litigator Nathaniel] Jones nor the NAACP had a clear idea at the outset. . . . they were more concerned about proving to the court and the country that a color line, every bit as wrong as Jim Crow, still divided America on a racial basis."[27] When it proposed a remedial plan, the NAACP concentrated on requiring the student body of each school to reflect the racial composition of the school district as a whole. On educational quality, it had little to say.[28]

Third, the longer desegregation orders remained in place, the more African American parents came to doubt that those orders were benefiting their children. It was usually black children who had the longest bus rides. Particularly galling was the fact that "white" seats at popular magnet schools often remained empty while African American students were stuck on waiting lists. Maintaining racial balance meant denying those students their choice of schools. Most disturbing was the fact that so many legally desegregated schools remained substandard. A 1994 Gallup poll found that 64 percent of African American parents favored local schools over more-distant integrated schools. By more than two to one, they thought the best way to improve education was more money rather than more busing.[29]

Judges overseeing desegregation orders heard the complaints of these parents, and sometimes responded by modifying desegregation plans. In 1980 the district court judge in Nashville offered this description of the "evolution of desegregation philosophy that has occurred among educators, sociologists, black parents, and plaintiffs in this litigation as well as similar litigation across the country":

> Historically, black plaintiffs felt the necessity to be in a majority white school in order to be assured of equal distribution of educational funding. . . . A

dramatic role reversal has taken place. In this case, we have a white majority of the school board, acting on the advice of a white desegregation expert, recommending to the Court *more* busing to achieve *more* racial balance. Equally contrary to earlier posture, the black plaintiffs urge upon the Court *less* busing, *more* neighborhood characteristics to the assignment plan, and the permissibility of majority black schools.[30]

He agreed with the black parents but was overruled by the Sixth Circuit.[31]

A year later the district court judge hearing the Dallas case allowed a group called the "Black Coalition" to intervene. This alliance he described as a "broad-based minority group composed of parents, patrons, and taxpayers with children in the [Dallas Independent School District], as well as representatives from a number of civic, political and ecumenical associations in the black community." The Coalition's testimony convinced him that "there is considerable difference of opinion among sizeable segments of the minority citizenry of Dallas over the type of relief that should be ordered," and that "no one party to this suit can lay claim any longer to speak on behalf of the entire minority population as a sacrosanct 'class.'" Intervention by the Black Coalition gave "formal recognition to the same undercurrents of tension and disunity among blacks that were experienced over the lengthy course of desegregation litigation in such large cities as Atlanta, Detroit, Nashville, and Boston."[32] In Kansas City, Judge Clark's ambitious and expensive desegregation order managed to unite the black community—against a plan that they believed had been formulated without their participation and that did little to improve their children's education. They eventually succeeded in forcing a return to neighborhood schools.[33]

The difficulty of identifying the interests of minority children increased as the number of Hispanic and Asian students rose. In Detroit, the trial judge refused to allow Hispanic parents to intervene. In Denver, Dallas, San Francisco, San Jose, and many other cities, the number of Hispanic students was too large to ignore. Hispanic and Asian organizations and parents were frequently among the most vocal opponents of busing plans, preferring neighborhood schools that would provide more assistance to English learners and reflect the ethnic culture of the neighborhood. In Denver, bilingual education came to dominate the *Keyes* litigation.

WHO SPEAKS FOR THE DEFENDANTS?

In some desegregation cases the named defendant was the school board. In others, the school district itself. In still others, the governor of the state. This variety points to a key question in desegregation cases: Who speaks for the school district? Within each of these complex organizations one finds a diversity of points of view about the best interest of its students, its teachers, and its leaders.

During the 1950s and 1960s the Fifth Circuit confronted many school districts intent upon delaying desegregation indefinitely. Such obstructionism had declined markedly by the 1970s. Yet school districts continued to differ in their eagerness to promote desegregation as defined by the federal courts. During the 1970s some northern school boards were as hostile to court action as their counterparts in the South had been decades before. For example, in Cleveland Judge Battisti complained that the school board's strategy had been "to resist at every step the letter and the spirit of the Court's orders . . . while at the same time attempting to publicly undermine the legitimacy of these proceedings by impugning the legitimacy of the Court and misrepresenting the facts and law." According to Kirp and Babcock, Battisti emerged from the fact-finding phase of the trial "persuaded that he was dealing with a system that combined obduracy and incompetence in equal and sobering proportions."[34] Much the same could be said about the school board in Boston, which added significant measures of vituperation and political opportunism.

Other school boards and superintendents were more cooperative, sharing the judges' general commitment to racial integration while recognizing the administrative and political obstacles to achieving that goal. That is why judges turned first to district personnel for proposed plans. According to one of the NAACP's attorneys in *Milliken v. Bradley*, the Detroit school board "held a national reputation as racially progressive."[35] Shortly before the NAACP sued the San Francisco Unified School District, its superintendent had proposed a new "School Complexes" plan to promote integration. The school board, "most of whose members were personal friends of and continuing collaborators with the civil rights movement," approved that plan.[36] In Kansas City the school board itself initiated *Missouri v. Jenkins*, blaming the states of Missouri and Kansas for school segregation. The judge subsequently realigned the district as a defendant, and then appointed a white attorney without any ties to civil rights organizations to represent African American students.[37] Similarly, the city of Wilmington, Delaware, initiated the desegregation case that culminated in a rare metropolitan-busing plan in that state. Most of the black members of the city council opposed the suit because they feared it would endanger recently secured black control over city schools; white members of the council supported it because they thought it would reduce the tax burden and draw more white families into the city.[38]

Even when listed as the nominal defendants, school boards and superintendents learned how to take advantage of litigation. For school boards in Detroit, Kansas City, and Wilmington, litigation provided an opportunity to increase funding from state governments. In San Francisco, it offered the school board a method for overcoming two political obstacles: the mayor's opposition to its "school complexes" plan, and a public referendum that had rejected school busing by a 3–1 margin.[39] Further north in the Bay Area, the Richmond school board instituted an ambitious desegregation plan in 1969. Then, "because the board knew that its decision might be overturned by the electorate," it "collaborated with the local legal services office to secure a state court decree insulating desegregation from the vagaries of politics."[40] The voters did indeed throw out those board members. In the first round of litigation, a state-court judge refused to take action because the case was so obviously collusive.[41] In Dayton, Ohio, school board members who had endorsed a desegregation plan with extensive busing were defeated by antibusing candidates. The lame-duck board and the superintendent then worked with the NAACP to protect their plan from revision, publicly announcing that the district had previously engaged in intentional segregation.[42]

In San Jose, the school superintendent who helped negotiate the court order told interviewers that she discovered how to "use it to leverage their 'doing the right thing' for Latino students."[43] The agreement committed the district to eliminating all tracking and self-contained gifted-and-talented classrooms, a move opposed by many parents. "It's very hard to get through the attitudes and expectations of more affluent parents who want their children accelerated," she explained. "I thought I could use the court order if it mandated the elimination of tracks. It became a buffer for me and my Board to say that it is an order of the court." Another part of the San Jose agreement committed the district to expanding its bilingual education program. When California approved Proposition 227, eliminating most bilingual programs, the consent decree allowed the program to continue: a federal-consent decree trumped state law. The superintendent also used the consent decree to change the curriculum in high school, to get rid of teachers who opposed those changes, and to campaign for a bond issue to upgrade science labs: "If people were unhappy, I had the hammer of the court to back me up."[44]

The San Jose experience points to one of the most interesting features of desegregation litigation: the way in which districts that had initially opposed court orders eventually came to embrace them. Nowhere was this reversal more evident than in Charlotte. After fighting the desegregation plan established by Judge McMillan in *Swann*, the school board and the rest of the district's leadership did an abrupt about-face, committing themselves to becoming "the premier integrated urban district in the country."[45] In subsequent years, school, city, and business leaders took pride in promoting Charlotte as "The City that Made It Work."

This about-face produced an odd situation when the federal courts considered whether the litigation had succeeded in creating a "unitary school system" that could be freed from judicial supervision. Insisting that after nearly thirty years it had yet to eliminate all the "vestiges" of the previously "dual" school system, the school board asked the court to retain jurisdiction. The district court judge noted that the Charlotte-Mecklenburg Schools (CMS) "takes a bizarre posture in this late phase of the case, arguing that it has not complied with the Court's order." Although CMS had instituted a number of programs to address the racial achievement gap and to hire more minority teachers, "the Court was unlikely to hear any of them from CMS, whose stance in the case was such that it offered no self-congratulatory evidence and strongly objected to anything that shed favorable light on the school system."[46] The Fourth Circuit noted that "CMS officials engaged in much self-recrimination and claimed that they had not pursued the dismantlement of the dual system with the requisite zeal."[47] The board's critics described this as the "We-Stink Defense."[48]

There was method to the school district's apparent madness. Once the system was deemed "unitary," the district would lose some state and federal funding. More importantly, it would become more difficult for it to take race into account when assigning students and teachers to schools. It could no longer establish racial targets for magnet schools. The trial judge charged that the district downplayed its accomplishments and sought to preserve the court order because it "wishes to use that order as a pretext to pursue race conscious, diversity enhancing policies in perpetuity."[49]

In this final chapter of the *Swann* case (commonly known as its *Swann* song), the Fourth Circuit noted that over time the school bureaucracy had been reshaped by judicial supervision: "the orders have been institutionalized to the point that CMS officials cannot imagine life without them."[50] In a similar vein, the superintendent of Denver schools observed that school principals subject to judicial orders would "use the judge as an excuse for everything. If they did something the parents didn't like, they would say, 'The court requires us to do it.'"[51] Court orders not only provide convenient political cover, but create new standard operating procedures, new funding streams, new organizational units, new constituencies, and a new sense of mission. In the 1960s and 1970s civil rights litigators and judges expected that once such reforms had been instituted, they would stick. By the 1990s and early 2000s, those who favored desegregation plans feared that without continuing judicial support these reforms would fade away. The reality was more complex. As we will see in chapter 8, those realities became apparent when judges began to terminate desegregation cases in the 1990s.

Diversity on the Bench

How have district court judges exercised their discretion in such widely varying circumstances? To what extent have the circuit courts limited that discretion? There are no simple answers to these questions. They vary from judge to judge, from appellate panel to appellate panel, and from decade to decade.

When the law is relatively clear, it makes little difference whether a judge is a liberal or conservative, a Democratic or Republican appointee. When the law is ambiguous, these factors loom larger. At the same time, in desegregation cases we see how the evidence that judges hear at trial can lead them to change their minds. Moreover, judges responsible for overseeing desegregation orders year after year—even those deeply committed to the cause—can tire of the matter, allowing it to languish on the docket or encouraging the parties to reach a final agreement. Some desegregation cases have lasted so long that the original judges have died, retired, or been removed from the case after antagonizing one side or the other. Their replacements are likely to have a different take on the central issues.

Perhaps the best known district court judges in desegregation cases are those who can be described as *reformers*. They view their job not just as following the letter of the law, but as correcting centuries of injustice done to minority children. Judges such as Frank Johnson, Jack Weinstein, J. Skelly Wright, and William Wayne Justice are celebrated not just for their rulings in school cases, but for their efforts to reform prisons, mental institutions, administrative law, and liability law. The judge in the San Francisco case, Stanley Weigel, issued controversial rulings on prison reform and the rights of tenants displaced by urban renewal projects. Although appointed by Richard Nixon, Judge Robert Duncan was an African American who had experienced segregation firsthand before taking aggressive action to desegregate the schools of Columbus, Ohio. NAACP attorney Paul Dimond described Judge Noel P. Fox, who ordered the desegregation of schools in Lansing, Benton Harbor, and Kalamazoo, Michigan, as "an aging but still fiery liberal long committed to the American dream of equality and opportunity."[52]

Somewhat more complicated are judges who can be described as *converts*: they began as skeptics but became deeply committed to reforming public schools. The leading example is Stephen Roth, who presided over the Detroit trial and issued the metropolitan plan overturned by the Supreme Court.

Roth came to the bench as a conservative Michigan Democrat. A few years before he decided *Milliken v. Bradley*, he had voiced his opposition to the involuntary reassignment of students to promote racial balance.[53] Early in the case he showed impatience with the NAACP's lawyers, publicly (and injudiciously) criticized them for bringing the case, and called them "outsiders [who] should go away and let Detroit solve its own problems."[54]

In her detailed study of the Detroit litigation, Eleanor Wolf convincingly argues that the evidence Judge Roth heard over the course of the forty-one-day trial—evidence she claims was badly skewed in favor of the plaintiffs—was responsible for his change of heart. The judge later told a reporter, "We all got an education during the course of the trial. It opened my eyes."[55] He refused to blame the Detroit school board for the condition of the city's educational system, preferring to decide the case on a no-fault basis and to dispense with the de jure/de facto distinction. His job was simply "to remedy a condition which we believe needs correction."[56]

Judge Russell Clark went through a similar conversion during the Kansas City litigation. During the trial, he sometimes treated the plaintiffs' lawyer in a dismissive, even contemptuous manner. At the end of the trial, he stated that the "plaintiffs simply failed to show that those defendants had acted in a racially discriminatory manner that substantially caused racial segregation."[57] But he still held that school authorities were operating a "dual" school system. Clark believed that otherwise he would have been overturned by the Eighth Circuit—and for good reason, as Joshua Dunn has shown.[58] With remarkable eagerness, Clark then threw himself into creating a model school system—one that by the end had cost $2 billion without improving achievement by minority students or drawing more white children into the city's schools. Judge Clark was understandably dismayed by the quality of Kansas City's schools and entranced by the notion that the federal judiciary could build a better educational system.

A judge can move in the other direction as well. This was true of one of the most aggressive, brilliant, innovative, and impetuous members of the federal bench, Judge Jack Weinstein of the Eastern District of New York. Faced with a case alleging that the Mark Twain Junior High School on Coney Island was unconstitutionally segregated, Judge Weinstein initially thought big. After finding that the local school board and the chancellor of the city school system had violated the Constitution, he appointed a special master to deal with a wide variety of issues. According to Robert Katzmann (himself later a judge on the Second Circuit),

> in an effort to achieve a comprehensive solution, the judge directed virtually all agencies that had even the slightest relation to education policy—schools,

housing, transit, park, and police authorities—to submit plans on March 1, 1974 that would be operative in September 1974. In particular, Judge Weinstein seemed committed to the view that a major restructuring of housing and other urban policies in the Coney Island area was essential to achieve the desegregation objectives; it was thus clear that the responses of the housing agencies would be of central importance.[59]

Weinstein's special master produced a lengthy, two-part report that called for housing subsidies to induce white lower-income families to move to the area; enforcement of housing codes; expansion of social services; a speed-up of urban renewal; and a "clean up Coney Island" campaign.[60] Not surprisingly, the plan encountered opposition from the agencies expected to make major changes in their priorities and to come up with the necessary money. Weinstein then backed down, conceding that "the [judicial] decretal tool is poorly designed for restructuring an entire community."[61] Instead he ordered that Mark Twain be converted into a magnet school for gifted children, with a 70–30 white-black student ratio. That limited endeavor proved successful.

A third category of trial judges can be called the *skeptics*. A good example is Judge Carl Rubin, who presided over the Dayton, Ohio, case that twice went to the Supreme Court. A Nixon appointee who had previously served as city attorney for Cincinnati, Rubin provided a vivid contrast to Judges Robert Duncan and Frank Battisti, who heard similar cases in Columbus and Cleveland at about the same time.[62] In his initial decision Rubin required limited reassignment of students, explaining that the neighborhood school is the "bedrock strength of public school systems and steps may properly be taken to preserve it."[63] The Sixth Circuit sent the case back to him because his plan had tolerated too many one-race schools. His next plan was similarly rejected by the appellate court. Only on his third try did Rubin require all schools in Dayton to be within 15 percent of the racial composition of the school district (that is, between 33 percent and 63 percent black). After the Supreme Court handed down *Dayton I*, Rubin dismissed the entire case. The Sixth Circuit again disagreed, and this time the Supreme Court upheld the circuit court (*Dayton II*). The racial-balance plan Rubin had with great reluctance issued in 1976 remained in place during these many appeals. With a touch of condescension, the NAACP's lawyers concluded, "Although we had tried to inform Judge Rubin from as many angles with as much evidence as possible, he had done much to avoid an education."[64]

Judge Robert Peckham of the northern district of California provides another example of a judicial skeptic. He ruled against the plaintiffs three times in the San Jose litigation, first in 1971 and again when the plaintiffs sought reconsideration in light of the Supreme Court's decision in *Keyes*. Peckham found that the district had followed a racially neutral and educationally sound policy of supporting neighborhood schools. After a long delay, the Ninth Circuit remanded the case, suggesting that he take another look at the inferences he had drawn from the facts. Peckham stood his ground, arguing that there was no evidence that the district had engaged in unconstitutional segregation. On the case's second trip to the Ninth Circuit, a three-judge panel upheld Peckham. But on rehearing the case en banc, the full Ninth Circuit ruled that San Jose had not taken sufficient steps to correct racial imbalance. By now it was 1984, thirteen years after the case was initially filed. Early in 1985, Judge Peckham rejected the plaintiff's mandatory student-reassignment plan in favor of one that focused on magnet schools and a "controlled choice" student-assignment plan.[65]

A final group of trial-court judges are the *replacements*, those assigned to a case after the liability phase and the first round of judicial orders. Examples include Judge Edward DeMascio, who took over in Detroit after Judge Roth died; Judge Avern Cohn, who took over for DeMascio after tension with the NAACP led to his recusal; Judge Richard Matsch in Denver after Judge Doyle was promoted to the Tenth Circuit; Judge William Orrick in San Francisco after Judge Weigel was promoted to the Ninth Circuit; Judge Barefoot Sanders in Dallas after the NAACP requested that Judge William Taylor be replaced. Although a varied lot, none showed the same zeal as the "reformers" described above. By the time they took over, the hope of educational transformation had faded, the issues had become more complex, and bickering among the parties had increased. In general, they were eager to negotiate agreements that would minimize the need for further judicial involvement.

A subcategory of replacements could be called *closers*. Like the relievers who come in during the ninth inning, they saw their job as mopping up and ending the game. Examples include Judge Dean Whipple, the "exit judge" in Kansas City; and Judge Robert Potter in Charlotte. Many of these decisions came in the 1990s and early in the first decade of the 2000s, when a number of Reagan and Bush appointees sat on the bench.

Between the Supreme Court and this varied lot of district court judges sit the circuit courts of appeal. The significance of the Fifth Circuit was described at length in chapter 4. As desegregation litigation moved north in the 1970s, the significance of that court declined and action moved to the Eighth Circuit (which includes Missouri, Arkansas, and Minnesota), the Ninth Circuit (which includes California), and especially the Sixth Circuit (Michigan, Ohio, Kentucky, and Tennessee). Because each case is heard by a randomly assigned panel of three appellate judges, none of these courts was a model of consistency. The Sixth Circuit affirmed quite different plans for Kalamazoo and Grand Rapids,

Michigan, and for Cincinnati and Cleveland, Ohio. These variations were in part the result of the luck of the draw and in part the result of the expectation that appellate courts should defer to trial courts in their evaluation of the facts and remedies. The Sixth Circuit was overruled by the Supreme Court in *Milliken* and *Dayton I* but upheld in *Dayton II* and *Columbus*—a good indication that the Supreme Court was no more predictable or consistent than the circuit courts. The Eighth Circuit made it clear that it expected district court judges to demand major changes in the St. Louis and Kansas City school systems. It was thrice overturned by the Supreme Court in *Missouri v. Jenkins*.[66] Weak appellate review produced enormous variation in desegregation plans.

The Law Personified

This chapter moved away from the grand abstractions of Supreme Court opinions to the complex and diverse realities facing district court judges. In theory, desegregation orders were based on the Equal Protection clause of the Fourteenth Amendment—a key component of "the supreme law of the land"—and Supreme Court interpretations thereof. In practice, though, lower court judges wielded enormous discretion both because the Court's decisions were so ambiguous and because the facts and parties before them were so diverse. The evolution of the structural injunction reflected not only the great exertion of federal authority required to reconstruct southern education and to reform urban education throughout the country, but also the need to tailor these extensive remedies to the peculiarities of each city and to revise them to reflect changing demographics and educational experiences.

In such a context, the exercise of judicial power is, as Owen Fiss has written, both "decentralized" and "peculiarly personalized." The creation, enforcement, and modification of the structural injunction "becomes an expression of a person, as much as it is an expression of an office."[67] That is why we can find important differences—ranging from "reformers" and "converts" to "skeptics"— among the ranks of the district court judges handling desegregation cases.

To some, these judges became heroes bravely upholding the Constitution. To others, they were villains tyrannically imposing their personal policy preferences on entire cities. Few stopped to consider the extraordinarily difficult position in which district court judges had been put by the Supreme Court's meandering, frequently ambiguous, poorly explained, and sometimes contradictory desegregation jurisprudence. The following chapter looks more closely at how these judges coped with this situation, and how their plans evolved over the decades.

7

Varieties of Desegregation Experiences

> Remedy-shaping is the centerpiece of the contemporary school desegregation case. The scope of the remedy is accordionlike. It can be confined to matters concerning the mix of students and teachers or expanded to encompass much of the ordinary business of the school district. That choice, while bounded by Supreme Court decisions, chiefly belongs to the district court judge: It is for him to describe the problem and to imagine a fit solution.
>
> DAVID KIRP AND GARY BABCOCK, "Judge and Company," 1981

Given the ambiguity of the term "unitary school system" and the many differences among cities and judges, describing how court-ordered desegregation efforts played out across the country is no easy task. Over the years journalists and legal scholars have provided detailed case studies that emphasize the unique features of each city, how judges' commands changed over time, and the gap that inevitably appeared between what the court had ordered and what actually happened in schools. Court opinions explaining why judicial supervision was eventually terminated provide additional histories of the desegregation efforts. What general patterns can one find in this sea of particularity?

By 1972 the court-agency alliance described in chapter 4 had largely succeeded in desegregating southern schools. Desegregation advocates then turned their attention to reducing racial isolation in northern and western school districts. In the South, desegregation had involved all kinds of school districts—rural, suburban, and urban. In the North, by contrast, the focus was almost entirely on the large urban districts where most minority students are enrolled.

The remainder of this chapter describes four phases of desegregation efforts by the lower courts. During the initial phase, roughly the first half of the 1970s, courts placed greatest emphasis on creating a racially balanced student body in each school. Doing so usually required busing. Although courts differed in the degree of variation they allowed, they agreed on the importance of eliminating schools that were overwhelmingly minority.

As the proportion of white students in these districts shrank, courts entered the second phase, permitting higher percentages of minority students in most schools and offering parents more choices among the schools their children could attend. During the third phase, judges' understanding of desegregation slowly shifted as they confronted a more racially and ethnically diverse student population. Earliest to face these new complexities were judges in the

West—especially San Francisco and Denver—where Hispanic students were more numerous than African Americans, and Asian students were becoming an increasingly important factor in the complex student equation. By the 1990s, desegregation could no longer be seen in black-and-white terms. This new set of circumstances required a new definition of racial "balance," and led judges to place more emphasis on programs for English learners.

Finally, over time the focus shifted once again, placing less emphasis on maintaining racial balance and more on improving the quality of education in urban school systems. It became apparent that merely shifting students and teachers from one school to another would not guarantee educational equality. This change in emphasis required judges to pay more attention to what happens *inside* schools: tracking, discipline, professional training, curriculum, bilingual education, special education, AP and gifted programs, and guidance and counseling programs—all these elements became subject to judicial scrutiny. At the extreme, a few judges tried to remake entire school systems. Others concluded that improving school quality was not a subject within the institutional capacity of judges. Once these issues were on the table, judges had to confront the question of whether a school district could be considered "unitary" if there remained a large achievement gap between white and minority students.

Phase 1: Desperately Seeking Balance

As lower court judges searched Supreme Court decisions for hints on what schools must do to attain "unitary status," they fastened on Justice Brennan's statement in *Green* that the "racial identification" of a school system extends "not just to the composition of student bodies," but "to every facet of school operations—faculty, staff, transportation, extracurricular activities and facilities." Of these six so-called *Green* factors, composition of the student body attracted by far the most attention. Assignment of faculty was addressed in most court orders, but incited less controversy, largely because fewer people were directly affected. Judges also faced more constraints on faculty assignment: union rules often allowed teachers to veto transfers; at the high school level specialization put limits on the pool of available black or white teachers.

Most desegregation orders established a maximum black/white range for all schools in the district. For example, if black students constituted 40 percent of the student body in a school district and the court order established a range of plus or minus 15 percent, then each school in the district should have a maximum of 55 percent black students and a minimum of 25 percent. A 1992 survey of desegregation plans conducted by the Department of Education found the following distribution in districts:

TABLE 7.1. Racial balance variation allowed in court orders

Variance allowed	Percentage of districts
None	18%
5% above or 5% below district average	09%
10% above or 10% below district average	12%
15% above or 15% below district average	24%
20% above or 20% below district average	28%
More than 20% above or below district average	10%

Source: Adapted from David J. Armor, *Forced Justice: School Desegregation and the Law* (New York: Oxford University Press, 1995), 160.

Most plans required student assignments to be modified as the district's demographics changed. The smaller the variation allowed, the more frequent the annual adjustments.

Some court orders—about one in ten—focused instead on reducing the number of predominantly black schools. For example, after the Supreme Court's decision in *Milliken*, district courts in St. Louis and Detroit tried to minimize the number of schools that were more than 50 percent black. Doing so in effect meant concentrating the remaining white students in a few schools, leaving the rest overwhelmingly minority. Other judges set more specific targets. Judge Garrity's plan for Boston specified that no school (except those in geographically isolated East Boston) could be more than 60 percent black or white. A more complex plan in Milwaukee set three initial targets: two-thirds of the city's schools would be 25–50 percent black; one-sixth 20–65 percent black; and one-sixth 15–75 percent black.[1] In the Wilmington, Delaware, case the court required all students to spend nine years in formerly white schools and three years in formerly black schools.[2] The Louisville, Kentucky, order required that the enrollment of all elementary schools be between 12 percent and 40 percent black; all secondary schools between 12.5 percent and 35 percent black.[3]

To achieve these goals, most desegregation plans initially relied on mandatory reassignments. These took many different forms: contiguous rezoning (in effect, gerrymandering attendance zones to produce greater racial balance); pairing/clustering (combining two or three schools with different racial characteristics and placing all students of the same age in the same school); and satellite zoning (placing noncontiguous areas with distinctive racial demographics in the same attendance zone). The extent of busing for each plan depended on the school district's geography and demography. These techniques were usually combined with an opportunity for voluntary "majority-to-minority transfers." That is, when seats were available, black students could transfer from majority-black to majority-white schools, and white students could transfer from majority-white to majority-black schools.[4]

Phase 2: Revisionism

Most school districts subject to judicial desegregation orders—even those in growing Sunbelt cities—faced the problem of declining white enrollment. This decline was in part the result of the broader demographic factors discussed previously, and in part the result of the "white flight" that followed most mandatory student-reassignment plans.[5] School officials were expected to revise attendance zones in accordance with the percentage-variance plans described above. Doing so meant that each year some students would be shifted to a new school. Frequent reassignments added to discontent among both black and white parents. Although the Supreme Court's decision in *Pasadena v. Spangler* seemed to limit federal judges' authority to order such revisions, the practice continued in most cities.

As the difficulty of avoiding predominantly minority schools increased, many school districts proposed major changes in their desegregation plans. These revisions usually combined magnet schools with an increase in the choices available to parents and their children. Magnet schools offer a specialty—science, computers, engineering, writing, the arts, theater, health care, even Greek and Roman history—with the promise of especially good training in these areas. Magnet schools are designed both to pull white, high socioeconomic status (SES) students into schools attended by minority students and to improve the quality of education for all students. They use "the carrot" rather than "the stick," as Christine Rossell, one of magnet schools' leading proponents, has put it.[6] Magnet schools are usually combined with "controlled choice" school assignment: students rank their choices; their choices are honored subject to availability of seats—and to an acceptable ratio of white to black students. The latter requirement sometimes means that for the most popular schools some seats remain empty while a number of students (often African Americans) remain on the waiting list. These restrictions have understandably been criticized by the parents of children denied their top choice.

Revisions proved to be as varied as the original orders. For example, in Wilmington and Dayton, judges allowed school districts to be broken down into three (Dayton) and four (Wilmington) subdistricts. Although individual schools would still be required to mirror the racial balance of each subdistrict, some of these subdistricts had a higher percentage of minority students than others. In Cleveland, Judge Battisti issued over five hundred separate orders between 1978 and 1992. After the school district experienced what he described as a "total fiscal and administrative collapse," he approved a new consent decree that increased the number of predominantly black schools.[7] Denver went through a long series of revisions that reflected not just the city's changing demographics, but also Hispanic leaders' push for more bilingual education and less busing.[8] This process led Denver superintendent James Scamman to complain that if the great Denver Broncos quarterback John Elway had faced such "moving goalposts," his famous touchdown drives wouldn't have succeeded either.[9]

Both the pressure for revision and the movement toward voluntary desegregation techniques are illustrated by developments in Mecklenburg County, the site of the *Swann* litigation. The Supreme Court approved Judge McMillan's ambitious plan in 1971. Within two years the judge found that his plan would be inadequate for "dealing with foreseeable problems," and he instructed the school district to design a new school-assignment plan. He approved the modified plan in 1974. The district continued to alter the assignment plan to prevent schools from becoming predominantly minority. White parents challenged these changes on the basis of *Pasadena v. Spangler*. In response, Judge McMillan pointed out that since the modifications had been made by the district, not the court, *Spangler* did not apply. In 1980 McMillan again modified his order, this time at the request of the district, to tolerate a few majority-minority schools. After that, the case became inactive for over a decade.

Meanwhile, the demographics of the district continued to change. As the region grew, more white families settled in previously rural areas far from the city of Charlotte, where minority families were concentrated. Complying with the 1971, 1974, and 1980 court orders became increasingly difficult as the proportion of minority students rose and the length of requisite bus rides increased. According to the judge who finally closed the case,

> by this time, the school board had 'institutionalized' the Court's racial balance guidelines such that the board was constantly adjusting boundaries, adding satellite zones, and reassigning students to different schools. This was a difficult process not just for the board members and the school staff but for the families who were required to send their children to different schools every couple of years.[10]

In 1992 the school board—by then considered one of the more reliably integrationist boards in the country—instituted a new "controlled choice" plan that relaxed mandatory reassignment rules and emphasized magnet schools. Each magnet school was to reflect the racial composition of the district as a whole: 40 percent black, 60 percent white. The district did not seek judicial approval of this major change, which was supported by both business and civil rights leaders in the county.

Although the new plan produced more predominantly minority schools, this time it was white parents who launched a legal challenge. They charged that the plan established racial quotas that had denied their children the opportunity to attend the magnet schools of their choice. Since schools under court order can (and often must) take race into account in assigning students to particular schools, the court was forced to decide whether after three decades of litigation and reform the district had achieved "unitary" status. The school board said "no": it had failed to achieve that goal. But the district court and the Fourth Circuit said "yes." They ruled that the school system was now "unitary," terminating the *Swann* desegregation orders and prohibiting the district from enforcing its 60/40 rule for magnet schools.

Phase 3: Beyond Black and White

The law of desegregation was developed to attack Jim Crow and its enduring vestiges. Before 1973 the Supreme Court did not hear any desegregation cases from outside the South. In 1970 the foreign-born percentage of the US population was at a twentieth-century low of 4.7 percent.[11] In southern states other than Texas and Florida, foreign-born residents were even rarer. As desegregation moved west and as immigration levels rose, judges were forced to wrestle with questions about how Mexican Americans, Chinese Americans, and many others fit into the desegregation equation.

The issue first rose to prominence in *Johnson v. San Francisco Unified School District*. San Francisco was ahead of the curve by having a substantial number of Hispanic and Asian students in its schools when the case was first litigated in 1970. Judge Stanley Weigel held that the Constitution requires the "desegregation of all races." Consequently, he required almost all schools to reflect the racial makeup of the entire district, with an allowable variance of plus or minus 15 percent. At the same time, he denied a motion to intervene filed by a lawyer representing Chinese parents who opposed the judge's order sending their children out of Chinatown. On this issue he was overturned by the Ninth Circuit.[12] Many of these parents responded to Weigel's desegregation order by enrolling their children in private "Freedom Schools." Eventually, the school district "tacitly exempted them from participation in the desegregation plan."[13]

A decade later, San Francisco's student population had become even more diverse: Anglos constituted only 17 percent of the student body; Chinese had risen to 20 percent, Hispanics to 17 percent, and African Americans to

23 percent; the remainder were Filipino (9 percent), Korean (1 percent), Japanese (1 percent), Native American (less than 1 percent), and a catchall "other non-white" at 12 percent. In 1983 Judge William Orrick approved a consent decree specifying that all San Francisco schools must include students from at least four of these nine groups, and that none of these groups should constitute more than 45 percent of the student population in any school. Despite years of negotiation, this arrangement did not please all the affected groups. Black parents in the isolated Hunters Point neighborhood objected to busing their children to more distant schools rather than improving the schools in their area. The Mexican American Legal Defense and Education Fund (MALDEF) complained that the consent decree did not pay sufficient attention to the special needs of Hispanic students. Judge Orrick responded that their "objection reflects a basic misunderstanding about the nature of this lawsuit and the objective of the Decree." This was a desegregation case, "*not* an action to establish an entitlement to a certain standard of academic excellence or to a right to certain programs to meet specific needs."[14] Efforts to "desegregate all races" proved increasingly challenging both administratively and politically.

Down the bay in San Jose, the number of African American students was tiny. There the desegregation case was initiated by Hispanic groups, not the NAACP. Their priority was improving the quality of education, not changing the racial balance in San Jose's schools. When Judge Robert Peckham's controlled choice/magnet schools plan went into effect in 1985, the district was 60 percent Anglo and 30 percent Hispanic. By 1992 the percentage of Anglo students had dropped to 30 percent, Hispanics had increased to 45 percent, and Asians reached 13 percent. By 2018 Anglos constituted only 24 percent of the student body, Hispanics 53 percent, and Asian and Pacific Islanders about 16 percent. As William Kolski and Jeannie Oakes explain in their perceptive case study, a series of agreements in the 1990s moved the litigation "away from ethnic balancing as the central meaning of equal educational opportunity and on to the creation of good neighborhood schools."[15] Especially for recent immigrants, this new focus meant above all helping their children learn English.

Demographic change complicated the desegregation equation in the South as well as the West. For example, in Dallas, white students outnumbered African Americans 58 percent to 33 percent in 1971, with only 8 percent Hispanic—promising numbers for racial integration. A decade later the numbers were Anglo 30 percent, African Americans 50 percent, and Hispanics 19 percent, with Hispanics projected to outnumber Anglos within five years.

Consequently, the judge in Dallas found little to be gained by distributing the declining number of white students in schools throughout the district. There were simply not "enough Anglo students to go around."[16] The NAACP generally agreed.

Nowhere was the role of Hispanic students, parents, and political leaders more prominent than in the long-running *Keyes* litigation. When desegregation first became an issue in Denver in 1967, the school population was 66 percent Anglo, 14 percent black, and 20 percent Hispanic. When court-ordered desegregation began a few years later, the Denver school system was already on its way to becoming predominantly Hispanic. By 1990, Hispanic students (39 percent) outnumbered Anglos (34 percent). A decade later Hispanic students constituted over half the student body, with Anglos and African Americans hovering around 20 percent each.[17] With their increasing numbers, Hispanic voters in Denver wielded significant clout, electing Federico Pena as the first Hispanic mayor of the city (1983–91). In his 1995 opinion finding the Denver system "unitary," Judge Matsch wrote,

> The Denver now before the court is very different from what it was when this lawsuit began. The current Mayor of Denver is Black. His predecessor was Hispanic. A Black woman has been Superintendent of Schools. Black and Hispanic men and women are in the city council, the school board, the state legislature and other political positions. . . . People of color are not bystanders. . . . Their voices will be heard in the Denver School system.[18]

For Matsch, this political change made continuing judicial supervision of the schools unnecessary.

If the Denver case demonstrates the potential for cross-racial political coalitions, it also illustrates the contrasting educational preferences of black and Hispanic voters. As Rachel Moran has noted, "prominent Hispanic activists in Denver strongly opposed integration at the outset of the [*Keyes*] case."[19] Throughout the extended litigation, Hispanic groups urged the judge to leave neighborhood schools intact, to focus on improving language instruction, and to hire more Hispanic teachers. Judge Doyle initially agreed, ordering reassignment of only a few Hispanic students. But the Supreme Court seemed to demand more extensive integration, and the Tenth Circuit held that bilingual education "is not a substitute for desegregation."[20] Nonetheless, bilingual education became a central component of the desegregation order. When the federal court oversight finally ended many years later, these programs persisted. "The ongoing commitment to bilingual programs," Moran writes, may be "the most lasting legacy of the case."[21]

Phase 4: The Shift to Educational Quality

For decades, the Supreme Court refused to address the relationship between racial balance and educational achievement. The justices seemed to assume that racial balance would significantly improve educational achievement by minority students—perhaps by equalizing tangible resources, more likely by mixing higher-SES white students with lower-SES black students. Initially, many trial judges endorsed the view that ending racial isolation would produce dramatic improvement in achievement by black students without harming white students. Unfortunately, even in school districts with a majority of white students, creating racially balanced schools did not come close to eliminating the racial achievement gap. Judges then had to decide whether to stick with the relatively well-defined goal of racial balance, or to shift their attention to reforms that promised to improve the educational achievement of minority students. Was racial balance the goal or a means to the end of equal educational opportunity?

In the first half of the 1970s, some judges dismissed as legally irrelevant the question of what policies were most likely to promote educational achievement. For example, in the Detroit case Judge Roth refused to allow the suburbs to present evidence claiming that a city-suburb busing plan was unlikely to improve the education of inner-city children: "Citation to such research ... misses the primary point: insofar as pupil assignments are concerned, the system of public schooling in every state must be run in a racially unified, nondiscriminatory fashion."[22] Responding to a district court judge who had argued that the busing plan for Nashville had proved counterproductive because it promoted white flight, disrupted students' lives, and drained financial resources, the Sixth Circuit chose to "remind the district court that the issue of achievement is irrelevant in a school system with a history of illegal segregation."[23]

Over time the educational effectiveness of desegregation orders became an issue judges could no longer avoid. What happens inside the classroom came to dominate negotiations over revisions. Reviewing the long history of the Wilmington, Delaware, litigation, Judge Sue Robinson wrote in 1995, "Most significantly, the focus of the relief has shifted from the desegregation process itself to the fact of a multicultural student body with varying educational problems."[24] As school quality replaced racial balance as the dominant issue, some judges sought to carry out wholesale restructuring of public school systems. Others decided that these were issues best left to politics and education experts.

It is not surprising that judges initially shied away from addressing the complex business of what goes on inside the schoolhouse. Not only had the Supreme Court stressed racial balance, but most judges recognized their limited familiarity with educational issues. Just as importantly, neither the NAACP nor other plaintiffs (including the Department of Justice) offered them much assistance. In their study of northern desegregation cases, Kirp and Babcock found that "when plaintiffs advanced a remedy at all, it spoke almost exclusively to the question of racial balance; questions of pedagogy and education programs on the one hand and community idiosyncrasy on the other at best received short shrift."[25] Even after it was clear that the district court would be forced to "desegregate" Detroit without bringing in white students from of the suburbs, the NAACP proposed no educational reforms—just greater busing within the city.[26]

Nonetheless, from the beginning a few judges had mandated changes in the internal operation of schools. Among them was Judge J. Skelly Wright, who curtailed the use of tracking and required the equalization of resources (especially experienced and specialty teachers) in the District of Columbia.[27] In Boston, Judge Garrity concluded that the city's entire public school system was inadequate. He rejected the NAACP's proposed plan because it failed to address the system's many flaws. The special master he appointed to formulate a remedial plan asked, "What the hell is the point in desegregation if there are no good schools?" Court-appointed experts proposed to remake the Boston system's administrative structure, revamp its special education and bilingual programs, and enlist local businesses and universities in an effort to improve educational quality. Although Garrity did not endorse all these changes, these experts convinced him to look beyond the reassignment of students.[28]

Much the same was true in Cleveland and Coney Island. During the remedial phase of the Cleveland litigation, Judge Battisti became alarmed at the "inferior education being meted out to those who were the victims of discrimination." As a result, the remedies he devised "addressed such educational policy concerns as educational testing, reading programs, counseling, extracurricular activities, and relations with universities, businesses and cultural institutions, as well as techniques of achieving a better racial mix."[29] In the Coney Island case, Judge Weinstein's remedial orders focused on turning the Mark Twain School into a high-quality magnet school that would attract both white and minority students.

One factor leading judges to pay more attention to what goes on inside school buildings was the Supreme Court's 1977 decision in *Milliken II*. There the Court held that the district court could require Detroit to establish—and the state of Michigan to help pay for—new magnet and vocational schools as well as "in-service training for teachers and administrators, guidance and counseling programs, and revised testing procedures." Such reforms, the Court claimed, would "restore the victims of discriminatory conduct to the position they would have enjoyed" had public officials not acted unconstitutionally. These changes might also "assure successful desegregation" and "minimize the possibility of resegregation."[30]

When Judge DeMascio took over the Detroit case after Judge Roth died, he saw educational reform as the only way to get out of the box in which the Supreme Court had placed him. In the words of Elwood Hain (who shared the NAACP's view that DeMascio was not aggressive enough in creating racially balanced schools), the court was "as enthusiastic about revitalizing the educational process as it was reluctant to desegregate it." The court "embraced most of the [school] board's proposed 'educational components,' drastically recast one and added one of its own."[31] DeMascio's education plan had nine components: reading; counseling and career guidance; bilingual education; vocational education; a uniform code of student conduct; school-community relations; in-service training; testing; and co-curricular activities.[32] He was especially committed to revamping the reading program, upgrading the vocational education program, and establishing a tougher school-discipline code. He ordered the state of Michigan to pay half the cost of this program, estimated to amount to about $400 million over the next decade. He also appointed a fifty-five-member Monitoring Commission to supervise the school district's implementation of the court-mandated initiatives. The commission frequently clashed with school administrators, who resented what they saw as its effort to micromanage school reform.[33]

The NAACP was never enthusiastic about DeMascio's emphasis on educational reform. In 1980 the Sixth Circuit noted that "bitter feelings" had developed between the judge and the plaintiff's lawyers.[34] Soon thereafter the chief judge for the eastern district of Michigan replaced DeMascio with a three-judge panel. That panel gradually wound down judicial oversight, approving termination in 1988. The member of the panel who played the largest role in winding up the case, Avern Cohn, later described his unease when trying to reshape education policy in Detroit. Judges, he confessed, are "frequently the last to know about the total environment in which a case exists. We only have, by and large, what the lawyers give us and generally in any particular case in court there is a much larger world surrounding it that we don't know very much about." He told an interviewer that "the court's thinking was that courts cannot perpetually keep it [the school district] under its authority." At some point the school district had to "walk on its own."[35] Judges who initiated education reforms with high hopes often left frustrated by the complexity of the task, the resistance from the school bureaucracy, the limits of their knowledge, and the paucity of measurable improvement.

Even in Wilmington, Delaware, the only city with court-ordered two-way urban-suburban busing, federal judges concluded that creating majority-white schools was not a sufficient remedy. The court's 1978 order specified eight elements of "ancillary relief."[36] In addition to familiar rules on the siting of new schools and the assignment of teachers, these items included:

1. "A comprehensive in-service training program for teachers, administrators, and other staff in order to train personnel to cope with the desegregation process."
2. "An affirmative reading and communication skills program . . . to remedy the effects of the past discrimination."
3. "Curriculum offerings and programs which emphasize and reflect the cultural pluralism of the students."
4. "An effective and nondiscriminatory counseling and guidance program . . . [that] insure[s] that students are counseled on a racially nondiscriminatory basis."
5. "An appropriate human relations" program designed "to protect the individual dignity of students and teachers and to prevent racial myths and stereotypes from prevailing in schools undergoing desegregation."
6. "A code of rights and responsibilities regarding such issues as student conduct and suspension and expulsion" that provides each student with "procedural and substantive due process required by existing law" and protects them "from unreasonable, discriminatory, and arbitrary rules."

Over the years the court often heard complaints about schools' failure to follow these guidelines. In 1990, it reprimanded one of the four subdistricts for tolerating racially skewed classrooms and "low minority achievement scores and college matriculation."[37] In 1995, though, the district court praised the overall performance of the school system and terminated judicial oversight. A year later the Third Circuit upheld that decision by a vote of 2–1.[38]

In the 1980s and 1990s many school districts proposed revisions to desegregation plans that combined relaxation of mandatory student-assignment rules with educational reform packages. Most of these revised plans included magnet schools, "controlled choice," increased spending (partially financed by state governments), and efforts to measure and boost student achievement. Asked to evaluate the adequacy of these proposals, judges tended to intersperse praise for the efforts of school boards with disappointment at the consequences of previous desegregation orders. For example, Judge Robert Krupansky argued that Cleveland's educational quality plan

> has received the enthusiastic support of the local community and has been endorsed by leading local scholars and educators and provides a blueprint for educational improvement... Scrapping this well-respected and accepted initiative in favor of demonstrated ineffective student assignments anchored in strict mathematical ratios is contrary to the admonition of Justice Kennedy that "[r]acial balance is not to be achieved for its own sake."

Krupansky noted that there was a sizable racial achievement gap "twenty years ago in Cleveland, ten years ago, and it remains to this day. Twenty years of transportation to achieve racial balance has not resulted in improved academic performance profiles." To make sure no one missed this point, he added, "it cannot be emphasized enough that transportation must be considered in the larger context of education, and the means of improving educational outcomes."[39]

When federal judges shifted emphasis from racial balance to educational quality, they did not always defer to the expertise of school boards and school administrators. Sometimes they relied on their own experts. The most dramatic example came in *Missouri v. Jenkins*, the long-running Kansas City desegregation suit. In no other case did educational quality loom so large. Judge Russell Clark explained that the "long term goal of this court's remedial order is to make available to *all* [Kansas City] students educational opportunity equal to or greater than those available" to the average student in suburban schools.[40] To accomplish this goal, Clark overhauled the entire school system, turning each city high school into a magnet school with a special theme, ranging from science and math to classical Greek, from visual and performing arts to agribusiness. By 1995 Kansas City was spending over $10,000 per student—more than any comparable school system in the country. The cost of these court-ordered reforms was about $2 billion, most of which came from the state of Missouri and the rest from tax increases mandated by the court. No other case so well illustrates the hazards of court-led educational reform.[41]

Missouri still segregated its schools in 1954. But Kansas City acted quickly to comply with *Brown*. In subsequent decades the black population expanded rapidly while whites moved to the suburbs. By the late 1970s nearly two-thirds of the students in the system were black. In 1975 HEW charged the Kansas City, Missouri, School District (KCMSD) with running a segregated system. The district responded by filing suit against the surrounding suburban school districts and the states of Missouri and Kansas, claiming that they had contributed to the racial isolation of city schools.

Although Judge Clark rejected the school district's argument, he did not throw out the suit. Rather, he realigned the school district as a defendant and appointed a new lawyer to represent a collection of KCMSD students who now became the official plaintiffs. The result was a three-way legal battle between the school district (which sought more financial assistance from the state), the state of Missouri (which funded most of the court' educational reforms), and the court-appointed lawyer for the recently named plaintiffs—who had his own vision for Kansas City schools.

As Joshua Dunn has convincingly shown, Clark did not become the $2 billion judge because he was a gung-ho advocate of desegregation or educational reform. Rather, the Eighth Circuit left him little choice. Its previous rulings in the St. Louis desegregation suit showed that it expected major efforts to combat racial isolation in the state's two largest school systems. The Eighth Circuit upheld Judge Clark's extensive reforms by a single vote: the minority expected him to go even further.

Clark found the school district guilty of unconstitutional segregation, but he refused either to order city-to-suburb busing (foreclosed by *Milliken*) or to use busing to spread around the city's few remaining white students (that, he believed, would merely accelerate white flight). Instead he instituted measures to improve dramatically the quality of education in Kansas City schools. This improvement, he hoped, would both pull white students back into city schools and provide the minority students left in those schools with the "equal educational opportunity" promised by *Brown*.

Despite all the money poured into the Kansas City school system, the court's plan never came close to working. Both the number of white students in city schools and the test scores of Kansas City students continued to decline. Judge Clark relied much too heavily on educational "experts" who had quickly thrown together the ambitious magnet-school plan. These education school professors made extravagant claims about the prospect for rapid improvement. Instituting their plans, they claimed, would raise Kansas City students' test scores to the national average within four or five years, and would draw in enough white students from the suburbs to make the school system 40 percent white.[42]

The judge repeatedly ignored the preferences and complaints of black parents whose children were the subject of his experiment. Many black parents objected to their children's long bus rides, and to the magnet schools' emphasis on exotic themes rather than on developing the basic skills so many of their children lacked. They were infuriated when the racial quotas established by the judge resulted in popular schools remaining under-enrolled while black children remained on waiting lists. When the black school superintendent, the black members of the school board, several dozen black pastors, and the local NAACP asked the court to institute a more modest magnet plan, they were rebuffed by Judge Clark.

To make matters worse, the school administrators who were handed this huge pile of money proved hopelessly incompetent and corrupt. Between 1969 and 1999 the school system went through twenty-one superintendents. The central staff ballooned: by 1990 the district spent less than half its budget on instruction. Eventually black parents—who had long opposed the court's emphasis on using magnet schools to draw whites back to the city—insisted upon a return to neighborhood schools.

Because *Missouri v. Jenkins* represented the most aggressive use of judicial authority since *Milliken*, it attracted the attention of the generally inattentive Supreme Court. The Court issued three separate rulings in the case, the most important of which came in 1995. The Eighth Circuit had announced that the KCMSD could not be declared "unitary" until the academic achievement of minority students improved significantly. Everyone recognized that this improvement would not happen soon. Until then, the appellate court ruled, the school district must remain under judicial supervision. In *Missouri v. Jenkins III*, a five-justice majority on the Supreme Court disagreed: achieving "unitary" status could not hinge on either increasing the "desegregative attractiveness" of urban schools or decreasing the black-white achievement gap.[43]

On remand, Judge Clark argued that even though the KCMSD could not be expected to eliminate the racial achievement gap, it could be required to eliminate that proportion of the gap attributable to unconstitutional segregation. He somehow calculated that proportion to be at least 26 percent. Clark then turned the case over to an "exit judge." Shortly thereafter the state's department of education stripped the district of its accreditation because its students were performing so poorly. This development led the replacement judge, Dean Whipple, to concede that the entire effort had been a failure: "Despite the expenditure of vast sums, the prolonged oversight of a federal court ... and the passage of forty years since the end of official *de jure* segregation in Kansas City, Missouri, the KCMSD still struggles to provide an adequate education to its pupils."[44]

After yet another round of litigation, Whipple ruled that the district had finally achieved unitary status. But not much had improved. The system continued to hemorrhage students as families both black and white left for the suburbs and private schools. Despite the influx of funding ordered by the court, in 2010 the KCMSD teetered on the verge of bankruptcy and was forced to close twenty-six schools.

Judicial Dilemmas

The most obvious takeaway from chapters 6 and 7 is the huge gap that separates the Supreme Court's abstractions and vague pronouncements from the complexities faced by district court judges in desegregation cases. In a country as large and diverse as the United States, school districts differ enormously in their composition, leadership, resources, and politics. Schools themselves are complex organizations that are difficult to control from the top or from outside. Moreover, the challenges facing public schools change over time. District court judges ignore these factors at their peril. They also face dilemmas never acknowledged by the Supreme Court, most importantly the extent to which steps to achieve racial balance can deprive schools of the political support and higher-SES students they need to improve educational opportunities for minority students.

A related theme is the weakness of hierarchical control within the federal judiciary. The Supreme Court hears few cases. Even during its flurry of desegregation activity from 1968 to 1979, it reviewed lower court decisions for only a few cities, and even in these cases it ignored crucial aspects of the district courts' orders. The circuit courts of appeal reviewed many more cases, but often disagreed among themselves. Only rarely would the Supreme Court resolve these conflicts.

Two factors added to the general weakness of hierarchical control within the judicial branch. One was the nature of the new form of "equitable remedies," the structural injunction. As its champions proclaim and its critics lament, the structural injunction lodges extensive power in the hands of trial judges who appoint experts and masters, supervise negotiations, sign off on lengthy orders and subsequent revisions, and monitor compliance. The other, obviously, was the ambiguity of Supreme Court doctrine documented in chapter 5.

This chapter has emphasized the untenable position in which district court judges were placed by the Supreme Court. On the one hand, the Court made it clear that it would not be enough for judges to stop school officials from engaging in discriminatory practices or to correct the most obvious and direct consequences of past discrimination. They were expected to eliminate "root and branch" all "vestiges" of "dual" school systems—which included not only every school district in the South, but almost every large school district in the country. Remedies that did not produce racial balance (of some sort) and reduce the number of predominantly black schools were unlikely to survive appellate review. On the other hand, the Court took away the one remedy capable of reducing "racial isolation" in many cities: city-to-suburb busing. As a result, achieving "racial balance" often meant a busing plan that inconvenienced minority students and drove away white families while leaving the schools majority black or Hispanic.

No longer linked to the larger goal of reducing racial isolation, the racial-balance requirement became a prime example of what students of bureaucracy call "goal displacement": the process by which a readily measurable means replaces the harder-to-measure objective it was originally designed to serve. Lower court judges faced a dilemma: should they choose a relatively simple remedy that might satisfy appellate courts (desegregation by the numbers); or should they take the riskier route of trying to improve educational opportunities for minority children—despite the fact that they had little understanding of how to accomplish this daunting feat?

Not surprisingly, this dilemma contributed to desegregation fatigue among the judges who had overseen desegregation orders for years, even decades. Most sought to broker a final deal among the parties to the litigation, and then be done with it. At the same time, many school constituencies were content with the status quo and reluctant to enter a new, supervision-free political world. Litigation over the termination of court orders highlighted just how far school systems were from providing equal educational opportunity to all their students. It also reignited the half-century-old debate over the meaning of "desegregation." That part of the desegregation story is the subject of the chapter that follows.

8

Termination without End

> The term 'unitary' does not have fixed meaning or content.
> JUSTICE KENNEDY, *Freeman v. Pitts*, 1992

When district court judges issued desegregation orders in the 1960s and 1970s, they gave little thought to how long those orders would remain in effect or how they would end. The task immediately before them was hard enough. Moreover, the structural injunction was an experiment borne of necessity, not a well-defined judicial tool. In most cities, initial court orders were followed by occasional adjustments and lengthy periods of judicial inaction. Only a few judges closed their desegregation cases in the 1980s, and even in those instances the status of their injunctions remained unclear. Toward the end of that decade the circuit courts began to address the question of when a school system can be declared "unitary." But they could not agree on key issues. Between 1991 and 1995 the Supreme Court handed down three opinions designed to resolve conflicts among the circuits. Although the Court noted that "the lower courts have been inconsistent in their use of the term 'unitary,'" it made little effort to explain when a "dual" school system had become "unitary." Once again the Court handed the hardest decisions over to district court judges.

Far from a technical matter, the determination of when a school system has achieved "unitary status" raises basic questions about the objectives of the entire desegregation effort. According to the "color-blind/limited intervention" position described in chapter 2, the extraordinary measures taken by the federal government to desegregate public schools should be temporary and designed to remedy specific measures taken by school officials to maintain racially segregated schools. If a school district has taken action—either overt or subtle—that produces racially identifiable schools, then it must adopt countermeasures to remove that racial identification. If for a decade or more the district has distributed students, teachers, and resources evenly across its many schools; if there is no substantial record of subsequent racial discrimination within these schools; and if new schools have been sited in a manner that promotes integration, then it is hard to see how any of these schools remains racially identifiable as the term was first used in *Green*. As successive generations of students cycle through these schools, any lingering stigma associated with formerly black schools would fade, leaving "just schools." At that point, the school district could be freed from judicial oversight and allowed to use any nonracial method for assigning students to schools—which usually means reverting to neighborhood schools. The fact that this reversion will often produce some schools that are predominantly minority should not prevent a "unitary" determination: that outcome is not the product of action by the school district, but of a complex mixture of economics, government action in the distant past, and private choice. To maintain judicial supervision until racial groups are distributed randomly across the district is to abandon the presumption that desegregation orders are temporary measures to address specific unconstitutional actions.

According to the "racial isolation/equal educational opportunity" framework, in contrast, the federal government has an obligation to eliminate *all* the lingering effects of past discrimination by *all* arms of government. Given the profound and lasting effects of slavery, Jim Crow, and many other forms of discriminatory behavior, we should not expect this effort to end within a few decades. The ultimate goal is equal educational opportunity. Minimizing the number of predominantly minority schools is one step in that direction, but far from the only one. Others include targeting more resources to schools with large numbers of poor and minority students; assigning more experienced teachers to these schools; ensuring that minority children are not disciplined more harshly than white students or assigned more frequently to special education; providing high-quality programs for English learners; expanding kindergarten and pre-K programs for disadvantaged children; and in general searching aggressively for reforms that promise to reduce the racial achievement gap. Courts should both prevent schools from reflecting the racial skew one finds in most urban neighborhoods, and spur them to place high priority on the needs of racial minorities. Under this understanding, "unitary status" becomes a distant goal and the structural injunction close to permanent.

One can find support for both these positions in the opinions issued by the Supreme Court between 1968 and 1979. When the Supreme Court briefly reentered the picture between 1991 and 1995, it again refused to endorse either view. Despite the weight the Court continued to place on the terms "unitary" and "dual," it cavalierly swatted away requests for clarification: "We are not sure how useful it is to define these terms more precisely."[1] While a bare majority on the Court seemed to indicate its preference for a more limited judicial role, in the end the Court said very little—which is one reason why so few school districts were released from court orders during the 1990s.

This chapter is divided into four parts. The first summarizes the Supreme Court's decisions on when school districts can be granted "unitary status." The second looks at how the lower courts have responded to these decisions. The third examines the extent to which these court decisions have promoted "resegregation." The fourth asks what we know about how termination of court orders has affected the academic achievement of minority students.

The Supreme Court: Still Hazy After All These Years

By 1990 most of the desegregation orders issued over the preceding three decades remained in effect. As the previous chapter explained, some had been revised to emphasize magnet schools and "controlled choice" rather than mandatory busing. Many cases remained inactive for long stretches. The Fourth Circuit upheld a few district court decisions finding school districts

---

BOX 8.1 Voting and Opinions in the Supreme Court's Termination Cases

Board of Education of Oklahoma City v. Dowell (1991), 5–3
Majority: Rehnquist, White, O'Connor, Scalia, and Kennedy
Dissent: Marshall, Blackmun, and Stevens
    (Souter did not participate)

Freeman v. Pitts (1992), 5–3
Majority: Kennedy, Rehnquist, White, Scalia, and Souter
    Scalia wrote a concurring opinion
    Souter wrote a concurring opinion
Concurring in judgment only: Blackmun, Stevens, and O'Connor
    (Thomas did not participate)

Missouri v. Jenkins III (1995), 5–4
Majority: Rehnquist, O'Connor, Scalia, Kennedy, and Thomas
    O'Connor wrote a concurring opinion
    Thomas wrote a concurring opinion
Dissent: Souter, Ginsburg, Breyer, and Stevens

Underlining indicates that the justice wrote an opinion

"unitary." The Eighth, Tenth, and Eleventh Circuits set a higher bar for termination of desegregation orders. In *Board of Education of Oklahoma City v. Dowell* (1991), *Freeman v. Pitts* (1992), and *Missouri v. Jenkins III* (1995), the Court attempted to explain the standards for ending judicial supervision.

These three cases are often portrayed as examples of the Rehnquist Court's retreat on civil rights and its weakening of remedies for constitutional violations. That account is incorrect on two counts. First, since the Court had been so divided and so ambiguous for so many years, it is impossible to identify a clear position from which it could retreat. Second, the Court's vague language in these cases reflected rather than resolved the competing understandings of "desegregation" described above. Instead of defining crucial terms, the Court strung together yet another string of platitudes. As Monika Moore pointed out in a perceptive *Yale Law Journal* article, the Court "has not provided the lower courts with any concrete standards to help them decide when they should release school districts from supervision."[2] The biggest effect of the three decisions was to shift power from circuit courts, which had tended to oppose efforts to terminate desegregation orders, to trial judges, some of whom had grown weary of periodically reviewing decades-old rulings.

In the twelve years that separated the Court's final attempt to define "desegregation" (*Columbus*, in 1979) from its first termination decision (*Dowell*, in 1991) its membership had changed without shifting its basic divisions on desegregation. Justices O'Connor, Scalia, Kennedy, and Souter had replaced Stewart, Burger, Powell, and Brennan, respectively. The only major change came in 1991, when Justice Thomas replaced Justice Marshall. Justice Marshall wrote an impassioned dissent in *Dowell*, the last desegregation case in which he participated. Justice Thomas's concurring opinion in *Missouri v. Jenkins* three years later presented an understanding of desegregation far different from that of his predecessor. One might have thought that the bloc sometimes known as the Federalist Five (Rehnquist, Scalia, O'Connor, Kennedy, and Thomas) would take further steps to limit the lower courts' supervision of school systems. But they did not. After 1995, the Court never said another word about the termination of desegregation orders. Once again, its efforts to clarify desegregation law largely failed.

OKLAHOMA CITY V. DOWELL

The 1991 *Dowell* case grew out of a disagreement between the Tenth Circuit and a district court judge over the status of Oklahoma City's desegregation plan. In 1972 the district court had established a busing plan to comply with the Court's *Swann* decision. Five years later that court ruled that the school district had achieved "unitary" status. It terminated the case; no one appealed its decision. In 1984 the school district sought to return grades 1–4 to neighborhood schools, arguing that demographic change required inner-city students to spend too much time on the bus. (Under the new plan busing would continue for grades 5–12.) The district court agreed, finding that the school district had complied in good faith for over a decade, and had done nothing to promote either school or residential segregation for a quarter of a century. All "vestiges" of segregation, the court claimed, had been eliminated.

The Tenth Circuit disagreed, claiming that "an injunction takes on a life of its own, and becomes an edict quite independent of the law it is meant to effectuate." Upon remand, the district court again found that the district had achieved unitary status. Again the Tenth Circuit reversed. The original order, it argued, required the school district to *maintain* racially balanced schools, something the district's revised plan clearly would not do. The appellate court placed a heavy burden on the school system to show why the court should approve a revision of the 1972 injunction: modification "requires nothing less than a clear showing of grievous wrong evoked by new and unforeseen circumstances." The school district "must demonstrate dramatic changes in conditions unforeseen at the time of the decree" that "impose extreme and unexpectedly oppressive hardship."[3] Not only would this burden of proof make it nearly impossible to terminate any desegregation order, it called into question the many revisions routinely approved by district court judges over the preceding decades. Its *Dowell* decision placed the Tenth Circuit at odds with the First, Fourth, and Ninth Circuits.[4]

This split in the circuits led the Supreme Court to reenter the field after more than a decade of silence. Writing for a five-justice majority, Chief Justice Rehnquist rejected the "test espoused by the Court of Appeals," which "would condemn a school district" that had once engaged in illegal segregation to "judicial tutelage for the indefinite future." Federal judges should show more respect for local control of education. But the chief justice's short, bland decision did little to establish a more adequate test. He acknowledged that "the lower courts have been inconsistent in their use of the term 'unitary,'" and that a school board is "entitled to a rather precise statement of its obligations under a desegregation decree." It would be "a mistake," he argued, "to treat words such as 'dual' and 'unitary' as if they were actually found in the Constitution."[5] Rather than provide the "precise standards" he promised, Rehnquist merely indicated that district courts should have substantial discretion to determine when school districts have adequately complied with court orders "in good faith." Beyond that he would not go. Judicial supervision should stop at some point, but since the Court could not specify what constitutes a "unitary" system, it could not say where that point was.

Dowell is best known not for what the majority held, but for what Justice Thurgood Marshall wrote in his spirited dissent. Here he offered an extensive defense of the "racial isolation/equal educational opportunity" understanding of desegregation described in chapter 2. Marshall decried the "particular social harm that racially segregated schools inflict on Afro-American children" as "stigmatic injury," "the message of racial inferiority implicit in the former policy of state-enforced segregation." Since the "reemergence of racial separation" in one-race schools "may revive" that message, such schools should be considered a "vestige" of segregation that must be eliminated. It is no excuse to say that one-race schools are the result of housing segregation, given "the roles of the State, local officials and the Board in creating what are now self-perpetuating patterns of residential segregation."[6]

Marshall's sweeping understanding of the "vestiges" of segregation did not end there. It "extends to *any condition* that is likely to convey the message of inferiority." It is not enough that the district itself had long ago stopped discriminating: "Our school desegregation jurisprudence establishes that the *effects* of past discrimination remain chargeable to the school district regardless of its lack of continued enforcement of segregation, and that the remedial decree is required until those effects have been finally eliminated." Appropriate remedies include "remedial education programs and other measures to redress the substandard communication skills of Afro-American students formerly placed in segregated schools." Since "predominately minority public schools typically receive fewer resources than other schools in the same district," courts must continue to monitor the distribution of teachers and money. "Indeed, the poor quality of a system's schools may be so severe that nothing short of a *radical transformation* of the schools within the system will suffice to achieve desegregation and eliminate all of its vestiges." (For this proposition Justice Marshall cites the Kansas City case described in the previous chapter.) Before terminating desegregation cases, judges must be convinced that "the stigmatic harm identified in *Brown* will not recur upon lifting the decree. Any doubt on the issue . . . should be resolved in favor of the Afro-American children affected by this litigation."[7]

Although the Supreme Court had "never contemplated perpetual judicial oversight" of schools subject to desegregation orders, Marshall rejected "the majority's suggestion that the length of federal supervision is a valid factor in assessing a dissolution."[8] The implication of his dissent was that courts must continue to adjust their decrees in order to eliminate racially identifiable schools as long as racial prejudice persists—which is likely to be as long as any of us remain alive. Justices Stevens and Blackmun joined Marshall's dissent.

FREEMAN V. PITTS

The following year the Court took another stab at explaining when lower courts can terminate desegregation decrees. Once again, a district court had tried to end a case, only to be reversed by a circuit court, this time the Eleventh. And again the Supreme Court held that the circuit court had imposed too many restrictions on the trial court. This time the Court was more candid in conceding that the term "unitary" has no "fixed meaning or content"—quite an admission for a Court that had put so much weight on the term since 1968.

Freeman v. Pitts raised important questions about the responsibility of school districts to respond to demographic change. The schools in DeKalb County, Georgia, had been legally segregated until 1969. Ordered by the court to dismantle its dual school system, the County closed its formerly black schools and assigned all students to neighborhood schools. Initially this action produced schools that were all majority white—an easy task in a district where fewer than 6 percent of the students were African American. But as large numbers of black families moved to southern DeKalb County from nearby Atlanta and many whites moved to northern parts of the County, schools in the south became predominantly black and those in the north predominantly white. The school district tried to mitigate the impact of these demographic changes by adjusting school-assignment zones and building new schools in the center of the county. But these measures were not sufficient to produce schools that reflected the racial composition of the county as a whole.

In 1986 the district court held that the school district had complied with four of the so-called "*Green* factors": transportation, extracurricular activities, physical facilities, and, most importantly, student assignment. But it also ruled that "vestiges of the dual system" remained in the areas of teacher assignment and resource allocation, as well as in a factor not mentioned in *Green*: quality of education. The court found the system "unitary" in regard to the first four factors and confined its supervision to the other three.

Twice the Eleventh Circuit reversed. It first held that a district could not be released incrementally from a desegregation order. To achieve unitary status, a court must find that the district has satisfied all six *Green* factors for at least three years. More importantly, the appellate court rejected the district court's refusal to require the school system "to eradicate segregation caused by demographic changes." Until the school district is deemed "unitary" in *all* respects, it must adjust school-assignment practices to compensate for the demographic change experienced by DeKalb County. Such adjustments might require actions that are "administratively awkward, inconvenient, or even bizarre in some situations"—including, most notably, extensive busing.[9]

Justice Kennedy's opinion in *Freeman v. Pitts* was more specific and more biting than the chief justice's opinion in *Dowell*. But only four members of the Court agreed with his standards for terminating desegregation decrees. Four others agreed that the case should be sent back to the lower courts for much different reasons. The concurring opinions of Justices Souter and Blackmun rejected Kennedy's central arguments. With the Court so closely divided, it was clear that the Court's newest member, Clarence Thomas, who did not participate in *Freeman v. Pitts*, would play a pivotal role in the future.

Conceding that "the term 'unitary' is not a precise concept," Justice Kennedy warned lower courts "not to attribute to the term a utility it does not have."[10] Rather than specify what "unitary" does mean, he harkened back to the Court's *Spangler* and *Dayton I* decisions to make three points. The first was that in desegregation cases the judge "has the discretion to order an incremental or partial withdrawal of its supervision and control." Because "the authority of the court is invoked at the outset to remedy *particular* constitutional violations," judicial authority evaporates once those violations are remedied.[11] None of the justices disagreed with this assertion.

Second and more controversially, Kennedy emphasized that judicial supervision of schools was "intended to be a temporary measure," and that "returning schools to the control of local authorities at the earliest practical date is essential to restore their true accountability in our governmental system." Partial release provides "a transition phase in which control is relinquished in a gradual way."[12]

Third, Kennedy insisted that racial balance "is not to be achieved for its own sake," but pursued only "when racial imbalance has been caused by a constitutional violation." School districts are "under no duty to remedy imbalance that is caused by demographic factors":

> When resegregation is a product not of state action but of private choices, it does not have constitutional implications. It is beyond the authority and beyond the practical ability of the federal courts to try to counteract these kinds of continuous and massive demographic shifts. To attempt such results would require ongoing and never ending supervision by the courts of school districts simply because they were once *de jure* segregated.[13]

Kennedy conceded that "vestiges of past segregation by state decree" remain "stubborn facts of history" that "linger and persist." In his characteristically oblique manner, he added that "though we cannot escape our history, neither must we overstate its consequences in fixing legal responsibility.... It is simply not always the case that demographic forces causing population change bear any real and substantial relation to a *de jure* violation. And the law need not proceed on that premise."[14]

In many other race-related cases, Justice Kennedy tried to find a middle ground between the Court's liberals and conservatives. But here he provided the clearest explanation of the position of those who sought to limit the role of the courts in desegregation cases.

The four concurring justices likewise made no attempt to define "unitary status" or to contest Kennedy's arguments about the wisdom of eventually returning control of schools to local government. Instead, they took issue with Kennedy's assumption that one can easily separate demographic change from the choices made by school officials, and they placed a heavy burden of proof on schools wishing to free themselves from court supervision. Justice Blackmun would require the lower courts to engage in exactly the type of sociopolitical investigation that Kennedy seemed intent upon foreclosing. "It is not enough," Blackmun maintained, for a school district "to establish that demographics exacerbated the problem; it must *prove* that its own policies did *not contribute*" to racial imbalance.[15] The district court recognized that "what might seem to be purely private preferences in housing may in fact have been created, in part, by actions of the school district." In this case, the way the school district assigned teachers and principal to particular schools "may have contributed to the demographic shift." It "could have started and expanded" several programs that promised to further integration. "But it did not."[16] Therefore, it had not carried the heavy burden of proving that its system was now "unitary."

Never one to let ambiguities and evasions pass unnoticed, Justice Scalia's concurrence pointed out how little guidance the Court had offered lower court judges and how much now rested on where courts placed the burden of proof. The Court, he charged, had never managed "to describe how one identifies a condition as the effluent of a violation, or how a 'vestige' or a 'remnant' of past discrimination is to be recognized." According to the Court's tangled jurisprudence, once a school district has been found guilty of segregation, "there arises a presumption, effectively irrebuttable (because the school district cannot prove the negative) that any current racial imbalance is the product of that violation."[17] At the time it was first established, Scalia conceded, this presumption was "extraordinary in law but not unreasonable in fact," given the ferocity of opposition to desegregation in many districts and the heavy burden "freedom of choice" plans placed on black families. "But granting the merits of this approach at the time of *Green*, it is now 25 years later." "We must acknowledge that it has become absurd to assume, without further proof, that violations of the Constitution dating from the days when Lyndon Johnson was President, or earlier, continue to have an appreciable effect upon current operation of schools." More than two decades after *Green* and *Swann*, Scalia insisted, it was "time for us to abandon our studied disregard of that obvious truth, and to adjust our jurisprudence to its reality." The Court should "revert to the ordinary principles of our law, of our democratic heritage, and of our educational tradition" by terminating cases where there has been no clear evidence of intentional racial discrimination by public officials.[18]

MISSOURI V. JENKINS

The Supreme Court's third effort to explain when a school system has achieved "unitary status" came in 1995, when it reviewed the Kansas City, Missouri, case described at the end of chapter 7. Because the facts of the Kansas City case were so unusual, five members of the Court (this time including Justice Thomas) could agree that some of the goals set by the lower courts were excessive. By the same token, because the remedial decree was so extraordinary, the limits set by the Supreme Court in *Missouri v. Jenkins III* affected few other school districts.

Chief Justice Rehnquist's majority opinion took aim at the two arguments used to justify the extensive remedies deployed in Kansas City. Judge Clark had based several elements of his plan, particularly the large number of magnet schools and the significant increase in teachers' pay, on the claim that they would increase the "desegregative attractiveness" of Kansas City schools. In other words, if you build new and improved urban schools, white children will come (especially if you provide them with free door-to-door taxi service from the suburbs, as Judge Clark's decree did). The Supreme Court held that federal judges could not use this rationale for ordering school districts to spend large sums of money on new school buildings and generous teacher contracts. Since there had been no finding that the city or the state had taken actions that drove white families to the suburbs, it was not the responsibility of the city or the state to lure them back. The "desegregative attractiveness" argument, Rehnquist suggested, was little more than a ploy to allow trial courts to circumvent "the limit on its remedial authority" imposed by the Court in *Milliken*. The "desegregative attractiveness" argument creates "too many imponderables," and is "so far removed from the task of eliminating the racial identifiability of the schools" that it lies "beyond the admittedly broad discretion of the District Court."[19]

The second argument rejected by the Supreme Court was that the district court must continue to supervise school districts as long as the achievement of minority students remained "at or below national norms at many grade levels." This novel claim, added at the last moment by the Eighth Circuit, implied that the less effective the court order, the longer it would remain in effect. According to Rehnquist, the "basic task" of federal courts is more limited: "to decide whether the reduction in achievement by minority students attributable to prior *de jure* segregation has been remedied to the extent practicable."[20] Rehnquist failed to note that both parts of his preferred test—the extent to which minority achievement had been reduced by prior discrimination and how much improvement is "practicable"—are nearly impossible to gauge.

The four dissenters pointed out that the Court had left plenty of room for lower courts both to retain jurisdiction over desegregation cases and to demand major educational reform and new spending. *Milliken II* had authorized district courts to mandate compensatory programs to "make whole" the students who had suffered from segregation and its vestiges. There is little difference between school improvements designed to increase "desegregative attractiveness" and those designed to compensate minority students for the lingering effects of segregation. As Justice Souter noted, "test scores will clearly be relevant in determining whether the improvement programs have cured a deficiency in student achievement to the practicable extent."[21] The "significance of scores" is the type of judgment that should be left to trial judges. Since Judge Clark had justified the salary hike for teachers "by reference to the quality of education alone," there was nothing in the majority opinion that "precludes those orders from remaining in effect."[22] In other words, by avoiding the arguments rejected by the Court in *Missouri v. Jenkins III* and relying instead on the language of *Green, Swann,* and *Milliken II,* lower courts can continue doing whatever they had been doing for as long as they want.

The three decisions of the early 1990s revealed deep, continuing divisions within the Court on the meaning of desegregation and the appropriate role of the federal judiciary. The Court limited the authority of district court judges to transform an entire school system as Judge Clark had attempted to do in Kansas City. But in light of the dismal results in that city, few judges were eager to go down that road anyway. District court judges retained broad authority to determine what constitutes a "vestige" of previous segregation, and now had the Court's permission to release school districts gradually from judicial supervision. The most important effect of these three decisions was to reduce the power of those circuit courts that had set a particularly high bar for school districts seeking release from court supervision.

The Diversity of "Unitary" Findings

Critics of the *Dowell, Freeman v. Pitts,* and *Missouri v. Jenkins* decisions charged that the Rehnquist Court was responsible for the "resegregation" of public schools. In 1996, Gary Orfield and Susan Eaton described these decisions as "a triumph for the decades-long powerful, politicized attacks on school desegregation" and "a victory for the conservative movement" that "turned the nation from the dream of *Brown* toward accepting a return to segregation."[23] Four years later, the NAACP Legal Defense Fund warned, "When there are findings of unitary status, as in Oklahoma City and Norfolk, resegregation has become the rule."[24] Orfield told the *Washington Post*, "We are losing many of the gains of desegregation. We are not back to where we were before *Brown*, but we are back to when King was assassinated [in 1968]."[25]

These pessimistic assessments are based on three assertions: (1) that the Supreme Court decisions led to an increase in "unitary" determinations by the lower courts; (2) that the release of so many school districts from court supervision led in turn to a significant burst of "resegregation"; and (3) that such "resegregation" has reduced the educational opportunities of minority students. The remainder of this chapter assesses these claims. The bottom line: (1) and (2) are incorrect; (3) is extremely hard to determine because we know so little about the long-term effects of various forms of desegregation.

THE TIMING OF TERMINATIONS

When researchers began to examine the frequency of "unitary" findings, they faced a daunting problem: because the litigation process had been so ad hoc and decentralized, no one knew how many school districts remained subject to desegregation plans. The Department of Education's biannual *Civil Rights Data Collection* reports demonstrate the confusion that surrounds this seemingly simple issue. In 2011–12, 1,200 school districts reported that they were operating under a desegregation plan. In 2013–14, this number dropped precipitously to 171. But two years later it doubled to 334. The *Education Week* article reporting on these perplexing statistics found that "the majority of districts reporting that they were in desegregation order or plans did so only once. Fewer districts reported that they were in them for all three years, and still fewer reported being in them for two years." Apparently, the school officials filling out these reports sometimes remembered they were subject to a desegregation plan, and sometimes forgot. After speaking to a variety of officials in both the Department of Education and the Department of Justice, the reporters concluded, "It's not clear that anyone—including federal education officials—can provide a clear answer to why those numbers have changed."[26]

In 2014 journalists at ProPublica spent months combing court records and calling school officials to discover the status of desegregation orders. They concluded that

> officials in scores of school districts do not know the status of their desegregation orders, have never read them, or erroneously believe that orders have been ended. In many cases orders have gone unmonitored, sometime for decades, by the federal agencies charged with enforcing them.

Moreover, "some federal courts don't even know how many desegregation orders still exist on their dockets."[27]

What we do know about the status of desegregation orders must be pieced together from several sources. In 2006 the US Commission on Civil Rights compiled detailed information on the number of southern school systems that had been released from supervision and the number still subject to court orders. Several other government agencies and scholars updated this list and added data from outside the South. The American Communities Project at Brown subsequently compiled a database of all known desegregation orders and their history. Relying on the data compiled by Reardon, the Commission on Civil Rights, the Brown project, and ProPublica, Rucker Johnson has provided the estimates of schools released from desegregation orders found in figure 8.1.

As figure 8.1 indicates, until the late 1990s, terminations remained rare. By 1990 about 1,100 school districts remained subject to court orders. Terminations seldom rose above five per year, almost all in the South. (The large number of northern districts attaining unitary status in 1998 is an anomaly; it reflects the fact that twenty-one districts in Indiana were released simultaneously as part of a thirteen-year phase-out plan.[28]) According to statistics compiled by the Commission on Civil Rights, of the 480 southern schools for which the DOJ had records in 2006, thirty-two were released in the 1970s, seventeen in the 1980s, and twenty-two in the 1990s.[29] These figures indicate that the Supreme Court's decisions on unitary status had little immediate effect.

Law professor Wendy Parker's investigation of court orders in the deep South from 1983 through 1999 provides further evidence that the Supreme Court's termination rulings had little initial impact. From 1983 through 1991 (the year *Dowell* was handed down), district courts in those states issued eighteen rulings on unitary status. Seventeen of these had been requested by the school district, one initiated by the court. In eleven of these cases

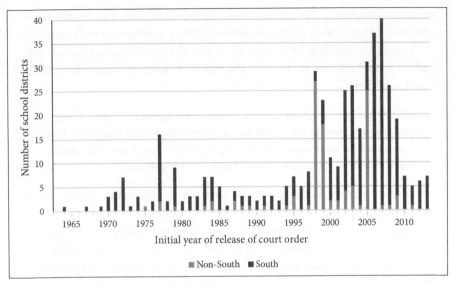

FIGURE 8.1. Dates of release from desegregation orders
Source: Rucker C. Johnson with Alexander Nazaryan, *Children of the Dream: Why School Integration Works* (New York: Basic Books, 2019), 207.

(61 percent), the district was found "unitary"; in seven (39 percent) the request was denied. In the eight years following *Dowell* only eight school districts requested termination of their court orders; in four other cases the district courts raised the issue *sua sponte*. Of these twelve, eight (67 percent) were granted and four (33 percent) rejected—little different from the success rate prior to *Dowell*, *Freeman v. Pitts*, and *Missouri v. Jenkins*. Moreover, in the six years following the Court's decision in *Freeman v. Pitts*, Parker found only a single instance where a district was granted partial unitary status. In short, as of the year 2000, "*Dowell* has *not* led to an increase in the number of school districts seeking or granted unitary status. Rather, the overall numbers actually dropped. Nor has *Freeman* resulted in many school districts attaining partial unitary status."[30]

WHO INITIATED TERMINATION?

Why did these Supreme Court decisions have such limited effect during the 1990s? The major reason, Parker shows, is that school districts were "largely unwilling to seek unitary status." In part this reluctance reflects the cost of litigation. Why pay lawyers to terminate orders that "may compel little that the school district finds adverse" or "may even be easily ignored"? Moreover, the divisiveness of school desegregation issues may make school districts hesitant to seek unitary status. Because the resurrection of dormant desegregation issues might lead to community unrest, a school district may appreciate the political cover provided by outstanding remedial orders. Court orders may provide the school districts with additional funding ... Even with the benefit of the pro-defendant stance of the Supreme Court, the outcome of any unitary status petition is still uncertain. School districts may prefer the known condition (i.e. the outstanding remedial order) to the unknown outcome of unitary status proceedings, which could impose new obligations or lead to closer judicial scrutiny.[31]

As we saw in the preceding chapter, many school officials had become comfortable with life under judicial supervision, finding it convenient to use court orders to justify their regular way of doing business.

In 2007 the Supreme Court gave school districts yet another reason to remain under court supervision. In *Parents Involved in Community Schools v. Seattle School District No. 1*, it held that unless a school district is subject to a remedial order, it cannot use race to assign students to particular schools.[32] One of the school districts in the case, Louisville, Kentucky, had been found "unitary" in 2000. Thereafter, Louisville voluntarily established a maximum (50 percent) and a minimum (15 percent) for black student enrollment in all schools. By a 5-4 vote the Court ruled that once Louisville had been declared "unitary" it could not voluntarily employ the type of race-based student-assignment plans it had previously been required to use. Consequently, school officials who support efforts to maintain racial balance thus have strong incentives to oppose unitary status. In Charlotte-Mecklenburg, for example, private litigants asked the court to terminate the desegregation order; the school district argued that the order should remain in effect. Like the desegregation orders themselves, efforts to terminate them depended heavily on local circumstances.

The second major trend evident in figure 8.1 is the upswing in terminations that began in the late 1990s and continued though the early years of the first decade of the 2000s. Reardon's figures show that of the nation's 483 large school districts (those with more than two thousand students) under court order in 1990, 215 (45 percent) had been released by 2009. Most of the released districts were in the South.[33] Examining the one hundred biggest cities in southern and border states, Clotfelter, Vigdor, and Ladd found that from 1993 to 1999 "the fraction of districts deemed unitary, weighted by enrollment, increased gradually, from about 12% to just over 20%." But "starting in 1999 and continuing over the next three years, the rate of growth increased markedly, with the (weighted) share of districts with unitary status increasing from just over 20% to 45%."[34]

What accounts for this acceleration? What do we know about the characteristics of the districts declared "unitary" and those remaining under judicial supervision? The answers to these questions, as usual, are complicated, reflecting local circumstances more than directives from the center. As Reardon et al. put it, "the timing of release is ultimately marked by 'an element of randomness.'"[35] They found few "differences between districts that were released from court orders between 1990 and 2009 and those that remained under order."[36] Large districts were somewhat more likely to request unitary status, but less likely to have their orders terminated.

Several factors contributed to the increase in terminations around the turn of the century. One was heightened review of desegregation orders by the Department of Justice. This trend began in the final year of the Clinton administration and gathered steam in the Bush administration. The DOJ took a more active role in advising districts that they were eligible for unitary status and joining them in requesting dismissal of desegregation orders.[37]

Second, Parker notes that "judges seemed exhausted from the decades-long effort and anxious to terminate their jurisdiction."[38] They frequently urged the parties to reach a deal. Some appointed special masters or mediators to facilitate negotiations. As a result, unitary status often came "with strings attached": more money for predominantly minority schools; expansion of magnet schools and "controlled choice" student-assignment plans; and within-school reforms designed to improve student performance and address discriminatory discipline and tracking. In Nashville-Davidson County, Tennessee, for example, the agreement allowed children to choose either neighborhood or magnet schools, but also required the district to spend $200 million over the next five years to construct and renovate schools in predominantly black neighborhoods. Lee County, Florida, was declared unitary in 1999, but agreed to keep all schools within 20 percent of the district's black-white distribution for at least five years. Pinellas County, Florida; Fulton County, Georgia; and East Baton Rouge, Louisiana, also combined a gradual phase-out of student-assignment plans with promises of further educational reform.[39]

As varied as these negotiated settlements were, they all reflected the sentiments expressed by the judges who granted unitary status to the Cleveland, Wilmington, and St. Louis school districts. According to Judge Robert Krupansky, "the importance of outdated policies to impose strict racial balancing continues to diminish as the age of state-imposed or de jure segregation recedes into the past."[40] Ending the Wilmington, Delaware, case, Judge Sue

Robinson wrote, "Most significantly, the focus of the relief has shifted from the desegregation process itself to the fact of a multicultural student body with varying educational problems."[41] Addressing these problems, she suggested, is a job for educators, not judges. In the St. Louis case Judge Stephen Limbaugh maintained that judges "are ill-equipped to implement [reforms], especially in fields such as education where judges have no expertise."[42]

Although most judges relied on the parties before them to negotiate a settlement, two district court judges in Alabama played much more active roles. Chief Judge Myron Thompson (who became the second African American judge to sit on the federal bench in Alabama when President Carter nominated him to replace the celebrated Frank Johnson) and his successor as chief judge, W. Harold Albritton III, required all of the thirty-eight school districts in the Middle District of Alabama still under court order to examine what they must do to attain unitary status. Not only did these two judges "actively promote the idea of settlement," but the magistrate for the district "closely managed the discovery process and the resulting settlement discussions." Within a few years each school had signed a consent decree that "focused more on quality-of-education concerns than with the racial makeup of schools." They covered not only the six *Green* factors, but "student assignment to classrooms (i.e. tracking and ability grouping); special education, including gifted and talented education; discipline; resource allocation; salary; curriculum; drop-out prevention and graduation rates."[43]

In some instances, it was a crisis that led school districts to seek unitary status. In 2002, twenty-six years after the Dayton school system had been placed under court supervision, the state of Ohio labeled Dayton an "academic emergency" due to the poor performance of its students. The district negotiated a settlement that would bring in more state money, and the NAACP agreed.[44] In nearby Cleveland, the school district experienced "total fiscal and administrative collapse" in 1992. This crisis led it to propose a set of educational reforms ("Vision 21") that included more school choice, more community schools, more magnet schools, and less emphasis on racial balance. Four years later the presiding judge closed the case, citing the quality of the city's magnet schools and its success in reducing the racial achievement gap.[45]

A third factor contributing to the termination of court orders was growing discontent among parents, both black and white, who objected not only to long bus rides (which are generally longer for black students than for whites), but also to the racial quotas established for many magnet schools. In Charlotte, it was a legal challenge by a white family to the strict 60/40 distribution of seats in magnet schools that led to a finding of unitary status. In Prince George's County, Maryland, and Lexington, Kentucky, African American parents objected to the district's policy of allowing "white" seats in magnet schools to sit empty while hundreds of black children remained on waiting lists.[46] In Kansas City, the parents of black students were the most persistent and vocal advocates for termination of judicial supervision.[47] African American mayors in Denver, Minneapolis, and Cleveland supported efforts to have their cities' schools declared unitary.[48]

These examples point to a final factor, the broader "standards and accountability" movement that gathered steam throughout the 1990s and culminated in enactment of No Child Left Behind in 2001. In part, this movement reflected disillusion with the national education policies of the preceding decades, which seemed to be doing little to improve the performance of American schools. Among those calling for a reset that focused on outcomes rather than inputs was a broad coalition of civil rights organizations that supported No Child Left Behind (see chapter 9.) Given the persistence of the racial achievement gap, the NAACP and local civil rights organizations were willing to accept termination of desegregation orders in exchange for promised improvements in the schools that serve minority children.[49]

The Supreme Court's three decisions on unitary status made it easier for lower courts to terminate desegregation orders. But they did not require those judges to do so. Nearly three decades after *Dowell*, hundreds of orders remained in place. Just as the content of the initial orders reflected diverse local circumstances and the disposition of lower court judges, so did termination proceed in an ad hoc manner with little control from the center. "Unitary status" remained as ambiguous as "desegregation," leaving key decisions in the hands of district court judges and the parties to individual cases.

Resegregation?

Has termination of desegregation orders contributed to the "resegregation" of public schools? The answer depends on the meaning of the highly contested word "segregation." The assumption underlying the Supreme Court's post-1991 rulings is that once a school system has complied in good faith with a desegregation order, the presence of racially imbalanced or predominantly minority schools does not in itself constitute the sort of segregation that violates the Equal Protection clause. At the heart of the "resegregation" argument, in contrast, lies the "racial isolation" counter-argument: schools that are predominantly minority are by that very fact inferior, segregated, and unconstitutional. According to this understanding, virtually any relaxation of desegregation orders that allows school districts to revert to neighborhood assignment will lead to "resegregation."

EVENNESS AND EXPOSURE: GENERAL TRENDS

What do we know about how the racial makeup of public schools has changed since 1991? In particular, what has happened in the school districts released from court supervision in the 1990s and thereafter? To address these questions, we must distinguish between two measures of segregation, "evenness" and "exposure." The first measures the extent to which various racial and ethnic groups are spread evenly throughout a school district. The second measures the extent to which one group goes to school with another group. (The important question of whether minority students actually sit in classrooms and interact with white students is not included in either measure.) If court decisions terminating desegregation orders have contributed significantly to "resegregation," we should see a major change in these measures starting in the early 2000s, when the pace of termination increased. Just as importantly, these measures should worsen more rapidly in districts deemed "unitary" than in those still under court order.

First, consider changes over time. From 1968 through the mid-1970s both measures of segregation showed significant improvement, especially in the South and Midwest. Progress continued, though at a slower rate, through most of the 1980s. Measures of "evenness" worsened slightly from the late 1980s through the late 1990s. But starting around 1998, they rebounded. In 2014, Reardon and Owen concluded that "it seems fair to say that the last 25 years have been characterized by largely stable patterns of sorting of students among schools (evenness)."[50] In their analysis of the hundred largest school districts in the South and border states between 1994 and 2004—years in which many court orders were terminated—Clotfelter, Ladd, and Vigdor found, "somewhat to our surprise, no evidence of resegregation."[51] Using a more complicated measure of evenness that includes the distribution of white, black, Hispanic, and Asian students, Kori Stroub and Meredith Richard found that in 350 major metropolitan areas, multiracial segregation increased by 2.3 percent between 1993 and 1998, but was "10.7% *lower* in 2009 than it was in 1993." "All three White/non-White comparisons," they report, reflect "worsening segregation through the 1990s followed by decreases in segregation thereafter."[52] Using a similar evenness measure, Brian An and Adam Gamoran's examination of national trends "found little evidence that school segregation has increased over time." Even in the South, the region most affected by both desegregation orders and their termination, "black-white school segregation did not significantly increase between 1990 and 2005.... If anything, there was evidence that school segregation decreased over time, especially between Latino and white students."[53]

In short, these studies provide scant support for the claim that the increasing number of "unitary" findings contributed to widespread "resegregation." Using the evenness or dissimilarity index, segregation increased *before* the surge of terminations, then *stabilized or even decreased* as more districts were released from court supervision—just the opposite of what proponents of the "resegregation" thesis claim. It seems likely that the combination of a gradual decline in housing segregation and continuing efforts by school districts to promote integrated schools (especially through magnet schools and "controlled choice") have offset the modest effects of relaxation of court-ordered busing.[54]

The "exposure" measures favored by the proponents of the resegregation thesis raise a more complicated set of questions. There is no doubt that the number of white students in schools attended by minority students has declined since the late 1980s. The main reason for this trend is the significant decline in the proportion of school-age children who are white, especially in urban areas. As a result of the sharp increase in the number of Hispanic and (to a lesser extent) Asian students, white students now constitute less than half the student body in many areas of the country. This demographic shift not only means that "exposure" measures will decline significantly without any change in public policy, but also that exposure to white students becomes a dubious measure of student diversity. For example, a school that goes from 60 percent white/40 percent black to 30 percent white/40 percent black/25 percent Hispanic/5 percent Asian (not an unusual scenario) would see its white/non-white "exposure" measure drop significantly. But would anyone consider the latter more "segregated" or less diverse than the former? Since these demographic shifts were taking place at about the same time as the courts were releasing districts from desegregation orders, untangling the two developments is difficult, yet essential.

A number of studies indicate that black students' decreasing levels of exposure to white students is due almost entirely to demographic shifts rather than policy change. In 2006 Clotfelter, Ladd, and Vigdor concluded that the change "appear to be driven by the general increase in the nonwhite percentage of the student population rather than district policies."[55] In the hundred southern and border cities they examined, "the share of black students attending 90–100% black schools fell slightly" due to the influx of Hispanic students. In 2004 Logan similarly found that "whites did not move toward increasingly white schools as minorities increasingly attended minority schools." Rather, demographic shifts "have resulted in schools with lower shares of white and higher shares of black, Hispanic, and Asian enrollment." "It is misleading," he concludes, "to label these trends as resegregation."[56] Using a more extensive data set, Byron Lutz reached a similar conclusion in 2011: "The decrease in black-white exposure over this period [1987–2006] is primarily the product of the demographic trends... not the end of court-ordered desegregation."[57]

BEFORE AND AFTER TERMINATION

These large-scale studies leave open two important questions. First, what happened to various measures of segregation in the school districts declared "unitary"? Second, how large are the differences between released and non-released school districts?

Since the main objective of most desegregation orders was to produce racially balanced schools, it would be surprising *not* to find at least some decrease in "evenness" in districts after they are deemed unitary. As Reardon et al. point out, since school districts usually agree to multi-year transition periods, we should not expect immediate change. They found that in large school districts, measures of unevenness "continue to grow steadily for at least 10 years" after release, exactly what "we would expect if most districts adopt neighborhood-based school assignment policies following the release from court order." They estimate that during this period the dissimilarity index for these districts typically rose 0.06—from about 0.34 to 0.40, where 0.0 represents a completely even distribution of black and white students among a district's schools and 1.0 represents complete separation. This increase is statistically significant, but does not come close to pre-*Brown* levels of 1.0. They also found that after ten years the difference between the evenness index for released and non-released districts had grown by 0.05, one quarter of a standard deviation.[58]

Examining the one hundred largest school districts in the South and border states from 1994 to 2004, Clotfelter, Ladd, and Vigdor also found districts released from judicial supervision had black/white evenness indices "almost 4 percentage points, roughly one-third of a standard deviation, higher than otherwise equivalent districts without unitary status." Measures of evenness that take into account Hispanic and Asian students were "also statistically significant, but smaller, roughly one-fifth of a standard deviation."[59]

Clotfelter, Ladd, and Vigdor did not, though, find higher levels of racial isolation in the districts declared unitary than in those still under court order. The effects of demographic change on exposure levels, they found, are so large as to swamp any differences resulting from unitary status. In these one hundred districts,

> black and white students alike now attend schools with greater proportions of Hispanic, Asian, and students of other races. The development creates the impression of increasing segregation when segregation is measured by one

widely-used index—the proportion of blacks attending 90–100% nonwhite schools—but the rise in this measure is the result of demographic change rather than any growing racial imbalance among schools.

They argue that "as a consequence of the increasing racial diversification of American schools, this particular measure of racial isolation may have lost much of its meaning as a measure of racial segregation." More adequate measures "point to a different conclusion": "the average level of segregation in large Southern school districts has not changed much over the last decade."[60] As An and Gamoran later explained, the effects of court decisions on termination are "too small and too few to affect the broader patterns of increasing racial isolation, which are dominated by the changing face of the US population."[61]

Termination and the Achievement Gap

School districts that ask to be released from desegregation orders almost always argue that they can do a better job educating children of all races and ethnicities if freed from racial-balance requirements established decades ago. In some cities African American parents have agreed, favoring neighborhood schools and school choice over mandatory assignment to schools at considerable distance from their homes. These claims raise the most important questions of all, but ones that are devilishly difficult to answer: To what extent have desegregation orders improved educational opportunities for minority children? Has termination improved or harmed the education of these children?

From the beginning, the ultimate purpose of desegregation has not been to produce racially balanced schools, but to improve the quality of education provided to minority students. State-sponsored segregation, Chief Justice Warren wrote in *Brown*, retards the "educational and mental development" of black students, depriving "them of some of the benefits they would receive in a racial[ly] integrated school system." The "racial isolation" thesis that undergirded so many of the federal judiciary's post-1968 decisions predicted that eliminating majority-minority schools would substantially improve the academic performance of African American children. Years later, civil rights organizations and school officials opposing termination argued that the stubborn gap in the math and reading test scores of white and black children constitutes a "vestige" of segregation that must be eliminated before a district is declared "unitary." Addressing the achievement gap may not have been the only goal of the desegregation effort, but it was certainly the most important one.

As noted in chapter 2, measured by standardized-test scores, the black-white achievement gap declined substantially in both math and reading for all age groups from 1970 until the mid- to late 1980s. Then progress stalled. During the first two decades of the twenty-first century, the gap narrowed somewhat for all age groups in math and reading.[62] High school graduation rates displayed a similar pattern: the white-black gap narrowed until the mid-1980s, when the graduation rate for white and black women and white men stabilized, but the rate for black men decreased significantly. In the first two decades of the twenty-first century, graduation rates among black students inched steadily upward, so that by 2017 the high school graduation rates among black and white eighteen-to-twenty-four-year-olds were close to equal.[63] The first and most significant round of progress coincided with massive desegregation of public schools, especially in the South. Progress ended well before many schools were deemed "unitary." The second round of progress began around 2000, at the same time that unitary findings were becoming more frequent. It is most likely that these improvements were the result of the post-2001 emphasis on testing and school accountability rather than of any changes in desegregation law.

Chapters 6 and 7 emphasized the many local factors that influenced the development of desegregation plans in school districts around the country. Desegregation was never a coherent policy applied uniformly across the country. Nor was there much study of the effectiveness of its many variants. As Roger Levesque has noted, only after a number of studies concluded that the effects of desegregation were disappointingly small in the aggregate did researchers try to isolate those "contextual and process factors" that might make the difference.[64] Unfortunately, those factors continue to elude educational researchers.

Chapter 7 closed with an examination of a costly failure: the court-led effort to remake the Kansas City, Missouri, school system. The termination of that desegregation case came as a relief to almost everyone. But what do we know about the effect of termination in the "city that made it work," Charlotte, North Carolina?

For many years after the *Swann* decision, the Charlotte-Mecklenburg School District (CMS) was "widely considered the epitome of a successfully desegregated school district—an example for the nation of how desegregation could be accomplished in ways that fostered student achievement, interracial civility, political stability, and economic growth."[65] CMS had a number of advantages: a geographically large district that included both the inner city and its suburbs; a white-black ratio that started at 70–30 and declined only to 50–40; a growing economy; and city, school, and business leadership that took pride in making desegregation succeed. Not surprisingly, when the district revised its desegregation plan to replace extensive busing with magnets and controlled choice, and again when the federal courts ruled (against the wishes of the district's leaders) that CMS had achieved unitary status, many interpreted the changes as a repudiation of what Justice Breyer called "the hope and promise of *Brown*."

A closer look at educational results in Charlotte, though, suggests that its success was more ambiguous than this common narrative maintains, and its termination less momentous than its critics had feared. In the early years of school desegregation in CMS, test scores for both black and white students rose significantly. But the racial achievement gap remained large. By the mid-1980s, CMS children had spent their entire elementary and secondary education in the desegregated system. Yet by then test scores had plateaued for both groups. The gap between white and black students remained not only large—one standard deviation—but somewhat greater than the national average.[66]

Starting in 1992 the district allowed greater variation in the racial composition of individual schools. The racial composition of those schools had no apparent effect on students' test scores. Test results for black students in schools that were less than 25 percent minority were virtually identical to those that were more than 75 percent minority. Perhaps the most distressing statistic about the educational system in Charlotte is one cited by Rucker Johnson. Despite many years under an ambitious desegregation plan and despite a booming regional economy, "a pioneering, influential study of intergenerational mobility published in 2013 [by Raj Chetty and his associates] found that Charlotte ranked last among the fifty largest cities in the United States in terms of a child's prospects for escaping poverty."[67]

Racial segregation (as measured both by evenness and exposure) started to grow in CMS in 1992, and increased significantly after 2002, the year it was released from judicial supervision. Yet, according to three critics of termination of the court order, during the following three years,

> CMS made modest progress in improving fifth- and eighth-grade math and reading proficiency scores of black, white, poor, and nonpoor students.... Importantly, the gains among poor students and black students were greater than the gains among nonpoor students and whites, suggesting that since 2000, the gaps between black and white . . . students have narrowed slightly.[68]

Most likely this progress was the result of CMS's "Equity Plus" spending increases in schools with high percentages of disadvantaged students. In subsequent years there was a slight increase in the black/white achievement gap for math, but not for reading. As Jacob Vigdor has shown, this increase was a continuation of a trend that had begun in the 1990s, prior to the end of judicial supervision. The gap remained smaller in Charlotte than in nearby Wake County, which continued its extensive busing program.[69] Vigdor's study suggests that desegregation policy was but one of many factors that affected achievement levels in these two counties.

Post-termination trends at the high school level were more troubling. Graduation rates for black and Hispanic students fell significantly after 2006.[70] This decline is consistent with David Liebowitz's 2018 analysis of all large school districts released from desegregation plans. He found an increased dropout rate of 2.7 percent among Hispanic students. The increase for African American students outside the South was smaller, and not quite statistically significant. Liebowitz did not, though, find a decline in black graduation rates in released southern school districts.[71]

The most serious negative consequence of the post-2002 CMS policy was a "large and statistically significant increase in crime" by poor African American males assigned to predominantly minority schools. This was the principal finding of a 2013 study by Billings, Deming, and Rockoff that compared similar groups of students who had, largely by chance, been assigned to schools with different racial compositions. Peer effects, their research suggests, are particularly powerful in middle school and high school, leaving a deeper imprint on nonacademic behavior than on test scores. They also found that poor white students (but not black students) are more likely to drop out if they attend a predominantly minority school.[72]

These mixed findings suggest that at least under optimal conditions, busing can improve the lot of some students living in poor neighborhoods, especially high school boys. At the same time, they suggest that providing more resources to primary and middle schools with high percentages of minority students can be at least as effective as increasing the number of white students in their classes—as Rucker Johnson's work has indicated.

Perhaps the best overall assessment of the effects of desegregation and termination is the one Reardon and his associates offered in 2012:

> Despite the evidence that desegregation in the 1960s and 1970s improved black students' educational attainment (and possibly their achievement), it is not clear that resegregation in the 1990s and 2000s will have the opposite effect. The changes in segregation levels that occurred in the 1960s and 1970s were substantially larger than our estimated changes following release from court orders. Moreover, the desegregation of public schools in the 1960s and 1970s was highly visible (and contentious, in many cases), led to significant changes in the quality of schooling available to black students, and occurred in an era when racial equality improved in many other domains as well.[73]

One could add that per-pupil spending levels are much higher now than several decades ago, that school funding is more evenly distributed between affluent and poor areas, and that federal reporting rules have focused attention on the achievement levels of racial minorities. Charlotte may have had its *Swann* song, but many of the accomplishments of decades of desegregation efforts remain in place.

Out with a Whimper

The most striking theme of this chapter is the continuing ambiguity of the key term "desegregation." A quarter century after the Supreme Court told lower court judges and school officials to convert "dual" school systems into "unitary" ones, it conceded that those pivotal terms have no clear meaning. Although advocates of the "color-blind/limited intervention" position wrote for the Court in the trilogy of cases decided between 1991 and 1995, there was never a solid majority on the Court for that stance. The justices inclined toward the "racial isolation/equal educational opportunity" position explained that the Court had not foreclosed that understanding of desegregation. Once again, the Court threw the hardest questions back to the lower courts, with little useful guidance on how they should proceed.

A second theme of this chapter is that federal district court judges are often more eager to terminate desegregation orders than are school officials. This pattern is not limited to judges appointed by Republican presidents. For example, Judge Myron Thompson, a distinguished African American jurist appointed by President Carter, led the effort to resolve all the desegregation cases in the Middle District of Alabama. Often these judges were weary of handling recurring disputes over desegregation orders that no longer seemed to improve the quality of education offered to minority students. They could also see the benefit of exchanging relaxation of busing requirements for educational reforms (such as additional funding and increased school choice) that seemed more promising.

Conversely, the termination story also shows that many school officials have been in no hurry to request an end to court orders. Many have grown comfortable with them and are loath to spend money for lawyers or to raise contentious racial issues. As we saw in chapter 6, some have been happy to respond to parents' criticism by saying "the judge made me do it." After the *Parents Involved* decision in 2007, school officials realized that a "unitary" finding would reduce their authority to take race into account in assigning students to particular schools. And some, it seems, did not even realize that desegregation orders were still in effect. In any case, by the late 1990s, we were no longer in 1960s Dixie, when the Fifth Circuit had to take extraordinary measures to overcome the obstructionism of avowed segregationists.

The third theme is that, in the aggregate, termination of desegregation orders had only a small effect on either measure of segregation, "evenness" or "exposure." That termination led to a small decrease in evenness measures is not surprising, since the central purpose of these orders was usually to spread white and black students evenly through the schools within a district. Returning to neighborhood schools would inevitably produce more "imbalanced" schools. Why, then, was the effect relatively small? In part this was because the change was usually spread out over several years. Moreover, school officials retained authority to use magnet schools, "controlled choice," the siting of new schools, and the drawing of attendance zones to offset the effects of residential segregation. Meanwhile, residential segregation was declining slightly for African Americans, more significantly for Hispanics and Asians.

To be sure, racial segregation as measured by "exposure" indexes did worsen during the period in which many desegregation orders were terminated. But this trend was largely the effect of demographic change. In many cities, there were just not enough white students for black and Hispanic students to be "exposed" to. Demography overwhelmed the small effect of policy change.

This circumstance does not, however, mean that termination had no important consequences in particular cities. As we saw in chapters 6–7, desegregation was a surprisingly ad hoc process, with major changes from one city to another. Just as importantly, within a city termination seemed to affect different groups of students in different ways. In Charlotte, for example, the return to neighborhood schools coupled with spending increases seemed to work well for elementary school students but increased dropout rates among high school males. The abstract categories of "desegregation" and "termination" included a variety of educational practices whose consequences were far from uniform.

The continuation or termination of desegregation orders was only one of many factors influencing school practices and results over the past three decades—and in most cases far from the most important. Not only was the composition of the student body changing significantly, but these were years with wave upon wave of education-reform efforts. Partly as a result of federal pressure, programs for English learners and students with disabilities improved significantly. Increased state aid reduced disparities between property-rich and property-poor school districts. The "standards and accountability" regime exemplified by No Child Left Behind increased the attention paid to testing and, consequently, to the stubbornly persistent racial achievement gap. The number of charter schools increased, as did the choices available to public school children and parents. As we will see in the next chapter, efforts to improve the educational opportunity of minority children and others previously underserved by local schools were not limited to the courts. Congress and federal agencies took action, too, in ways quite different from the courts.

9

Looking Beyond Courts: ESEA and Title VI

From the mid-1960s through the 1970s, school desegregation was the most important and most controversial education issue addressed by the federal government. For a brief moment, Congress, the executive branch, and the federal courts were united in an effort to end de jure segregation in the South. By 1970, presidential and congressional hostility to busing had removed federal administrators from most northern desegregation cases. Thereafter, almost all the action on desegregation took place in the federal courts. At the same time, though, Congress and federal administrators were taking a number of steps to address related issues of educational opportunity. In 1965 Congress passed the Elementary and Secondary Education Act (ESEA), which based federal grants in part on the number of poor children in each school district. Soon thereafter Congress enacted new laws to improve educational opportunities for English learners, children with disabilities, and female students. Meanwhile, the Office of Education (soon to become the Department of Education) was establishing its own Title VI guidelines for bilingual education, and promulgating extensive regulations under ESEA, the Education for All Handicapped Children Act of 1975, Title IX of the 1972 Education Amendments (prohibiting sex discrimination in federally funded programs), and §504 of the Rehabilitation Act of 1973 (prohibiting discrimination against the handicapped in federally funded programs). These laws and regulations often provided more specific rules on matters the courts had already encountered in desegregation cases: resource inequalities, specialized programs for English learners, criteria for assigning students to special education, discrimination in tracking and discipline, and racial harassment. Different institutions brought different perspectives and different policy tools to bear on these common problems.

The combination of separation of powers, bicameralism, and decentralization within both houses of Congress creates multiple veto points in the legislative process. For many years this feature of our political institutions stymied efforts to expand the federal role in education. But after the policy breakthrough of 1965, it became clear that our fragmented political system also creates multiple opportunity points for the expansion of federal programs. An increasingly entrepreneurial Congress acted incrementally to create a variety of new programs and mandates. Combined with the broad commands of the 1964 Civil Rights Act, these new laws and funding streams created new opportunities for federal administrators to regulate the activities of state and local education officials. They also enhanced the authority of federal judges in education matters. By the early 1980s, the furor over court-ordered desegregation had died down, but many other efforts to promote equal educational opportunity were firmly established and—after a brief lull in the early Reagan years—still expanding. The 2001 reauthorization of ESEA known as "No Child Left Behind" was designed to draw more attention to the racial achievement gap and to require states to take more aggressive steps to restructure failing schools. The Obama administration not only expanded these efforts but issued a number of Title VI guidelines to address issues that had previously arisen in desegregation cases.

ESEA and Civil Rights

"Education is the civil rights issue of our time."
GEORGE W. BUSH, BARACK OBAMA, DONALD TRUMP, ARNE DUNCAN,
MITT ROMNEY, and JOHN MCCAIN, among others

The Elementary and Secondary Education Act and civil rights law were entwined in many ways. Had it not been for the 1964 Civil Rights Act, ESEA could not have been enacted the following year. Conversely, if not for ESEA, Title VI of the Civil Rights Act would not have become such a potent regulatory instrument. The combination of the two statutes made possible the institutional alliance for southern school desegregation described in chapter 4.

Prior to 1964, congressional consideration of education legislation was complicated by acrimonious debate over the "Powell amendment." Named after Harlem congressman Adam Clayton Powell, it prohibited disbursement of federal money to segregated schools. Southern Democrats would not vote for a bill that contained the Powell amendment; northern Democrats and Republicans were reluctant to vote for one that did not. The Civil Rights Act paved the way for ESEA by taking the issue off the table.

In a subtler but equally important way, the mid-decade ferment over civil rights shaped the underlying purposes of ESEA, especially its major funding provision, Title I. Prior to 1965, advocates of federal aid had pushed for general aid to local school systems, money to help all districts pay for school construction and teachers' salaries. ESEA, in contrast, was sold as a federal effort to help disadvantaged children. As a congressional staffer who worked on education issues for many years put it, "The War on Poverty was the ascendant discussion at the time, and so the theory was that you could gear aid to poverty as a way to get something enacted. . . . This was the way to break the log jam over enacting federal aid."[1] Funding would be apportioned on the basis of the number of poor students in each school district. At the same time, though, the funding formula provided some money to almost every congressional district in the country—increasing its political popularity while limiting the amount targeted to districts with large numbers of minority students. Moreover, the federal government exercised little control over how the money was spent: ESEA explicitly barred the federal government from meddling in curricular matters.

In 1969 a report issued by the NAACP Legal Defense Fund revealed the extent to which federal funds were being used to replace rather than supplement state and local funding, and to provide services and amenities for the entire student body rather than disadvantaged children. Over the next decade and a half, Congress and federal administrators took a number of steps to require school districts to demonstrate that they were directing federal money to poor children. Many schools responded by creating "pull-out" programs that provided disadvantaged children with small-group tutoring—while potentially stigmatizing the "pull-outs."[2]

Throughout the 1970s, "prominent studies were released that found that ESEA funds and programs had largely failed to improve educational opportunities for disadvantaged students."[3] Nor was there much federal administrators could do to improve the situation. As David Cohen and Susan Moffitt have pointed out, it is hard to improve the quality of instruction when you have no legal control over the substance of instruction.[4] The basic problem was that Congress had assumed that local schools knew how to do better by these students and were eager to do so—they just needed more money. One major study concluded that "in 1965 Congress was apparently not aware of the immensity of the problem of developing and implementing a program to deal successfully with educational disadvantage on a national scope."[5]

Despite these disappointing results, ESEA was an immediate political success. The congressional politics of education turned on a dime. From 1961 through 1965 Democratic presidents prodded and cajoled Congress to spend more on education. Thereafter the White House was usually trying to restrain congressional spending—a trend that started while Lyndon Johnson was still president. In 1963–64 the federal share of spending on K–12 education was 4.4 percent. That number rose to 7.9 percent in 1965–66 and nearly 10 percent by the end of the 1970s. In 2016 Susan Moffitt noted that "Title I has developed durable constituencies and appetites for federal funds."[6] As spending grew, so too did the number of federal rules: in the decade after enactment of ESEA, federal laws on education expanded in length from eighty pages to 360; the number of pages of federal regulations increased from ninety-two to nearly one thousand.[7]

Since ESEA comes up for reauthorization on a regular basis, it provides congressional entrepreneurs ample opportunity to initiate new programs. This trend first became evident in 1967 when Senator Ralph Yarborough (D-TX) introduced legislation to create a categorical grant for schools with a large number of Spanish-speaking students. Despite opposition from the Johnson White House, Congress created a new Division of Bilingual Education within the Office of Education to distribute such grants.[8] Similar congressional entrepreneurship got the ball rolling on federal assistance for students with disabilities. Again over the objection of the White House, Congress created the Bureau of Education for the Handicapped to distribute another categorical grant to state and local education authorities. In 1975, Congress enacted the Education for All Handicapped Children Act, which at the time was the most demanding federal education law on the books.[9] Over the years Congress also added to ESEA special provisions on the education of migratory children; neglected, delinquent, or at-risk children; Native Americans, Native Hawaiians, and Alaskan Natives; and rural and low-income schools. Once Congress had crossed the "legitimacy barrier" on education, incremental expansion became the norm.

The so-called "equity regime" that characterized federal education policy in the decades after 1965 had two key features: it focused on "inputs," primarily money; and it sought to improve educational opportunities for the previously underserved—the poor, racial minorities, English learners, female students, and those with disabilities. Armed with the "power of the purse," Congress could do forthrightly what courts could do only indirectly: provide more resources to school districts with large numbers of disadvantaged students. Congress could also avoid the perilous politics of race by appealing to broader constituencies.

Despite its political popularity, the "equity regime" did little to close the achievement gap between white and black students or between relatively affluent and relatively poor students. By the late 1980s progress in reducing the racial achievement gap stalled. The gap between high and low socioeconomic status (SES) students appeared to widen. As Jesse Rhodes has shown, leaders of civil rights organizations such as the NAACP Legal Defense Fund, the National Council of La Raza, the Leadership Conference on Civil Rights, the Citizens Commission on Civil Rights, the Children's Defense Fund, and the Education Trust came to believe that simply providing more money to existing school systems would do little to improve the educational opportunities provided to poor and minority students.[10] These groups wanted to call attention to achievement gaps, and to force poorly performing schools either to change fundamentally or be shut down. Along with business groups and back-to-basics advocates, they formed the diverse coalition that produced the new "standards and accountability regime" exemplified by No Child Left Behind.

This standards and accountability regime differed from the equity regime in two regards: it focused on "outputs"—primarily test results—rather than inputs; and it aimed at improving education for all children, not just the disadvantaged. The US was spending much more money per student than ever before, but, it seemed to many, not producing better results. In the words of *A Nation at Risk*, the famous report commissioned by President Reagan's Secretary of Education,

> Our once unchallenged preeminence in commerce, industry, science, and technological innovation is being overtaken by competitors throughout the world. . . . The educational foundations of our society are presently being eroded by a rising tide of mediocrity . . . We have, in effect, been committing an act of unthinking, unilateral educational disarmament.[11]

This crisis called for federal efforts to improve American education across the board—an even more ambitious undertaking than that announced in 1965.

NCLB was the product of a bipartisan coalition that stretched from George H. W. Bush and Bill Clinton to George W. Bush, Barack Obama, Ted Kennedy, and House Education Committee chair George Miller. Bush '41 and '43 broke with Republican orthodoxy by advocating a more forceful federal role in education. According to Patrick McGuinn, "with NCLB, the federal government for the first time pressured states in a sustained way to undertake systemic change in their education systems and held them accountable for the academic performance of their students."[12]

NCLB's Democratic supporters had to withstand opposition from a major party constituency—teachers' unions—and address their contention that the law placed too much emphasis on standardized tests. Many Democrats were willing to vote for NCLB, and the Obama administration was eager to build upon it because it had strong support from civil rights organizations. In 2008, the Leadership Conference on Civil Rights declared that "NCLB is a civil rights law, and that some of the requirements of NCLB constitute, in essence, the rights of children to obtain a quality education."[13] Phyllis McClure, who worked for the NAACP Legal Defense Fund for many years and coauthored the influential 1969 critique of Title I practices, maintained that "NCLB has grabbed the education community's attention like no previous ESEA reauthorization. It has really upset the status quo in state and local offices.... For the first time, district and school officials are actually being required to take serious and urgent action in return for federal dollars."[14] Christopher Edley, who held major civil rights positions in the Clinton and Obama administrations, testified that with NCLB, "for the first time the academic achievement of the major racial and ethnic groups, socioeconomically disadvantaged students, English language learners, and children with disabilities, will be at the core of whether our schools are judged to be successful."[15] Although many of NCLB's mandates were relaxed when Congress passed the Every Student Succeeds Act (ESSA), that 2015 reauthorization of ESEA strengthened the rules on reporting test results for those groups—a key demand of civil rights organizations.

Although Congress repeatedly passed statutory provisions and appropriation riders to limit busing, it was hardly unsympathetic to the plight of students who had not been well served by state and local school systems. Its first instinct was to throw money at the problem. That tendency was evident not only in ESEA, but also in the Emergency School Aid Act of 1972, which provided additional funding to schools undergoing desegregation. Unfortunately, Congress is notoriously bad at targeting aid to schools and students most in need. Maintaining congressional coalitions requires spreading funding around to a large number of congressional districts. Another limitation was that Congress was hesitant, at least initially, to tell school districts how to spend that money.

Slowly, though, that reluctance began to diminish. With money came strings, and then mandates, both funded and unfunded. Such mandates first became apparent in the Education for All Handicapped Children Act (EAHCA) of 1975, which required schools to establish extensive procedures and provide numerous services to students with a wide variety of disabilities. The trend reached its apogee in NCLB. Meanwhile, under the little known Equal Educational Opportunity Act—an odd offshoot of Congress's effort to limit busing in 1974—federal administrators and judges were supervising school programs for English learners.

A common characteristic of congressional action on education was the effort to build coalitions that bridged racial and economic divides. That effort was particularly evident with the EAHCA (later renamed the Individuals with Disabilities Education Act). It developed a strong constituency among middle-class and affluent parents. Programs for English learners gained support not just among Hispanic and Asian groups, but from professional organizations representing teachers and language-acquisition experts. The most successful of these programs provided services to some students without imposing readily traceable costs on others. That usually means applying established techniques (for example, bilingual education or English as a second language) to a subset of students (English learners or those with a specific disability) without changing the structure or the culture of the larger school system. As Congress and presidents learned from NCLB—and as many judges learned from their desegregation cases—efforts at systemic reform are much less likely to succeed than isolated add-ons. That generalization about the prospects for organizational change holds true even for a legislative body that has the power of the purse.

The Transformation of Title VI

As noted in chapter 3, Title VI received little attention during the long debate over the Civil Rights Act of 1964. Prohibiting the national government from providing financial support for unconstitutional practices by state and local governments—the avowed purpose of the provision—was a stance hard to oppose by any but the most unreconstructed segregationists. Moreover, the final version of Title VI provided a number of checks on the power of the federal agencies charged with enforcing it. How, then, did Title VI prove to be (in Hugh Davis Graham's words) "the sleeper that would become by far the most powerful weapon of them all"?[16] Partly through administrative evasion of the procedural requirements of Title VI, partly through judicial willingness to enforce agency guidelines, and partly through an unexpected change in the standard operating procedures of civil rights offices, effected by a decades-long court case.

Title VI gives agencies that dispense federal funds two powers. First, it authorizes (but does not explicitly require) federal agencies to terminate funding to recipients who discriminate on the basis of "race, color, or national origin." Compliance with the statute and rules issued under it "*may* be effected (1) by the termination of or refusal to grant or to continue [financial] assistance . . . or (2) by any other means authorized by law." Those "other means" include referring the case to the Department of Justice for prosecution. The 1964 law did not explicitly create a "private right of action," that is, authorize private citizens to file suit to enforce its requirements.

Second, Title VI empowers agencies to issue "rules, regulations, and orders of general applicability" to carry out the purposes of the statute. It adds the unusual provision that "no such rule, regulation, or order shall become effective unless and until approved by the President." The statute also specifies the procedures agencies must follow before terminating funding: they must first give the funding recipient an opportunity to come into compliance voluntarily; termination can proceed only after the agency has made an "express finding on the record after opportunity for hearing"; the funding cutoff shall not take effect until thirty days after the agency has made a full report to the committees in Congress with jurisdiction over the program in question; and any person, organization, or political subdivision adversely affected by the termination shall have the opportunity to challenge it in federal court. Until Congress amended Title VI in 1988, it also limited the funding cutoff "to the particular program . . . in which noncompliance has been found." In short, the new powers granted to federal administrators were accompanied by substantial procedural guardrails.

In chapter 4 we saw how the Office for Civil Rights (OCR) used its Title VI authority to assist the Fifth Circuit in the desegregation of southern schools. Two features of that effort illustrate how the actual operation of Title VI has departed from its textual structure. First, OCR did not issue rules and regulations signed by the president. Nor did the agency follow the notice-and-comment rulemaking procedures laid out by the Administrative Procedure Act (APA). This flouting of legal procedures continued for decades under Title IX and §504 as well as Title VI.

Second, OCR seldom instituted proceedings to terminate federal funds, and almost never actually pulled the trigger. The only exception was for a handful of particularly recalcitrant southern school districts in the mid-1960s. In the half century following enactment of Title IX in 1972, the federal government has never terminated funds to enforce its ban on sex discrimination. For reasons laid out in chapter 4, the funding cutoff proved too administratively cumbersome and politically dangerous to use in any but the most extreme circumstance. Instead, enforcement took place through court action, almost always in cases brought by private parties.

Originally viewed as a means to replace time-consuming litigation with quick executive action, during the initial phase of southern school desegregation Title VI was *transformed into a mechanism for establishing administrative guidelines enforceable in court*. Whether informal agency guidance would be considered legally binding depended on the courts' willingness to defer to administrators' interpretation of the statute. As Commissioner of Education Francis Keppel put it in 1967, the success of the court-agency alliance rested on their ability to move along "parallel tracks." In the late 1980s, those "tracks" began to diverge as the Supreme Court became more skeptical of disparate-impact analysis. Meanwhile, federal judges in the District of Columbia were experimenting with another form of court-agency interaction in litigation that shaped Title VI regulation in unexpected ways.

EXIT PANETTA, ENTER *ADAMS*

On February 17, 1970, Leon Panetta, the Nixon administration's first OCR director, learned that the White House had accepted his resignation—despite the fact that he had never offered one. Thus ended a year-long struggle between OCR, which was continuing its aggressive drive for southern school desegregation, and the White House, which sought to deflect criticism by shifting responsibility to the judiciary. Nixon's effort to curtail OCR's role in desegregation provoked an unusually public conflict between civil servants and the White House: nearly two thousand HEW officials protested Panetta's firing; two-thirds of the lawyers in the Department of Justice's civil rights division condemned the administration for "subordinat[ing] clearly defined legal requirements to non-legal considerations."[17]

Panetta's firing had two important consequences. First, OCR abandoned its single-minded focus on school desegregation, and (in the words of Panetta's replacement, Stanley Pottinger) began "to look for other problems to solve."[18] It didn't take long. Three months after Panetta's unceremonious exit, Pottinger issued a memo to school districts across the country announcing that failure to provide special assistance to English learners constituted discrimination on the basis of "national origin" under Title VI. Two years later, Congress enacted Title IX of the Education Amendments of 1972, barring sex discrimination in educational institutions receiving federal funding. The next year Congress passed §504 of the Rehabilitation Act of 1973, prohibiting discrimination on the basis of disability. OCR bore responsibility for carrying out these statutory mandates. Starting in 1970, Gary Orfield has noted, "OCR searched for and found enthusiastic new constituencies with real need and with intellectuals who had a vision of educational change." This shift "gave the agency important tasks free from the treacherous politics of busing."[19] These new regulatory efforts commanded OCR's attention for years to come. Not until the Obama administration did OCR turn its attention back to racial issues in a major way.

The second consequence was the filing of *Adams v. Richardson*. Washington lawyers affiliated with the NAACP Legal Defense Fund argued that Panetta's dismissal was part of the Nixon Administration's "virtually complete abandonment of HEW school aid terminations—the teeth of Title VI."[20]

Federal district court judge John H. Pratt agreed, finding that OCR had "no discretion to negate the purpose and intent" of Title VI "by a policy described in another context as one of 'benign neglect.'"[21] The DC Circuit upheld Pratt, charging that OCR's "consistent failure" to take enforcement action against recalcitrant school districts constituted "an abdication of its statutory duty."[22]

Over the next two decades Judge Pratt placed OCR in virtual receivership, issuing multiple orders that shaped the agency's sense of mission and standard operating procedures. His initial order set deadlines for OCR to review desegregation plans for several hundred school districts in southern and border states. He subsequently issued an injunction requiring OCR to begin formal enforcement proceedings against seventy-four school districts that had failed to carry out their approved desegregation plans, against another 127 districts that had not complied with the racial balance standards established in *Swann*, and against the higher-education systems of ten states. He also required the agency to investigate vocational schools and schools for deaf, blind, and developmentally disabled children in seventeen states, and to monitor 640 school districts' compliance with judicial desegregation orders. By 1976 his orders had expanded to include Title IX, §504, and discrimination against linguistic minorities. With the inclusion of each new law came a new set of parties to the lawsuit.[23]

In a ruling that marked the beginning of the end of *Adams v. Richardson*, DC Circuit judge Ruth Bader Ginsburg noted that the case

> has grown ever larger in the two decades since initiation. Eventually, the action cast the district court as nationwide overseer or pacer of procedures government agencies use to enforce civil rights prescriptions. . . . Over the past two decades, the once contained action expanded to colossal proportions: the litigation came to encompass enforcement by units of the Department of Education and the Department of Labor of four civil rights measures as they pertain to the education systems of all fifty states.[24]

A case that came in with a bang eventually went out with a whimper: after nearly twenty years and many rulings, Judge Pratt found that the original plaintiffs lacked standing to bring the case. "I think what really happened," one federal appellate judge told Stephen Halpern, "was that Judge Pratt just got tired of being the Czar of civil rights enforcement."[25]

THE UNEXPECTED CONSEQUENCES OF THE ADAMS LITIGATION

The immediate goal of the *Adams* lawsuit was to reinvigorate the desegregation effort by forcing OCR to make greater use of the funding cutoff. Elliot

Lichtman, the attorney who did much of the day-to-day work on *Adams*, explained this point of view in testimony before Congress:

> The whole theory of title VI has been that the *credible threat* of cutoff will make the difference, that it won't actually be necessary to cut off the funds or if the funds are ever cut off, the discrimination will cease very quickly, and the funds will start again, and that indeed has been the history.... [There were] a lot of cutoffs in the sixties, just a handful in the early seventies. In every case where there were cutoffs ... the funds were restored almost immediately in most cases because the discrimination ceased.... The statute isn't working, because OCR is today a paper tiger, but no one wants these funds ultimately to be cut off. I think history tells us that a credible threat of cutoff yields a cessation of the discrimination.[26]

During the "reconstruction of southern education" described in chapter 4, federal courts relied upon OCR's guidelines, but wielded a big "stick" (i.e., the structural injunction) themselves rather than waiting for OCR to terminate federal funding. With *Adams* the judicial role shifted to a futile effort to induce federal agencies to wield the only stick available to administrators.

A defining feature of the *Adams* litigation was the plaintiffs'—and the judge's—studied avoidance of substantive issues. From the beginning the case was based on the fiction that OCR has at its disposal clear rules for determining whether a school system had complied with Title VI and other civil rights statutes. As we have seen in the preceding chapters, that was almost never the case. *Adams*'s emphasis on procedure was the product of the plaintiffs' lawyers' litigational calculations: they recognized the danger of becoming embroiled in arguments about the substantive requirements of Title VI and how they should apply to particular cases. Emphasizing procedures and deadlines for investigating complaints would assure Judge Pratt that they were not asking him to second-guess an "expert" agency. Just as importantly, they realized that they had no independent capacity to monitor the status of thousands of schools. As one of the *Adams* lawyers later explained, their strategy was based on "framing the issues as procedural issues—using OCR's own data—careful not to give information on particular cases."[27]

Judge Pratt's procedural mandates had the unanticipated consequence of turning OCR into a complaint-investigating agency that would be evaluated on the basis of the number of complaints it resolved in a timely fashion. The pivotal event came in 1975 when the judge issued a "supplemental order" that contained an appendix known as "Part F."[28] Responding to the plaintiffs' claim that OCR had once again failed to take action against scores of school districts that had not complied with their desegregation plans, Judge Pratt found that "HEW has often delayed too long in ascertaining whether a complaint or other information of racial discrimination constitutes a violation of Title VI." By then, Nixon was gone, and most southern school systems had been successfully desegregated. Pratt later explained that OCR was no longer "charged with a policy of non-enforcement, but rather with assisting in the unlawful practices of educational institutions by *failing to promptly process complaints and compliance reviews according to certain time frames*."[29] Pratt took the fateful step of requiring the agency to investigate all complaints submitted to it. He then established a "90–90–30" rule: the agency had ninety days from the receipt of a complaint to determine whether a district had complied with Title VI; if it found a violation, it had an additional ninety days to seek compliance through negotiations; and if voluntary compliance was not forthcoming, it had thirty days to initiate formal enforcement proceedings.

Judge Pratt established the Part F framework just as a variety of new constituencies were demanding attention from OCR. After the Supreme Court's 1974 decision in *Lau v. Nichols*, the Mexican American Legal Defense and Education Fund (MALDEF) and other groups representing Spanish-speaking families demanded that OCR devote more attention to the language issue. The Women's Equality Action League (WEAL) sued OCR to force it to issue regulations under Title IX and to devote more resources to Title IX enforcement. Soon thereafter, groups representing the disabled filed a suit demanding that OCR issue regulations under §504. All these groups sought to intervene in *Adams v. Richardson*. Pratt said yes to MALDEF, but initially said no to WEAL, claiming that expanding the case to include Title IX threatened to "overload the boat."[30] On this point he was overruled by the DC Circuit. By then *Adams* had become, in Jeremy Rabkin's words, an exercise in "interest group management."[31]

Nothing in Title VI itself or any of its "clones" requires OCR to investigate the thousands of complaints it receives each year. But starting with Judge Pratt's 1975 order and continuing for more than forty years thereafter, such investigations became OCR's top priority and the chief measure of its performance. In the late 1970s OCR devoted about 80 percent of its resources to processing complaints.[32] By 1993, the agency reported, "nearly 90 percent of OCR resources" were still being spent "in a complaint mode."[33] In its FY 2018 budget request, it blandly stated, "OCR's performance measures are based on the percentage of complaints resolved within 180 days and the percentage of complaints pending after 180 days."[34] Stephen Halpern has noted that an agency that had only a few years earlier "led a social revolution" was by the mid-1970s "preoccupied with management efficiency in the processing of complaints."[35]

A central irony of the *Adams* litigation was the fact that the Reagan administration—which repeatedly sought to terminate the case—quickly became comfortable with the complaint-resolving mission for OCR. The focus on processing individual complaints was consistent with the administration's emphasis on "disparate treatment" rather than "disparate impact." Disparate-impact analysis requires examining a school district as a whole, rather than the treatment of particular individuals who file complaints. Moreover, the focus on prompt resolution of complaints created pressure for constricting the scope of OCR's investigation and promoting quick settlements. Throughout the 1980s OCR developed administrative practices that complied with the procedural mandates of *Adams*, facilitated the prompt resolution of complaints, sharply reduced the number of compliance reviews—and simultaneously infuriated civil rights groups and Democrats on oversight committees. The average time for processing a complaint plummeted from 1300 days in 1982 to 230 in 1984, and the average age of pending compliance reviews dropped from a little over a thousand days to 270.[36] The number of complaints missing at least one *Adams* deadline declined from five hundred in 1984 to only one hundred in 1988.[37]

The major disadvantage of the heavy emphasis on resolving complaints is that it reduces the resources available for more systematic investigations (or, in the administrative lexicon, "compliance reviews"). Soon after Judge Pratt established his Part F deadlines, the Department of Health, Education, and Welfare (HEW) warned that "investigations, negotiations, and enforcement action concerning isolated incidents of discrimination by a grantee can consume as much staff time as monitoring the operation of, for example, some entire school systems." Moreover, "complaints received by the Department" often are not "broadly representative of the spectrum of the Department's civil rights enforcement program." Rather than follow a "reactive" approach "geared toward securing individual relief for persons claiming discrimination," HEW insisted that it should be allowed to develop "a methodical approach geared toward identifying and eliminating systemic discrimination."[38]

Democratic appointees repeated this argument. David Tatel, appointed head of OCR by President Carter, told Judge Pratt that OCR could not "plan systematically if we must respond to each group's attempts to compel OCR to commit the bulk of its resources to enforcement of a particular law, or to enforcement in a particular set of institutions in a particular manner." If the agency's limited resources "continue to be allocated and consumed by the duty to comply with individual and uncoordinated court orders," he warned, the new administration would be unable "to develop a balanced enforcement program."[39] When the Clinton administration took power after twelve years of Republican rule, the newly installed leaders of OCR charged that they had "inherited a reactive approach to civil rights enforcement" that had failed "to protect students from egregious cases of discrimination." "Because the vast majority of the agency's resources were spent reacting to complaints that arrived in the morning mail," the agency charged, "glaring instances of long-standing discrimination went unredressed."[40]

OCR generally conducted more compliance reviews under Democratic than Republican administrations. No matter who controlled the White House, though, after 1975 the bulk of the agency's resources were devoted to complaint investigations. Resolving individual complaints remained its central bureaucratic task and the principal way in which those outside the agency judged its performance.

BACK TO THE FUTURE: THE TRIUMPH OF PRIVATE ENFORCEMENT

Although the *Adams* litigation had a huge influence on the bureaucratic task structure of OCR, it failed to induce administrators to make greater use of the funding cutoff. Instead OCR reverted to the enforcement strategy it first used in the 1960s: relying on private rights of action and judicial injunctions.

In the 1990 circuit-court opinion that finally ended the case, Judge Ruth Bader Ginsburg compared two methods for addressing the lethargy and inaction alleged in the *Adams case*: (1) nondiscretionary duty suits against civil rights agencies; and (2) private rights of action targeting those alleged to have engaged in discriminatory behavior. Judge Ginsburg argued that federal judges should not attribute to Congress an intent to authorize the first type of suit because Congress had already provided for the second. To be sure, the private right of action had not been mentioned in the text of Title VI, Title IX, or §504. But in *Cannon v. University of Chicago*, the Supreme Court had "confirmed an implied private remedy" under these statutes, and had "simultaneously" discouraged federal judges from recognizing "broad-gauged rights of action against federal enforcement agencies." That the Supreme Court recognized "implied private rights of action" in Title VI and its clones, she argued, "suggests that Congress considered private suits to end discrimination not merely adequate but in fact the proper means for individuals to enforce title VI and its sister antidiscrimination statutes."[41] Judge Ginsburg's opinion was the last word in a long debate among civil rights advocates, administrators, and judges over the usefulness of the funding cutoff. After 1990, her approach prevailed; private rights of action replaced the threat of termination of federal funds as the primary enforcement tool for Title VI, Title IX, and §504.

By the late 1970s OCR had also foresworn APA rulemaking. It preferred to make policy on an incremental, case-by-case basis as it investigated the individual complaints that constituted its standard bureaucratic fare. When it did issue general policy statements, they took the form of "interpretations," "guidelines," "technical support," and "Dear Colleague" letters. The last time OCR went through the transparent, participatory, and time-consuming notice-and-comment rulemaking process under Title VI was 1968. Under extreme duress—including lawsuits and, in the case of §504, occupation of the office of the Secretary of HEW—OCR did issue formal rules under Title IX in 1975 and §504 in 1977. The next time OCR used the notice-and-comment process for a major Title IX rule was 2020.

In 2001 the Supreme Court addressed for the first time the regulatory regime that had grown up under Title VI, Title IX, and §504. *Alexander v. Sandoval* involved a challenge to rules issued by the Departments of Justice and Transportation. Those federal departments maintained that state laws requiring drivers' license tests to be administered in English have a "disparate impact" on those who do not speak English, and thus discriminate on the basis of "national origin." Such discrimination, they argued, violates Title VI. Nearly thirty years before, the Supreme Court had accepted a similar reading of Title VI in the famous case of *Lau v. Nichols*.[42]

In *Sandoval*, Justice John Paul Stevens composed the following ode to the "integrated remedial scheme" that had slowly developed over the preceding decades:

> This legislative design reflects a reasonable—indeed inspired—model for attacking the often-intractable problem of racial and ethnic discrimination. On its own terms the statute supports an action challenging policies of federal grantees that explicitly or unambiguously violate antidiscrimination norms (such as policies that on their face limit benefits or services to certain races). With regard to more subtle forms of discrimination (*such as schemes that limit benefits or services on ostensibly race-neutral grounds but have the predictable and perhaps intended consequence of materially benefiting some races at the expense of others*), the statute does not establish a static approach but instead empowers the relevant agencies to evaluate social circumstances to determine whether there is a need for stronger measures. Such an approach builds into the law flexibility, an ability to make nuanced assessments of complex social realities, and an admirable willingness to credit the possibility of progress.[43]

Under this "inspired model," civil rights agencies would investigate complaints, slowly develop general policies, occasionally institute broader compliance reviews, and rely on private suits rather than funding cutoffs to impose sanctions on institutions that fail to comply.

Despite the fact that Justice Stevens and his three allies could cite a variety of precedents in support of this "integrated remedial scheme," they lost. Justice Scalia's majority opinion in *Sandoval* continued the Rehnquist and Roberts Courts' attack on the two major judicial doctrines upon which it rested: the disparate-impact interpretation of civil rights statutes; and judicial creation of "implied private rights of action" to enforce federal mandates. Scalia maintained that the Equal Protection clause and the 1964 Civil Rights Act forbid only intentional discrimination. He also insisted that federal court normally cannot hear private enforcement suits unless Congress has explicitly authorized them. This limitation on private enforcement is especially important, he argued, in cases against state and local governments.

On both these issues, Scalia admitted, the Court had been wildly inconsistent for years.[44] "Although Title VI has often come to this court," he wrote, "it seems fair to say (indeed perhaps an understatement) that our opinions have not eliminated all uncertainty regarding its commands."[45]

Scalia argued that although the Court had frequently recognized a private right of action to enforce the commands of Title VI itself, it had never explicitly recognized a private right of action to enforce agency rules that sweep more broadly than the text of Title VI. It is "beyond dispute," he asserted, that Title VI's ban on discrimination in federally funded programs "prohibits only intentional discrimination." Consequently, the disparate-impact regulations issued by federal administrators in the case at hand "proscribed activities" that are "permissible" under Title VI.

Surprisingly, though, Scalia did not strike down the agencies' disparate-impact rules. Since Alabama had not challenged the regulations themselves, the Court was forced to "assume for the purposes of deciding this case" that "regulations proscribing activities that have disparate impact on the basis of race are valid." They just are not enforceable *in court*. In other words, while the private right of action the Court had previously read into Title VI no longer extended to agencies' disparate-impact rules, the Court might not prevent agencies from using alternative enforcement methods.

In the eight years following the *Sandoval* decision, the Bush administration did little to expand or enforce disparate-impact rules similar to those challenged in that case. But the Obama administration took a number of steps that went beyond the Court's interpretation of Title VI, Title IX, and the Equal Protection clause. Recognizing that often it could not count on judicial enforcement, OCR experimented with a new mechanism for inducing compliance: investigations so expensive and potentially embarrassing that schools would sign detailed compliance agreements simply to end them.

This approach was abandoned by the Trump administration but is likely to be revived under President Biden. The final section of this chapter examines the power and the limitations of the enforcement strategy under President Obama.

The Revival of Title VI Regulation

In 2010, Secretary of Education Arne Duncan traveled to Selma, Alabama, to commemorate the forty-fifth anniversary of "Bloody Sunday," the day state troopers viciously attacked peaceful voting-rights marchers. Secretary Duncan charged that the Bush administration had failed to enforce civil rights laws: "The hard truth is that, in the last decade, the Office for Civil Rights has not been as vigilant as it should have been in combating gender and racial discrimination and protecting the rights of individuals with disabilities. But that is about to change."[46]

And change it did. Over the next six years the Department of Education backed Duncan's words with a flurry of actions. Its Office for Civil Rights issued "Dear Colleague" letters (DCLs) on bullying, sexual harassment, the rights of transgender students, affirmative action in college admissions, the use of race in assigning students to public schools, school districts' allocation of financial resources, racial disparities in school discipline, the instruction provided to students not fluent in English, and much more.

As table 9.1 indicates, the number of policy pronouncements issued by OCR between 2009 and 2016 exceeded the total number issued during the terms of Obama's seven predecessors. To be sure, the number of guidelines issued under Title VI, Title IX, §504, the Americans with Disabilities Act, and other nondiscrimination statutes also increased under George W. Bush. But these Bush guidelines tended to be relatively small-bore. And they entailed little concerted enforcement activity. By contrast, the Obama-era guidelines were both sweeping and (especially in the case of school discipline and sexual harassment) backed by aggressive enforcement action.

The Title VI policies announced by OCR between 2010 and 2016 were notable not just for their number and scope, but also for the extent to which they were designed to limit the impact of Supreme Court decisions. For decades, OCR had stuck relatively close to Supreme Court rulings, sometimes going a few steps beyond with the expectation that federal courts would follow—which they often did. But once the Supreme Court began to narrow its interpretation of civil rights statutes, Democratic administrations looked for ways to move in the opposite direction.

TABLE 9.1. Number of policy guidance documents issued by OCR, by category

President	Title VI, race	Title IX	Disability	Language	Multiple	Other	Total
Nixon/Ford	0	1	0	1	0	0	2
Carter	0	1	2	0	1	0	4
Reagan	0	0	1	0	1	0	2
G. H. W. Bush	0	0	1	2	0	0	3
Clinton	3	3	1	0	1	0	8
G. W. Bush	6	7	3	0	1	3	20
Obama	10	8	15	1	5	0	39
Trump	#	1, #	0	0	0	5	6
Biden (1 year)	0	3	1	0	0	1	4

Between 2017 and 2020, OCR withdrew multiple guidance documents under Titles VI and XI.

Source: These figures are based on material available on the Office for Civil Rights' "Policy Guidance Portal" (www2.ed.gov/about/offices/list/ocr/frontpage/faq/rr/policyguidance/index.html?perPage=100), accessed May 20, 2022, and supplemented by the author's knowledge of a few additional policy documents. Given the variety of forms such policy statements take, deciding what to include required a few judgment calls.

RACIAL PREFERENCES AND ASSIGNMENTS

The new relationship between OCR and the Supreme Court was most obvious in five documents the Obama administration issued on the use of racial classifications in school assignments and college admission. Four of these guidance documents explained how colleges and graduate schools could increase racial diversity within the confines of the Supreme Court's decisions in *Grutter v. Bollinger, Gratz v. Bollinger, Schuette v. Coalition to Defend Affirmative Action,* and *Fisher v. University of Texas at Austin I and II.*[47] OCR and the Department of Justice made it clear that their main objective was to maximize schools' ability to institute affirmative-action programs.

The longest of these guidance documents was the 2011 joint OCR/DOJ "Guidance on the Voluntary Use of Race to Achieve Diversity and Avoid Racial Isolation in Elementary and Secondary School." It offered OCR's first defense of the "racial isolation" argument that had been so central to the courts' desegregation jurisprudence in the 1960s and 1970s:

> Racially diverse schools provide incalculable educational and civic benefits by promoting cross-racial understanding, breaking down racial and other stereotypes and eliminating bias and prejudice . . . [W]here schools lack a diverse student body or are racially isolated (i.e. are composed overwhelmingly of students of one race), they may fail to provide the full panoply of benefits that K-12 schools can offer. The academic achievement of students at racially isolated schools often lags behind that of their peers at more diverse schools. Racially isolated schools often have fewer effective teachers, higher teacher

turnover rates, less rigorous curricular resources (e.g. college preparatory courses,), and inferior facilities and other educational resources.[48]

For OCR and DOJ, encouraging schools' efforts to reduce racial isolation meant minimizing the impact of the Supreme Court's opinion in the 2007 *Parents Involved* case.

To do so, they emphasized that Justice Kennedy's concurring opinion in *Parents Involved* offered more flexibility to school districts than did Chief Justice Roberts' plurality opinion: "Together with the four dissenting Justices, Justice Kennedy recognized that K-12 school districts have compelling interests both in achieving diversity and in avoiding racial isolation, and he concluded that school districts could voluntarily adopt measures to pursue these goals." These measures include (1) "generalized race-based approaches [that] employ expressly racial criteria, such as the overall racial composition of neighborhoods" and (2) "individual racial classifications," so long as race is just one "plus factor" in "individualized review." The guidance document offered many examples of legal methods for reducing racial isolation. For example, "in evaluating requests to transfer into a predominantly Asian-American school, a school district could give priority to students who live in a neighborhood comprised predominantly of non-Asian-American households, regardless of the race of the particular student requesting the transfer." If this step doesn't do enough to reduce racial isolation, a school district "may consider using an individual student's race as one factor among others in considering whether to approve or deny the student's transfer request." Such a combination of "generalized race-based" policies and highly discretionary, "individualized" use of race by school officials drained the *Parents Involved* decision of much of its significance.

It is hard to judge the impact of these guidance documents on the use of race in admissions and school assignments. Colleges and graduate schools had never made much effort to change their affirmative-action policies in response to the Supreme Court's meandering and loophole-filled opinions on the subject. Moreover, any school districts with halfway-decent legal advice would realize that Justice Kennedy's concurrence in *Parents Involved* left them with plenty of leeway. The Trump administration withdrew all these documents in July 2018.[49] The Biden administration did not reinstate them during its first year in office. But it did announce that the 2018 withdrawal letter "and the underlying issues are under review by the U.S. Department of Education and the U.S. Department of Justice." This action did "not have the effect of rescinding this document or reinstating prior guidance."[50] It is likely that the informal advice OCR gives to school officials will be more important than its formal policy statements.

THE RESOURCES QUAGMIRE

Explaining that the president could not "continue to wait" for Congress to act "on behalf of vulnerable children," on October 1, 2014, Secretary Duncan announced the Obama administration's "Guidance to Ensure All Students have Equal Access to Educational Resources." The guidance came in the form of a thirty-seven-page DCL signed by Assistant Secretary of Education Catherine E. Lhamon, who had previously been the lead attorney for the American Civil Liberties Union in a major California school-finance case.[51] To justify its policy, OCR drew on the findings of a 2012 report by the congressionally commissioned Commission on Equity and Excellence in Education.

School finance has long been a central concern of education reformers and civil rights advocates. Behind the Court's decision in *Brown* lay the undeniable fact that "separate but equal" had always been a fraud: spending on white schools was far higher than on black schools; racial segregation was a mechanism for channeling funds to the former rather than the latter. Not only do states differ in the support they provide to public schools, but school districts vary markedly in their tax base and tax revenue. ESEA was designed in part to reduce such inequities. The same was true of school finance litigation. Although the US Supreme Court has refused to address the issue under the federal Constitution, state courts have heard challenges to state funding laws in forty-three states, and have required substantial changes in almost half of these cases. Over time the percentage of funding coming from state governments has increased and local funding decreased, diminishing the gap between property-rich and property-poor jurisdictions. Yet substantial differences between school districts remain.

At the heart of the 2014 DCL lay a disparate-impact argument: school districts and state governments "violate Title VI if they adopt facially neutral policies that are not intended to discriminate," but that nonetheless "have an unjustified, adverse disparate impact on students based on race, color, or national origin."[52] According to the DCL, once federal officials determine that the distribution of *any* educational resource disadvantages a protected minority, schools must not only "demonstrate that the policy or practice is *necessary* to meet an *important* educational goal," but also show that there is no "comparably effective alternative policy or practice that would meet the school district's stated educational goal with less of a discriminatory effect." This language originated in Title VII court decisions on hiring practices. In the education context, this formulation grants substantial authority to federal regulators to decide what constitutes an "important educational goal" and a "comparably effective alternative."

Years of experimentation and study have failed to uncover a clear and direct relationship between money and school quality. Since the early 1980s, real per-capita spending on K–12 public education has nearly doubled, yet student performance has barely budged, and the US has fallen further behind other nations. Despite Title I and state-level funding changes, the achievement gap between black and white students and between poor and more affluent students remains distressingly large.[53] Addressing that gap was a key factor in the federal government's pivot from the input-based "equity regime" to the output-based "standards and accountability regime" described above. As the 2012 report issued by the Commission on Equity and Excellence put it,

> It's not that America hasn't increased spending on education over time—it has. By some measures, we spend as much as or even more as a share of our GDP than do other nations, which underscores that the amount of money spent is not the only factor affecting student achievement. . . . it is critical to spend money strategically on things that work. A look at certain local school districts proves the point: Some districts spend enormous sums with poor results, showing that *how* money is spent can be as important as *how much* is available.[54]

Recognizing this fact, the 2014 DCL focused not on money alone, but on a wide variety of school resources, ranging from curriculum to leadership to teachers to extracurricular activities.

Complex Comparisons

The DCL started from the relatively uncontroversial argument that money *well spent* can "make a dramatic difference in children's lives." Listed in the DCL's sixty-three footnotes are a number of studies indicating how "high-quality" programs can help disadvantaged children. But the DCL offers little insight on the crucial question: How do we know what constitutes a high-quality program? Moreover, the material in the DCL's footnotes sometimes casts doubt on the bold pronouncements made in the text. For example, to support its claim about "high-quality arts programs," it cites four articles, one titled "Mute Those Claims: No Evidence (Yet) for a Causal Link between Arts Study and Academic Achievement."[55]

By focusing on the quality of programs and not just their cost, the guidelines required OCR and school officials to make complex comparisons among schools. School districts were expected both to demonstrate equitable distribution of each type of resource and to engage in a "holistic" analysis of the quality of education provided to all students. Not only are most of the resources described in the DCL hard to quantify, but the letter fails to explain how schools should assign weights to each resource to arrive at the "holistic" analysis it demands. Collecting all this information for every school in a district would be difficult; providing a nonarbitrary comparison of the quality of education provided by multiple schools even harder.

The central mandate of the school resources DCL is for school districts to undertake "periodic self-evaluations" to "identify barriers to equal educational opportunity." The DCL lists seven criteria that must be included in this "self-evaluation" and are subject to OCR review:

- *Curriculum.* To assess the quality of the education provided to students of different races, OCR will examine "a range of specialized programs, such as early childhood programs including preschool and Head Start, Advanced Placement and International Baccalaureate courses, gifted and talented programs, career and technical education programs, language immersion programs, online and distance learning opportunities, performing and visual arts . . . science, technology, engineering, and mathematics (STEM) courses . . . [and] the overall quality and adequacy of special education programs."[56]
- *Teachers.* OCR review will include "teachers' licensure and certification status, whether teachers have completed appropriate training and professional development, whether teachers are inexperienced, [and] whether they are teaching out of their field."[57] OCR can either "focus on a small subset of these criteria where appropriate," or "rely upon a holistic analysis of these criteria to better gauge the totality of teacher and staff characteristics and the quality of instruction." It conceded that "the current state of the empirical research has demonstrated only weak support for the importance of teacher qualifications (such as route of certification, experience, subject matter expertise, and other training) to teachers' effectiveness in the classroom."[58]
- *School leadership.* OCR will investigate whether there are racial disparities "in student access to effective, well-prepared, and stable school leadership." The guidance did not explain how schools can identify "effective" leaders, noting only that it would consider "their levels of experience, their credentials and certification, [and] whether they have completed appropriate training and professional development"—none of which have proven particularly useful in identifying effective principals in the past.[59]
- *Support staff.* OCR will examine "the staff-to-student ratios, training, certification, and years of experience of the support staff."[60] This category includes not just guidance counselors, psychologists, librarians, and specialized therapy providers for students with disabilities, but also social workers, health professionals, and paraprofessionals.

- *School facilities.* Declaring that "research has shown that the quality and condition of the physical spaces of a school are tied to student achievement and teacher retention," OCR will evaluate "the overall physical condition of the school, including features such as paint, maintenance of carpet and lockers, and the absence of vandalism." Among the factors it will consider are "the location and surrounding environment of school buildings," "the availability and quality of transportation services," and "specialized spaces such as laboratories, auditoriums, and athletic facilities."[61]
- *Extra- and co-curricular programs.* OCR will evaluate whether students of different races "participate in a comparable variety of specialized programs—whether curricular, co-curricular, or extracurricular." To do so it will consider "the number of extracurricular activities as well as their intensity and content," "the expertise of teachers, coaches, and advisors," and "the availability of the necessary materials." Left unaddressed was how OCR will measure the "intensity" of a drama club or a school band or the "expertise" of a baseball coach or a school-newspaper adviser.[62]
- *Technology and instructional materials.* OCR will "evaluate whether all students, regardless of race, have comparable access to the technological tools given to teachers and students." This analysis will include such matters as the speed of internet access, the technical training of teachers, how many hours a day students have access to computers, whether this technology is available to students with disabilities, and whether "students have access to necessary technology outside of school and how school districts support students who do not have Internet access at home."[63]

Although most of the DCL is devoted to differences among schools in the same district, OCR emphasizes that it will also examine differences *within schools*. How it would do so was left unclear. Would it look at the racial composition of each class and at the "quality" of each teacher? At the racial composition of AP and advanced math courses, drama clubs, sports teams, and school newspapers? If, as is likely to be the case, fewer black and Hispanic students are enrolled in advanced courses, will that finding be interpreted as discriminatory or a consequence of the racial achievement gap we are trying to reduce? In short, OCR made its investigatory power so open-ended that it could look at everything and anything that goes on in a school.

Buried in a footnote early in the DCL is another implicit expansion of OCR's investigative authority: "State education officials should examine policies and practices for resource allocation *among districts* to ensure that differences among districts do not have the unjustified effect of discriminating on the basis of race."[64] According to OCR, any disparity in resources must be justified by an "important educational goal." Funding differences among school districts are based in large part on the differing tax bases of the districts and the political choices made by voters and school boards. In other words, they do not reflect "important educational goals." The language of the DCL seems to imply that all education-funding decisions should be made at the state level, with no room for local discretion. The DCL never explicitly admits that its new rules are at odds with the basic structure of the American educational system—but based on the standards it announced, it is hard to see how local control could survive.

The DCL's concluding section on remedies adds yet another level of complexity: it emphasizes that OCR expects states to spend more money on schools with high percentages of black and Hispanic children than on those that serve primarily white students. Correcting discriminatory practices "may require significant financial investment from the district," and "lack of funding is not a defense for noncompliance with Federal civil rights obligations." Comparative spending levels should reflect the "extra costs often associated with educating low-income children, English language learners, and students with disabilities." OCR stated that it "will not consider Title I funds in a resource equity analysis"—despite the fact that those federal funds are specifically designed to help school districts meet the needs of such disadvantaged students.[65]

Legal Authority

How did the resources DCL justify this ambitious assertion of federal authority? It opened with the obligatory nod to *Brown v. Board of Education*. But since Chief Justice Warren's opinion consciously avoided the question of school resources, that decision quickly disappeared from sight. In its copious footnotes, the DCL also cited a number of desegregation cases handed down by the Supreme Court and the lower courts. All these cases involved school systems that had already been found guilty of intentional racial segregation.[66] OCR implied that the scrutiny applied to schools operating under desegregation orders would now apply to every school district in the country. If anything is clear from the federal courts' desegregation jurisprudence, though, it is that the remedies for school districts that come before the court with dirty hands far exceed the legal requirements for school districts that have not been found guilty of intentional segregation.

In another footnote, the DCL also claimed support from school-finance cases decided at the state level. It correctly noted that "numerous State courts have also deemed inequitable access to these educational resources unlawful under their State constitutions."[67] But school finance reformers turned to *state* courts after 1973 because in that year the US Supreme Court handed down *San Antonio v. Rodriguez*, the landmark case in which the Court refused to enter the school-finance thicket.[68] Not once in the DCL's footnotes does the name of that famous case appear. Its omission is the specter that haunts the entire document: the DCL was in effect an effort to achieve through administrative means what the Supreme Court had refused to do in *San Antonio*.

In the end, OCR's legal argument rested on the claim that the thirty-seven-page DCL was nothing more than a clarification of a 1980 Department of Justice regulation stating that Title VI prohibits recipients from "utiliz[ing] criteria or methods of administration which have the *effect* of subjecting individuals to discrimination because of their race, color, or national origin."[69] OCR conceded that "the Supreme Court in *Alexander v. Sandoval* held that private individuals have no right to sue to enforce the disparate-impact provision of the Title VI regulations," yet insisted that *Sandoval* "did not undermine the validity of the regulations or otherwise limit the government's authority and responsibility to enforce Title VI regulations."[70]

Investigations

OCR's reading of *Sandoval* was accurate. But it left the agency with a basic enforcement problem: since it had long abandoned the funding cutoff as impractical, how could it enforce its guidelines without relying on the courts? OCR's general response to this problem was to use lengthy, reputation-damaging investigations to induce school leaders to make changes in their programs.[71]

Tracking OCR's enforcement of its resources DCL is no easy task. Nowhere does it list the investigations it has initiated or indicate their status. From data included in OCR's reports to Congress, the resolution agreements it posts on its website, and testimony from Department of Education officials, it is possible to piece together an outline of the office's investigations and negotiated settlements. Three features stand out.

First, in the years following publication of the resources guidance, the number of systemic investigations remained small. Agency documents mention only six compliance reviews on the school resources issue, three resolved in FY 2015 and three initiated that year. Moreover, the number of complaints OCR received on resource disparities constituted a tiny fraction of the thousands it receives each year. In the two-year period before the DCL (FY 2013 and 2014), OCR received a total of thirty-six complaints on resources, eighteen per year.[72] This number increased to twenty-six in FY 2015, but dropped to just nine in FY 2016, the last year of the Obama administration.[73] By comparison, in FY 2015 the total number of complaints OCR received exceeded ten thousand, including nearly 2,200 on Title VI alone. Starting in 2014, the agency placed highest priority on investigating Title IX sexual harassment complaints. 2014 was also the year OCR began to focus on investigating racial disparities in school discipline. With a declining number of staff members and a burgeoning enforcement agenda, OCR could not devote sufficient resources to an initiative it had announced with great fanfare.

Second, most of the agreements OCR reached with school districts did not require major reallocation of resources, but focused narrowly on access to AP courses, gifted and talented programs, and the International Baccalaureate. This constricted focus was apparent in three of the four school systems highlighted in OCR's congressional reports and testimony: Arlington, Texas; Elk Grove, California; and South Orange-Maplewood, New Jersey.[74] In light of enforcement realities, it is not surprising. The number of minority students in such classes and programs is easy to count. Moreover, these numbers are readily apparent to students and their parents, the main source of Title VI complaints. And complying with these demands is relatively easy for schools since doing so does not require a major reallocation of resources. Focusing on access to advanced courses, though, has the disadvantage of distracting attention from the question of whether schools have adequately prepared minority students for those courses in the first place.

Third, in the rare case in which OCR did undertake a "holistic" review of a school district's allocation of resources, the investigation lasted for many years but produced only a milquetoast compliance agreement that required the district to continue its ongoing efforts and to report back to OCR on its progress. The agreement with the Toledo, Ohio school system was the only one disclosed by OCR that went much beyond access to advanced courses. The Toledo investigation began in September 2010, sparked by a major reorganization of the primary and secondary schools in that city. It culminated in a resolution agreement announced five and a half years later.

OCR's letter of findings shows how extensive its Toledo investigation had become. The nineteen-page single-spaced letter described the agency's review of fifteen of the district's forty-one K–8 schools and five of its eight high schools. OCR investigators visited all these schools, interviewing "the principal, librarian, counselor, staff person responsible for computer technology, and teachers" at each. They collected data on the racial composition of each school; the qualifications, experience, and tenure of teachers and staff; the number of books in each library; and the courses offered.[75]

OCR compared the resources at three types of schools: majority white; majority black; and those close to the district average, 43 percent black and

42 percent white. Its investigation uncovered little evidence of systematic discrimination against predominantly black schools. Although the three K–8 schools with the lowest percentage of teachers with master's degrees were predominantly black, the school with the highest level of MA degrees was also predominantly black. At the high school level, the school with the lowest percentage of MA teachers was predominantly white; the predominantly black schools were close to the median. Moreover, "there were no significant differences in the percentage of core classes taught by properly certified teachers between racially identifiable white and African American K-8 schools." Predominantly black schools had more guidance counselors and psychologists than white schools. The libraries in predominantly black schools had more books but shorter hours. OCR found school facilities "were comparable with respect to amenities."

This lengthy investigation culminated in an agreement that demanded little of the school district. It would "continue to implement" its programs to ensure that qualified and effective teachers and leaders are "equitably distributed throughout the District." The district would find more volunteers to extend library hours in predominantly black schools. It would also provide in-person (as opposed to online) AP courses in predominantly black schools, even if only one or two students signed up for them. The only other specific requirements involved record-keeping and reporting.[76]

None of the agreements OCR negotiated with school districts required them to change the way they assign teachers to particular schools. Citing multiple studies by reputable scholars, the 2014 DCL reported that schools with large numbers of minority students tend to employ less-experienced and less-effective teachers, and that this trend adversely affects student achievement. Secretary Duncan had repeatedly emphasized this crucial source of inequality. The central problem is that employment contracts and union rules give experienced teachers the opportunity to move to schools with fewer at-risk students. The DCL bravely announced, "When a district's adherence to collective bargaining agreements or State law has caused or contributed to discrimination against students on the basis of race, color, or national origin, Federal civil rights obligations may require a school district to renegotiate agreements, revise its personnel policies, or take other steps to remedy the discrimination." But it never tried to do so. Although the National Education Association and the American Federation of Teachers enthusiastically endorsed the Obama administration's equity initiative, they have fervently opposed such attacks on collective bargaining agreements. Recognizing the tenuous legal basis for the DCL, OCR avoided court battles on this issue.

During the Trump administration, OCR withdrew its guidance documents on affirmative action and on school discipline. It did not, though, withdraw the DCL on resources. It continued to investigate a small number of resources complaints. But it did not consider any of those investigations significant enough to mention in the agency's annual report.[77]

The school-resources issue illustrates three features of OCR's reliance on onerous investigations to enforce its guidelines. First and most obviously, investigations are resource-intensive for the agency as well as schools. That limits the number of guidelines OCR can enforce at one time. The Obama administration placed highest priority on enforcing its Title IX DCL on sexual harassment and its Title VI DCL on school discipline. The school-resources DCL fell by the wayside.

Second, a new administration can neutralize its predecessors' guidelines merely by reducing the resources it devotes to investigations. It need not take the potentially controversial step of revoking them.

Third, and more subtly, the extent to which the investigation strategy produces a significant shift in the behavior of school districts is inversely proportional to the complexity of the calculations it requires. As we will see in the next section, OCR structured investigations of school discipline in such a way that no major school district was likely to pass its test. It could continue to apply pressure until the district signed an agreement—as so many did. But the school-resources calculation was so complicated that it was never clear what compliance required. In the end, compliance was largely procedural: even the school districts subject to extensive investigations were merely required to file further reports.

DISCIPLINING SCHOOLS

A few months earlier in 2014, OCR joined with the Department of Justice to issue a DCL on "Nondiscriminatory Administration of School Discipline."[78] In announcing the letter, Secretary Duncan asserted that the "overuse of suspensions and expulsions" has taken "a terrible toll on students, families, schools, and communities." Suspended students are "less likely to graduate on time— and more likely to repeat a grade, drop out of school, and become involved in the criminal justice system." Black students are "more than three times as likely as their white peers to be expelled or suspended." This disparity, he confidently asserted, "is not caused by differences in children; it is caused by differences in training, professional development, and discipline policy." It is "adult behavior that needs to change."[79] The DCL was one part of the Obama administration's broader effort to address the "school-to-prison pipeline" by discouraging the use of suspensions and expulsions by public schools. The administration was not alone: more than twenty states have revised their laws to discourage use of out-of-school punishments; nearly a quarter of the county's largest school systems have limited the use of suspensions.[80]

One could defend the 2014 DCL simply by saying that kicking students out of school is bad educational policy. What students with behavioral problems need is more time in school and more sustained attention from teachers, not less. The federal government, though, has no authority to set disciplinary policy for local school systems. When Congress enacted ESEA in 1965, it prohibited the national government from exercising any control over instructional matters. What happened inside the schoolhouse was left to teachers, principals, local school boards, and state boards of education to decide.

In the late 1960s and early 1970s federal courts carved out two exceptions to this hands-off approach regarding school discipline. The first was constitutional. The Due Process clause of the Fourteenth Amendment gives students the right to "some sort of hearing" before being subjected to serious punishment. Moreover, students cannot be punished for exercising their right to free speech in a manner that does not disrupt educational programs. After 1975, though, federal courts became more hesitant to second-guess school officials on disciplinary matters.[81] Second, as courts were drawn deeper into the difficult job of desegregating public schools, they faced a plethora of so-called "second-generation" issues, including discriminatory disciplinary practices. This form of judicial oversight was confined to district found guilty of operating a "dual" school system.

As a result, OCR only has authority to prohibit disciplinary practices deemed racially discriminatory. Its DCL charged that many school systems have violated Title VI by punishing black and Hispanic students more frequently and more punitively than white and Asian students engaged in similar behavior. It promised to investigate school systems whose disciplinary policies and practices have a disparate impact on minority students—which meant nearly every large school district in the country.

Different Treatment and Disparate Impact

The discipline DCL was divided into two parts, one on "different treatment" and the other on "disparate impact." The discussion of "different treatment" was relatively uncontroversial, essentially a restatement of previous court and agency applications of Title VI. If a school's rules are designed to disadvantage minority students or if (more likely) "the school administers the policy in a discriminatory manner," then the school has violated federal law. Almost all the examples described in the DCL involved some form of disparate treatment. And nearly all the two hundred to three hundred discipline complaints OCR investigates each year also allege different treatment.

The problem is that "different treatment" is hard to prove. How does one determine if two students who received different punishments had engaged in similar behavior? Usually infractions are observed by only a few people, and many involve judgment calls. Moreover, the punishment meted out to a particular student will depend in part on past behavior—is this a first offense, or the third or fourth? To the extent that OCR focuses on "different treatment," it is drawn into detailed and often inconclusive investigations of complicated individual cases. And it will not be able to address the broader issue of schools' use of out-of-school punishments.

More significant, therefore, was the DCL's assertion that schools "also violate Federal law when they *evenhandedly* implement *facially neutral* policies and practices that, although not adopted with the intent to discriminate, nonetheless have an *unjustified effect* of discriminating on the basis of race."[82] A school's disciplinary policies and practices will be deemed to have an "adverse impact" on minority students if those students "are disproportionately" punished at higher rates or "subject to longer sanctions or more severe penalties." Once that prima facie case has been made, the school bears the burden of demonstrating that its policy is "necessary to meet an important educational goal," and that there exist no "comparably effective alternative policies or practices that would meet the school's stated educational goal with less of a burden or adverse impact on the disproportionately affected racial group." OCR explained that it would take a particularly hard look at policies that "impose mandatory suspension, expulsion or citations" for specified offenses, especially truancy.

Secretary Duncan and OCR insisted that out-of-school punishments do not work, and that alternatives such as "restorative justice" and "positive behavioral interventions and supports" do. Consequently, under the DCL's disparate-impact rule, school districts would find it nearly impossible to convince the agency that they have met their burden of proof. In fact, during its lengthy investigation of school districts' disciplinary policies, OCR rarely inquired as to their justification for their policies. For example, a full two years into its investigation of the Oklahoma City schools, it noted that "in order to make findings" to conclude its review, "interviews would need to be conducted to establish whether or not there is a legitimate nondiscriminatory reason for the disparate numbers."[83] OCR never got around to conducting those interviews because the school district agreed to a settlement. The easiest way for districts to avoid or resolve expensive and politically embarrassing

OCR investigations was to eliminate or substantially reduce out-of-school punishments. This reduction was clearly the agency's overriding goal.

The Debate over Evidence

OCR had no difficulty showing that African American students "tend to be disciplined more than their peers." In fact, they are three to four times more likely to be suspended or expelled from school than white students. (Asian American students are disciplined less frequently than whites; Hispanic students more than whites but less than African Americans.) The big question is: Why this huge racial difference? OCR and the Department of Justice acknowledged that these disparities "may be caused by a range of factors." But according to the key sentences in the lengthy letter, "research suggests that the substantial racial disparities are not explained by more frequent or more serious misbehavior by students of color."

The DCL cited a number of academic studies to buttress this claim. Some of those studies tried to control for factors that are likely to be correlated with misbehavior, most importantly poverty. They showed that poor black students are disciplined more severely than poor white children. But these studies were not able either to consider the exact nature of the misbehavior that led to disciplinary action or additional risk factors likely to increase misbehavior—such as growing up in a single-parent family, living in a high-crime neighborhood, being subjected to parental abuse or neglect, or being exposed to lead in the air or in drinking water.

Several subsequent studies cast doubt on the assumption that the discipline gap is largely the product of racial discrimination. For example, a 2014 article published in the *Journal of Criminal Justice* factored in previous behavioral patterns identified by parents and teachers, and found that accounting for "prior problem behavior reduced to statistical insignificance the odds differential in suspensions between black and white youth." The authors concluded that "difference in rates of suspension between racial groups thus appears to be a function of differences in problem behavior that emerge early in life, that remain relatively stable over time, and that materialize in the classroom." They criticize advocacy groups and government agencies (especially the Department of Justice) for taking "great liberties" in "linking racial differences in suspensions to the racial discrimination" of teachers and other school officials.[84]

A later study suggested that the well-documented racial disparities "are primarily due to differences in discipline practices across schools, rather than within schools." Racial disparities "diminished greatly when school fixed effects were included." Within a particular school, "Black students are only slightly more likely than white students to receive exclusionary discipline."[85] To be sure, some schools might be too harsh in their discipline (perhaps because they experience higher levels of violence and disorder), but they do not apply those harsh penalties in a discriminatory manner.

One could reply to these studies that "implicit" racial bias leads young minority students to be labeled and stigmatized in ways that affect both their later behavior and school officials' image of them. Or that schools with a large number of minority students adopt an unnecessarily punitive approach toward discipline. The major take-away is that disparate-impact analysis inevitably leads to extended debates over what social-science evidence can demonstrate—and what it leaves unresolved.

Remedies and Enforcement

An appendix to the DCL offers multiple "Recommendations for School Districts, Administrators, and Staff" on alternatives to out-of-school punishments. It warns that these alternatives are "illustrative" only, "not intended to be exhaustive or exclusive." Schools that "choose to implement one or more of these recommendations might still be found to be in violation of Federal law(s)." Despite these disclaimers, schools clearly felt pressure to adopt at least some of the appendix's five pages of recommendations.

In a 2018 Brookings Institution report, Nora Gordon notes that "while the DCL relies heavily on research to support its assertion that disparities are a result of discrimination, it does not do so in its policy and practice recommendations." Its appendix "outlines a number of ideas with popular support, but a limited research base to date." Gordon warned that "schools will need to adopt alternative practices, rather than eliminating or dramatically reducing the use of exclusionary discipline in a policy void." Unfortunately, "recent studies shed light on the difficulty of actually implementing changes in these practices."[86] Doing so will be particularly difficult when schools' "street-level bureaucrats," namely teachers, find the new policies ineffective or even dangerous.

Given the Supreme Court's insistence that Title VI bans only intentional discrimination and that federal courts will not enforce agencies' disparate-impact regulations, how did OCR manage to convince so many school districts to change their discipline policies? The answer lies in its particularly aggressive use of lengthy investigations. By early 2017 OCR had conducted well over three hundred investigations, focusing on large urban school districts. It signed compliance agreements with school districts throughout the country, including Oklahoma City; Oakland, California; and Minneapolis and Rochester, Minnesota. Many other districts, including Los Angeles, San Francisco, Philadelphia, Baltimore, Chicago, New York City, and Pittsburgh, also made major changes in their disciplinary policies after the DCL was announced.[87]

The nature of these investigations was laid out in an unusually detailed 2014 internal-enforcement document that eventually became public.[88] Running to twenty-one single-spaced pages, it emphasized five features of OCR's enforcement program. First, even in "complaints alleging *only* individual discrimination in discipline, OCR will investigate both the individual allegation *and* will open a class-based investigation" either of the particular school in question or of the entire school district, depending on how the district's disciplinary statistics compare with national averages. This "class-based" investigation must continue "regardless of whether the relief provided" by the district "fully addresses the individual complaint."[89]

Second, investigation of disciplinary complaints will involve "an examination and analysis of *all* components of the disciplinary process; the investigations are broad-based and systemic." They must cover not just "disciplinary actions of a substantial nature," but "other types of minor disciplinary responses." OCR will interview teachers (including both those with particularly high and particularly low rates of disciplinary referrals), students, administrators, and law-enforcement personnel. The document devotes six full pages to describing the elements of the investigation, which must include collecting three years of data on fifteen different items. It also requires investigators to compare the disciplinary records of schools within the district.

Third, the document devotes less than a third of a page to explaining how schools can meet their burden of proof for showing that their policies are "necessary" for meeting "an important educational goal" and that no "comparably effective alternative policies" would have less of an "adverse impact." It simply repeats the cursory language of the DCL. The elaborate flowchart at the end of the document does not include the opportunity for schools to defend their policies. Clearly, once OCR concludes that a school district's policies have a disproportionate impact on minority students, no defense is realistically available.

Fourth, the internal-guidance document provided nearly four pages of instruction on what resolution letters must contain. These include fourteen separate items. The item on data collection and evaluation lists twenty-two pieces of information that must be reported on each disciplinary action taken by the school district subsequent to signing the agreement.

Fifth, the settlement agreement must be followed by "ongoing interactions with the recipient," i.e., the school district. The document explained that

Given the breadth of the discipline agreements, it is essential for OCR to be proactive in establishing and maintaining a productive working relationship with the recipient . . . Monitoring of discipline resolution agreements is very detailed and long-term; it requires on-going communications not only with administrators, but also with teachers, other staff, students and parents/guardians in order to determine whether the remedies are effective in addressing discrimination.

Such federal oversight will continue into the indefinite future: "OCR will review any changes that a district proposes"; "if OCR is not satisfied with them, we will require further correction."[90]

None of OCR's hundreds of investigations culminated in a finding that a school district had violated Title VI, and therefore should lose federal funding. Such a finding would provide the district with the opportunity to seek judicial review, with the risk that a court would rule that the 2014 DCL exceeded OCR's statutory authority. Instead, OCR kept its investigations open until the school district signed an agreement.

Not surprisingly, OCR's investigations often produced resentment among those subject to them. In 2018 the School Superintendents' Association conducted an extensive survey of school-district leaders targeted by OCR. One key finding was that "the more generalized pressure from OCR has changed local policies and practices in a different and more substantial way than the [2014] guidance."[91] In interviews designed to illuminate the nature of the pressure generated by OCR's investigations, the association's staff heard the following statements "expressed multiple times":

- "Investigations into individual complaints quickly morphed into district-wide investigations that required school personnel to compile information on discipline infractions and policies in every grade and school."
- Gathering the data demanded by OCR "was commonly described as unprecedented, intimidating and costly. Multiple districts estimated it cost tens of thousands of dollars to meet the paperwork and personnel demands of OCR investigations."
- The investigations frequently lasted well over a year, "leading to considerable uncertainty and unease in districts. As school leaders, personnel and school boards awaited an answer from OCR, they felt unable to change disciplinary interventions, adjust policies and practices and were unsure as to whether current professional development activities and programs for students were appropriate or maintainable."
- Even in schools found to be in compliance with Title VI, "teachers and principals discussed feeling undermined and scared by the process. . . .

There was a noticeable decline in staff morale after these investigations concluded that did not fade once the district was found to be legally compliant."
- School officials interviewed by the association's staff "described the scope of the investigatory process as overwhelming and intimidating for school personnel."

In short, as was the case with OCR's investigations of colleges' compliance with its Title IX DCL on sexual harassment, the process was the punishment.

Consequences

It is one thing to announce a new policy, quite another to carry it out in an effective manner. For highly discretionary matters such as discipline, successful implementation requires buy-in from the teachers and principals who will apply the new rules. In many districts, policies curtailing out-of-school punishments generated strenuous opposition from teachers. For example, in Oklahoma City and Baton Rouge, Louisiana, 60 percent of teachers surveyed by the local school union reported that discipline had declined since new policies were instituted to limit out-of-school punishments. In some cities teachers expressed alarm at the extent to which new policies reduced their ability to control their classrooms and keep students (and themselves) safe.[92]

Most teachers think that alternative programs can work if provided the necessary resources, but that out-of-school suspensions remain an important tool for dealing with students who repeatedly commit serious offenses. When asked by pollsters in 2016 whether they supported or opposed "policies that prevent schools from expelling or suspending black and Hispanic students at higher rates than other students," 58 percent of teachers answered "opposed," only 24 percent "support." The general public was similarly negative, with 51 percent opposed and 20 percent supporting. Among African Americans and Hispanics, opinion was nearly equally divided: for the former, 29 percent supporting and 31 percent opposing; for the former, 36 percent for each position.[93] Many teachers also claim that their schools have complied with new mandates by underreporting the number of actual out-of-school punishments.[94]

Given teachers' distrust of reforms imposed from the top, what have been the consequences in school districts that have announced new discipline policies? A detailed 2017 study of the School District of Philadelphia (SDP) by Matthew Steinberg and Johanna Lacoe provides some unexpected answers. During the 2012–13 school year the SDP made "dramatic changes to its code of conduct," most importantly, "a ban on out-of-school suspensions (OSS) for low-level 'conduct' offences—such as profanity or failure to follow classroom rules—and reduced the length of OSS for more serious infractions."[95] This directive came from the school district's leaders, not OCR. Among Steinberg and Lacoe's findings are the following:

- The number of suspensions for conduct infractions targeted by the reform initially declined, but this reduction did not persist.
- "The degree of adherence to the policy varied across schools. Some schools fully complied by eliminating conduct suspensions while others partially complied by reducing but not eliminating these suspensions. And some schools actually increased conduct suspensions."[96]
- "Revising the district's code of conduct was associated with an *increase* in racial disproportionality at the district level." Although "the black-white gap in suspensions for conduct infractions decreased in the wake of the policy change," that decline "was more than offset by an increase in suspensions for more serious incidents, among black students." Overall, "black students experienced an average *increase* in suspension days of eight days per one hundred students relative to white students."[97]
- Academic achievement by students with previous suspensions—the group most likely to have been suspended again if the old policy had remained in place—did not increase. Achievement by students without previous suspensions declined somewhat, but only in schools that did not comply with the SDP's directives.[98]

In other words, complying with the new policy did not seem either to hurt most students academically or help those with a history of disciplinary trouble. But compliance was highly variable, and the goal of reducing racial disparities became even more distant.

We do not know whether the experience of other school systems was similar. The extent of noncompliance in Philadelphia is particularly notable given that the change originated in the leadership of the school district and was not imposed from outside. Above all, the Philadelphia case reminds us of the decentralized nature of American public education and the large gap that can emerge between publicly announced policies and what actually happens in the classroom.

After Obama

The Trump administration's initial action on the discipline issue was to alter enforcement policy, not withdraw the 2014 DCL. In June 2017, acting assistant secretary Candice Jackson informed the regional offices that they were no longer required to turn each individual complaint into a class-wide investigation. Nor need they collect three years of data for each investigation.[99] A year and a half later, OCR withdrew the 2014 DCL along with several accompanying documents and reports.[100]

During the summer of 2021 the Departments of Education and Justice announced that the 2018 withdrawal and the "underlying issues" were "under review," explaining that this reassessment did not "have the effect of rescinding the document or reinstating prior guidance." In 2022 Catherine Lhamon, the author of the 2014 DCL, was nominated by President Biden's nominee to become assistant secretary of education for civil rights once again. Asked about the discipline issue in her confirmation hearing, Lhamon replied, "It's crucial to reinstate guidance on the topic and I think it's crucial to be clear with school communities about what the civil rights obligations are and how best to do the work in their classrooms."[101] Given Lhamon's strong commitment on the topic, it would be surprising if OCR did not eventually reinstate central elements of the former policy. Yet by the end of 2022, OCR had issued no new guidance.

Government Institutions and Policy Strategies

Court-ordered school desegregation was just one strategy federal officials employed to improve educational opportunity for disadvantaged children. As support for busing declined, Congress and administrators focused their attention on alternative approaches. The strengths and weaknesses of these strategies in part reflected the peculiar features of their institutional sponsors.

Congress's initial impulse was to increase federal funding—to "throw money at the problem," as it so often does. The landmark Elementary and Secondary Education Act of 1965 was sold as an effort to provide more resources to schools with large number of poor children. Similarly, the 1972 Emergency School Aid Act offered more money to schools undergoing desegregation. Passing such legislation usually required spreading the money around to a large number of congressional districts, reducing the amount available to districts that needed it most. This broad distribution of funds was especially apparent with ESEA. Over the years the law was amended to do a somewhat better job targeting of funds to schools with a disproportionate number of low-income students. But the need to build broad congressional majorities continues to limit such targeting.

The other major limitation has been Congress's reluctance to provide specific guidance on how that money should be spent. In 1965 it prohibited any form of federal control over instruction. Although that restriction changed somewhat with the "standards and accountability" regime that began to take shape in the 1990s, federal control over what goes on in the classroom remained minimal. The more demanding requirements of No Child Left Behind of 2001 remained unattained in practice and largely repudiated by the Every Student Succeeds Act of 2015.

There were two partial exceptions to this generalization, one the product of congressional and judicial action, the other a joint product of administrators and judges. The first was education for students with disabilities. The litigation that provided both the policy model and the political stimulus for the 1975 Education for All Handicapped Children Act grew out of early desegregation cases. Initially the concern was that too many minority children were being relegated to special-education programs that did little more than warehouse them. Soon the effort to improve education for children with disabilities gained two sets of allies: middle-class parents of children with disabilities; and organizations representing professions providing services to those children. Here the federal government provided more mandates than money. Most of the cost was borne by state and local government. There is no doubt, though, that the quality of special-education programs improved significantly.[102]

The second partial exception was programs for English learners. Here, too, desegregation litigation played a major role in calling attention to students not well served by state and local school systems. Once again Congress began by simply providing money to schools with a significant number of English learners. Adding to the political appeal of this effort was the competition of Republicans and Democrats for the votes of the increasing number of Hispanic voters. In the mid-1970s Congress timidly encouraged school districts to adopt a particular pedagogical approach: bilingualism. When OCR and the courts made a stronger push in this direction, the resistance was quick and strong. Congress retreated, forsaking all efforts to prescribe a particular pedagogical approach.

Congress has one obvious institutional advantage: the power of the purse. It can provide more money to schools that are either underfunded or serve children who need special services. For better and for worse, Congress usually needs to build broad coalitions that reach beyond a specific racial or ethnic group. This coalition-building produces more resilient political support, but at the same time reduces the extent to which funding is targeted to those most in need. Just as importantly, in most cases Congress has proven unable to ensure that federal funds are used in a way that actually improves the education of the targeted population.

Federal administrative agencies have demonstrated greater ability to change the behavior of local school systems, provided they have substantial support from federal courts. This capacity was most evident with southern school desegregation in second half of the 1960s. It again became apparent in the 1970s when OCR, backed by the Supreme Court's opinion in *Lau v. Nichols* and injunctions issued by district court judges, required many schools to institute bilingual programs for English learners. This effort eventually collapsed in the face of congressional and presidential opposition, and a change in heart among federal judges. In the long run, though, the combination of judicial and administrative action has created a regulatory regime designed to insure the quality—but not determine the methods—of instruction for English learners.

The Title VI initiatives of the Obama administration raise the question of how effective administrative action can be when it cannot count on support from federal courts. Given the ineffectiveness of the funding cutoff, judicial enforcement through private rights of action has long been the most important sanction lurking behind agency guidelines. Since the Supreme Court has indicated that it will not authorize private suits to enforce disparate-impact rules, OCR has tried to substitute the threat of long and costly investigations to induce compliance with its rules on educational resources and school discipline. This strategy met with considerable success on the school-discipline issue, both because those guidelines were relatively clear and because the effort to reduce out-of-school punishments already had significant support at the state and local level. The same cannot be said of the resources DCL, which lacked both clear standards and support at the state and local level. In both instances OCR had to contend with the thinness of the DCLs' statutory foundations, lack of support in Congress, and the omnipresent threat of judicial reversal.

Given the prominence that the Biden administration has given to racial equity, it is quite possible that it will reinstate and possibly expand upon the Obama administration's use of Title VI. Since it is unlikely that a Supreme Court with six Republican appointees will back away from the *Alexander v. Sandoval* decision, OCR will again face the challenge of finding ways to enforce its guidelines without the help of—and perhaps against the opposition of—the federal courts.

10

What Have We Learned?

Since the 1950s, the federal government has instituted a variety of programs designed to improve the quality of public education provided to underserved students. Title I of the 1965 Elementary and Secondary Education Act distributes federal funding to school districts with a high proportion of poor students. Head Start offers preschool programs to millions of poor families. The Individuals with Disabilities Education Act has substantially improved the education we offer to students with a wide array of disabilities. Federal money and mandates have similarly improved the quality of instruction offered to the growing number of English learners. No Child Left Behind and the Every Student Succeeds Act have highlighted the racial achievement gap, and pressured state and local school systems to focus attention on the most poorly performing schools. Title IX helped sweep away barriers to education for women and girls. Meanwhile, state governments—often under pressure from court suits—have restructured school-funding formulas to increase the money available to districts with many disadvantaged students. In short, school desegregation was only the most visible and controversial part of a much larger effort to promote equality of educational opportunity.

That educational opportunities for female students, students with disabilities, and English learners has improved significantly is beyond dispute. Unfortunately, for African American students the picture is mixed. The racial achievement gap decreased significantly from the late 1960s to the late 1980s, but since then improvement has been modest. The gap between high and low socioeconomic status (SES) students has (depending on the measures used) either failed to narrow or widened.[1] Meanwhile, the economic significance of these gaps has increased. The economy of the early twenty-first century rewards skills developed in school more than did the economy of the 1950s.

"Differences in basic skills" as measured by standardized tests, Ronald Ferguson has estimated, accounts for half to three-quarters of the white/black wage differential.[2] In recent decades, the well-educated have become richer and the poorly educated poorer, making the quality of public education more important than ever before.

The Elusive Pursuit of Equal Educational Opportunity

In one of the most evocative pronouncements in *Brown v. Board*, Chief Justice Warren wrote,

> In these days, it is doubtful that any child may reasonably be expected to succeed in life if he is denied the opportunity of an education. Such an opportunity, where the state has undertaken to provide it, is a right which must be made available to all on equal terms.

It is hard to disagree with this statement. But how do we know when educational opportunity has been "made available to all on equal terms"? Does this proposition mean that all students should be treated the same? Even if such a thing were possible, it is hardly clear that students with different backgrounds, abilities, interests, motivations, and habits should be treated similarly. Since we expect educational institutions to respond to such individual differences, and we realize that some students will progress faster than others, how do we measure educational opportunity?

At the very least, "equal educational opportunity" means not distributing educational resources on an arbitrary basis—which was obviously the case with racially segregated schools, schools that refused to enroll students with disabilities, and programs that excluded female students. These clear-cut inequalities were rejected by the Court in *Brown* and addressed by Congress when it enacted Title IX in 1972 and the 1975 Education for All Handicapped Children Act.

Unfortunately, many forms of unequal treatment take more subtle forms: bias in evaluating students for tracking or assignment to special-education courses; different expectations of white and black, affluent and poor students; disciplinary rules that fall more heavily on some students than others; allocation of resources that favors some activities, schools, and students over others. This list could be extended at length. Rooting out such forms of unequal treatment requires intimate knowledge of the operation of particular schools. And it often requires overseers to second-guess the multitude of discretionary judgments made by the teachers and principals who do the day-to-day work of providing public education.

Rather than delve into the daily practices of school officials, we could ask whether schools are devoting equal resources to all students. Even if equal allocation were possible in our highly decentralized educational system, quantifying "resources" is difficult—as chapter 9's analysis of the Department of Education's 2014 "Dear Colleague" letter shows. More money does not guarantee higher quality education: today the United States spends four times as much per student as it did in the 1960s, but it is doing a poorer job preparing those students for future employment, and is falling behind countries that spend far less. We know that the most important school-based determinant of how much a student learns is the quality of his or her teachers. While we have made some progress in developing useful measures of teachers' performance, we are still a long way from being able to identify which teachers get the best results and why. Equalizing resources, especially the most crucial ones, is far easier said than done.

Then we come to the difficult question of the responsibility of public schools to compensate for educational difficulties they do not create. The most obvious example here is disability: should schools be expected to spend much, much more on students with severe impairments, even if the result is only a modest improvement in their skills? In the US since the mid-1970s, the answer to this question has been "yes." To what extent are schools expected to provide special classes to English learners, helping them to master a new language while keeping up with their regular schoolwork? That is what federal law requires, though not usually what schools achieve. And to what extent should we expect schools to help low-SES students overcome the multiple challenges created by poverty, unsafe neighborhoods, single-parent families, and health risks? Within states and within districts, spending on schools with a high proportion of black students is now slightly higher than spending on predominantly white schools.[3] Yet the racial achievement gap remains large—indicating either that we are not spending enough or that we are not spending in the right way. We know that the educational level of parents has a huge effect on the academic achievement levels of their children, larger than any school-based factors. We also know that students enter kindergarten and first grade with much different capacities, and that these differences tend to accelerate rather than fade over time. Try as we might, we still do not know how to overcome these family-based differences except in very small-scale, high-quality programs.

Recent writing on race and education has emphasized that *equality* (in the sense of formally equal treatment) often does not produce *equity* in the sense of equal outcomes. That is hard to deny. But what do we mean by "equal outcomes"? One possibility is equal academic achievement as measured by standardized tests such as the federal government's National Assessment of Education Progress. Reducing the racial and SES achievement gap has been the goal of education leaders for decades, yet progress has stalled.

The persistence of the racial achievement gap has led some proponents of a new "antiracist" agenda to break with established civil rights groups, and to condemn these tests rather than acknowledge the underlying problem they expose. According to the most prominent such voice, Ibram X. Kendi,

> the use of standardized tests to measure aptitude and intelligence is one of the most effective racist policies ever devised to degrade Black minds and legally exclude Black bodies. We degrade Black minds every time we speak of an "academic-achievement gap" based on these numbers. The acceptance of an academic-achievement gap is just the latest method of reinforcing the oldest racist idea: Black intellectual inferiority.[4]

The civil rights organizations that fought to require schools to break down test results by race and to make those statistics public, of course, did not seek to reinforce stereotypes of racial inferiority. They sought to highlight the deficiencies in the schools so many minority students attend. Reducing the prominence of test results in public schools will hide rather than address the central problem: that African American and Hispanic students leave school with fewer basic skills than their white and Asian peers. Shooting the messenger serves only to divert attention from the urgent need for educational improvement.

The bottom line is that "equal educational opportunity" is a noble aspiration, but far from a guide for action. It raises more questions than it answers. At best it is the beginning of a long examination of what we want from our public educational system and what we can realistically expect it to achieve.

Another American Dilemma

In the long struggle over school desegregation, two central features of American political life have collided: our creedal commitment to equality of opportunity and our decentralized educational institutions. Compared to other advanced liberal democracies, Americans are more accepting of large inequalities of income and wealth. For most Americans, what counts is not equal results but equal opportunity to achieve the "American Dream" of upward mobility. We expect public schooling to help children overcome obstacles to social and economic advancement—regardless of what those obstacles might be. And we have great faith in the power of schooling to "level the playing field." In short, as Jennifer Hochschild and Nathan Scovronick put it, Americans "want the educational system to help translate the American dream from vision to practice."[5] We also expect public schools to prepare citizens for democratic self-government and to develop a common sense of American identity in a large, diverse country that has welcomed immigrants from many countries and cultures.

This commitment to public education goes beyond mere rhetoric. Among advanced industrial democracies, the United States is generally considered a "welfare state laggard," a country exceptionally committed to limited government, to a market economy, and to individual liberty. But when it comes to public education, the US has been a leader rather than a laggard. Hochschild and Scovronick note that, "here public schools started earlier and have always included more people and taken a larger share of resources."[6] In the nineteenth century we led the world in making elementary education widely available to those of modest means. After visiting America in 1830, Tocqueville wrote, "I do not know a people who have succeeded in establishing schools as numerous and as efficacious."[7] In the early twentieth century we sprinted ahead again, offering the high school education needed to produce skilled workers for an evolving economy.[8] Today we spend more per K–12 student than almost any country in the world. Land-grant colleges, the GI Bill, Pell grants, student loan guarantees, and generous research grants helped the US develop a higher education system that draws students from all over the globe.

Public education began in the US when virtually all politics was local, and the federal government still for the most part "at a distance and out of sight." Until the 1960s, American public schools were almost entirely under the control of state and local governments. In 1920, 80 percent of elementary and secondary school funding came from local taxation, 20 percent from state taxes, and almost nothing from the federal government. By 1980 the local contribution had dropped to 40 percent, and the states' risen to 50 percent. Despite the massive growth of regulation, the federal government's financial contribution has seldom risen above 10 percent.[9] Federal law continues to prohibit federal control of curricular matters. The US Department of Education, the smallest federal department, employs fewer than 4,500 people—a fraction of the number employed by local school systems and state education offices.

For most of American history, public support for education was closely connected to its local roots. Schools were controlled by elected school boards, one for each of the more than one hundred thousand school districts. Local control may have produced schools rife with patronage and provincialism, but, as Paul Peterson has pointed out, it also "provided a robust, democratic base for a rapidly expanding system that commanded broad support throughout the political community."[10] In an enormously diverse country, local school districts could tailor their programs to the peculiar demands, interest, and prejudices of their constituencies. "Prior to the 1960s," the historian Hugh Davis Graham has written, "one of the most distinctive attributes of American political culture has been the tenacity with which the United States, unlike most nations, had resisted a national education policy."[11]

The problem, of course, was that this localism also created numerous forms of inequality. Not only did some states provide separate and unequal schools for African Americans, but real estate–poor districts could not spend as much as their more affluent neighbors. Discrimination against religious groups—from Catholics to Jehovah's Witnesses—remained common. School districts were similarly free to exclude students they considered "uneducable" and to expect English learners to "sink or swim." For those determined to make "equal educational opportunity" a reality, localism was *the* problem.

Before the policy breakthrough of the mid-1960s, opposition to federal involvement in education had strong and persistent constitutional overtones. Unlike state constitutions, which bestow upon state and local governments responsibility for public education, the federal Constitution says nothing on the topic, neither explicitly granting Congress power in this field nor denying it to them. According to a Senate staff member who supported federal aid in the 1960s, his opponents "clung on to some mythical constitutional principle: the last thing that could happen in the United States was for the federal hand to be laid on local education, which belongs in the hands of the school boards and local councils of education . . . it was a religious faith."[12] Although hostility to federal intervention diminished after 1965, it did not completely disappear. It reappeared in Republican demands for the elimination of the Department of Education in the early 1980s and again in the mid-1990s.

It is no coincidence that the most important expansion of the federal role in education came at the height of the civil rights revolution. Only extraordinary federal action could put an end to the obviously unjust and unconstitutional educational system of the South. The prestige of the federal government was at an all-time high, educational inequalities were particularly salient, and states-rights arguments had been all but discredited by the actions of Bull Connor, George Wallace, and other defenders of white supremacy. The 1960s, Graham notes, "witnessed federal intervention on an unprecedented scale into realms of education policy that had hitherto been almost the exclusive preserve of state and local and private jurisdictions."[13]

Without doubt, Americans' understanding of federalism has undergone a vast change since the early 1960s. The responsibilities and expectations of the national government have grown exponentially. But especially in the field of education, the federal *institutions* charged with ensuring that local schools comply with federal policy remain small, with uncertain enforcement powers. The increasingly empty threat of funding cut-offs was not enough to ensure compliance with the torrent of regulations, guidelines, and compliance orders generated by federal regulators. Those administrators relied on federal courts to provide the enforcement teeth. But, as we have seen throughout this book, the federal judiciary is itself a decentralized institution, especially when the Supreme Court fails to provide lower court judges with clear rules. With federal judges and administrators searching for ways to reconcile their expansive mandates with their uncertain enforcement powers, the American civil rights state was built on the fly, the product of decades of institutional experimentation.

Two central features of education policy added to this problem. One is the fact that schools are what James Q. Wilson has termed "coping organizations": the most important work in these large bureaucracies is performed by teachers in separate classrooms, usually with little direct supervision.[14] Rules issued from above—whether the superintendent's office, the state board of education, the federal Department of Education, or a judge—can be ignored, subverted, or followed only in a formal manner. Getting buy-in from teachers and principals requires patience, steadfastness, and persuasiveness. The quality of a school probably depends at least as much on its leadership and its sense of organizational mission than on its resources or its rules. As noted above, although the quality of teaching is crucial, we still have no reliable methods for predicting teacher effectiveness.

The second is the hard truth that the academic performance of students is determined more by their family and neighborhood background than by what they learn in school. As much as we might hope that schools will create a "level playing field" that will allow everyone to succeed, in reality the advantages that some children bring to school help them advance more rapidly than those lacking those advantages. We have yet to discover scalable methods for developing schools that overcome rather than accentuate these differences.

School desegregation was the federal government's first major effort to change educational practices in primary and secondary schools. What first seemed like a question of "simple justice" soon became a matter of complex institutional reform as judges, administrators, and educators confronted the difficulties highlighted above. It is understandable that half a century ago federal judges and administrators believed they could use federal mandates to remake public education. With the benefit of decades of hindsight, we are no longer justified in taking such a leap of faith.

The Contested Meaning of "Desegregation"

A central theme of this book is that the Supreme Court has demanded "desegregation" without ever explaining what that key term means. Given the moral standing of *Brown v. Board of Education*, claiming that your understanding of that term reflects the true meaning of *Brown* was more appealing than explicitly stating and defending a policy prescription. Chief Justice Warren's opinion in that case contains enough ambiguity to provide some support for vastly different educational policies.

Chapter 2 laid out the two major understandings of desegregation that for decades have dominated the debate: the "color-blind/limited intervention" approach; and the "racial isolation/equal educational opportunity" approach. The former is what most of the litigants and justices had in mind when *Brown* first came before the Court. By the early 1970s, the latter had become dominant, both in the lower courts and in the Supreme Court. As the implications of this expansive understanding became evident, though, judges began to pull back. The result was an uneasy compromise that pleased almost no one: the immediate goal became achieving racial proportionality within urban school districts that were hemorrhaging affluent white students and a growing number of middle-class black families. Lower court judges slowly shifted their focus from maintaining racial balance to improving school quality, with only moderate success. In chapters 4–8 we saw how judges and administrators oscillated between these two understandings of *Brown*, usually without appreciating the implications of the choices they had made.

Current use of the term "resegregation" illustrates the underlying problem. We have obviously not returned to a time in which states mandate separate schools for black and white children. Nor has there been much change in the extent to which white, black, Hispanic, and Asian students are distributed among schools within school districts (the "evenness" measure). Rather, the increase in the number of Hispanic and Asian students combined with the declining number of white students has reduced the percentage of white students in schools attended by black, Hispanic, and Asian students (the "exposure index"). At the same time, though, white students now go to school with more non-white students than ever before, and the racial and ethnic diversity in many schools has increased. Employing the politically loaded terms "segregation," "resegregation," and "desegregation" does little to help us understand these new realities. These terms are deployed largely to invoke the authority of *Brown* to encompass issues the initial supporters of that decision could never have envisioned.

The main reason neither of these competing interpretations has displaced the other is that each has an Achilles heel. The "color-blind/limited intervention" approach proved too easy to evade. That is why it was abandoned by the Fifth Circuit in *Jefferson County*, the Supreme Court in *Green*, and HEW in its influential 1965 and 1966 guidelines. The more fiercely southern officials fought desegregation, the more judges departed from the earlier, more limited understanding of *Brown*. That is the story of chapter 4 and the first half of chapter 5. Without some degree of desegregation by the numbers, the Jim Crow system of education would have remained in place. Not even the most fervent advocates of the "color-blind/limited intervention" position can deny that racial assignments are sometime necessary as a remedial measure.

At a time of both racial unrest and optimism about the capacity of government to address inequality, it is not surprising that in the late 1960s and early 1970s many government officials, civil rights advocates, educational experts, and legal scholars saw judicial desegregation injunctions as a convenient mechanism for restructuring American education. Expert witnesses assured judges that they could quickly improve the quality of education for black and white students. For a few years it seemed that Congress, the executive branch, and the courts were moving along "parallel tracks." Even President Nixon's appointments to the Court initially endorsed this ambitious project. Opposition seemed to come only from politically discredited southern segregationists and white bigots in ethnic enclaves in the Northeast and Midwest.

Eventually the inherent difficulty of reforming educational institutions from above became evident. The academic consensus on the benefits of racial balance collapsed. White flight demonstrated the limits of judicial control. Opposition to busing turned Congress from a quiet ally into a vocal critic. HEW was relegated to the sidelines. While it is fashionable to blame the failure of this phase of desegregation on the Supreme Court's decision in *Milliken*, it is likely that a contrary ruling would have led to a more thoroughgoing attack on the federal courts and on all forms of desegregation.

By the late 1970s, most judges recognized that simply increasing the number of white students in schools attended by minority children would not significantly improve the quality of education offered to the latter. After *Milliken*, lower court judges focused more attention on determinants of school quality other than racial ratios. In doing so, they came to appreciate both the inherent difficulty of that undertaking and the limited expertise and reach of the judicial branch. That is the story of chapters 6 and 7.

As chapter 2 explains, the differences between the "color-blind/limited intervention" approach and the "racial isolation/equal educational opportunity" approach go beyond constitutional interpretation to encompass competing understandings of institutional capabilities and the reliability of social-science evidence. The former displays greater respect for American federalism, and greater skepticism about the ability of judges to understand and improve educational practices. It questions the extent to which social science can provide a reliable source of guidance to judges, who lack both political accountability and practical experience working in schools. The latter interpretation places more trust in courts in part because it has more faith in social science, and in part because it views American federalism more as a source of inequality than as a forum for local self-government. Its adherents recognized that the power of courts to change educational practices was not set in stone: over the course of the decade, judges used structural injunctions in ways never before envisioned. But the amount of attention busy federal judges could devote to these cases was severely limited. As we saw in chapter 8, most of these injunctions remained in place for decades—long after judges had lost interest in supervising them.

Thinking Institutionally

Another major theme of this book, then, is the importance of thinking about the shape of the government institutions charged with carrying out ambitious mandates announced by the Supreme Court and Congress. As obvious as this might seem in retrospect, neither the Court nor the legislative branch paid much attention to this topic at the start of the desegregation process. At the time of *Brown* both Chief Justice Warren and Justice Frankfurter worried that the Court had handed district court judges a task that exceeded their institutional capacity. The chief justice thought that to "let them flounder" with only such vague guidance would be "rather cruel." Frankfurter feared that to "unload responsibility upon lower courts most subject to community pressure without any guidance for them except our decision of unconstitutionality" would lead to "drawn-out, indefinite delay without even colorable compliance."[15] Nonetheless, Warren and Frankfurter signed a decision in *Brown II* that offered lower courts few clues about how to proceed. And on the crucial question of the form and reach of structural injunctions—the central mechanism for devising and enforcing desegregation orders—the Supreme Court has had almost nothing to say.

By enacting Title VI of the Civil Rights Act, Congress created a mechanism for interpreting and enforcing the nondiscrimination mandate of the Constitution and the 1964 law. Unfortunately, the young, inexperienced administrators charged with implementing Title VI were thrown into a sea of controversy without an institutional compass. The head of the newly created civil rights office later admitted a "general lack of appreciation of the monstrousness of the task before us."[16] Wilbur Cohen, the elder statesman who served as undersecretary and secretary of HEW during those years, concluded that while "all these young lawyers" had "good ideas," their "concept of enforcement and administration was juvenile."[17]

It soon became clear that Title VI's central enforcement mechanism, the funding cut-off, would seldom work. By the late 1960s it had been all but abandoned. Federal administrators similarly diverged from the initial statutory framework by refusing to follow the Administrative Procedure Act's rulemaking procedures. HEW published its first desegregation guidelines in the *Saturday Review of Literature*, rather than the *Federal Register*, without any opportunity for public comment or judicial review. More recently the Department of Education's Title VI rules have been announced in unilateral "Dear Colleague" letters. The expectation that federal regulators explain their proposal, accept and respond to comments, and revise their initial rule in light of public input never took hold in the Office for Civil Rights. In short, federal administrators' actual role under Title VI (and Title IX) bears little relationship to that envisioned by the statute. Yet Congress has done nothing to address the issue of administrative authority. None of the three branches has made a significant effort to evaluate, revise, or even acknowledge the structure of our jerry-built civil rights state.

During the heyday of the Warren Court, faith in the federal courts' ability to bring about what was routinely described as "social change" was strong, especially in the legal academy. "What informed the enterprise" of the Warren Court, Alexander Bickel wrote in 1970, "was the idea of progress." Belief in "man-made progress was the new faith and the supremacy of judges as its carriers and executors was not denied."[18] Nowhere was this conviction more evident than in the desegregation cases of 1965–74.

Disappointment with the failure of litigation to produce the promised transformation of public education eventually led many on the left to conclude that expecting the judiciary to achieve egalitarian reforms was a "hollow hope"—to use Gerald Rosenberg's famous phrase.[19] Rosenberg convincingly demonstrated that Judge Wisdom was right when he concluded in 1966 that "the courts acting alone have failed," and that the intervention of federal administrators was crucial in achieving the "reconstruction of southern education." What Rosenberg failed to acknowledge, though, was that the federal courts remained the senior partner in an institutional alliance that not only produced substantial desegregation in the late 1960s and early 1970s, but served as a model for federal regulation under Title IX and federal efforts to improve instruction of English learners. The central theme of chapter 4 of this book is the success of what Steven Halpern has described as "the synergistic power of the bench and bureaucracy's working together."[20]

No description of the federal courts is cited more frequently than Alexander Hamilton's claim in *Federalist* #78 that the judiciary "has no influence over either the sword or the purse.... It may truly be said to have neither FORCE nor WILL, but merely judgment." Usually overlooked is the fact that in his newspaper articles defending the proposed constitution, Hamilton was trying to assuage Anti-federalists' fears of a powerful judiciary, or that under Chief Justice John Marshall the Supreme Court took many of the steps most feared by the Anti-federalists. Hamilton had strong political reason for understating the potential power of the federal judiciary.

In desegregation cases federal judges demonstrated that in fact they *do* wield substantial influence over both the purse and the sword. They required large increases in spending on schools—indeed, $2 billion more in Kansas City. Rarely was the "sword" used to enforce desegregation orders as directly as in Little Rock, Arkansas, in 1957, when President Eisenhower sent in paratroopers to protect black students who sought to enroll in Central High School. But officials who refuse to comply with court orders are routinely threatened with contempt of court, punishable not just by fines but imprisonment. Behind "mere judgment" lies the threat of FORCE. That these orders did not always produce the salutary change their authors envisioned should not hide from us their coercive nature.

Federal judges often found unacknowledged allies for gaining compliance with desegregation orders: supporters within the targeted school systems. Many administrators and teachers welcomed efforts to bring more white students and more resources into schools attended by minority students. In fact, school officials were often the most influential participants in the process of writing and revising structural injunctions. At times the initial litigation was collusive, with local school leaders working with civil rights organizations to squeeze more money out of state governments and to pull in white students from the suburbs. School officials could use court rulings to insulate themselves from elected officials and public opinion. Chapters 6–8 provide many examples of these patterns. In the "public law litigation" that desegregation exemplifies, lawsuits are "polycentric," involving a large number of players with divergent interests. The parties named in a case's title tell us little about the array of these interests and likely alliances among them.

Desegregation cases also requires us to rethink the common claim that the Supreme Court is limited to deciding what Article III of the Constitution terms "cases and controversies." The Court's many desegregation decisions are notable for their *failure* to explain how the controversies before them should be resolved. *Brown I* was altogether silent on remedies; *Brown II* said little more. In subsequent decisions the Court seldom did more than compose commentaries on lower court decisions, first insisting that lower court judges create "unitary" school systems and later denying that the crucial term "unitary" has any clear meaning. Typically, the Court would remand the case to the lower courts requiring them to reconsider their prior ruling in light of its ambiguous advice—hardly a resolution of the underlying "case or controversy."

Chapter 5 shows how the Supreme Court could live in a world of legal abstractions, far away from the hard and complex choices facing district court judges. As the number of important cases decided by the federal judiciary rose in the second half of the twentieth century, the number of cases reviewed by the Supreme Court shrank. Meanwhile, the number of dissenting and concurring opinions increased, and the clarity of the Court's decisions further declined. We should acknowledge that rather than decide actual "cases and controversies," the Supreme Court usually limits itself to writing convoluted commentaries on cases, often without a clear majority position.

A related theme of this book is that in order to provide uniform application of the "supreme law of the land"—that is, the federal Constitution and federal statutes—our highly decentralized political system relies upon an institution—the federal judiciary—that in practice is itself notably decentralized. Judicial decentralization was most apparent in the decade after *Brown*, when federal district court judges chosen by segregationist Senators tolerated endless delay. A few engaged in blatant insubordination. Having for years "gone to bed and waked up with school segregation problems on their minds," judges on the Fifth Circuit were finally forced to institute unprecedented methods for supervising district court judges, and, at times, even taking over parts of their jobs. Such extraordinary review could not be sustained for long. It stands out as one of the temporary expedients required to destroy the well-defended racial caste system of the South.

Appellate review of trial-court rulings is particularly difficult in cases that are highly fact-specific, and when judges must fashion complex remedies. Both factors characterized desegregation litigation. Appellate judges do not hear witnesses. Seldom do they have time to review in full the long records generated in desegregation cases. Structural injunctions are usually the product of long negotiations to which appellate judges are not privy. Appellate judges have long given trial-court judges broad discretion in determining what constitutes "equitable remedies." Chief Justice Burger surely went too far when he proclaimed "that words are poor instruments to convey the sense of basic fairness inherent in equity." Since words are the only instruments of control at appellate judges' command, Burger's words in *Swann* constituted an abdication of responsibility—one he later regretted. Always challenging, appellate review of complex remedies becomes all but impossible when those appellate courts cannot agree on the central purpose of the endeavor. Nowhere was the fatal combination of complex remedies and ambiguous standards more evident than in desegregation cases.

Over the decades the relationship between courts and agencies on civil rights matters has shifted substantially. Within a few years, the institutional alliance that emerged in the late 1960s had frayed. When the Department of Education reentered the picture decades later, it confronted a judiciary with more Republican appointees. In the Obama years, the Department sought to limit the influence of decisions such as *Parents Involved*, and to enforce the disparate-impact guidelines it issued under Title VI without any help from the courts. Damage control replaced symbiosis.

The Obama administration's school-resource and school-discipline guidelines discussed in chapter 9 illustrate the many ways in which Title VI can be invoked to address important educational issues. When interpreted to prohibit any practice that has a "disproportionate impact" on minority children, Title VI offers federal administrators authority to scrutinize virtually every feature of schools, particularly those in cities with a substantial number of minority students. To do so, though, it must define the issues it chooses to tackle in racial terms: the Department has authority to prohibit only policies that are discriminatory, not those it believes are merely unwise.

There are many reasons to believe that out-of-school suspensions and expulsions do more educational harm than good. But the federal government has no authority to establish a national policy on disciplinary matters. The Department therefore engaged in an analysis of the distribution of out-of-school punishments that ignored key factors—most importantly, the nature of the misbehavior and the student's history of infractions—to conclude that these sanctions have routinely been applied in a discriminatory fashion. Not surprisingly, these charges of racial discrimination provoked resentment and opposition among many of the teachers and administrators responsible for carrying out the agreements negotiated by the Department. Similarly, the Department could not order school systems to devote more resources to schools with minority students. They could forbid only discriminatory allocation of resources: the result was the complex and largely unenforceable 2014 "Dear Colleague" letter. If these disparate-impact guidelines show how the federal government can use civil rights laws to issue rules on almost every aspect of public education, they also illustrate the limits of federal control in practice.

Chapter 9 also reviewed some of the steps Congress has taken to address educational inequalities. Most of these measures involve money: providing either aid to school districts with underserved students or programs such as Head Start to supplement regular school programs. A few have provided more sticks than carrots: the leading examples are the Individuals with Disabilities Education Act and No Child Left Behind. The results of these many initiatives have at best been mixed. The most effective and politically popular policies appear to be "add-ons," that is, those that create separate programs for a defined constituency rather than attempting to restructure entire schools or school systems.[21] Head Start and special education are examples of the former; No Child Left Behind the leading example of the latter.

Whether one looks at the judiciary, administrative agencies, or Congress, the same theme emerges: achieving beneficial change for poor and minority students is excruciatingly hard, especially in our highly decentralized education system. Cooperation among these national institutions clearly helps, but is seldom sufficient to guarantee results. And in American politics, moments of consensus on educational issues are rare.

Reassessments

In a report appended to the NAACP's 1991 brief in *Freeman v. Pitts*, fifty-two prominent social scientists wrote that "assigning minority and white students to the same school is no panacea for educational inequality. The creation of racially mixed rather than racially segregated schools is *just the beginning of the long-term process* of interracial schooling." They explained that "brief exposure to whites, in schools that do nothing else to produce equal opportunity, will not cure the harms created by a history of segregation." Court-ordered changes "in student assignment cannot be understood in isolation from changes in the curriculum, the adjustments of teachers and administrators, the reaction in the community, the changes in housing patterns, or the consequences of past segregation." Consequently, "the way in which desegregated schools are structured is crucial."[22] A decade and a half later, the 553 social scientists who signed a brief urging the Supreme Court to allow racial assignment of students to facilitate integration repeated this warning, distinguishing "desegregation"—which "generally describes the creation of schools containing substantial percentages of students from two or more racial and ethnic groups"—from "integration"—which "refers to the positive implementation of desegregation with equal status for all groups and respect for all cultures."[23] These candid statements underscore the complexity of the task of reforming public education to make equal educational opportunity a reality.

Negotiating this difficult policy terrain requires us to achieve greater clarity on three issues. First, what are the goals of this effort? Why do we consider this project worth undertaking? Second, what are the pedagogical changes that will move us in that direction? And third, what institutional mechanisms does the federal government have at its disposal to achieve these changes in public schools? The history of federal desegregation efforts is in large part the story of well-meaning judges and administrators failing to pay sufficient attention to these crucial questions.

THE "NEW WAVE"

In recent years, a number of school districts across the country have taken a new look at the school desegregation question, devising programs more modest than the judicial decrees discussed in chapters 6 and 7. In a series of reports, the Century Fund (TCF) has described this "New Wave of School Integration" to help us understand "What School Integration in America Looks Like Today."[24] These reports focus on 185 school districts with "active integration policies," that is, "places where the work of integration has begun" under the constraints created by the Supreme Court's *Parents Involved* decision of 2007.

As diverse as they are, these plans share several characteristics. First, most of them are local initiatives. A few are the product of state-court decisions, most notably in Hartford, Connecticut. Others resulted from the revision of old judicial orders negotiated by current school leaders, civil rights organizations, and federal officials. "But many more of these active integration policies," the authors of the Fund's reports write, "are in districts that have taken matters into their own hands and embraced the work of integrating the schools." Evidence reviewed in chapter 2 indicates that voluntary plans are more effective than those imposed by judicial or administrative fiat. Given the complexity of the task, support for the plan within the local school system is crucial.

Second, the plans seldom mandate extensive busing. Most are intra-district efforts that forego extensive mixing of students from cities and suburbs. Although many redraw student assignment lines and site new schools in locations most likely to draw from diverse neighborhoods, they do not employ the sort of pairing and satellite zones so common in the busing orders of the 1970s.

Third, these plans focus more on SES than on race. According to TCF, more than 90 percent of these 185 programs (171) take SES into account in assigning students to particular schools. In only fourteen of the 185 are assignments "based solely on race/ethnicity." Another twelve "consider both socioeconomic factors and race/ethnicity." Focusing on SES allows almost all these plans to stay within the bounds established by the Supreme Court in *Parents Involved*. It also encourages schools to address the educational problems faced by poor children of every race and ethnicity.

Fourth, all the programs include multiple choices for students and their parents. They rely on magnet schools, charter schools, and "controlled choice." Rather than being assigned to schools on the basis of geography, students and their parents list their preferences. School officials then try to honor those preferences subject to the constraint of achieving SES (and, to a lesser extent, racial) balance within each school.

A crucial question, of course, is how much constraint such "controlled choice" plans impose. Do these districts use the patina of "controlled choice" to cover an effort to distribute students on the basis of SES and race? Or do high-SES white families retain enough choice to keep them in the public schools? According to TCF's 2016 report, this is a hard question to answer:

> Our interactions with many district officials revealed that socioeconomic school integration is still often a fragile political issue, limiting administrators' desire to publicly discuss the existence and success of assignment plans and other programs that promote integration. . . . Because school board members are typically elected, they are understandably sensitive to the desires and concerns of voters who benefit from and promote segregated systems. This relatively prevalent mindset likely explains why specific information about assignment plans that disrupt this pattern is often inaccessible online or in public records, and why many officials are hesitant about providing details of their plans. Furthermore, some district and charter leaders may believe it is in the best interest of their integration strategies to operate under the radar rather than attract attention that may subject them to renewed scrutiny.[25]

In other words, political support for these programs remains tenuous. And, as the Fund points out, this lack of transparency makes it more difficult to evaluate the effectiveness of various types of assignment practices.

Another key feature of this "new wave" is that it has taken place outside the large cities that have been the focus of so many desegregation plans in the past. 60 percent of the 185 plans are in cities, 30 percent in suburbs. Unlike overwhelmingly minority school districts such as New York, Los Angeles, Chicago, Houston, Dallas, Philadelphia, Boston, Miami, and San Francisco, these districts have retained a significant number of white students: whites are the largest racial group in half these districts, Hispanics the largest group in a quarter of the districts, and black students in only one sixth. Retaining higher-SES students, of course, is one of the biggest challenges school leaders face in these districts. They start out in a better position than our largest cities.

The Century Fund lauds these districts for putting such plans in place. What we do not yet know is whether these school districts will succeed in enhancing the quality of education for minority children, improving race relations within these communities, or retaining a significant number of higher-SES students. In coming years, we will have the opportunity to learn if these modest efforts will produce modest improvements. In contrast to the desegregation orders of the 1960s and 1970s, it is likely that the consequences of these plans will be carefully scrutinized by researchers interested in determining which of their components work and which don't.

A CRITICAL PERSPECTIVE

A key political advantage of the current practice of framing educational issues in terms of "diversity" rather than invoking the older, more laden terms "desegregation" and "integration" is that it is hard to be against diversity. What's not to like? We are frequently told that opposition to integration stems from one basic fact: white parents' racism. In one of her several articles on desegregation, Nikole Hannah-Jones declared that while "court-ordered desegregation worked," "white racism made it hard to accept." White parents might invoke the alleged American tradition of neighborhood schools, but such considerations "never outweighed their desire to maintain racially homogeneous environments for their children." White Americans, Hannah-Jones claims, "opposed busing precisely because it was so effective." The majority of whites simply "did not want their children to share schools with large numbers of black children."[26]

Without a doubt, white racism was a major component of opposition to desegregation not only in the South, but throughout the country. But is that all there was to it? A powerful counter-argument has come from an unlikely source: Derrick Bell, the noted black scholar widely credited with founding Critical Race Theory within the legal academy. Before joining the faculty at Harvard Law School, Bell worked on desegregation cases both for the NAACP and at the Department of Justice. His 1976 *Yale Law Journal* article, "Serving Two Masters: Integration Ideals and Client Interests in School Desegregation Litigation," questioned the wisdom of the NAACP's decision to place highest priority on racial balance and, in effect, urged judges not to accept that organization's understanding of desegregation.[27] Derrick Bell can hardly be accused of promoting white supremacy.

Bell's central argument was that his former colleagues' preoccupation with racial balance and their reluctance to address issues of school quality led them to ignore the interests of the clients they claimed to represent. NAACP lawyers had devoted so much effort to establishing racial balance as the principal measure of whether a school district had become "unitary" that it was unwilling to back away, even when the results in many cities "served to make concrete what many parents had long sensed and what new research has suggested: court orders mandating racial balance may be (depending on the circumstances) educationally advantageous, irrelevant, or even *disadvantageous*." Yet civil rights lawyers continued to advocate racial balance "without regard to the educational effects of such assignments."[28]

Bell describes how this intransigence led to disputes between NAACP lawyers and local black leaders in Boston, Detroit, and Atlanta. In Boston and Detroit, district court judges addressed on their own initiative the educational issues the NAACP had pointedly refused to include in their proposed remedies. In Atlanta the local branch of the NAACP accepted a compromise that the national NAACP strongly opposed, in effect calling for more black control of the school district rather than more busing. The Atlanta Compromise Plan was defended by Dr. Benjamin E. May (described by Bell as "one of the most respected black educators in the country") as "the most viable plan for Atlanta." "More importantly," May wrote,

> Black people must not resign themselves to the pessimistic view that a nonintegrated school cannot provide Black children with an excellent educational setting. Instead, Black people, while working to implement *Brown*, should recognize that integration alone does not provide a quality education, and that much of the substance of quality education can be provided to Black children in the interim.

Bell's article opens with a similar statement from "black community groups in Boston":

> In the name of equity, we . . . seek dramatic improvement in the quality of the education available to our children. Any steps to achieve desegregation must be reviewed in light of the black community's interest in improving pupil performance as the primary characteristic of educational equity. We define educational equity as the absence of discriminatory pupil placement and improved performance for all children who have been the objects of discrimination. We think it neither necessary, nor proper to endure the dislocations of desegregation without reasonable assurances that our children will instructionally profit.

Although Bell's principal argument is that the racial-balance approach to school desegregation "fails to encompass the complexity of achieving equal educational opportunity for children to whom it so long has been denied," he does not say much about what judges and litigants *should* do in the face of such complexity. He notes some of the problems that commonly accompanied desegregation: "Low academic performance and large numbers of disciplinary and expulsion cases are only two of the predictable outcomes in integrated schools where the racial subordination of blacks is reasserted in, if anything, a more damaging form." And he calls attention to the issue of political control: in many cities, desegregation orders threatened to limit the extent to which black mayors, school board members, superintendents, and parents could control what went on in their schools.

As we saw in chapter 2, the leading argument regarding the educational benefits of racial balance holds that in majority-white schools, the more affluent white students will establish a school culture that values hard work, discipline, order, and academic achievement. Advocates of this theory paid little attention to the consequences of the fact that black students would usually enter these schools less well prepared academically than their higher-SES white peers. Often the result was that tracking within these schools separated white and black children into different classrooms—and different school environments. Rather than promote the sense of comradery proponents of integration had hoped to see, this divide can demoralize black students, create resentment, and promote the belief that doing well academically is "acting white."

Often this circumstance led black students to conclude—correctly in many cases—that they no longer attended "their school," but one attuned to the interests and culture of white students. As the recent podcast "Nice White Parents" demonstrates, integration efforts sometimes led schools to emphasize themes (such as "global citizenship" or, in the case of Kansas City, Greek history) of little use to students struggling to gain proficiency in math and reading.[29] (Of course, it is not evident that focusing on esoteric subjects is good for affluent white students either.) The rationale has been that such innovations are necessary to keep affluent white students in the school system. Black and Hispanic parents, like students, could see this—and understandably resented it.

Although the Supreme Court studiously avoided the issue, the question of whether and how minority students might benefit from attending majority-white schools was the subject of considerable debate in the lower courts in the late 1960s and early 1970s. Simon Sobeloff was the US Solicitor General who presented the arguments of the government in *Brown II*, a well-respected federal judge, and the author of a critique of "freedom of choice" plans quoted approvingly by the Supreme Court in *Green*. In a 1970 concurring opinion, Sobeloff offered the following blunt description of the then-dominant view on the educational superiority of majority-white schools:

Essentially, the theory postulates that the quality of a school depends largely on its "class climate," and that middle class schools are better. Therefore, it is important to create dominantly middle class school populations. The optimum level, which would include enough middle class students to establish the class character of the school and at the same time include a substantial number of lower class children to benefit from it, would be about 70% middle class and 30% lower class. In general, the theory continues, "white" is synonymous with "middle class," "black" is the same as "lower class." Accordingly, the educationally sound objective is to achieve majority white schools (optimally 70–30).[30]

According to Judge Sobeloff, the "central proposition" of this "invidious" thesis

> is that the value of a school depends on the characteristics of a majority of its students and superiority is related to whiteness, inferiority to blackness. Although the theory is couched in terms of "socio-economic class" and the necessity for the creation of a "middle-class milieu," nevertheless, at bottom it rests on the generalization that, educationally speaking, white pupils are somehow better or more desirable than black pupils. This premise leads to the next proposition, that association with white pupils helps the blacks and so long as whites predominate does not harm the white children. But once the number of whites approaches minority, then association with the inferior black children hurts the whites and, because there are not enough of the superior whites to go around, does not appreciably help the blacks.[31]

This statement by the "liberal" Judge Sobeloff and the arguments of the "radical" Professor Bell bears a striking similarity to a well-known statement penned by the "conservative" Justice Clarence Thomas a quarter of a century later:

> It never ceases to amaze me that the courts are so willing to assume that anything that is predominantly black must be inferior . . . [The district] court has read our cases to support the theory that black students suffer an unspecified psychological harm from segregation that retards their mental and educational development. This approach not only relies upon questionable social science research rather than constitutional principle, but it also rests on an assumption of black inferiority . . . The mere fact that a school is black does not mean that it is the product of a constitutional violation.[32]

All other things being equal, racially integrated schools are good for students and good for democracy. Unfortunately, other things are not always equal. For example, when southern schools were desegregated in the 1960s and 1970s, the number of black teachers plummeted. Under Jim Crow, black schools were severely underfunded. Partly for that reason, they were also largely ignored by white-controlled school boards, with the result that "Black school leaders were generally free to make independent on-site decisions." Black schools were expected to hire exclusively black teachers. The result, according to a recent study by Seth Gershenson, Michael Hansen, and Constance Lindsay, was to establish

> the dignified position of Black schools—and of Black teachers in Black communities. There was a shared ownership and pride in Black schools among teachers, parents, students, and community members. These schools enjoyed a robust supply of quality and experienced Black teachers, structured curricula, and extracurricular activities, parent support and buy-in, and strong leadership.[33]

Desegregation put an end to that. Of the eighty-two thousand black teachers employed in 1954, thirty-eight thousand had lost their jobs by 1964. Between 1964 and 1972, the years of most rapid southern desegregation, the number of black teachers declined by another 31 percent. Gershenson, Hansen, and Lindsay maintain that black and Hispanic students benefit significantly from having some black and Hispanic teachers. They conclude that "while the long-run, social benefits of the *Brown* decision probably outweighed the costs, there were definitely real and immediate consequences for Black students and for the diversity of the teaching force that linger to this day."[34] In politics and social policy, unalloyed goods are dreadfully hard to find.

The Long Haul

The protests that swept the nation after the murder of George Floyd in 2020 placed issues of racial fairness near the top of the national agenda. At the same time, theories that frame these issues in stark terms of "antiracism" versus "white supremacy" have challenged previous understandings of the value of racial integration. On the one hand, by questioning the merits of "whiteness," the new breed of advocates and writers has emphasized the undeniable fact that the presence of white bodies in a school does not necessarily help to develop the minds of non-white students. On the other hand, denigration of skills needed to prosper in the economy as components of "white supremacy," hostility to the testing that demonstrates the extent to which we are shortchanging minority students, and the implicit theme that racial oppression is inescapable all threaten to derail the crucial task of improving educational opportunities for these children. It is hard to think of more destructive messages to send to children of any race, ethnicity, or SES level.

This book has frequently called attention to the mismatch between the ambitious goals of those who adopt a broad reading of *Brown* and the institutional tools available to them. Too often the result of this mismatch has been a slew of unintended consequences. Nonetheless, the two central goals of school integration remain worthy of sustained attention. One is to improve the education provided to minority children in order to increase social mobility, promote economic advancement, and spur political engagement. The other is to improve race relations by combatting racial and ethnic stereotypes, helping students to see their peers as individuals rather than as members of a rigidly defined group.

As we once again confront questions of racial justice in education—nearly three-quarters of a century after *Brown*—we should keep in mind two features of this story. The first is the importance of the twin goals described in the previous paragraph. The second is the difficulty of achieving them. If we learn anything from the long history of desegregation, it is to be wary of quick fixes. Educational reform requires sustained effort, clarity about goals, appreciation of modest improvements, attentiveness to unintended consequences, and regular evaluation of results. These were all in short supply during the first phases of school desegregation. We should work to ensure they are more common in those to come.

Notes

Preface

1. Lyndon B. Johnson, "To Fulfill These Rights," commencement address at Howard University, June 4, 1965, Washington, DC, posted online via Gerhard Peters and John T. Woolley, American Presidency Project, https://www.presidency.ucsb.edu/documents/commencement-address-howard-university-fulfill-these-rights.

2. Frederick M. Hess, *Letters to a Young Education Reformer* (Cambridge, MA: Harvard Education Press, 2017), 30 (emphasis added) and 26.

Chapter One

1. Quoted in Matt Viser, "Biden Tough Talk on 1970s Desegregation Plan Could Get New Scrutiny in Today's Democratic Party," *Washington Post*, March 7, 2019, https://www.washingtonpost.com/politics/bidens-tough-talk-on-1970s-school-desegregation-plan-could-get-new-scrutiny-in-todays-democratic-party/2019/03/07/9115583e-3eb2-11e9-a0d3-1210e58a94cf_story.html. A transcript of the TV interview had been placed in the *Congressional Record* by Senator Frank Church (D–ID), 94th Cong. (1st sess.), 121 Cong. Rec. pt. 24, S31341–44 (daily ed. October 2, 1975).

2. Joseph Biden, quoted in Astead Herndon and Sheryl Gay Stolberg, "The Long Run: How Joe Biden Became the Democrats' Anti-Busing Crusader," *New York Times*, July 15, 2019, https://www.nytimes.com/2019/07/15/us/politics/biden-busing.html.

3. "Gallup Finds Few Favor Busing for Integration," *New York Times*, September 9, 1973, www.nytimes.com/1973/09/09/archives/gallup-finds-few-favor-busing-for-integration.html.

4. David Weakliem, "More on Busing," *Just the Social Facts, Ma'am* (blog), July 1, 2019, http://justthesocialfacts.blogspot.com/2019/07/more-on-busing.html; Mark Gillespie, "Americans Want Integrated Schools, but Oppose School Busing," *Gallup*, September 27, 1999, https://news.gallup.com/poll/3577/americans-want-integrated-schools-oppose-school-busing.aspx; Christine H. Rossell, "The Convergence of Black and White Attitudes on School Desegregation Issues During the Four Decade Evolution of the Plans," 36 *William and Mary Law Review* 613, 639–45 (1995).

5. Rossell, "The Convergence of Black and White Attitudes," 641–45.

6. Chelsea Janes, "Harris's Views on Busing Come Under Question after Her Debate Criticism of Biden's Past Position," *Washington Post*, July 4, 2019, https://www.washingtonpost.com/politics/harriss-views-on-busing-come-under-question-after-her-debate-criticism-of-bidens-past-position/2019/07/04/b197c6cc-9e71-11e9-b27f-ed2942f73d70_story.html.

7. Sherrilyn Ifill, "The Same Myths that Thwarted Busing Are Keeping School Segregation Alive," *Slate*, July 5, 2019, https://slate.com/news-and-politics/2019/07/joe-biden-kamala-harris-busing-debate-2020-primary.html.

8. Nikole Hannah-Jones, "It Was Never About Busing," *New York Times*, July 12, 2019, https://www.nytimes.com/2019/07/12/opinion/sunday/it-was-never-about-busing.html.

9. Matthew Delmont, "The Lasting Legacy of the Busing Crisis," *Atlantic*, March 29, 2016, https://www.theatlantic.com/politics/archive/2016/03/the-boston-busing-crisis-was-never-intended-to-work/474264/.

10. Will Stancil, "The White Suburbs That Fought Busing Aren't So White Anymore," *Atlantic*, July 12, 2019, https://www.theatlantic.com/education/archive/2019/07/kamala-harris-busing-politics/593797/. An NPR piece on the Supreme Court's 1974 decision in *Milliken v. Bradley* followed suit with the misleading title, "This Supreme Court Case Made School District Lines a Tool for Segregation" (Elissa Nadworny and Cory Turner, *NPR*, July 25, 2019, https://www.npr.org/2019/07/25/739493839/this-supreme-court-case-made-school-district-lines-a-tool-for-segregation).

11. Paul Barton and Richard Coley, *The Black-White Achievement Gap: When Progress Stopped* (Princeton, NJ: Education Testing Service, 2010), https://www.ets.org/Media/Research/pdf/PICBWGAP.pdf; and "Racial and Ethnic Achievement Gaps," Educational Opportunity Monitoring Project, Stanford Center for Education Policy Analysis, accessed May 23, 2022, https://cepa.stanford.edu/educational-opportunity-monitoring-project/achievement-gaps/race/#first.

12. Ron Haskins and Isabel Sawhill, *Creating an Opportunity Society* (Washington, DC: Brookings Institution Press, 2009), ch. 3–4; Greg Duncan and Richard Murnane, *Restoring Opportunity* (Cambridge, MA: Harvard Education Press, 2014), ch. 2–3; Isabel Sawhill, *The Forgotten Americans* (New Haven, CT: Yale University Press, 2018), ch. 2–3.

13. "Racial/Ethnic Enrollment in Public Schools," National Center for Educational Statistics, last updated May 2022, https://nces.ed.gov/programs/coe/indicator/cge#:~:text=In%20fall%202018%2C%20of%20the,and%20186%2C000%20were%20Pacific%20Islander. Also see William H. Frey, *The Diversity Explosion: How New Racial Demographics Are Remaking America* (Washington, DC: Brookings Institution Press, 2015), 22.

14. National Center for Education Statistics, "Indicator 6: Elementary and Secondary Enrollment," in *Status and Trends in Education of Racial and Ethnic Groups 2018*, February 20, 2019, https://nces.ed.gov/programs/raceindicators/indicator_rbb.asp.

15. See the map in Kate Rabinowitz, Armand Emamdjomeh, and Laura Meckler, "How the Nation's Growing Racial Diversity Is Changing Our Schools," *Washington Post*, September 12, 2019, https://www.washingtonpost.com/graphics/2019/local/school-diversity-data/.

16. National Center for Education Statistics, "Percentage Distribution of Public School Enrollment in the United States and 20 Largest Public School Districts, by Race/Ethnicity: 2004," table 7.3 in *Status and Trends of Racial and Ethnic Minorities 2007* (Washington, DC: US Department of Education, September 2007), https://nces.ed.gov/pubs2007/minoritytrends/tables/table_7_3.asp?referrer=report.

17. Laura Meckler and Kate Rabinowitz, "The Changing Face of School Integration: Millions More American Children Are Attending School with Students of Other Races, Even as Many

NOTES TO PAGES 6–14

Urban Schools Remain Deeply Segregated," *Washington Post*, September 12, 2019, https://www.washingtonpost.com/education/2019/09/12/more-students-are-going-school-with-children-different-races-schools-big-cities-remain-deeply-segregated/.

18. Frey, *Diversity Explosion*, 149.

19. Parents Involved in Community Schools v. Seattle School District No. 1, 551 U.S. 701 (2007).

20. Halley Potter and Michelle Burris, "Here Is What School Integration in America Looks Like Today," *Century Fund*, December 2, 2020, https://tcf.org/content/report/school-integration-america-looks-like-today/.

21. Keyes v. School District No. 1, Denver, 413 U.S. 189, 225 (1973).

22. Green v. County School Board of New Kent County, 391 U.S. 430, 442 (1968).

23. Freeman v. Pitts, 503 U.S. 467, 487 (1992).

24. Coalition to Save Our Children v. State Board of Education of the State of Delaware, 901 F. Supp. 784, 822 (D. Del., 1995).

25. Plessy v. Ferguson, 163 U.S. 537, 559 (1896).

26. Brown v. Board II, 349 U.S. 294, 300–01(1955), emphasis added.

27. Brief for Appellants in Brown v. Board of Education O.T. 1952, no. 1, 5; and Brief for Appellants in Brown v. Board of Education O.T. 1953, nos. 1, 2, and 4, 65, quoted in Thomas's concurring opinion in *Parents Involved in Community Schools*, 551 U.S. at 772.

28. Transcript of oral argument in *Brown v. Board of Education*, reprinted in Leon Friedman, ed., *Argument: The Oral Argument before the Supreme Court in Brown v. Board of Education of Topeka, 1952–55* (New York: Chelsea House Publishers, 1969), 14. Also see Richard Kluger, *Simple Justice* (New York: Vintage, 1975), 564.

29. Thurgood Marshall, quoted in Kluger, *Simple Justice*, 571–72.

30. Remarks of Judge Motley, "In Memoriam: Honorable Thurgood Marshall," Proceedings of the Bar and Officers of the Supreme Court of the United States X (1993), cited by Justice Thomas in his concurrence in *Parents Involved in Community Schools*, 551 U.S. at 773.

31. United States Commission on Civil Rights, *Racial Isolation in the Public Schools*, vol. 1 (Washington, DC: GPO, 1967), 193.

32. Keyes v. School District No. 1, Denver 313 F. Supp. 61, 81 (D. Colo., 1970).

33. Johnson v. San Francisco Unified School District, 339 F. Supp. 1315, 1331 (N.D. Cal., 1971).

34. Swann v. Charlotte-Mecklenburg Board of Education, 300 F. Supp. 1358, 1369 (W.D. N.C., 1969).

35. Milliken v. Bradley, 418 U.S. 717, 802 and 783 (1974).

36. Board of Education of Oklahoma City v. Dowell, 498 U.S. 231, footnote 5 of Marshall dissent (1991).

37. *Parents Involved in Community Schools*, 551 U.S. at 803, emphasis added.

38. *Parents Involved in Community Schools*, 551 U.S. at 838–40.

39. Richard Matsch, quoted in James Fishman and Lawrence Strauss, "Endless Journey: Integration and the Provision of Equal Educational Opportunity in Denver's Public Schools: A Study of *Keyes v. School District No. 1*," in *Justice and School Systems: The Role of the Courts in Education Litigation*, ed. Barbara Flicker (Philadelphia: Temple University Press, 1990), 201.

40. Gary Orfield, *The Reconstruction of Southern Education: The Schools and the 1964 Civil Rights Act* (New York: Wiley-Interscience, 1969).

41. Felix Frankfurter, quoted in Kluger, *Simple Justice*, 572.

42. *Green v. County School Board*, 391 U.S. at 435.

43. David L. Kirp and Gary Babcock, "Judge and Company: Court-Appointed Masters, School Desegregation, and Institutional Reform," 32 *Alabama Law Review* 313, 354, 357 (1981).

44. Joshua M. Dunn, *Complex Justice: The Case of Missouri v. Jenkins* (Chapel Hill: University of North Carolina Press, 2008), ch. 4.

45. Lawrence Kenny and Amy Schmidt, "The Decline in the Number of School Districts in the US, 1950–1980," *Public Choice* 79, no. 1–2 (1994): 1–18.

46. James Q. Wilson, *Bureaucracy: What Government Agencies Do and Why They Do It* (New York: Basic Books, 1989), ch. 9. I have discussed the significance of schools as coping organizations in "Taking Remedies Seriously," in *From Schoolhouse to Courthouse: The Judiciary's Role in American Education*, eds. Joshua Dunn and Martin West (Washington, DC: Brookings Institution Press, 2009), 17–48.

47. Frederick M. Hess, *Spinning Wheels: The Politics of Urban School Reform* (Washington, DC: Brookings Institution Press, 1999).

48. Owen M. Fiss, *The Civil Rights Injunction* (Bloomington: Indiana University Press, 1978), 26–28, emphasis in the original.

49. Swann v. Charlotte-Mecklenburg Board of Education, 402 U.S. 1, 15, 31 (1971), internal punctuation omitted.

50. Kirp and Babcock, "Judge and Company," 329.

51. Sean Reardon, Elena Tej Grewal, Demetra Kalogrides, and Erica Greenbert, "Brown Fades: The End of Court-Ordered Desegregation and the Resegregation of American Public Schools," *Journal of Policy Analysis and Management* 31, no. 4 (2012): 881. A year earlier, Byron Lutz found "no accurate statistics are available concerning the number of court-ordered desegregation plans in place or the number of dismissals." "The End of Court-Ordered Desegregation," *American Economic Journal: Economic Policy* 3, no. 2 (2011): 135.

52. Nikole Hannah-Jones, "Lack of Order: The Erosion of a Once-Great Force for Integration," *ProPublica*, May 1, 2014, https://www.propublica.org/article/lack-of-order-the-erosion-of-a-once-great-force-for-integration. Other stories on the uncertainty about the status of desegregation orders include Will Stancil, "Is School Desegregation Coming to an End?," *Atlantic*, February 28, 2018, https://www.theatlantic.com/education/archive/2018/02/a-bittersweet-victory-for-school-desegregation/554396/; and Rachel Cohen, "School Choice and the Chaotic State of Racial Desegregation: Why No One Can Say for Sure If Some School Districts Are Still under Federal Desegregation Orders," *American Prospect*, September 15, 2015, https://prospect.org/education/school-choice-chaotic-state-racial-desegregation/.

53. Kirp and Babcock, "Judge and Company," 324.

54. Roger J. R. Levesque, *The Science and Law of School Segregation and Diversity* (New York: Oxford University Press, 2018), 85.

55. Charles R. Epp, *Making Rights Real: Activists, Bureaucrats, and the Creation of the Legalistic State* (Chicago: University of Chicago Press, 2010).

56. Robert C. Lieberman, "Weak State, Strong Policy: Paradoxes of Race Policy in the United States, Great Britain, and France," *Studies in American Political Development* 16, no. 2 (2002): 139.

57. Abigail C. Saguy, *What is Sexual Harassment? From Capitol Hill to the Sorbonne* (Berkeley: University of California Press, 2003); Kathrin S. Zippel, *The Politics of Sexual Harassment: A Comparative Study of the United States, the European Union, and Germany* (Cambridge: Cambridge University Press, 2006).

58. Erik Bleich, *Race Politics in Britain and France: Ideas and Policymaking since the 1960s* (New York: Cambridge University Press, 2003), ch.4. Also see Steven Teles, "Positive Action

or Affirmative Action? The Persistence of Britain's Antidiscrimination Regime," and Erik Bleich, "The French Model: Color-Blind Integration," both in *The Color Lines: Affirmative Action, Immigration, and Civil Rights Options for America* ed. John Skrentny (Chicago: University of Chicago Press, 2001); Nicholas Pedriana and Robin Stryker, "The Strength of a Weak Agency: Enforcement of Title VII of the 1964 Civil Rights Act and the Expansion of State Capacity, 1965–71," *American Journal of Sociology* 110, no. 3 (2004): 709; Frank Dobbin and John R. Sutton, "The Strength of a Weak State: The Rights Revolution and the Rise of Human Resources Management Divisions," *American Journal of Sociology* 104, no. 2 (1998): 441–76; and Frank Dobbin, *Inventing Equal Opportunity* (Princeton, NJ: Princeton University Press, 2009). The first chapter of Dobbin's book is titled "Regulating Discrimination: The Paradox of a Weak State."

59. John Skrentny "Law and the American State," *Annual Review of Sociology* 32 (2006): 213–44; and Paul Frymer, "Law and American Political Development," 33 *Law and Social Inquiry* 779 (2008).

60. Paul Gewirtz, "Remedies and Resistance," 92 *Yale Law Journal* 585, 588 (1983).

61. R. Shep Melnick, *The Transformation of Title IX: Regulating Gender Equality in Education* (Washington, DC: Brookings Institution Press, 2018); and Melnick, "Separation of Powers and the Strategy of Rights: The Expansion of Special Education," in *The New Politics of Public Policy*, eds. Marc K. Landy and Martin A. Levin (Baltimore, MD: Johns Hopkins University Press, 1995).

Chapter Two

1. Brown v. Board of Education of Topeka, 347 U.S. 483, 489 (1954).
2. *Brown*, 347 U.S. at 492–93 (emphasis added) and 495.
3. *Brown*, 347 U.S. at 494. The material in brackets was added by Chief Justice Warren.
4. *Brown*, 347 U.S. at 494.
5. Bolling v. Sharpe, 347 U.S. 497, 499 (1954).
6. Muir v. Louisville Park Theatrical Association, 347 U.S. 971 (1954); Florida ex rel Hawkins v. Board of Control, 350 U.S. 413 (1956); Tureaud v. Board of Supervisors of L.S.U., 347 U.S. 971 (1954); Dawson v. Mayor and City Council of Baltimore, 350 U.S. 877 (1955); Holmes v. City of Atlanta, 350 U.S. 879 (1955).
7. Goss v. Board of Education, 373 U.S. 683, 687 (1963).
8. McLaughlin v. Florida, 379 U.S. 184 (1964).
9. *Brown*, 347 U.S. at 493.
10. Missouri v. Jenkins III, 515 U.S. 70, 120–21 (1995)
11. Adarand Construction v. Pena, 515 U.S. 200, 214 (1995), quoting from Hirabayashi v. U.S. 320 U.S. 81, 100 (1943).
12. Fullilove v. Klutznick, 448 U.S. 448, 537 (1980).
13. Parents Involved in Community Schools v. Seattle School District No. 1, 551 U.S. 701, 795 and 797 (2007).
14. *Parents Involved in Community Schools*, 551 U.S at 795.
15. City of Richmond v. J. A. Croson Co., 488 U.S. 469, 498 (1989).
16. *Parents Involved in Community Schools*, 551 U.S at 756–57.
17. Justice O'Connor in Grutter v. Bollinger, 539 U.S. 306, 324 (2003).
18. *Parents Involved in Community Schools*, 551 U.S. at 759, Justice Thomas concurring.
19. League of United Latin American Citizens v. Perry, 548 U.S. 399, 511 (2006).
20. *Grutter v. Bollinger*, 539 U.S. at 371.

21. Justice O'Connor, dissenting in Metro Broadcasting, Inc. v. FCC, 497 U.S. 547, 609 (1990). In a footnote in *Parents Involved in Community Schools*, Justice Thomas wrote, "Justice Breyer's good intentions, which I do not doubt, have the shelf life of Justice Breyer's tenure. Unlike the dissenters, I am unwilling to delegate my constitutional responsibilities to local school boards and allow them to experiment with race-based decisionmaking on the assumption that their intentions will forever remain as good as Justice Breyer's." 551 U.S. at 781, n30.

22. Milliken v. Bradley, 418 U.S. 717, 741–42 (1974).

23. Board of Education of Oklahoma City v. Dowell, 498 U. S. 231, 248 (1991).

24. Columbus Board of Education v. Penick, 443 U.S 449, 489 (1979)

25. Keyes v. School District No. 1, Denver, 413 U.S. 189, 250 (1973)

26. *Columbus Board of Education v. Penick*, 443 U.S. at 487.

27. Freeman v. Pitts, 503 U.S. 469, 495 (1992).

28. Avern Cohn, quoted in Joseph Feldman et al., *Still Separate, Still Unequal: The Limits of Milliken II's Educational Compensation Remedies*, report of the Harvard Project on School Desegregation, Harvard Graduate School of Education, Cambridge, MA, April 1994, 21, https://eric.ed.gov/?id=ED371070.

29. In 1968 Justices White and Harlan objected to similar language in Justice Brennan's draft opinion in *Green* because it was based on dubious social-science evidence. Brennan agreed to delete it. Mark Whitman, *The Irony of Desegregation Law 1955–1995: Essays and Documents* (Princeton, NJ: Markus Wiener Publishers, 1998), 101 and 123.

30. *Parents Involved in Community Schools*, 551 U.S. at 757.

31. *Parents Involved in Community Schools*, 551 U.S. at 780–81.

32. Scalia concurring in Freeman v. Pitts, 498 U.S. 467, 505–506 (1992).

33. Owen M. Fiss, "The Fate of An Idea Whose Time Has Come: Antidiscrimination Law in the Second Decade after *Brown v. Board of Education*," 41 *University of Chicago Law Review* 742, 764–65 (1974).

34. Quoted in Raymond Wolters, *The Burden of Brown: Thirty Years of School Desegregation* (Knoxville: University of Tennessee Press, 1984), 157.

35. NAACP brief in *Green*, quoted in Wolters, *The Burden of Brown*, 156.

36. Michael Klarman, *From Jim Crow to Civil Rights: The Supreme Court and the Struggle for Racial Equality* (New York: Oxford University Press, 2004), 457.

37. Bell v. Maryland, 378 U.S. 266, 311, 288 (1964), emphasis added.

38. The most forceful and famous presentation of this argument was Charles L. Black Jr., "The Supreme Court, 1966 Term—Foreword: 'State Action,' Equal Protection, and California's Proposition 14," 81 *Harvard Law Review* 69 (1967).

39. Adickes v. Kress and Co., 398 U.S. 144, 190, 192 (1970).

40. *Bell v. Maryland*, 378 U.S. at 288. He and Justice Douglas repeated this claim a few months later when they voted to uphold Congress's power to enact Title II in Heart of Atlanta Motel, Inc. v. United States, 379 U.S. 241 (1964).

41. Reva B. Siegel, "Equality Talk: Antisubordination and Anticlassification Values in Constitutional Struggles Over *Brown*," 117 *Harvard Law Review* 1470 (2003–2004): 1472–73.

42. Jack M. Balkin and Reva B. Siegel, "The American Civil Rights Tradition: Anticlassification or Antisubordination?," 58 *University of Miami Law Review* 9 (2003).

43. Balkin and Siegel, "The American Civil Rights Tradition," 11.

44. Singleton v. Jackson Municipal Separate School District, 348 F.2d 729 (1965).

45. U.S. v. Jefferson County, 372 F.2d 836, 847 (5th Cir., 1966), emphasis added.

46. Green v. County School Board of New Kent County, 391 U.S. 430, 439 (1968), emphasis in the original.

47. John Skrentny *The Ironies of Affirmative Action: Politics, Culture, and Justice in America* (Chicago: University of Chicago Press, 1996), ch. 5.

48. *Racial Isolation in the Public Schools* (Washington DC: GPO, 1967), vol. 1, 193, emphasis added.

49. *Racial Isolation*, 209–10.

50. Keyes v. School District No. 1, Denver, 313 F. Supp. 61, 81–82 (1970), emphasis added.

51. Milliken v. Bradley, 338 F. Supp. 582, 592 (E.D. Mich., 1971).

52. Milliken v. Bradley, 418 U.S. 717, 783 (1974).

53. *Parents Involved in Community Schools*, 515 U.S. at 839–40.

54. *Milliken v. Bradley*, 418 U.S. at 783.

55. Johnson v. San Francisco Unified School District, 339 F. Supp. 1315, 1331 (N.D. Cal., 1971). The defendant school board did not challenge the plaintiffs' argument on these issues. David Kirp, *Just Schools: The Idea of Racial Equity in American Education* (Berkeley: University of California Press, 1982), 95.

56. Swann v. Charlotte-Mecklenburg Board of Education, 243 F. Supp. 1358, 1369 (1969).

57. Eleanor P. Wolf, *Trial and Error: The Detroit School Segregation Case* (Detroit, MI: Wayne State University Press, 1981), 82.

58. *Green v. County School Board*, 391 U.S. at 436.

59. Milliken v. Bradley II, 433 U.S. 267, 282–83, 272–76 (1977).

60. Richard Matsch, quoted in James Fishman and Lawrence Strauss, "Endless Journey: Integration and the Provision of Equal Educational Opportunity in Denver's Public Schools: A Study of *Keyes v. School District No. 1*," in *Justice and School Systems: The Role of the Courts in Education Litigation*, ed. Barbara Flicker (Philadelphia: Temple University Press, 1990), 201.

61. "School Desegregation: A Social Science Statement," June 1991, appendix to brief of the NAACP, DeKalb County, Georgia in *Freeman v. Pitts*, 498 U.S., 14a (emphasis added), 2a, 17a, https://blackfreedom.proquest.com/freeman-v-pitts-brief-of-the-naacp-dekalb-county-georgia-branch-of-the-naacp-american-jewish-committee-childrens-defense-fund-fund-for-an-open-society-mexican-american-legal-defense-and-educ/.

62. "Parents Involved in Community Schools v. Seattle School District No. 1, et al.: Brief of 553 Social Scientists as Amici Curiae in Support of Respondents" (filed October 16, 2006), 2, https://blackfreedom.proquest.com/parents-involved-in-community-schools-v-seattle-school-dist-no-1-et-al-brief-of-553-social-scientists-as-amici-curiae-in-support-of-respondents/.

63. *Board of Education of Oklahoma City v. Dowell*, 498 U.S. at 260 n.5.

64. David L. Kirp and Gary Babcock, "Judge and Company: Court-Appointed Masters, School Desegregation, and Institutional Reform," 32 *Alabama Law Review* 313, 325 (1981).

65. Abram Chayes, "The Role of the Judge in Public Law Litigation," 89 *Harvard Law Review* 1281 (1976).

66. Janet Ward Schofield, "School Desegregation and Intergroup Relations: A Review of the Literature," in *Review of Research on Education*, ed. Gerald Grant, vol. 17 (Washington, DC: American Educational Research Association, 1991), 363.

67. Roger J. R. Levesque, *The Science and Law of School Segregation and Diversity* (New York: Oxford University Press, 2018), 82.

68. Stuart W. Cook, "The 1954 Social Science Statement and School Desegregation: A Reply to Gerard," *American Psychologist* 39, no. 8 (1984): 823; M. Deutscher and I. Chein, "The

Psychological Effects of Enforced Segregation: A Survey of Social Science Opinion," *Journal of Psychology* 26 (1948): 268; Schofield, "School Desegregation and Intergroup Relations," 342.

69. Quoted in Richard Kluger, *Simple Justice* (New York: Vintage, 1975), 321. According to another member of the team, Jack Weinstein (later a prominent federal judge), "I may have used the word 'crap' to describe the doll tests." Kluger, *Simple Justice*, 555.

70. Kluger, *Simple Justice*, 555; Fred B. Rothman, "Grade School Segregation: The Latest Attack on Racial Discrimination," 61 *Yale Law Journal* 730 (1952); Harold B. Gerard, "School Desegregation: The Social Science Role," *American Psychologist* 38, no. 8 (1983): 869–77.

71. Levesque, *The Science and Law of School Segregation*, 61. David Armor provides a similar review of this literature in *Forced Justice: School Desegregation and the Law* (New York: Oxford University Press, 1995), 99–101. See also Wolters, *The Burden of Brown*, 134–35.

72. Cook, "The 1954 Social Science Statement and School Desegregation," 823.

73. James S. Coleman *Equality and Achievement in Education* (Boulder, CO: Westview, 1990), 129–30.

74. James Coleman, Sara D. Kelley, and John A. Moore, *Trends in School Integration, 1968–73* (Washington: Urban Institute, 1975).

75. American Sociological Association, *Footnotes* 4, no. 8 (November 1976): 4; and *Footnotes* 17, no. 1 (January 1989): 4. Also see Raymond Wolters, *Race and Education, 1954–2007* (Columbia: University of Missouri Press, 2009), 255.

76. Not only was the initial correlation weak, it was based on a coding error. See James J. Heckman and Derek Neal, "Coleman's Contributions to Education: Theory, Research Styles and Empirical Results," in *James S. Coleman*, ed. Jon Clark (London: Falmer Press, 1996), 81–102.

77. David Armor, "The Evidence on Busing," *Public Interest* no. 28 (1972): 90–126; Thomas Pettigrew et al., "Busing: A Review of 'The Evidence,'" *Public Interest* no. 30 (1973): 88–118; David Armor, "The Double Double Standard: A Reply," *Public Interest* no. 30 (1973): 119–31.

78. Levesque, *Science and Law*, 63.

79. Nancy H. St. John, *School Desegregation: Outcomes for Children* (New York: Wiley-Interscience, 1975), 85.

80. Schofield, "School Desegregation and Intergroup Relations," 356, citations omitted.

81. See, for example, Levesque, *Science and Law*, 73.

82. Levesque, *Science and Law*, 79, emphasis added.

83. Robert Putnam, "E Pluribus Unum: Diversity and Community in the Twenty-First Century," *Scandinavian Political Studies* 30, no. 2 (2007): 137–74.

84. David Armor, "Why is Black Educational Achievement Rising?," *Public Interest* no. 108 (1992): 77–78.

85. Robert Putnam with Shaylyn Romney Garrett, *The Upswing: How America Came Together a Century Ago and How We Can Do It Again* (New York: Simon and Schuster, 2020), 205–10.

86. St. John, *School Desegregation*, 119.

87. R. I. Crain and R. Mahart, "The Effect of Research Methodology on Desegregation Achievement Studies: A Meta-Analysis," *American Journal of Sociology* 88, no. 5 (1983): 839–54.

88. Thomas Cook et al., *School Desegregation and Black Achievement* (Washington, DC: National Institute for Education, 1984): 40–41, emphasis added.

89. Janet Ward Schofield, "Review of Research on School Desegregation's Impact on Elementary and Secondary School Students," in *Handbook of Research on Multicultural Education*, eds. James A. Banks and Cherry A. McGee Banks (New York: MacMillan, 1995), 610.

90. Charles T. Clotfelter, *After Brown: The Rise and Retreat of School Desegregation* (Princeton, NJ: Princeton University Press, 2004), 187.

91. Sean Reardon, Elena Tej Grewal, Demetra Kalogrides, and Erica Greenberg, "Brown Fades: The End of Court-Ordered Desegregation and the Resegregation of American Public Schools," *Journal of Policy Analysis and Management* 31, no. 4 (2012): 900.

92. Stephen Billings, David Deming, and Jonah Rockoff, "School Segregation, Educational Attainment, and Crime: Evidence from the End of Busing in Charlotte-Mecklenburg," *Quarterly Journal of Economics* 129, no. 1 (2014): 435–76.

93. Schofield, "Review of Research," 604.

94. "Brief of 553 Social Scientists," 13–14.

95. Levesque, *Science and Law*, 75–78; Armor, *Forced Justice*, 71–72.

96. Rucker C. Johnson, "Long-Run Impacts of School Desegregation" (National Bureau of Economic Research Working Paper no. 16664, 2011), http://www.nber.org/papers/w16664; Garrett Anstreicher, Jason Fletcher, and Owen Thompson, "The Long Run Impacts of Court-Ordered Desegregation" (National Bureau of Economic Research Working Paper no. 29926, 2022), http://www.nber.org/papers/w29926. The findings of Johnson's paper are presented in Rucker Johnson with Alexander Nazaryan, *Children of the Dream: Why School Integration Works* (New York: Basic Books, 2019).

97. Johnson with Nazaryan, *Children of the Dream*, 55.

98. Johnson with Nazaryan, *Children of the Dream*, 63–65.

99. Johnson with Nazaryan, *Children of the Dream*, 60.

100. Johnson with Nazaryan, *Children of the Dream*, 133.

101. Anstreicher, Fletcher, and Thompson, "The Long Run Impacts of Court-Ordered Desegregation," 23.

102. Anstreicher, Fletcher, and Thompson, "The Long Run Impacts of Court-Ordered Desegregation," 2 and 14–15.

103. Anstreicher, Fletcher, and Thompson, "The Long Run Impacts of Court-Ordered Desegregation," 23.

104. Anstreicher, Fletcher, and Thompson, "The Long Run Impacts of Court-Ordered Desegregation," 23–24.

105. Sean F. Reardon and Ann Owens, "60 Years after *Brown*: Trends and Consequences of School Segregation," *Annual Review of Sociology 40 (2014)*: 214.

106. Schofield, "School Desegregation and Intergroup Relations," 346.

107. Schofield, "School Desegregation and Intergroup Relations," 357.

108. Schofield, "School Desegregation and Intergroup Relations," 358.

109. Levesque, *Science and Law*, 65, 71, and 77.

110. Levesque, *Science and Law*, 85.

Chapter Three

1. Quoted in Michael Klarman, *From Jim Crow to Civil Rights: The Supreme Court and the Struggle for Racial Equality* (New York: Oxford University Press, 2004), 317.

2. Cooper v. Aaron, 358 U.S. 1, 6 (1958).

3. Shuttlesworth v. Birmingham Board of Education, 358 U.S. 101 (1958). Also see Kelly v. Board of Education of Nashville, 361 U.S. 924 (1959); and Klarman, *From Jim Crow to Civil Rights*, 329–31.

4. Gerald Rosenberg, *The Hollow Hope: Can Courts Bring About Social Change?*, 2nd ed. (Chicago: University of Chicago Press, 2008), 50.

5. Stephan and Abigail Thernstrom, *America in Black and White: One Nation, Indivisible* (New York: Simon and Schuster, 1997), 316.

6. Goss v. Board of Education, 373 U.S. 683, 687 (1963).

7. Griffin v. School Board, 377 U.S. 218, 229 (1964).

8. Education Amendments of 1974, section 215(a). Gary Orfield provides a detailed history of congressional efforts to limit busing in *Must We Bus? Segregated Schools and National Policy* (Washington, DC: Brookings Institution Press, 1978), 244–68.

9. Hugh Davis Graham, *The Civil Rights Era: Origins and Development of National Policy* (New York: Oxford University Press, 1990), 83.

10. U.S. v. Jefferson County Board of Education, 372 F.2d 836, 847 (5th Cir., 1966). Subsequently referred to as *Jefferson County I*.

11. *Jefferson County I*, 372 F.2d at 847.

12. Gary Orfield, *The Reconstruction of Southern Education: The Schools and the 1964 Civil Rights Act* (New York: Wiley-Interscience, 1969).

13. *Jefferson County I*, 372 F.2d at 847.

14. *Jefferson County I*, 372 F.2d at 866, emphasis added.

15. Quoted in Gareth Davies, *See Government Grow: Education Politics from Johnson to Reagan* (Lawrence: University Press of Kansas, 2007), 112–13.

16. 45 C.F.R. §181.54 (1966), emphasis added. While the 1966 guidelines were included in the official Code of Federal Regulations, the 1965 guidelines retained their nebulous status, and were never published in any formal way. They are included in the appendix of Price v. Denison Independent School District, 348 F.2d 1010 (5th Cir., 1965).

17. Lino A. Graglia, *Disaster by Decree: The Supreme Court Decisions on Race and the Schools* (Ithaca, NY: Cornell University Press, 1976), 101. Graglia provides a list of some of these cases, 301 n.25.

18. Quoted in Beryl Radin, *Implementation, Change, and the Federal Bureaucracy: School Desegregation Policy in H.E.W., 1964–68* (New York: Teachers College Press, 1977), 129.

19. Milliken v. Bradley, 418 U.S. 717, 746–47 (1974).

20. See the discussion of Pasadena City Board of Education v. Spangler, 427 U.S. 434 (1976) and Dayton Board of Education v. Brinkman I, 433 U.S. 406 (1977) in chapter 5.

21. Columbus Board of Education v. Penick, 443 U.S. 449, 490 (1979).

22. Board of Education of Oklahoma City v. Dowell, 498 U.S. 231, 246 (1991). It would be "a mistake," Chief Justice Rehnquist argued in the 1991 case, "to treat words such as 'dual' and 'unitary' as if they were actually found in the Constitution." At 245.

23. Freeman v. Pitts 503 U.S. 469, 489–90 (1992).

24. *Board of Education of Oklahoma City v. Dowell*, 498 U.S. at 259–62 and 266.

25. US Commission on Civil Rights, *Becoming Less Separate? School Desegregation, Justice Department Enforcement, and the Pursuit of Unitary Status* (Washington, DC: Government Printing Office, 2007), 37, table 4.6.

26. Wendy Parker, "The Decline of Judicial Decisionmaking: School Desegregation and District Court Judges," 81 *North Carolina Law Review* 1623, 1652 (2003).

27. Parker, "The Decline of Judicial Decisionmaking," 1634–35.

28. Wendy Parker, "The Future of School Desegregation," 94 *Northwestern University Law Review* 1157, 1181 (1999–2000).

NOTES TO PAGES 78-86

29. Leadership Conference on Civil Rights, quoted in Jesse Rhodes, *An Education in Politics: The Origins and Evolution of No Child Left Behind* (Ithaca, NY: Cornell University Press, 2012), 174.

30. For some reason the full text of the speech has disappeared from the Department of Education's website. Some of Duncan's key phrases are reported by Sam Dillon, "Officials Step Up Enforcement of Rights Laws in Education," *New York Times*, March 8, 2010, https://www.nytimes.com/2010/03/08/education/08educ.html.

31. US Department of Education (OCR) and US Department of Justice (Civil Rights Division), *Guidance on the Voluntary Use of Race to Achieve Diversity in Postsecondary Education*, December 2, 2011, https://www2.ed.gov/about/offices/list/ocr/docs/guidance-pse-201111.html.

32. "Dear Colleague" letter from Assistant Secretary of Education Catherine Lhamon, October 1, 2014, https://www2.ed.gov/about/offices/list/ocr/frontpage/pro-students/issues/roi-issue01.html.

33. Departments of Education and Justice, joint "Dear Colleague" letter, "Nondiscriminatory Administration of School Discipline," January 8, 2014, 7, emphasis added, https://www2.ed.gov/about/offices/list/ocr/letters/colleague-201401-title-vi.html.

Chapter Four

1. Stephan and Abigail Thernstrom, *America in Black and White: One Nation, Indivisible* (New York: Simon and Schuster, 1997), 316.

2. Griffin v. School Board of Prince Edward County, 377 U.S. 218, 229 and 234 (1964).

3. Charles Clotfelter, *After Brown: The Rise and Retreat of School Desegregation* (Princeton, NJ: Princeton University Press, 2004), 6 and 56.

4. Gary Orfield, *The Reconstruction of Southern Education: The Schools and the 1964 Civil Rights Act* (New York: Wiley-Interscience, 1969), 1.

5. We are fortunate to have a number of detailed studies of OCR in the second half of the 1960s, several of them based on personal interviews as well as review of official documents. This section of the chapter relies on the following works: Orfield, *The Reconstruction of Southern Education*; Beryl Radin, *Implementation, Change, and the Federal Bureaucracy: School Desegregation Policy in H.E.W., 1964-68* (New York: Teachers College Press, 1977); Allan Wolk, *The Presidency and Black Civil Rights: Eisenhower to Nixon* (Vancouver: Fairleigh Dickinson University Press, 1971); and Stephen C. Halpern, *On the Limits of the Law: The Ironic Legacy of Title VI of the 1964 Civil Rights Act* (Baltimore, MD: Johns Hopkins University Press, 1995). Halpern's chapter 3 is particularly good on examining cooperation between the Fifth Circuit and OCR.

6. Hugh Graham, *The Uncertain Triumph: Federal Education Policy in the Kennedy and Johnson Years* (Chapel Hill: University of North Carolina Press, 1984), xvii.

7. Quoted in Orfield, *The Reconstruction of Southern Education*, 56.

8. Orfield, *The Reconstruction of Southern Education*, 59.

9. Wolk, *The Presidency and Black Civil Rights*, 111.

10. David Seeley, quoted in Wolk, *The Presidency and Black Civil Rights*, 114; and in Orfield, *The Reconstruction of Southern Education*, 76.

11. Wilbur Cohen, quoted in Gareth Davies, *See Government Grow: Education Politics from Johnson to Reagan* (Lawrence: University Press of Kansas, 2007), 112-13.

12. Orfield, *The Reconstruction of Southern Education*, 116 and 248; Radin, *Implementation, Change, and the Federal Bureaucracy*, 165; Note, "The Courts, HEW, and Southern School

Desegregation," 77 *Yale Law Journal* 321, 344 (1967); and Orfield, *Must We Bus? Segregated Schools and National Policy* (Washington, DC: Brookings Institution Press, 1978), 297. Orfield notes that OCR's growth was inversely proportional to its emphasis on school desegregation. Most of the work of this growing staff focused on issues other than desegregation.

13. Orfield, *The Reconstruction of Southern Education*, 72–75; Radin, *Implementation, Change, and the Federal Bureaucracy*, 106–107; Wolk, *The Presidency and Black Civil Rights*, 126.

14. Francis Keppel, quoted in Wolk, *The Presidency and Black Civil Rights*, 116.

15. Wolk, *The Presidency and Black Civil Rights*, 116; Orfield, *The Reconstruction of Southern Education*, 93–94.

16. Orfield, *The Reconstruction of Southern Education*, 80–81.

17. Orfield, *Must We Bus?*, 280–90; Frank T. Read and Lucy S. McGough, *Let Them Be Judged: The Judicial Integration of the Deep South* (Metuchen, NJ: Scarecrow Press, 1978), 516.

18. Halpern, *On the Limits of the Law*, 56.

19. Radin, *Implementation, Change, and the Federal Bureaucracy*, 14.

20. Halpern, *On the Limits of the Law*, 51–52; Orfield, *The Reconstruction of Southern Education*, 241–43.

21. Quoted in Wolk, *The Presidency and Black Civil Rights*, 140. Also see Orfield, *The Reconstruction of Southern Education*, ch. 6; Orfield, *Must We Bus*, ch. 8; and Wolk, *The Presidency and Black Civil Rights*, 120–42.

22. Radin, *Implementation, Change, and the Federal Bureaucracy*, 105.

23. Radin, *Implementation, Change, and the Federal Bureaucracy*, 109.

24. Orfield, *The Reconstruction of Southern Education*, 142.

25. Orfield, *The Reconstruction of Southern Education*, 111–16.

26. Harold Howe II, quoted in Wolk, *The Presidency and Black Civil Rights*, 120.

27. 45 C.F.R. §181.54 (1966), emphasis added. The 1965 guidelines are included in the appendix of *Price v. Denison Independent School District*, 348 F.2d 1010 (5th Cir., 1965).

28. Orfield, *The Reconstruction of Southern Education*, 92.

29. Halpern, *On the Limits of the Law*, 54.

30. Halpern, *On the Limits of the Law*, 53–57.

31. Singleton v. Jackson Municipal Separate School District, 348 F.2d 729, 730 (5th Cir., 1965).

32. Price v. Denison Independent School District, 348 F.2d 1010 (5th Cir., 1965).

33. John Skrentny, *The Ironies of Affirmative Action: Politics, Culture, and Justice in America* (Chicago: University of Chicago Press, 1996), 112.

34. U.S. v. Jefferson County Board of Education, 372 F.2d 836, 858 (5th Cir., 1966).

35. Jack Greenberg, *Crusaders in the Courts: Legal Battles of the Civil Rights Movement*, anniversary ed. (New York: Twelve Tables Press, 2004), 324.

36. US Department of Justice, "Report of Assistant Attorney General John Doar in Charge of the Civil Rights Division," in *Annual Report of the Attorney General of the United States for the Fiscal Year Ending June 30, 1966* (Washington, DC: Government Printing Office, 1966), 196; and Orfield, *The Reconstruction of Southern Education*, 333.

37. US Department of Justice, "Report of Assistant Attorney General John Doar in Charge of the Civil Rights Division," in *Annual Report of the Attorney General of the United States for the Fiscal Year Ending June 30, 1967* (Washington, DC: Government Printing Office, 1967), 174.

38. See Read and McGough, *Let Them Be Judged*, ch. 10; and J. W. Peltason, *Fifty-Eight Lonely Men: Southern Federal Judges and School Desegregation* (Urbana: University of Illinois Press, 1971).

39. Read and McGough, *Let Them Be Judged*, provides an excellent examination of the judges on the Fifth Circuit during this period and a detailed history of their often acrimonious relations. At one point, Judge Cameron threw the court into tumult by accusing "the Four" of manipulating assignments to favor civil rights litigants, a charge that was never substantiated. Judges Tuttle, Wisdom, and Brown were Eisenhower Republicans. Rives, a Democrat, was close to Justice Black. Tuttle was chief judge of the circuit from 1961 to 1967, when he was replaced by Brown. Together they were responsible for many of the procedural innovations described below.

40. Read and McGough, *Let Them Be Judged*, 376. The procedural changes are described on 186–88 and 450.

41. Singleton v. Jackson Municipal Separate School District, 348 F.2d 729, 729–30 (5th Cir., 1965).

42. U.S. v. Jefferson County Board of Education, 372 F. 2d 859 (5th Cir., 1966) (original three-judge panel; subsequently referred to as *Jefferson County I*); and U.S. v. Jefferson County Board of Education, 380 F.2d 385 (5th Cir., 1967) (en banc; subsequently referred to as *Jefferson County II*).

43. Frank Read, "Judicial Evolution of the Law of School Integration since Brown v. Board," 39 *Law and Contemporary Problems* 7, 20 (1975).

44. *Jefferson County I*, at 847.

45. Briggs v. Elliott, 132 F. Supp. 776, 777 (E.D. S. C., 1955) (three-judge panel).

46. *Jefferson County I*, at 847.

47. *Jefferson County I*, at 866, emphasis added.

48. *Jefferson County I*, at 847.

49. *Jefferson County II*, at 389. It is likely that Judge Wisdom wrote the per curiam opinion as well, and that he omitted much of the lengthy explanation he provided in *Jefferson I* in order to corral a majority on the twelve-member en banc court.

50. *Jefferson County II*, at 419.

51. *Jefferson County II*, at 410.

52. *Jefferson County II*, at 403.

53. *Jefferson County II*, at 397.

54. *Jefferson County II*, footnote 9 of Godbold dissent.

55. *Jefferson County I*, at 876.

56. J. Harvie Wilkinson III, *From Brown to Bakke: The Supreme Court and School Integration: 1954–1978* (New York: Oxford University Press, 1981), 113–14.

57. Read, "Judicial Evolution," 31–32, n.106.

58. Read and McGough, *Let Them Be Judged*, provides an extensive review of these procedural changes in chapter 12, appropriately named "The Era of the Super Court."

59. Not only was Ramsey Clark more passionate about desegregation litigation than this predecessor, but President Johnson had used his appointment as a way to replace his relatively conservative father, Justice Tom Clark, with Thurgood Marshall on the Supreme Court.

60. Greenberg, *Crusaders in the Courts*, 411.

61. Lino Graglia, *Disaster by Decree: The Supreme Court Decisions on Race and the Schools* (Ithaca, NY: Cornell University Press, 1976), 101 and 301 n.25.

62. Lee v. Macon County Board of Education, 267 F. Supp. 467 (M.D. Ala, 1967) (three-judge panel).

63. Read and McGough, *Let Them Be Judged*, 469; Read, "Judicial Evolution of the Law of School Integration," 32.

64. Owen M. Fiss, *Injunctions*, University Casebook Series (Mineola, NY: Foundation Press, 1972), 415–81.

65. See Paul Gewirtz, "Remedies and Resistance," 92 *Yale Law Journal* 585, 588 (1983).

66. William A. Fletcher, "The Discretionary Constitution: Institutional Remedies and Judicial Legitimacy," 91 *Yale Law Journal* 635, 682 (1982)

67. Quoted in Halpern, *On the Limits of the Law*, 74.

68. Radin, *Implementation, Change, and the Federal Bureaucracy*, 117; Halpern, *On the Limits of the Law*, 74.

69. Halpern, *On the Limits of the Law*, 73.

70. "The Courts, HEW, and Southern School Desegregation," 77 *Yale Law Journal* 321, 349–50 (1967). The journal did not name the author but noted that the article won an award for "the most outstanding piece of faculty-designated student work."

71. "The Courts, HEW, and Southern School Desegregation," 353–54.

72. Radin, *Implementation, Change, and the Federal Bureaucracy*, 129, emphasis added.

73. Mannings v. Board of Public Instruction, 427 F.2d 874 (5th Cir., 1970).

74. Ellis v. Board of Public Instruction of Orange County, 423 F. 2d 203 (5th Cir., 1970).

75. Ross v. Eckels, 434 F.2d 1140, 1147 (5th Cir., 1970).

76. Andrews v. City of Monroe, 425 F.2d 1017, 1020 (5th Cir., 1970).

77. Henry v. Clarksdale, 433 F. 2d 387 (5th Cir., 1970).

Chapter Five

1. Griffin Bell, quoted in Bernard Schwartz, *Swann's Way: The School Busing Case and the Supreme Court* (New York: Oxford University Press, 1986), 186.

2. Bowman v. County School Board, 382 F.2d 326, 327 (4th Cir., 1967). A peculiar feature of the *Green* case is that one never learned which school the nominal plaintiff attended. If he or she attended the formerly white school, it would be hard to claim denial of the right to attend a desegregated school. If he or she attended the formerly black school, the remedy would seem to be the right to attend the formerly white school, an option previously offered but not exercised. What the Court implied but did not say is that Mr. or Ms. Green has the right to attend a school that reflected the racial balance of the school district as a whole. The fact that individual plaintiffs disappeared from sight in these cases made it easier for the justices to be vague about the nature of the underlying right.

3. In addition to Bowman, the lower court decisions were Monroe v. Board of Commissioners, 380 F.2d 955 (6th Cir., 1967); Kemp v. Beasley, 389 F.2d 178 (8th Cir., 1968); Clark v. Board of Education of Little Rock, 374 F.2d 569 (8th Cir., 1967); and Raney v. Board of Education, 381 F.2d 252 (8th Cir., 1967).

4. Owen Fiss, "The Charlotte-Mecklenburg Case—Its Significance for Northern School Desegregation," 38 *University of Chicago Law Review* 697, 699 (1970).

5. Green v. County School Board, 391 U.S. 430, 439 (1968).

6. *Green v. County School Board*, 391 U.S. at 440, quoting Judge Sobeloff's concurring opinion in Bowman.

7. *Green v. County School Board*, 391 U.S. at 439, emphasis in the original.

8. *Green v. County School Board*, 391 U.S. at 437–38.

9. *Green v. County School Board*, 391 U.S. at 435.

10. *Green v. County School Board*, 391 U.S. at 442, emphasis added.

11. *Green v. County School Board*, 391 U.S. at 440 n.5.

12. Quoted in Raymond Wolters, *The Burden of Brown: Thirty Years of School Desegregation* (Knoxville: University of Tennessee Press, 1992), 157.

13. Quoted in Wolters, *The Burden of Brown*, 156.

14. *Green v. County School Board*, 391 U.S. at 442 n.6.

15. Louis Claiborne, quoted in J. Harvie Wilkinson III, *From Brown to Bakke: The Supreme Court and School Integration: 1954–1978* (New York: Oxford University Press, 1981), 115.

16. The language of the draft opinion is reprinted in Mark Whitman, *The Irony of Desegregation Law* (Princeton, NJ: M. Wiener, 1998), 123.

17. Frank T. Read and Lucy S. McGough, *Let Them Be Judged: The Judicial Integration of the Deep South* (Metuchen, NJ: Scarecrow Press, 1978), 472–94.

18. Quoted in Gary Orfield, *Must We Bus? Segregated Schools and National Policy* (Washington, DC: Brookings Institution Press, 1978), 352. As we will see in chapter 9, it quickly found them.

19. *Adams v. Richardson*, 351 F. Supp. 630, 642 (D.D.C., 1972). This case is discussed in chapter 9.

20. Kevin J. McMahon, *Nixon's Court: His Challenge to Judicial Liberalism and Its Political Consequences* (Chicago: University of Chicago Press, 2011), 84 and 91.

21. Rowland Evans and Robert Novak, quoted in McMahon, *Nixon's Court*, 93.

22. Gareth Davies, *See Government Grow: Education Politics from Johnson to Reagan* (Lawrence: University Press of Kansas, 2007), 123–24.

23. Quoted in Davies, *See Government Grow*, 128.

24. Quoted in McMahon, *Nixon's Court*, 76.

25. Davies, *See Government Grow*, 138–40.

26. *U.S. v. Montgomery County Board of Education*, 289 F. Supp. 647 (M.D. Ala., 1968); *U.S. v. Montgomery County Board of Education*, 400 F.2d 1 (5th Cir., 1968).

27. *U.S. v. Montgomery County Board of Education*, 395 U.S. 225, 236 (1969).

28. These events are recounted in a variety of sources. Read and McGough add two interesting details. First, HEW secretary Robert Finch sent a private letter to the Chief Judge Brown of the Fifth Circuit asking him to delay the order—an ex parte communication of dubious propriety. The Fifth Circuit ignored that request but accepted the DOJ's formal request for a temporary stay. Second, Judge Brown later decided that granting the stay was one of the worst mistakes the court had made in the long desegregation saga. See Read and McGough, *Let Them Be Judged*, 487.

29. *Alexander v. Holmes County Board of Education*, 396 U.S. 19 (1969).

30. Bob Woodward and Scott Armstrong, *The Brethren: Inside the Supreme Court* (New York: Simon and Schuster, 1979), 43.

31. Woodward and Armstrong, *The Brethren*, 50.

32. Woodward and Armstrong, *The Brethren*, 51–56.

33. *Singleton v. Jackson Municipal*, 419 F.2d 1211, 1217 (5th Cir, 1969).

34. *Carter v. West Feliciana Parish School Board*, 396 U.S. 290, 292–93 (1970). Justice Fortas had resigned and had not yet been replaced.

35. Frank Read, "Judicial Evolution of the Law of School Integration since Brown v. Board," 39 *Law and Contemporary Problems* 7, 31 (1975).

36. *Singleton v. Jackson Municipal Separate School District*, 425 F. 2d 1211, 1214–16 (5th Cir., 1970).

37. *Northcross v. Board of Education*, 420 F.2d 546, 548 (1969). One of the three members of the panel was former HEW secretary Celebrezze.

38. Northcross v. Board of Education, 397 U.S. 232, 236–37 (1970).

39. Swann v. Charlotte-Mecklenburg Board of Education, 300 F. Supp. 1358, 1369 (W.D.NC, 1969).

40. Quoted in Schwartz, *Swann's Way*, 186.

41. Schwartz, *Swann's Way*, ch. 6–12; Woodward and Armstrong, *The Brethren*, 95–112.

42. Lino Graglia, *Disaster by Decree: The Supreme Court Decisions on Race and the Schools* (Ithaca, NY: Cornell University Press, 1976), 140–41.

43. Schwartz, *Swann's Way*, 122–29; and Woodward and Armstrong, *The Brethren*, 101.

44. Swann v. Charlotte-Mecklenburg Board of Education, 402 U.S. 1, 15 (1971), internal quotation marks removed.

45. *Swann v. Charlotte-Mecklenburg Board of Education*, 402 U.S. at 28.

46. *Swann v. Charlotte-Mecklenburg Board of Education*, 402 U.S. at 23–24, emphasis added.

47. *Swann v. Charlotte-Mecklenburg Board of Education*, 402 U.S. at 25.

48. *Swann v. Charlotte-Mecklenburg Board of Education*, 402 U.S. at 23.

49. *Swann v. Charlotte-Mecklenburg Board of Education*, 402 U.S. at 26 and 28.

50. *Swann v. Charlotte-Mecklenburg Board of Education*, 402 U.S. at 29–31.

51. *Swann v. Charlotte-Mecklenburg Board of Education*, 402 U.S. at 31.

52. Davis v. Bd. of School Commissioners of Mobile County, 402 U.S. 33, 37–38 (1971).

53. In the letter he sent to lower-court judges a few months later, Chief Justice Burger stated that "nothing could be plainer" than that the Supreme Court had "disapproved of the 71%-29% racial composition found in the Swann case as the controlling factor in assignment of pupils." This claim is particularly bizarre in light of his opinion in *Davis*.

54. Orfield, *Must We Bus?*, 25.

55. Read and McGough, *Let Them Be Judged*, 530–31.

56. Keyes v. School District No. 1, Denver, 303 F. Supp. 279 (D. Colo., 1969); 313 F. Supp. 61 (D. Colo., 1970); and 445 F.2d 990 (10th Cir., 1971).

57. Keyes v. School District No. 1, Denver, 413 U.S. 189, 201, 203 (1973).

58. *Keyes v. School District No. 1*, Denver, 413 U.S., at 210, emphasis added.

59. *Keyes v. School District No. 1*, Denver, 413 U.S. at 236, emphasis added.

60. *Keyes v. School District No. 1*, Denver, 413 U.S. at 250.

61. *Keyes v. School District No. 1*, Denver, 413 U.S. at 258.

62. Wright v. Council of City of Emporia, 407 U.S. 451, 462 (1972), emphasis added.

63. Quoted in U.S. v. Scotland Neck Board of Education, 407 U.S. 484, 489 (1972).

64. *Wright v. Council of City of Emporia*, 407 U.S. at 472.

65. *Wright v. Council of City of Emporia*, 407 U.S. at 466,

66. *Wright v. Council of City of Emporia*, 407 U.S. at 474.

67. Milliken v. Bradley 484 F.2d 215, 249–50 (6th Cir., 1973), emphasis added.

68. Bradley v. Richmond School Board. 462 F. 2d 1058, 1060 (4th Cir., 1972). Merhige was not trying to achieve "racial balance" in the way the term was used in *Swann*. There, it meant having each school reflect the racial balance of the school district as a whole. Merhige rejected that option because it would produce predominantly black schools in Richmond. He was trying to produce majority-white schools.

69. Justice Powell recused himself because he had previously been chairman of the Richmond School Board. The vote was not recorded, but it almost certainly found Burger, Rehnquist, Blackmun, and Stewart on one side and Brennan, Marshall, Douglas, and White on the other. Richmond remained a separate—and predominantly black—school district. See James E. Ryan,

Five Miles Away, a World Apart: One City, Two Schools, and the Story of Educational Opportunity in Modern America (New York: Oxford University Press, 2011).

70. Milliken v. Bradley 338 F. Supp. 582, 592 (E. D. Mich., 1971).
71. Milliken v. Bradley, 418 U.S. 717, 746 (1974), emphasis added.
72. *Milliken v. Bradley*, 418 U.S. at 747.
73. *Milliken v. Bradley*, 418 U.S. at 802.
74. *Milliken v. Bradley*, 418 U.S. at 783.
75. *Milliken v. Bradley*, 418 U.S. at 755.
76. Spangler v. Pasadena City Board of Education, 311 F. Supp. 501, 505 (C.D. CA, 1970).
77. Quoted in Spangler v. Pasadena City Board of Education, 427 U.S. 424, 433 (1976).
78. *Spangler v. Pasadena City Board of Education*, 427 U.S. at 438.
79. See chapter 6 for more details on the Dayton case.
80. Dayton Board of Education v. Brinkman I, 433 U.S. 406, 417–18 (1977).
81. *Dayton Board of Education v. Brinkman I*, 433 U.S. at 420, emphasis added.
82. Washington v. Davis, 429 U.S. 229, 239–40 (1976).
83. Arlington Heights v. Metro Housing Corp., 429 U.S. 252, 264–65 (1977).
84. Brennan v. Armstrong 433 U.S. 672 (1977); School District of Omaha v. U.S. 433 U.S. 667 (1977).
85. Columbus Board of Education v. Penick, 443 U.S. 449, 479 (1979).
86. *Columbus Board of Education v. Penick*, 443 U.S. at 480.
87. *Columbus Board of Education v. Penick*, 443 U.S. at 483.
88. *Columbus Board of Education v. Penick*, 443 U.S. at 492.
89. *Columbus Board of Education v. Penick*, 443 U.S. at 525.
90. Dissent from dismissal of certiorari, Estes v. Metropolitan Branch, Dallas NAACP, 444 U.S. 437, 439, 444, 450–51 (1980).
91. Delaware State Board of Education v. Evans, 446 U.S. 923, 925–26 (1980).
92. Milliken v. Bradley II, 433 U.S. 267, 274, 283 (1977).

Chapter Six

1. Swann v. Charlotte-Mecklenburg Board of Education, 379 F. Supp. 1102, 1103 (W.D. NC, 1974).
2. Capacchione v. Charlotte-Mecklenburg Board of Education, 57 F. Supp. 2d 228, 242–43 (W.D. NC, 1999).
3. Coalition to Save Our Children v. State Board of Education of the State of Delaware, 901 F. Supp. 784, 822 (D. Del., 1995).
4. Owen M. Fiss, *The Civil Rights Injunction* (Bloomington: Indiana University Press, 1978): 1.
5. Fiss, *Civil Rights Injunction*, 7.
6. Fiss, *Civil Rights Injunction*, 7.
7. David L. Kirp and Gary Babcock, "Judge and Company: Court-Appointed Masters, School Desegregation, and Institutional Reform," 32 *Alabama Law Review* 313, 325 (1980–81).
8. Fiss, *Civil Rights Injunction*, 26–28, emphasis in the original.
9. Kirp and Babcock, "Judge and Company," 325.
10. David L. Kirp, *Just Schools: The Idea of Racial Equality in American Education* (Berkeley: University of California Press, 1982), 55.
11. Kirp and Babcock, "Judge and Company," 382.

12. See below, chapter 6, 153–55.

13. Kirp and Babcock, "Judge and Company," 327.

14. John Finger, quoted in Robert C. Wood and Clement E. Vose, eds., *Remedial Law: When Courts Become Administrators* (Amherst: University of Massachusetts Press, 1990), 27.

15. Rule 53, discussed in Kirp and Babcock, "Judge and Company," 383 ff.

16. Kirp and Babcock, "Judge and Company," 365–66.

17. William A. Fletcher, "The Discretionary Constitution: Institutional Remedies and Judicial Legitimacy," 91 *Yale Law Journal* 635, 681–82 (1982).

18. Kirp and Babcock, "Judge and Company," 324.

19. Brown v. Board of Education II, 349 U.S. 294, 298–300 (1955)

20. Swann v. Charlotte-Mecklenburg Board of Education, 402 U.S. 1, 28 (1971).

21. William H. Frey, *Diversity Explosion: How New Racial Demographics Are Remaking America* (Washington, DC: Brookings Institution Press, 2015), 22.

22. Frey, *Diversity Explosion*, 26–27.

23. "Racial/Ethnic Enrollment in Public Schools," National Center for Educational Statistics, last updated May 2022, https://nces.ed.gov/programs/coe/indicator/cge#:~:text=In%20fall%20 2018%2C%20of%20the,and%20186%2C000%20were%20Pacific%20Islander.

24. Abram Chayes, "The Role of the Judge in Public Law Litigation," 89 *Harvard Law Review* 1281 (1976); and Donald Horowitz, *Courts and Social Policy* (Washington, DC: Brookings Institution Press, 1976), ch. 2.

25. Joseph Radelet, "Stillness at Detroit's Racial Divide: A Perspective on Detroit's School Desegregation Court Order—1970–1989," *Urban Review* 23, no. 3 (1991); and Joyce A. Baugh, *The Detroit School Busing Case: Milliken v. Bradley and the Controversy over Desegregation* (Lawrence: University Press of Kansas, 2011), 182.

26. Derrick Bell, "Serving Two Masters: Integration Ideals and Client Interests in School Desegregation Litigation," 85 *Yale Law Journal* 470 (1976).

27. Paul R. Dimond, *Beyond Busing: Inside the Challenge to Urban Segregation* (Ann Arbor: University of Michigan Press, 1985), 63 and 30.

28. Dimond, *Beyond Busing*, ch. 2; and Eleanor P. Wolf, *Trial and Error: The Detroit School Segregation Case* (Detroit, MI: Wayne State University Press, 1981), 212–38.

29. The polling data is cited in James Ryan and Thomas Saunders, "Foreword to Symposium on School Finance Litigation," 22 *Yale Law and Policy Review* 463, 480 (2009). Drew Days, a former NAACP litigator who filed desegregation suits against several cities while in the Department of Justice, also developed doubts about focusing on racial balance rather than educational quality: "In Search of Educational E/Quality Forty-Six Years after *Brown v. Board of Education*," 54 *Southern Methodist University Law Review* 2089 (2001). Polling data cited by Christine Rossell indicates that black parents' support for mandatory reassignment of children beyond neighborhood schools dropped below 50 percent in the 1990s. Christine H. Rossell, "The Convergence of Black and White Attitudes on School Desegregation Issues during the Four Decade Evolution of the Plans," 36 *William and Mary Law Review* 613 (1995). See also Stephan Thernstrom and Abigail M. Thernstrom, *America in Black and White: One Nation, Indivisible* (New York, NY: Touchstone, 1999), 330–31; and David J. Armor, *Forced Justice: School Desegregation and the Law* (New York: Oxford University Press, 1995), 198–203.

30. Kelley v. Metropolitan County Board of Education, 492 F. Supp. 167, 184 (M.D. Tenn., 1980).

31. Kelley v. Metropolitan Board of Education, 687 F.2d 814 (6th Cir., 1982).

NOTES TO PAGES 155–161

32. Tasby v. Wright, 520 F. Supp. 683, 689–90 (N.D. Tex., 1981); upheld in Tasby v. Wright, 713 F.2d 90 (5th Cir., 1983).

33. Joshua M. Dunn, *Complex Justice: The Case of Missouri v. Jenkins* (Chapel Hill: University of North Carolina Press, 2008), ch. 6.

34. Kirp and Babcock, "Judge and Company," 350. The quotation from Judge Battisti comes from an unpublished hearing, the key portion of which can be found in Kirp and Babcock, "Judge and Company," 350, n.116.

35. Dimond, *Beyond Busing*, 28.

36. Kirp, *Just Schools*, 91.

37. Dunn, *Complex Justice*, 53–55.

38. Raymond Wolters, *The Burden of Brown: Thirty Years of School Desegregation* (Knoxville: University of Tennessee Press, 1992): 206–12.

39. Kirp, *Just Schools*, 92–93.

40. Kirp, *Just Schools*, 117.

41. Kirp, *Just Schools*, 131.

42. Dimond, *Beyond Busing*, 124–25.

43. William S. Kolski and Jeannie Oakes, "Equal Educational Opportunity, School Reform, and the Courts: A Study of the Desegregation Litigation in San Jose," in *From the Courtroom to the Classroom: The Shifting Landscape of School Desegregation*, eds. Claire E. Smrekar and Ellen B. Goldring (Cambridge, MA: Harvard Educational Press, 2009), 88.

44. Superintendent Linda Murray, quoted in Kolski and Oakes, "Equal Educational Opportunity," 90 and 98.

45. Raymond Wolters, *Race and Education, 1954–2007* (Columbia: University of Missouri Press, 2008), 269–70. Also see Roslyn Arlin Mickelson, Stephen Samuel Smith, and Amy Hawn Nelson, eds., *Yesterday, Today, and Tomorrow: School Desegregation and Resegregation in Charlotte* (Cambridge, MA: Harvard Education Press, 2015), ch. 1; and David Armor, "Desegregation and Academic Achievement," in *School Desegregation in the 21st Century*, eds. Christine Rossell, David Armor, and Herbert Walberg (Westport, CT: Praeger, 2002), 169–71.

46. Capacchione v. Charlotte-Mecklenburg Schools, 57 F. Supp. 2d 228, 282 (W.D. NC, 1999).

47. Belk v. Charlotte-Mecklenburg Board of Education, 269 F. 3d 305, 333 (4th Cir., 2001).

48. Wolters, *The Burden of Brown*, 276–77.

49. *Capacchione v. Charlotte-Mecklenburg Schools*, 57 F. Supp. 2d at 232.

50. *Belk v. Charlotte-Mecklenburg Board of Education*, 269 F. 3d at 333–34.

51. Denver school superintendent James P. Scamman, quoted in Wood and Vose, *Remedial Law*, 29.

52. Dimond, *Beyond Busing*, 122.

53. Wolf, *Trial and Error*, 18–19.

54. Baugh, *The Detroit School Busing Case*, 88–90.

55. Quoted in Dimond, *Beyond Busing*, 72.

56. Milliken v. Bradley, 338 F. Supp. 582, 592 (E.D. Mich., 1971).

57. Dunn, *Complex Justice*, 74.

58. Dunn, *Complex Justice*, ch. 3.

59. "Judicial Intervention and Organizational Theory: Changing Bureaucratic Behavior and Policy," 89 *Yale Law Journal* 513, 528 (1980).

60. Kirp and Babcock, "Judge and Company," 362. See also James J. Fishman, "The Limits of Remedial Power: Hart v. Community School Board 21," in *Limits of Justice: The Courts' Role in*

School Desegregation, ed. Howard I. Kalodner and James J. Fishman (Cambridge, MA: Ballinger Publishing, 1978).

61. Hart v. Community School Board, 383 F. Supp. 699, 775 (E.D. NY, 1974).

62. For detailed comparisons of these judges, see Kirp and Babcock, "Judge and Company"; and Dimond, *Beyond Busing*, ch. 6, 7, and 11.

63. Brinkman v. Gilligan, 503 F.2d 684, 688 (6th Cir., 1974), quoting Judge Rubin's July 13, 1973, order.

64. Dimond, *Beyond Busing*, 146.

65. Most of the details in this section come from the excellent case study by Kolski and Oakes, "Equal Educational Opportunity, School Reform, and the Courts."

66. Missouri v. Jenkins, 491 U.S. 274 (1989); Missouri v. Jenkins, 495 U.S. 33 (1990); Missouri v. Jenkins, 515 U.S. 70 (1995).

67. Fiss, *The Civil Rights Injunction*, 26–28.

Chapter Seven

1. David J. Armor, *Forced Justice: School Desegregation and the Law* (New York: Oxford University Press, 1995), 159.

2. Coalition to Save Our Children v. State Board of Education, 90 F.3d 752, 790–791 (3rd Cir., 1996).

3. Kristie Phillips, Robert Rodosky, Marco Munoz, and Elisabeth Larsen, "Integrated Schools, Integrated Futures? A Case Study of School Desegregation in Jefferson County, Kentucky," in *From the Courtroom to the Classroom: The Shifting Landscape of School Desegregation*, eds. Claire E. Smrekar and Ellen B. Goldring (Cambridge, MA: Harvard Educational Press, 2009), 240.

4. Armor, *Forced Justice*, 161–63; Christine Rossell, "The Effectiveness of Desegregation Plans," in *School Desegregation in the 21st Century*, eds. Christine Rossell, David Armor, and Herbert Walberg (Westport, CT: Praeger, 2002), 69 ff.

5. Charles T. Clotfelter, *After Brown: The Rise and Retreat of School Desegregation* (Princeton, NJ: Princeton University Press, 2006), ch. 3; Armor, *Forced Justice*, 174–80.

6. Christine H. Rossell, *The Carrot or the Stick for School Desegregation Policy: Magnet Schools or Forced Busing* (Philadelphia: Temple University Press, 1990).

7. Reed v. Rhodes, 422 F. Supp. 708 (N.D. Ohio, 1976); 500 F. Supp. 363 (1980); 934 F. Supp. 1533, 1539 (1996); and 1 F. Supp. 2d 705 (1998).

8. The long history of the case is described in Keyes v. School District No. 1, Denver, 902 F. Supp. 1274 (D. Colo., 1995).

9. Quoted in Robert C. Wood and Clement E. Vose, eds., *Remedial Law: When Courts Become Administrators* (Amherst: University of Massachusetts Press, 1990), 39.

10. Capacchione v. Charlotte-Mecklenburg Schools, 57 F. Supp. 2d 228, 249 (W.D. NC, 1999), citations omitted.

11. William A. Kandel, *The U.S. Foreign Born Population: Trends and Selected Characteristics*, Congressional Research Service report, January 18, 2011, p. 2, fig. 1, https://sgp.fas.org/crs/misc/R41592.pdf.

12. Johnson v. San Francisco Unified School District, 339 F. Supp. 1315, 1319 (N.D. Cal., 1971); Johnson v. San Francisco Unified School District, 500 F. 2d 349 (9th Cir., 1974). In an oral history, Weigel stated, "One thing I erred in was I treated Asians as the equivalent of whites." Interview

conducted by William Fletcher, Bancroft Library, Berkeley, 1989, p. 118, http://digitalassets.lib.berkeley.edu/rohoia/ucb/text/litigatorstanley00weigrich.pdf.

13. David L. Kirp, *Just Schools: The Idea of Racial Equality in American Education* (Berkeley: University of California Press, 1982), 108.

14. San Francisco NAACP v. San Francisco Unified School District, 576 F. Supp. 34, 49 (1983).

15. Kolski and Oakes, "San Jose," in *From the Courtroom to the Classroom*, eds. Smrekar and Goldring (Cambridge, MA: Harvard Educational Press, 2009), 92. As one of the original plaintiffs in the case stated, "This suit was never filed for desegregation. . . . We wanted equal opportunity."

16. Tasby v. Wright, 713 F.2d 90, 91 (5th Cir., 1983).

17. Catherine Horn and Michael Kurlaender, "The End of Keyes: Resegregation Trends and Achievement in Denver Public Schools," in *From the Courtroom to the Classroom*, eds. Smrekar and Goldring, 228.

18. Keyes v. Congress of Hispanic Educators, 902 F. Supp. 1274, 1307 (D. Colo., 1995).

19. Rachel F. Moran, "Getting a Foot in the Door: The Hispanic Push for Equal Educational Opportunity in Denver," 2 *Kansas Journal of Law and Public Policy* 35, 38 (1992).

20. Quoted in Rachel F. Moran, "Untoward Consequences: The Ironic Legacy of Keyes v. School District No. 1," 90 *Denver Law Review* 1209, 1216 (2013).

21. Moran, "Untoward Consequences," 1221.

22. Stephen Roth, quoted in Eleanor P. Wolf, *Trial and Error: The Detroit School Segregation Case* (Detroit, MI: Wayne State University Press, 1981), 278–79.

23. Kelly v. Metropolitan Board of Education, 687 F.2d 814, 824 (6th Cir., 1982).

24. Coalition to Save Our Children v. State Board of Education of the State of Delaware, 901 F. Supp. 784, 823 (D. Del., 1995).

25. David L. Kirp and Gary Babcock, "Judge and Company: Court-Appointed Masters, School Desegregation, and Institutional Reform," 32 *Alabama Law Review* 313, 334 (1980–81).

26. Elwood Hain, "Sealing Off the City: School Desegregation in Detroit," in *Limits of Justice: The Courts' Role in School Desegregation*, eds. Howard Kolodner and James Fishman (Cambridge, MA: Ballinger, 1978), 275.

27. Donald Horowitz, *Courts and Social Policy* (Washington, DC: Brookings Institution Press, 1976), ch. 4.

28. Ralph Smith, "Two Centuries and Twenty-Four Months: A Chronicle of the Struggle to Desegregate the Boston Public Schools," in *Limits of Justice*, eds. Kolodner and Fishman; Kirp and Babcock, "Judge and Company," 347–48.

29. Kirp and Babcock, "Judge and Company," 357. The first quotation comes from their interview with the judge.

30. Milliken v. Bradley II, 433 U.S. 267, 272, 274, and 280 (1977).

31. Hain, "Sealing Off the City," 292. The Sixth Circuit did not share his enthusiasm. When it reviewed DeMascio's remedies, it offered little guidance and only a "reluctant and qualified affirmance." The appellate court maintained that "genuine constitutional desegregation cannot be accomplished within the school boundaries of the Detroit School District." Milliken v. Bradley, 540 F.2nd 229, 240 (6th Cir., 1976).

32. Joseph Radelet, "Stillness at Detroit's Racial Divide: A Perspective on Detroit's School Desegregation Court Order—1970–1989," *Urban Review* 23, no. 3 (1991): 181.

33. Hain, "Sealing Off the City," and Radelet, "Stillness at Detroit's Racial Divide."

34. Milliken v. Bradley, 620 F. 2d 1143, 1150 (6th Cir., 1980).

35. Avern Cohn, quoted in Joseph Feldman et al., *Still Separate, Still Unequal: The Limits of Milliken II's Educational Compensation Remedies*, report of the Harvard Project on School Desegregation, Harvard Graduate School of Education, Cambridge, MA, April 1994, 21, https://eric.ed.gov/?id=ED371070.

36. Listed in Coalition to Save Our Children v. State Board of Education, 901 F. Supp. 784, 791 (D. Del., 1995).

37. Coalition to Save Our Children v. State Board of Education, 757 F. Supp. 328, 349–50 (D. Del., 1990).

38. Coalition to Save Our Children v. State Board of Education, 90 F. 3d 752 (3rd Cir., 1996).

39. Reed v. Rhodes, 934 F. Supp. 1533, 1544–45 (N.D. Ohio, 1996).

40. Russell Clark, quoted in Missouri v. Jenkins, 495 US 22, 60 (1990), emphasis in Judge Clark's opinion.

41. The following review of the Kansas City case is based on Joshua M. Dunn's excellent case study, *Complex Justice: The Case of Missouri v. Jenkins* (Chapel Hill: University of North Carolina Press, 2008).

42. Dunn, *Complex Justice*, 88 and 99.

43. Missouri v. Jenkins III, 515 U.S. 70 (1995), discussed at greater length in the next chapter.

44. Dean Whipple, quoted in Dunn, *Complex Justice*, 173.

Chapter Eight

1. Board of Education of Oklahoma City v. Dowell, 498 U.S. 237, 245 (1991).

2. Monica L. Moore, "Unclear Standards Create an Unclear Future: Developing a Better Definition of Unitary Status," 112 *Yale Law Journal* 311 (2002–2003).

3. Dowell v. Board of Education of Oklahoma City, 890 F.2d 1483, 1490, 1496, and 1520 (10th Cir., 1989).

4. Spangler v. Pasadena City Board of Education, 611 F.2d 1239 (9th Cir., 1979); Riddick v. School Board of City of Norfolk, 784 F.2d 521 (4th Cir., 1986); and Morgan v. Nucci, 831 F.2d 313 (1st Cir., 1987). The Ninth Circuit opinion was written by Judge, later Justice, Anthony Kennedy.

5. *Board of Education of Oklahoma City v. Dowell*, 498 U.S. at 249, 245–46.

6. *Board of Education of Oklahoma City v. Dowell*, 498 U.S at 257, 260, 251, 265.

7. *Board of Education of Oklahoma City v. Dowell*, 498 U.S. at 268, 262, 259, n.5 (emphasis added), 266.

8. *Board of Education of Oklahoma City Public Schools v. Dowell*, 498 U.S. at 266.

9. Freeman v. Pitts, 755 F.2d 1423 (11th Cir., 1985), and Freeman v. Pitts, 887 F.2d 1438 (11th. Cir., 1989).

10. Freeman v. Pitts, 503 U.S. 467, 487 (1992).

11. *Freeman v. Pitts*, 503 U.S. at 489.

12. *Freeman v. Pitts*, 503 U.S. at 490.

13. *Freeman v. Pitts*, 503 U.S. at 496.

14. *Freeman v. Pitts*, 503 U.S. at 495–96.

15. *Freeman v. Pitts*, 503 U.S. at 512, emphasis added.

16. *Freeman v. Pitts*, 503 U.S. at 518.

17. *Freeman v. Pitts*, 503 U.S. at 505.

18. *Freeman v. Pitts*, 503 U.S. at 506.

19. Missouri v. Jenkins III, 515 U.S. 70, 100 (1995).

NOTES TO PAGES 191-196

20. *Missouri v. Jenkins III*, 515 U.S. at 101.
21. *Missouri v. Jenkins III*, 515 U.S. at 154.
22. *Missouri v. Jenkins III*, 515 U.S. at 158.
23. Gary Orfield and Susan E. Eaton, *Dismantling Desegregation: The Quiet Reversal of Brown v. Board of Education* (New York: New Press, 1996), 1.
24. Quoted in Charles Clotfelter, Jacob Vigdor, and Helen Ladd, "Federal Oversight, Local Control, and the Specter of 'Resegregation' in Southern Schools," *American Law and Economics Review* 8, no. 2 (2006): 349.
25. Michael Dobbs, "U.S. School Segregation Now at '69 Level." *Washington Post*, January 18, 2004, https://www.washingtonpost.com/archive/politics/2004/01/18/us-school-segregation-now-at-69-level/442bfc77-d328-452d-966f-2356e11e213c/?utm_term=.2bacc497664a.
26. Andrew Ujifusa and Alex Harwin, "There Are Wild Swings in School Desegregation Data. The Feds Can't Explain Why," *Education Week*, May 2, 2018, https://www.edweek.org/policy-politics/there-are-wild-swings-in-school-desegregation-data-the-feds-cant-explain-why/2018/05.
27. Nikole Hannah-Jones, "Lack of Order: The Erosion of a Once-Great Force for Integration," *ProPublica*, May 1, 2014, https://www.propublica.org/article/lack-of-order-the-erosion-of-a-once-great-force-for-integration. In 2012, Stanford education professor Sean Reardon and his associates wrote, "The number of U.S. school districts that were ever under court order is not clear. Until relatively recently, no comprehensive accounting of districts under order existed." Sean Reardon, Elena Tej Grewal, Demetra Kalogrides, and Erica Greenbert, "Brown Fades: The End of Court-Ordered Desegregation and the Resegregation of American Public Schools," *Journal of Policy Analysis and Management* 31, no. 4 (2012): 881. A year earlier, Byron Lutz had found "no accurate statistics are available concerning the number of court-ordered desegregation plans in place or the number of dismissals." See Byron Lutz, "The End of Court-Ordered Desegregation," *American Economic Journal: Economic Policy* 3, no. 2 (2011): 135.
28. Reardon et al., "Brown Fades," 886. The case was *US v. Board of School Commissioners of Indianapolis*, 506 F.Supp. 657 (S.D. Ind., 1979).
29. US Commission on Civil Rights, *Becoming Less Separate? School Desegregation, Justice Department Enforcement, and the Pursuit of Unitary Status* (Washington, DC: Government Printing Office, 2007), 37, table 4.6.
30. Wendy Parker, "The Future of School Desegregation," 94 *Northwestern University Law Review* 1157, 1194 (1999-2000), emphasis in the original.
31. Parker, "The Future of School Desegregation," 1212-13.
32. *Parents Involved in Community Schools v. Seattle School District No. 1*, 551 U.S. 701 (2007).
33. Reardon et al., "Brown Fades," 882.
34. Clotfelter, Vigdor, and Ladd, "Federal Oversight," 374.
35. Reardon et al., "Brown Fades," 879. The internal quotation comes from Lutz, "The End of Court-Ordered Desegregation," 134. Clotfelter, Vigdor, and Ladd similarly emphasize the "local particularity" of desegregation cases, "Federal Oversight," 368.
36. Reardon et al., "Brown Fades," 886. Lutz similarly found no discernable differences between districts dismissed from court supervision and those remaining under court order; see "The End of Court-Ordered Desegregation," 139.
37. US Commission on Civil Rights, *Becoming Less Separate?*, 37; and Reardon et al., "Brown Fades," 878.
38. Wendy Parker, "The Decline of Judicial Decisionmaking: School Desegregation and District Court Judges," 81 *North Carolina Law Review* 1623, 1652 (2002-2003).

39. Clotfelter, Vigdor, and Ladd, "Federal Oversight," 370–72.

40. Reed v. Rhodes, 934 F. Supp. 1533, 1545 (N.D. Ohio, 1996).

41. Coalition to Save Our Children v. State Board of Education of the State of Delaware, 901 F. Supp. 784, 823 (D. Del., 1995).

42. Liddell v. The Board of Education of the City of St. Louis, Missouri, memorandum and order, March 2, 1999, 18, www.clearinghouse.net/chDocs/public/SD-MO-0001-0002.pdf.

43. Parker "The Decline of Judicial Decisionmaking," 1653–55.

44. Joetta Sack, "Last Minute Deal Ends 26-Year-Old Dayton Desegregation Case," *Education Week*, April 24, 2002.

45. Reed v. Rhodes, 1 F. Supp. 2d 705 (N.D. Ohio, 1996).

46. Parker, "The Decline of Judicial Decisionmaking," 1634–35; and "The Future of School Desegregation," 1183–84.

47. Dunn, *Complex Justice*, ch. 6.

48. Parker, "The Future of School Desegregation," 1181.

49. For examples, see the discussion of Cleveland and Dallas in chapter 7 above; and Clotfelter, Vigdor, and Ladd, "Federal Oversight," 370–72.

50. Sean F. Reardon and Ann Owens, "60 Years After *Brown*: Trends and Consequences of School Segregation," *Annual Review of Sociology* 40 (2014): 204.

51. Clotfelter, Vigdor, and Ladd, "Federal Oversight," 350.

52. Kori J. Stroub and Meredith P. Richards, "From Resegregation to Reintegration: Trends in the Racial/Ethnic Segregation of Metropolitan Public Schools, 1993–2009," *American Educational Research Journal* 50, no. 2 (June 2013): 509–10, emphasis added.

53. Brian P. An and Adam Gamoran, "Trends in School Racial Composition in the Era of Unitary Status," in *From the Courtroom to the Classroom: The Shifting Landscape of School Desegregation*, eds. Claire E. Smrekar and Ellen B. Goldring (Cambridge, MA: Harvard Educational Press, 2009), 43.

54. Reardon and Owens, "60 Years After," 206–07; US Commission on Civil Rights, *Becoming Less Separate?*, 79–80. According to the Commission's report, "looking at differences in integration from the early 1990s to 2004/5, the results suggest that fears of substantial increases in levels of racial concentration arising from districts obtaining unitary status are unfounded."

55. Clotfelter, Vigdor, and Ladd, "Federal Oversight," 347.

56. John Logan, *Resegregation in American Public Schools? Not in the 1990s*, Lewis Mumford Center for Comparative Urban and Regional Research, University of Albany, April 26, 2004, 1, https://s4.ad.brown.edu/Projects/usschools/reports/report1.pdf.

57. Lutz, "The End of Court-Ordered Desegregation, 141.

58. Reardon et al., "Brown Fades," 899 and 893.

59. Clotfelter, Vigdor, and Ladd, "Federal Oversight," 376.

60. Clotfelter, Vigdor, and Ladd, "Federal Oversight," 381.

61. An and Gamoran, "Trends in School Racial Composition," 44.

62. "Racial and Ethnic Achievement Gaps," The Educational Opportunity Monitoring Project, Stanford Center for Education Policy Analysis, https://cepa.stanford.edu/educational-opportunity-monitoring-project/achievement-gaps/race/#first; and M. Danish Shakeel and Paul E. Peterson, "A Half Century of Progress in US Student Achievement: Agency and Flynn Effects, Ethnic and SES Differences," *Educational Psychology Review* (March 2022).

63. National Center for Education Statistics, *Trends in High School Dropout and Completion Rates in the United States: 2019*, compendium report, January 2020, US Department of Education, Washington, DC: 28, fig. 3.2, https://nces.ed.gov/pubs2020/2020117.pdf.

64. Roger J. R. Levesque, *The Science and Law of School Segregation and Diversity* (New York: Oxford University Press, 2018), 85.

65. Roslyn Arlin Michelson, Stephen Samuel Smith, and Stephanie Southworth, "Resegregation, Achievement, and the Chimera of Choice in Post-Unitary Charlotte Mecklenburg Schools," in *From the Courthouse to the Classroom*, eds. Smrekar and Goldring, 129. One chapter of Rucker Johnson's book is titled, "How Charlotte (Briefly) Got It Right."

66. David Armor, "Desegregation and Academic Achievement," in *School Desegregation in the 21st Century*, eds. Christine Rossell, David Armor, and Herbert Walberg (Westport, CT: Praeger, 2002), 169–73.

67. Johnson with Nazaryan, *Children of the Dream*, 185.

68. Michelson, Smith, and Southworth, "Resegregation," 144, n.53.

69. Jacob Vigdor, "School Desegregation and the Black-White Test Score Gap," in *Whither Opportunity: Rising Inequality and Children's Life Chances*, eds. Greg Duncan and Richard Murnane (New York: Russell Sage, 2011), 453–59.

70. Michelson, Smith, and Southworth, "Resegregation," 151.

71. David Liebowitz, "Ending to What End? The Impact of the Termination of Court-Desegregation Orders on Patterns of Residential Segregation and School Dropout Rates," *Educational Evaluation and Policy Analysis* 40, no. 1 (March 2018): 103–28.

72. Stephen Billings, David Deming, and Jonah Rockoff, "School Segregation, Educational Attainment, and Crime: Evidence from the End of Busing in Charlotte-Mecklenburg," *Quarterly Journal of Economics* 129, no. 1 (2014): 435–76.

73. Reardon et al., "Brown Fades," 900–01.

Chapter Nine

1. John F. Jennings, quoted in David K. Cohen and Susan L. Moffitt, *The Ordeal of Equality: Did Federal Regulation Fix the Schools?* (Cambridge, MA: Harvard University Press, 2009), 49.

2. Cohen and Moffitt, *The Ordeal of Equality*, 73–80 and 107–08.

3. Patrick McGuinn, "Schooling the State: ESEA and the Evolution of the U.S. Department of Education," *RSF: The Russell Sage Foundation Journal of the Social Sciences* 1, no. 3 (2015): 84, citing numerous studies.

4. Cohen and Moffitt, *The Ordeal of Equality*, 74.

5. Donald McLaughlin, *Title I, 1965–1975: A Synthesis of the Findings of Federal Studies* (Palo Alto, CA: American Institute for Research, 1977), 4.

6. Susan L. Moffitt, "The State of Educational Improvement: The Legacy of ESEA Title I," *History of Education Quarterly* 56, no. 2 (May 2016): 375.

7. The figure on statutory pages comes from McGuinn, "Schooling the State," 82. The figure on pages of regulation is based on the author's examination of the Code of Federal Regulations.

8. Susan Gilbert Schneider, *Revolution, Reaction or Reform: The 1974 Bilingual Education Act* (Washington, DC: Center for Applied Linguistics, 1976), 21–27; John Skrentny, *The Minority Rights Revolution* (Cambridge, MA: Harvard University Press, 2002), 192–93, 206–07; Gareth Davies, *See Government Grow: Education Politics from Johnson to Reagan* (Lawrence: University Press of Kansas, 2007), 142–43.

9. R. Shep Melnick, *Between the Lines: Interpreting Welfare Rights* (Washington, DC: Brookings Institution Press, 1994), ch. 7; Davies, *See Government Grow*, 171–72 and 188–92.

10. Jesse Rhodes, *An Education in Politics: The Origins and Evolution of No Child Left Behind* (Ithaca, NY: Cornell University Press, 2012); and Jesse Rhodes, "Progressive Policy Making in a Conservative Age? Civil Rights and the Politics of Federal Education Standards, Testing, and Accountability," *Perspectives on Politics* 9, no. 3 (2011): 528–33.

11. National Commission on Excellence in Education, *A Nation at Risk: The Imperative for Educational Reform: A Report to the Nation and the Secretary of Education, United States Department of Education,* April 1983, 9, https://edreform.com/wp-content/uploads/2013/02/A_Nation_At_Risk_1983.pdf. Davies provides an excellent review of the history and significance of the report; *See Government Grow,* 270–75.

12. Patrick McGuinn, "From No Child Left Behind to the Every Student Succeeds Act: Federalism and the Education Legacy of the Obama Administration," *Publius: The Journal of Federalism* 46, no. 4 (2016): 393.

13. Leadership Conference on Civil Rights, quoted in Rhodes, *An Education in Politics,* 174.

14. Phyllis McClure, "Grassroots Resistance to NCLB," Fordham Institute's *Education Gadfly,* March 17, 2004, https://fordhaminstitute.org/national/commentary/grassroots-resistance-nclb.

15. Quoted in Rhodes, "Progressive Policy Making in a Conservative Age?," 531.

16. Hugh Davis Graham, *The Civil Rights Era: Origins and Development of National Policy* (New York: Oxford University Press, 1990), 83.

17. Quoted in Stephen Halpern, *On the Limits of the Law: The Ironic Legacy of Title VI of the 1964 Civil Rights Act* (Baltimore, MD: Johns Hopkins University Press, 1995), 89.

18. Stanley Pottinger, quoted in Gary Orfield, *Must We Bus? Segregated Schools and National Policy* (Washington, DC: Brookings Institution Press, 1978), 352.

19. Orfield, *Must We Bus?,* 298 and 309.

20. Plaintiffs' "Amended Complaint for Declaratory and Other Relief," Adams v. Richardson, Civil Action # 3095-70, 6. The brief is contained in a report by the Majority Staff of the Committee on Education and Labor, *Investigation of the Civil Rights Enforcement Activities of the Office for Civil Rights,* House of Representatives, 100th Cong., 2 sess. (Washington, DC: Government Printing Office, 1988): 193–227.

21. Adams v. Richardson, 351 F. Supp. 630, 642 (D.D.C., 1972). "Benign neglect" was the term Nixon advisor Daniel Patrick Moynihan had famously used to describe a strategy designed to turn down the heat on racial issues. Judge Pratt, like so many others, distorted Moynihan's argument.

22. Adams v. Richardson, 480 F.2d 1159, 1162 (D.C. Cir., 1973).

23. These many additions are described in Halpern, *On the Limits of the Law,* ch. 4–5.

24. WEAL v. Cavazos, 906 F.2d 742, 744–45 (D.C. Cir., 1990).

25. Quoted in Halpern, *On the Limits of the Law,* 221.

26. *Civil Rights Enforcement by the Department of Education: Hearings before a Subcommittee of the Committee on Government Operations, House of Representatives,* 100th Cong. 1 sess. (April 23, 1987), 254–55, emphasis added.

27. Quoted in Rosemary Salomone, "Judicial Oversight of Agency Enforcement: The *Adams* and *WEAL* Litigation," in *Justice and School Systems: The Role of the Courts in Education Litigation,* ed. Barbara Flicker (Philadelphia, PA: Temple, 1990), 129. Lichtman made a similar point in an interview with the author.

28. Adams v. Weinberger, 391 F. Supp. 269, 273 (D.D.C., 1975).

29. Adams v. Bennett, 675 F. Supp. 668, 677 (D.D.C., 1987), emphasis added.

30. John H. Pratt, quoted in Jeremy Rabkin, *Judicial Compulsions: How Public Law Distorts Public Policy* (New York: Basic Books, 1989), 165.

NOTES TO PAGES 220-227

31. Rabkin, *Judicial Compulsions*, 167.

32. Rabkin, *Judicial Compulsions*, 168.

33. US Department of Education, Office for Civil Rights, *Annual Report to Congress: Fiscal Year 1993* (Washington, DC: Office for Civil Rights, 1994), 10, https://files.eric.ed.gov/fulltext/ED422667.pdf.

34. Department of Education Office for Civil Rights Fiscal Year 2018 Budget Request, Z-13, https://www2.ed.gov/about/overview/budget/budget18/justifications/z-ocr.pdf.

35. Halpern, *On the Limits of the Law*, 133 and 151. According to Rosemary Salomone, "the court had framed the order in 'procedural' terms, and the agency was offering a 'procedural response.' By addressing the processing failures identified by the court, the agency was left free to make the fewest 'substantive changes' possible." "Judicial Oversight," 130.

36. Testimony of Assistant Secretary for Civil Rights Harry M. Singleton, *Investigation of Civil Rights Enforcement by the Department of Education: Hearings before the Subcommittee on Intergovernmental Relations and Human Resources, House Committee on Government Operations*, 99th Cong. 1 sess. (July 18 and September 11, 1985): 93-95.

37. Majority Staff of the Committee on Education and Labor, *Investigation of the Civil Rights Enforcement Activities of the Office for Civil Rights*, 103-14.

38. 40 *Federal Register* 24149 (June 4, 1975).

39. These statements come from Tatel's affidavit in the Adams litigation, as quoted in Halpern, *On the Limits of the Law*, 140.

40. Office for Civil Rights, *Annual Report to Congress: Fiscal Year 1995* (Washington, DC: Office for Civil Rights, 1996), 1, www2.ed.gov/about/offices/list/ocr/AnnRpt95/edlite-ocr95rp1.html.

41. *WEAL v. Cavazos*, 906 F. 2d at 747 and 751.

42. *Lau v. Nichols*, 414 U.S. 563 (1974).

43. *Alexander v. Sandoval*, 532 U.S. 275, 306 (2001), emphasis added.

44. On private rights of action, compare *J. I. Case Co. v. Borak*, 377 U.S. 426 (1964) with *Pennhurst State School and Hospital v. Halderman*, 451 U.S. 1 (1981); *Middlesex Co. Sewage Authority v. National Seaclammers Association*, 453 U.S. 1 (1981); and *California v. Sierra Club*, 451 U.S. 287 (1981).

45. *Alexander v. Sandoval*, 532 U.S. at 279-81.

46. Sam Dillon, "Officials Step Up Enforcement of Rights Laws in Education," *New York Times*, March 8, 2010, https://www.nytimes.com/2010/03/08/education/08educ.html.

47. US Department of Education (OCR) and US Department of Justice (Civil Rights Division), *Guidance on the Voluntary Use of Race to Achieve Diversity in Postsecondary Education*, December 2, 2011, https://www2.ed.gov/about/offices/list/ocr/docs/guidance-pse-201111.html; *Questions and Answers about* Fisher v. University of Texas at Austin, September 27, 2013, https://www2.ed.gov/about/offices/list/ocr/letters/colleague-201309.html; *"Dear Colleague" letter* on *Schuette v. Coalition to Defend Affirmative Action*, May 6, 2014, https://www2.ed.gov/about/offices/list/ocr/letters/colleague-201405-schuette-guidance.pdf; *Questions and Answers about* Fisher v. University of Texas at Austin II, September 30, 2016, https://www2.ed.gov/about/offices/list/ocr/docs/qa-fisher-ii-201609.pdf.

48. US Departments of Education and Justice, "Guidance on the Voluntary Use of Race to Achieve Diversity and Avoid Racial Isolation in Elementary and Secondary School," December 2, 2011, 1, https://www2.ed.gov/about/offices/list/ocr/docs/guidance-ese-201111.html.

49. US Departments of Education and Justice, "Dear Colleague" letter, July 3, 2018, www2.ed.gov/about/offices/list/ocr/letters/colleague-title-vi-201807.pdf.

50. US Departments of Education and Justice, "Dear Colleague" letter, July 3, 2018.

51. "Dear Colleague" letter from Assistant Secretary of Education Catherine Lhamon, October 1, 2014, https://www2.ed.gov/about/offices/list/ocr/letters/colleague-resourcecomp-201410.pdf, hereafter referred to as 2014 School Resources DCL.

52. 2014 School Resources DCL, n.33.

53. Paul E. Peterson, Eric Hanushek, Laura Tapley, and Ludgen Woessmann, "The Achievement Gap Fails to Close," *Education Next* 19, no. 3 (2019); Sean Reardon, "The Widening Academic Achievement Gap Between the Rich and the Poor: New Evidence and Possible Explanations," in *Whither Opportunity: Rising Inequality, Schools, and Children's Chances*, ed. Greg J. Duncan and Richard J. Murnane (New York: Russell Sage Foundation, 2011).

54. US Department of Education, Equity and Excellence Commission, *For Each and Every Child: A Strategy for Education Equity and Excellence* (Washington, DC: Government Printing Office, 2013), 15, emphasis in the original, https://oese.ed.gov/files/2020/10/equity-excellence-commission-report.pdf.

55. 2014 School Resources DCL, 27, n.6.

56. 2014 School Resources DCL, 11.

57. 2014 School Resources DCL, 12–13.

58. 2014 School Resources DCL, 34, n.47.

59. 2014 School Resources DCL, 15.

60. 2014 School Resources DCL, 16.

61. 2014 School Resources DCL, 17.

62. 2014 School Resources DCL, 12.

63. 2014 School Resources DCL, 18.

64. 2014 School Resources DCL, second note at bottom of first page, emphasis added.

65. 2014 School Resources DCL, 5.

66. 2014 School Resources DCL, notes 36–40 and 44.

67. 2014 School Resources DCL, 33, n.40.

68. San Antonio Independent School District v. Rodriguez, 411 U.S. 1 (1973).

69. 34 *Code of Federal Regulations* 100.3(b)(2), emphasis added. It should be noted that this section of the 1980 regulations does not claim that disparate impact constitutes proof of discrimination. Rather it makes the more ambiguous claim that an institution violates Title VI when its policies have the "effect" of discriminating. What that odd formulation means is anyone's guess.

70. 2014 School Resources DCL, 32, n.33.

71. For an example outside Title VI, see my discussion of OCR's Title IX sexual harassment investigations. Melnick, *The Transformation of Title IX: Regulating Gender Equality in Education* (Washington, DC: Brookings Institution Press, 2018), 211–18.

72. OCR, *Protecting Civil Rights, Advancing Equity: Report to the President and Secretary of Education, Fiscal Years 2013–14* (Washington, DC: April 2015), 18, https://www2.ed.gov/about/reports/annual/ocr/report-to-president-and-secretary-of-education-2013–14.pdf.

73. OCR, *Delivering Justice: Report to the President and Secretary of Education, Fiscal Year 2015* (Washington, DC: Government Printing Office, May 2016), 18, https://www2.ed.gov/about/reports/annual/ocr/report-to-president-and-secretary-of-education-2015.pdf; *Securing Equal Educational Opportunity: Report to the President and Secretary of Education, Fiscal Year 2016* (Washington, DC: Government Printing Office, December 2016), 17, https://www2.ed.gov/about/reports/annual/ocr/report-to-president-and-secretary-of-education-2016.pdf.

74. These three cases are discussed in the 2015 and 2016 reports listed in notes 72 and 73 above, and in the testimony of three Department of Education officials, Tanya Clay House, Ary Amerikaner, and Jessie Brown, before the US Commission on Civil Rights, *Briefing on Public Educational Funding Inequality in an Era of Increasing Concentration of Poverty and Resegregation*, May 20, 2016. Other than the Toledo case discussed below, they are the only enforcement actions described in OCR's reports or testimony.

75. Meena Morey Chandra, regional director, OCR region XV, to Jennifer Dawson, Esq., Toledo Public Schools, January 20, 2016, https://www2.ed.gov/documents/press-releases/toledo-resolution-letter.pdf.

76. Resolution Agreement, Toledo Public Schools, OCR docket no. 15-10-5002, https://www2.ed.gov/documents/press-releases/toledo-resolution-agreement.pdf.

77. OCR, *Annual Report to the Secretary, the President, and the Congress, Fiscal Years 2017–18* (Washington, DC: Government Printing Office, March 2020), https://www2.ed.gov/about/reports/annual/ocr/report-to-president-and-secretary-of-education-2017-18.pdf.

78. US Departments of Education and Justice, joint "Dear Colleague" letter, "Nondiscriminatory Administration of School Discipline," January 8, 2014, https://www2.ed.gov/about/offices/list/ocr/letters/colleague-201401-title-vi.html, hereafter referred to as "2014 Discipline DCL."

79. Arne Duncan, "Rethinking School Discipline," speech delivered at the Academies at Frederick Douglass High School, Baltimore, MD, January 8, 2014.

80. Matthew P. Steinberg and Johanna Lacoe, "What Do We Know about School Discipline Reform? Assessing the Alternatives to Suspension and Expulsions," *Education Next* 17, no. 1 (2017): 44.

81. The leading Supreme Court case was *Goss v. Lopez*, 419 U.S. 565 (1975). Richard Arum provides an overview of these shifts in *Judging School Discipline: The Crisis of Moral Authority* (Cambridge, MA: Harvard University Press, 2003), 5–23.

82. 2014 Discipline DCL, 7, emphasis added.

83. Quoted in Max Eden, "'Disparate Impact' for School Discipline? Never Has Been, Never Should Be," *Flypaper*, https://fordhaminstitute.org/national/commentary/disparate-impact-school-discipline-never-has-been-never-should-be.

84. J. P. Wright et al., "Prior Problem Behavior Accounts for the Racial Gap in School Suspensions," *Journal of Criminal Justice* 42, no. 3 (2014): 263.

85. Kaitlin P. Anderson and Gary W. Ritter, "Disparate Use of Exclusionary Discipline: Evidence on Inequities in School Discipline from a U.S. State," *Education Policy Analysis Archives* 25, no. 49 (2017): 27, https://files.eric.ed.gov/fulltext/EJ1144442.pdf.

86. Nora Gordon, "Disproportionality in Student Discipline: Connecting Policy to Research," *Brookings Institution*, January 18, 2018, https://www.brookings.edu/research/disproportionality-in-student-discipline-connecting-policy-to-research/.

87. For a list of investigations and resolution agreements, see Gail Heriot and Alison Somin, "The Department of Education's Obama-Era Initiative on Racial Disparities in School Discipline: Wrong for Students and Teachers, Wrong on the Law," 22 *Texas Review of Law and Politics* 471, 481–83, notes 17–34 and 37 (2018).

88. OCR, "OCR's Approach to the Evaluation, Investigation and Resolution of Title VI Discipline Complaints," February 12, 2014, https://media4.manhattan-institute.org/sites/default/files/OCR-disciplineguide-2014.pdf.

89. OCR, "OCR's Approach to the Evaluation, Investigation and Resolution of Title VI Discipline Complaints," 2, emphasis in the original.

90. "OCR's Approach to the Evaluation, Investigation and Resolution of Title VI Discipline Complaints," 20.

91. AASA: The School Superintendents Association, "The 2018 AASA Discipline Survey" (Alexandria, VA: AASA, 2018), https://aasa.org/uploadedFiles/AASA_Blog(1)/AASASurvey DisciplineGuidance2014.pdf.

92. Max Eden, "Studies and Teachers Nationwide Say School Discipline Reform is Harming Students' Academic Achievement and Safety," *The 74*, June 10, 2019, https://www.the74million.org/article/eden-studies-and-teachers-nationwide-say-school-discipline-reform-is-harming-students-academic-achievement-and-safety/. Eden has written some of the most detailed critiques of the Obama administration's school-discipline policies. See also *Safe and Orderly Schools: Updated Guidance on School Discipline*, Manhattan Institute report, 2019; *Enforcing Classroom Disorder: Trump Has Not Called Off Obama's War on School Discipline*, Manhattan Institute issue brief, August 2018.

93. "2016 EdNext Poll Interactive," *Education Next*, updated August 3, 2016, https://www.educationnext.org/2016-ednext-poll-interactive/. Also see Paul E. Peterson et al., "Common Core Brand Taints Opinion on Standards: 2016 Findings and 10-Year Trends from the EdNext Poll," *Education Next* 17, no. 1 (Winter 2017): 15.

94. David Griffith and Adam Tyner, "Discipline Reform through the Eyes of Teachers," Fordham Institute/RAND report (July 2019), https://fordhaminstitute.org/sites/default/files/publication/pdfs/20190730-discipline-reform-through-eyes-teachers.pdf.

95. Matthew P. Steinberg and Johanna Lacoe, *The Academic and Behavioral Consequences of Discipline Policy Reform: Evidence from Philadelphia*, Fordham Institute report (December 2017), 6, https://files.eric.ed.gov/fulltext/ED598616.pdf.

96. Steinberg and Lacoe, "Evidence from Philadelphia," 31.

97. Steinberg and Lacoe, "Evidence from Philadelphia," 29, emphasis added.

98. Steinberg and Lacoe, "Evidence from Philadelphia," 26.

99. US Department of Education, "OCR Instructions to the Field re Scope of Complaints," memo, June 8, 2017, https://www.documentcloud.org/documents/3863019-doc00742420170609111824.html.

100. US Departments of Education and Justice, "Dear Colleague" letter, December 21, 2018, https://www2.ed.gov/about/offices/list/ocr/letters/colleague-201812.pdf.

101. Catherine Lhamon, quoted in Kimberly M. Richey, *Enforcing Disciplinary Leniency: How the Office for Civil Rights Dictated School Disciple Policy and How It Could Again*, American Enterprise Institute report, December 15, 2021, https://www.aei.org/research-products/report/enforcing-disciplinary-leniency-how-the-office-for-civil-rights-dictated-school-discipline-policy-and-how-it-could-again/. The hearings are available at https://www.help.senate.gov/hearings/nominations-of-catherine-lhamon-to-be-assistant-secretary-for-civil-rights-at-the-department-of-education-elizabeth-brown-to-be-general-counsel-of-the-department-of-education-and-roberto-rodriguez-to-be-assistant-secretary-for-planning-evaluation-and-policy-development-of-the-department-of-education.

102. See R. Shep Melnick, "Separation of Powers and the Strategy of Rights: The Expansion of Special Education," in *The New Politics of Public Policy*, eds. Marc K. Landy and Martin A. Levin (Baltimore, MD: Johns Hopkins University Press, 1995).

Chapter Ten

1. Paul E. Peterson, Eric Hanushek, Laura Tapley, and Ludgen Woessmann, "The Achievement Gap Fails to Close," *Education Next* 19, no. 3 (2019); Sean Reardon, "The Widening

Academic Achievement Gap between the Rich and the Poor: New Evidence and Possible Explanations," in *Whither Opportunity: Rising Inequality, Schools, and Children's Chances*, eds. Greg J. Duncan and Richard J. Murnane (New York: Russell Sage Foundation, 2011).

2. Ronald F. Ferguson, *Toward Excellence with Equity: An Emerging Vision for Closing the Achievement Gap* (Cambridge, MA: Harvard Education Press, 2008), 27.

3. Kenneth Shores, Hojung Lee, and Nell Williams, "Increasing Title I Funds Should Target Largest Sources of School Spending Inequalities—Across States," Brookings Institution's Brown Center Chalkboard, August 6, 2021, https://www.brookings.edu/blog/brown-center-chalkboard/2021/08/06/increasing-title-i-funds-should-target-largest-sources-of-school-spending-inequalities-across-states/.

4. Ibram X. Kendi, *How to Be an Antiracist* (New York: One World Press, 2019), 101.

5. Jennifer Hochschild and Nathan Scovronick, *The American Dream and the Public Schools* (New York: Oxford University Press, 2004), 11.

6. Hochschild and Scovronick, *The American Dream*, 19.

7. Alexis de Tocqueville, *Democracy in America*, trans. and ed. Harvey C. Mansfield and Delba Winthrop (Chicago: University of Chicago Press, 2000), 87 (vol. 1, part 1, ch. 5).

8. Claudia Goldin and Lawrence Katz, *The Race Between Education and Technology* (Cambridge, MA: Harvard University Press, 2008), ch. 5.

9. Paul Peterson, "Education," in *Understanding America: The Anatomy of an Exceptional Nation*, eds. Peter Schuck and James Q. Wilson (New York: Public Affairs, 2008), 422–23.

10. Peterson, "Education," 419.

11. Hugh Davis Graham, *The Uncertain Triumph: Federal Education Policy in the Kennedy and Johnson Years* (Chapel Hill: University of North Carolina Press, 1984), xvii.

12. Stuart McClure, quoted in Gareth Davies, *See Government Grow: Education Politics from Johnson to Reagan* (Lawrence: University of Kansas Press, 2007), 11.

13. Graham, *The Uncertain Triumph*, xv.

14. James Q. Wilson, *Bureaucracy: What Government Agencies Do and Why They Do It* (New York: Basic Books, 1991), ch. 9.

15. Warren and Frankfurter, quoted in Michael Klarman, *From Jim Crow to Civil Rights: The Supreme Court and the Struggle for Racial Equality* (New York: Oxford University Press, 2004), 317.

16. David Seeley, quoted in Allan Wolk, *The Presidency and Black Civil Rights: Eisenhower to Nixon* (Vancouver: Fairleigh Dickinson University Press, 1971), 114; and in Gary Orfield, *The Reconstruction of Southern Education: The Schools and the 1964 Civil Rights Act* (New York: Wiley-Interscience, 1969), 76.

17. Wilbur Cohen, quoted in Davies, *See Government Grow*, 112–13.

18. Alexander Bickel, *The Supreme Court and the Idea of Progress* (New York: Harper and Row, 1970), 13 and 19.

19. Gerald Rosenberg, *The Hollow Hope: Can Courts Bring About Social Change?* (Chicago: University of Chicago Press, 1993).

20. Stephen C. Halpern, *On the Limits of the Law: The Ironic Legacy of Title VI of the 1964 Civil Rights Act* (Baltimore, MD: Johns Hopkins University Press, 1995), 74.

21. Wilson, *Bureaucracy*, ch. 12.

22. "School Desegregation: A Social Science Statement," June 1991, appendix to brief of the NAACP, DeKalb County, Georgia in *Freeman v. Pitts*, at 17a, 2a, and 14a, https://blackfreedom.proquest.com/freeman-v-pitts-brief-of-the-naacp-dekalb-county-georgia-branch-of-the

-naacp-american-jewish-committee-childrens-defense-fund-fund-for-an-open-society-mexi can-american-legal-defense-and-educ/, emphasis added.

23. "Parents Involved in Community Schools v. Seattle School District No. 1, et al.: Brief of 553 Social Scientists as Amici Curiae in Support of Respondents" (filed October 16, 2006), 2, https://blackfreedom.proquest.com/parents-involved-in-community-schools-v-seattle-school -dist-no-1-et-al-brief-of-553-social-scientists-as-amici-curiae-in-support-of-respondents/.

24. Richard Kahlenberg, Halley Potter, and Kimberly Quick, "A Bold Agenda for School Integration," Century Fund, April 8, 2019, https://tcf.org/content/report/bold-agenda-school -integration/; Halley Potter, Kimberly Quick, and Elizabeth Davies, "A New Wave of School Integration: Districts and Charters Pursuing Socioeconomic Diversity," Century Fund, February 9, 2016, https://tcf.org/content/report/a-new-wave-of-school-integration/?agreed=1; Amy Stuart Wells, Lauren Fox, and Diana Cordova-Cobo, "How Racially Diverse Schools and Classrooms Can Benefit All Students," Century Fund, February 9, 2016, https://tcf.org/content/report/how -racially-diverse-schools-and-classrooms-can-benefit-all-students/.

25. Potter, Quick, and Davies, "A New Wave of School Integration," 7.

26. Nikole Hannah-Jones, "It Was Never About Busing," *New York Times*, July 12, 2019, https://www.nytimes.com/2019/07/12/opinion/sunday/it-was-never-about-busing.html.

27. Derrick Bell, "Serving Two Masters: Integration Ideals and Client Interests in School Desegregation Litigation," 85 *Yale Law Journal* 470 (1976).

28. Bell, "Serving Two Masters," 480, emphasis in the original.

29. Chana Joffe-Walt, *Nice White Parents*, produced by Julie Snyder, podcast series, July 23–August 20, 2020, https://www.nytimes.com/column/nice-white-parents.

30. Brunson v. Board of Trustees of School District #1 of Clarendon County, 429 F.2d 820, 824 (4th Cir., 1970).

31. *Brunson v. Board of Trustees*, 429 F.2d 820 at 826.

32. Missouri v. Jenkins III, 515 U.S. 70, 114–15 (1995).

33. Seth Gershenson, Michael Hansen, and Constance A. Lindsay, *Teacher Diversity and Student Success: Why Racial Representation Matters in the Classroom* (Cambridge, MA: Harvard Education Press, 2021), 71.

34. Gershenson, Hansen, and Lindsay, *Teacher Diversity and Student Success*, 72.

Index

academic performance, 12, 15, 28, 42, 51–57, 91, 134–35, 160, 172–75, 229, 250–51. *See also* achievement gap; education; standards and accountability regime
accountability. *See* standards and accountability regime; tracking
achievement gap, xi, xiii, 4, 51–54, 176, 198, 203–5, 213, 231, 248, 251
Adams v. Richardson, 217–22
administrative pragmatism, 40, 93
Administrative Procedure Act (APA), 216, 223, 258, 280n16
admissions policies, 7, 10–11, 14, 28, 35–37, 165–66, 195, 262–63. *See also* attendance zones; "freedom of choice" plans
affirmative action, 31–32, 65, 70, 95–96, 226, 236
Agnew, Spiro, 118
Albritton, W. Harold, III, 197
Alexander v. Holmes County Board of Education, 109, 118, 121–22, 125
Alexander v. Sandoval, 223–24, 233
Allport, Gordon, 48, 50–51
American Dilemma (Myrdal), 28
American Dream, 6, 251
American Federation of Teachers, 235
American Sociological Association, 48
An, Brian, 199, 202
Anstreicher, Garrett, 55–56
antiracism, 4, 251, 269. *See also* racism
Arlington Heights v. Metropolitan Housing Corp., 138
Armor, David, 49–50
Armstrong, Scott, 120, 125
Asian students: and busing, 31; growing population of, 75, 152, 165; and interest groups, 155; and measuring segregation, 200, 290n12; and racial balance, 7, 123
Atlanta Compromise, 154, 266
attendance zones, 7, 29, 45, 89, 104–5, 114, 123, 127–29, 148, 166, 187. *See also* admissions policies; racial gerrymandering

Babcock, Gary, 18, 44, 147, 149–50, 156, 164, 173
Bakke, 32
Balkin, Jack, 38–39
Battisti, Frank, 156, 161, 167–68
Bell, Derrick, 265–66, 268
Bell, Griffin, 94, 97, 99, 105, 108
benign neglect, 117–18
Bickel, Alexander, 258
Biden, Joe, 1–3, 8, 21, 62, 80, 225, 227, 247
bilingual education, 21, 43, 129, 155–57, 168–73, 209–15, 246. *See also* English proficiency
Billings, Stephen, 205
Black, Hugo, 67, 119–21
black city/white suburb paradigm, 6
Black Coalition, 155
Blackmun, Harry, 72, 108, 110, 125, 139, 141, 143, 187–89
black pride, 48
Board of Education of Oklahoma City v. Dowell, 76–77, 109, 183, 188, 193–94
Bolling v. Sharpe, 28
Bork, Robert, 135
Brennan, William, 38, 108, 113–14, 121, 125, 129, 136, 139, 165, 184
Breyer, Stephen, 11–12, 34, 38, 41, 43, 204, 276n21
Briggs doctrine, 95–96, 98
Brown, John R., 94, 101, 285n28
Brown, Linda, 10

INDEX

Brown v. Board of Education I: ambiguity of, 10, 66–67, 142; and available remedies, 32, 260; critics of, 115; divergence from, xi, 48, 130; and educational quality, 12, 202, 228, 249; interpretation of, 29, 43, 59, 70–71; legacies of, 22, 24, 26, 29–30, 36, 232, 269–70; legal strategy of, 66, 153; moral standing of, 255; public support for, 153; responses to, 63, 82, 136, 176, 269; social-science evidence, 34, 46–48, 77, 133; Supreme Court's role following, 102; unanimity of, 27

Brown v. Board of Education II: ambiguity of, 27, 257, 260; and color-blindness, 10; flexibility of solutions, 74, 150; legal strategy of, 96; responses to, 63; and school admission policies, 28

Buchanan, Pat, 118
Burger, Warren, 17, 32, 72–73, 108, 110, 124–36, 142–43, 184, 260–61
Bush, George H. W., 213
Bush, George W., 5, 8, 62, 77–80, 196, 213, 224–25
busing: authority to mandate, 73; critics of, 1–2, 6, 23, 31, 64, 67, 72, 152, 157, 168, 170, 265, 288n29; effectiveness of, 141, 172, 205; effects on education, 33; length of rides, 154, 168, 177, 185, 197; limits on, 72, 124, 127, 136–37, 148, 152, 154, 177, 180, 214, 263; necessity of, 100, 105, 123, 129, 134, 138, 184–85; proliferation of, 22, 64, 128, 135, 166, 173. *See also* desegregation

Cameron, Ben, 94, 283n39
Cannon v. University of Chicago, 222
Carter, Jimmy, 62, 206, 221
Carter, Robert, 11
Carter v. West Feliciano School Board, 121–22
Celebrezze, Anthony, 85
Century Fund (TCF), 263
Chayes, Abram, 44
Children of the Dream (Johnson), 55
circuit courts: differing approaches, 151; practical applications of desegregation, 39–40, 150–51; relation with Supreme Court, 23; reliance on trial judges, 17. *See also* federal courts; Fifth Circuit
City of Emporia, 134
Civil Rights Act of 1964, 21–22, 29, 32, 63, 67–68, 82, 88, 92, 210, 224. *See also* funding termination; Title VI
Civil Rights Data Collection (Department of Education), 192
Civil Rights movement, x–xi, 24. *See also* specific legislation and SCOTUS cases
civil rights state, ix, 9, 19, 24, 67. *See also* United States
Clark, Kenneth, 28, 47
Clark, Mamie, 28
Clark, Ramsey, 101, 283n59

Clark, Russell, 160, 176–78, 190–91
Clark, Tom, 67, 283n59
Clinton, Bill, 5, 62, 77–78, 196, 213, 221–22
Clotfelter, Charles, 195–96, 199–201
Cohen, David, 211
Cohen, Wilbur, 70, 85, 258
Cohn, Avern, 34, 162, 174
Coleman, James, 48, 94, 98, 122, 124
Coleman, William, 47
Coleman report, 41, 49, 59
color-blind/limited intervention position, ix, xi, xii, 10–12, 22–36, 59–68, 108, 181, 206, 255. *See also* racial isolation/equal educational opportunity position
Columbus Board of Education v. Penick, 139–40, 145, 163
compensatory education programs, 129, 142
Congress: allocation of funding, 23, 83, 211–12, 245–46, 261–62; coalitions within, 214–15; and color-blindness, 68; perceived role of, 40–41; political makeup of, 63–64, 67
Connor, Bull, 253
contact theory, 48–51
"controlled choice" plans, 7, 65, 162, 167–70, 175, 183, 196, 200–207, 264. *See also* "freedom of choice" plans
Cook, Stuart, 47–48
Cox, William, 94
crime rates, 205
Critical Race Theory, 265
curriculum, 43, 79, 129, 157, 211, 230, 252. *See also* education

Daley, Richard J., 85
Davis v. Board of School Commissioners of Mobile County, 128
Dayton Board of Education v. Brinkman I, 107, 138–39, 142, 161, 163, 188
Dayton Board of Education v. Brinkman II, 107, 139–40, 161, 163
"Dear Colleague" letters (DCLs), 21, 79–80, 225–38, 250, 258, 261
de jure/de facto distinction, xi, 11, 35, 39, 60, 74–75, 88–89, 99–100, 123–24, 130, 139, 152, 160. *See also* segregation
Delmont, Matthew, 4
DeMascio, Edward, 162, 174, 291n31
Deming, David, 205
Democratic Party, 2–3, 67
demographic changes, 5–6, 16, 34, 65, 75, 77, 152–53, 165–71, 207. *See also* resegregation; white flight
Department of Education, 16, 21, 79, 192, 209, 252–53, 260
Department of Health, Education, and Welfare (HEW): authority of, 103; critics of, 92; and

"freedom of choice" plans, 112; and funding termination, 69, 83–84; guidelines from, 14, 20, 40, 64, 71, 97, 112–13, 121, 256, 258; staffing of, 70, 85–86. *See also* Office for Civil Rights
Department of Justice, 67–68, 77, 85–86, 93, 196, 215
desegregation: ambiguous definition of, x, 5–6, 9–13, 22, 26, 44, 50, 58, 67–68, 72, 76, 95, 100, 107, 136, 142, 153, 180, 198, 206, 255–57; benefits of litigation, 156–57, 194–95, 206; beyond education, 146; definitions of success, ix, xi, 13, 18–19, 37, 50, 53–54, 90–91, 106, 114, 164, 203–4; effectiveness of, 50, 172, 192, 205; goals of, 5, 10, 15–16, 31, 35, 45, 62, 104–5, 115–16, 122, 128, 131–32, 136–37, 141, 182, 188, 201–2; jurisprudence of, 35, 38; in the North, 128–29; official guidelines for, 85–86; pace of, 13, 62, 90, 93, 113–14, 116–17, 119–22, 144, 159; perceptions of, ix, 3, 24, 29, 62–63; requirements of, 71; resistance to, xi–xii, 13–14, 20, 22, 34–35, 37, 66, 102, 156, 207, 256; responsibility for, 7, 18, 85; strategies of, 7, 36, 51, 54, 57, 71, 74–75, 126–27, 150; unclear status of decrees, 18, 192–93. *See also* busing; integration; segregation; structural injunctions; unitary status
desegregative attractiveness, 190–91
Dimond, Paul, 154, 159
discipline, x, 8, 54, 80, 234, 236–41, 243–44, 261. *See also* out-of-school punishments; school to prison pipeline
discrimination: and the civil rights state, 9; definitions of, 68; effects of, xii, 39, 77, 114; evidence of, 239; forms of, 20, 38, 209, 217, 253; and intent, 136, 139, 190, 224. *See also* racism; segregation
disparate-impact analysis, 80, 261
diversity, as slogan, xi, 265
Douglas, William O., 38, 121, 125
Doyle, William, 12, 41, 129, 149, 162, 171
Duncan, Arne, 79, 225, 228, 236, 238
Duncan, Robert, 159, 161
Dunn, Joshua, 160, 177

Eaton, Susan, 192
Edley, Christopher, 214
education: as constitutional right, 73–74; economics of, 4–5, 248–49; equal opportunity, 12, 41, 44, 48, 57, 73, 81, 100, 169–70, 182, 192, 251; funding, 21, 55, 80, 84, 104, 156–58, 175, 178, 211–12, 229, 231–32, 246, 250, 252, 259, 268–69; political structure of, 14–15; prioritization of, xii, 213; quality of, xi–xii, 6–7, 13–15, 32, 34, 39, 42, 45, 75, 124, 129, 154, 160, 165, 173, 177, 187, 197, 202, 229–30, 248, 254, 265, 269. *See also* academic performance; curriculum; school districts; schools
Education for All Handicapped Children Act of 1975, 21, 209, 212, 214–15, 246, 249. *See also*

Individuals with Disabilities Education Act of 1990
Education Week, 192
Ehrlichman, John, 118
Eisenhower, Dwight, 66
Elementary and Secondary Education Act of 1965, 16, 63, 67, 84, 209–12, 245
Emergency School Aid Act of 1972, 214, 245
English proficiency, 21, 129, 152, 165, 170, 215, 217, 246, 250. *See also* bilingual education
Epp, Charles, 19
Equal Educational Opportunity Act of 1974, 214
Equal Protection clause, xi, 10–11, 27, 29–30, 38, 86, 138, 198, 224. *See also* Fourteenth Amendment
evenness index, 51, 199–204, 207, 255
Every Student Succeeds Act of 2015, 214, 248
evidence (in court). *See* social-science evidence
exposure indexes, 51, 199–201, 204, 207, 255

Fair Housing Act of 1968, 67
Faubus, Orval, 66
Faulkner, William, x
federal courts: and abstraction, 60; authority of, 1–3, 26, 33–35, 59–60, 73, 98–99, 146–47, 174, 184, 188; decentralization of, 16–17, 23, 62, 150, 163, 179, 260; distrust of southern officials, 37; initiating education reform, 14–15, 32, 34, 44, 75–76, 103–4; political makeup of, 8, 93, 159–60; relationship with agencies, 20–22, 44, 102–3; role of, 57, 191, 259; uniform standards for, 94–95. *See also* circuit courts; institutions; Supreme Court
Federalist Five, 184
Federal Register, 85, 258, 280n16
Federal Rules of Civil Procedure, 149, 153
Ferguson, Ronald, 249
Fifth Circuit: caseload of, 94, 101; confronting obstruction, 156; critiques of, 120–21; jurisdiction of, 39–40, 101–2; prominent figures of, 93–94, 283n39; relationship with Department of Health, Education, and Welfare, 44, 64, 69–70, 83, 88, 97; structural changes of, 71, 103–4, 121. *See also* circuit courts
Finch, Robert, 285n28
Finger, John, 149
Fiss, Owen, 17, 36, 102, 113, 146, 163
Fletcher, Jason, 55–56
Fletcher, William A., 102, 150
Floyd, George, 269
Ford, Gerald, 62
Fortas, Abe, 38, 116
Fourteenth Amendment, 27–28, 32, 38–39, 237. *See also* Equal Protection clause
Fox, Noel P., 159
Frankfurter, Felix, 13–14, 47, 66, 257

"freedom of choice" plans, 35–37, 63–64, 70–71, 89–101, 112, 114, 120, 123, 267. *See also* admissions policies; "controlled choice" plans
Freeman v. Pitts, 43, 76–77, 183, 187–90, 194, 262
Frey, William, 6
From Jim Crow to Civil Rights (Klarman), 37
funding termination, 20–21, 63, 69, 83–88, 103–4, 210–22, 233, 242, 247, 254–58. *See also* Civil Rights Act of 1964

Gamoran, Adam, 199, 202
Gardner, John, 92, 102–3
Garment, Leonard, 118
Garrity, W. Arthur, Jr., 147, 166, 173
Gershenson, Seth, 269
gifted-and-talented programs, 157
Ginsburg, Ruth Bader, 218, 222
globalization, 5
goal displacement, xii, 180
Godbold, John Cooper, 100
Goldberg, Arthur, 38
Gordon, Nora, 240
Graglia, Lino, 125
Graham, Hugh Davis, 68, 84, 215, 253
Green v. County School Board of New Kent County, 10, 37–43, 64, 72–74, 95, 105–16, 123–36, 182, 187, 190, 197, 256, 284n2

Hain, Elwood, 174
Halpern, Stephen, 103, 218, 258–59
Hamilton, Alexander, 259
Hannah-Jones, Nikole, xi, 3–4, 265
Hansen, Michael, 269
Harlan, John Marshall, 10–11, 27–28, 115, 121, 125
Harris, Kamala, 1–3
Haynsworth, Clement, 112
Heckman, James, 49
Hess, Frederick, xiii, 16
Hispanic students: and busing, 31, 170; growing population of, 7, 62, 75, 152, 165; and interest groups, 155; and measuring segregation, 200; and racial balance, 123, 131. *See also* bilingual education
Hochschild, Jennifer, 251–52
housing subsidies, 161
Howe, Harold, II, 85, 90, 92
Humphrey, Hubert (senator), 86

Ifill, Sherrilyn, 3
"I Have a Dream" (King), 19
individuality, 30, 38, 96, 112–13. *See also* racial identity
Individuals with Disabilities Education Act of 1990, 21, 262. *See also* Education for All Handicapped Children Act of 1975

institutions: building of, ix; capacity of, 44; and division of labor, 106; failures of, 142–43; and federalism, 32–33; structure of, 9, 13–19, 60–61, 101, 179, 209–10, 257–58. *See also* federal courts; *and specific institutions*
integration: definitions of, 5–6, 44, 50, 96, 262; requirement of, 95; unclear guidance for, 27. *See also* desegregation

Jackson, Candice, 245
Jim Crow, xi, xii, 13, 31, 34, 46–48, 101, 169, 182. *See also* racism; segregation
Johnson, Frank, 93, 102, 119–20, 147, 159
Johnson, Lyndon B., xii, 36, 62, 68, 85, 116, 212, 283n59
Johnson, Rucker, 55, 193, 204–5
Johnson v. San Francisco Unified School District, 169
Jones, Nathaniel, 154
Justice, William Wayne, 159

Kansas City, Missouri, School District, 156, 176–78
Katzenbach, Nicholas, 93
Katzmann, Robert, 160–61
Kendi, Ibram X., 251
Kennedy, Anthony, 7, 10, 30, 34, 77, 143, 184, 188, 227
Kennedy, Ted, 213
Keppel, Francis, 70, 85–86, 88, 216–17
Kerner Commission, 112
Keyes v. School District No. 1, Denver, 9–12, 64–65, 73–74, 107–8, 123–31, 137, 152–57, 171
King, Martin Luther, Jr., 19, 29–30, 72, 108, 112, 192
Kirp, David, 18, 44, 147, 149–50, 156, 164, 173
Klarman, Michael, 37
Kolski, William, 170
Krupansky, Robert, 176, 196

Lacoe, Johanna, 243
Ladd, Helen, 195–96, 199–201
Latino students. *See* Hispanic students
Lau v. Nichols, 220, 223, 247
Leadership Conference on Civil Rights, 78
Lee County, 101
legal abstraction, 115–16, 125, 127–28, 143, 260, 284n2
Let Them Be Judged (Read and McGough), 283n39
Levesque, Roger, 18, 46–47, 50, 59, 203
Lhamon, Catherine E., 228
Lichtman, Elliot, 218–19
Lieberman, Robert, 19–20
Liebowitz, David, 205
Limbaugh, Stephen, 197
Lindsay, Constance, 269
Little Rock, AR, 66, 151, 259
Lutz, Byron, 274n51

INDEX

MacMillan, James, 12, 42, 75, 124, 126, 145, 157–58, 168
Maddox, Lester, 118
majority-to-minority transfers, 128, 166
Marshall, John, 259
Marshall, Thurgood, 11–12, 28, 41–47, 77, 115, 121, 125, 136, 139, 184–87, 283n59
Matsch, Richard, 13, 43, 162, 171
May, Benjamin E., 266
McClure, Phyllis, 214
McDaniel v. Barresi, 109
McGough, Lucy, 94, 283n39
McGovern, George, 2
McGuinn, Patrick, 213
McMahon, Kevin, 118
Merhige, Robert, 134
Mexican American Legal Defense and Education Fund (MALDEF), 170, 220
Miller, George, 213
Milliken v. Bradley, 12, 32, 41, 64–65, 73, 107–8, 123, 132–42, 156, 163, 173, 178, 190–91, 256
Missouri v. Jenkins, 76, 109, 156, 163, 176, 178, 183–84, 190–91, 194
Mitchell, John, 118
Moffitt, Susan, 211
Moore, Monika, 184
Moran, Rachel, 171
Moynihan, Pat, 118
Myrdal, Gunner, 28

National Assessment of Educational Progress (NAEP), 4, 57
National Association for the Advancement of Colored People (NAACP): accepting termination orders, 198; and busing, 173; caseload of, 67–68, 93, 101; and changing demographics, 171; and color-blindness, 10–12, 28; contemporary positions of, 3; and defining desegregation, 100; disagreements among, 266; and "freedom of choice" plans, 37, 114, 120; legal strategy of, 66, 122, 134, 153–54, 156–57; and racial isolation, 43, 45; report on federal funding, 211; and resegregation, 192; and social-science evidence, 34, 46, 262
National Bureau of Economic Research (NBER), 55
National Education Association, 235
Nation at Risk, A, 213
New Kent County, 115–16. See also *Green v. County School Board of New Kent County*
New Republic, 125
Nixon, Richard, 2, 16–17, 62, 72, 106, 108, 116–20, 217–18, 220, 256
No Child Left Behind (NCLB), 78–80, 198, 208, 210, 213–15, 248, 261
NYC v. Harris, 109

Oakes, Jeannie, 170
Obama, Barack, x, 5, 8, 21, 23, 62–65, 78–80, 210–13, 224, 235–37, 244–47, 261
O'Connor, Sandra Day, 30–31, 143, 184
Office for Civil Rights (OCR), 16, 44; authority of, 83–84, 216, 258; creating desegregation plans, 87; critics of, 87–88; guidelines from, 88, 223, 231; investigatory power, 219–22, 224–25, 231, 233, 236, 240–42; and local conditions, 103–5; priorities of, 117–18. See also Department of Health, Education, and Welfare; Office of Education
Office of Education (OE), 70, 85–86. See also Office for Civil Rights
Oklahoma City v. Dowell, 184–87
Orfield, Gary, 4, 13, 82, 84, 87, 89–92, 128, 192, 217
Orrick, William, 162, 169–70
out-of-school punishments, x, 238–39, 243–44. See also discipline
Owens, Ann, 56

Panetta, Leon, 106, 117, 217
parallel tracks, 70, 86, 102–4, 209, 256
Parents Involved in Community Schools v. Seattle School District No. 1, 7–8, 11–12, 29–31, 65, 79, 195, 206, 227, 261, 263, 276n21
Parker, Wendy, 193
Pasadena v. Spangler, 137, 167–68, 188
Peckham, Robert, 161–62, 170
Pena, Federico, 171
Peterson, Paul, 252–53
Pettigrew, Thomas, 49–50, 124
Pettigrew thesis, 49
Plessy v. Ferguson, 10–11, 27–28, 66
Potter, Robert, 162
Pottinger, Stanley, 117, 217
poverty, 39, 80, 211, 239, 248, 250. See also socioeconomic status
Powell, Adam Clayton, 210–11
Powell, Lewis, 10, 32–33, 72, 107–8, 110, 130, 134, 138, 140–41, 151, 184
Pratt, John H., 217–19, 221
preventative injunction, 147
private litigation, 87, 215–16, 222–25, 247
private schools, 16, 33, 151, 169, 178–79
psychology, 28
public interest litigation, 153–57
"pull-out" programs, 211–12
Putnam, Robert, 51

Quigley, James, 84
quotas, xii, 14, 31, 71, 78, 93–98, 119, 126–33, 137, 143–44, 165–69, 177–78, 197, 256. See also racial balance; racial identification of schools

Rabkin, Jeremy, 220
Race to the Top, 78–80

racial balance: ambiguity of, 104–6, 114, 145, 165, 179; consequences of, 154, 180, 202; critics of, 77, 92, 126, 188; educational benefits, 1–7, 12, 57, 267; ideal of, 63–64; maintenance of, 185, 255; measurement of, 34–35, 40, 42, 167; as ongoing process, 31; prioritization of, 71, 74–75, 122, 128, 141, 172, 265–66. *See also* quotas
racial gerrymandering, 123, 166. *See also* attendance zones
racial identification of schools, 14, 17, 74, 96, 113, 115, 134, 139, 165, 182
racial identity, 5, 10–11, 28–31, 38, 96, 155, 170. *See also* individuality
racial isolation, xi, 11–14, 22, 38–50, 54, 62–64, 74, 115, 123–36, 176–180, 124, 128–36, 176–77, 180, 198, 201, 226–27. *See also* white flight
racial isolation/equal educational opportunity position, 22, 26, 35–44, 59, 73, 79, 108, 182, 186, 206, 255. *See also* color-blind/limited intervention position
Racial Isolation in the Public Schools (United States Commission on Civil Rights), 11–12, 40–41
racial mixing, 126
racism: acceptance of, 4; contemporary forms of, x–xi, 4; legacies of, xii, 265; and morality, 62–63, 119; in northern states, x–xi; systemic forms, 4, 7–8. *See also* antiracism; discrimination; Jim Crow; white supremacy
Radin, Beryl, 87–90, 103
Raleigh, NC, 87
Read, Frank, 94, 101, 121, 283n39
Reagan, Ronald, 213, 221
Real, Manuel, 137
Reardon, Sean, 18, 56, 193, 201, 205
Rehabilitation Act of 1973, 209, 217
Rehnquist, William, 32–33, 72–76, 108–10, 130, 137–46, 184–91, 224
remedial education programs, 77, 186
reparative injunction, 147
resegregation, x, 4, 6, 23, 65, 77, 192, 198–202, 255. *See also* segregation
resource equity, 212–13, 229–32
Richard, Meredith, 199
Rives, Richard, 94
Roberts, John, 31, 224, 227
Robinson, Sue, 10, 146, 172, 196–97
Rockoff, Jonah, 205
Rossell, Christine, 167, 288n29
Roth, Stephen, 134–36, 159–60, 162, 172, 174
Rubin, Carl, 140–41, 161
Ryan, James, 288n29

Saguy, Abigail, 20
Salomone, Rosemary, 297n35
San Antonio v. Rodriguez, 233

Sanders, Barefoot, 162
San Francisco Unified School District, 156
Saturday Review of Literature, 85–86, 258, 280n16
Saunders, Thomas, 288n29
Scalia, Antonin, 36, 184, 189, 224
Scamman, James, 168
Scarlett, Frank, 94
Schofield, Janet Ward, 46, 50–51, 57–58, 60
school districts: accreditation of, 178; boundaries of, 123–24, 132–33; court authority over, 149; demographics of, 124; differences among, 150; direct negotiation with, 88; embrace of litigation, 157–59, 194–95, 206; independence of, 8, 15, 18; sizes of, 56, 73, 87, 99, 115, 152, 164; supervision of, 45, 59–60, 77, 102, 149, 171, 174, 184, 194–95; unknown number under court order, 18, 77, 192, 274n51. *See also* education
schools: as coping organizations, 274n46; facilities, 231; local conditions in, xiii, 50–51, 57, 60–61, 74–75, 80, 103–4, 150, 165, 173–74; local control over, 32, 45, 57, 153–55, 178, 185, 252, 266; locations of, 148, 175, 182; racial mixing in, 43; student assignment to classrooms, 197. *See also* education; teachers
School Superintendents' Association, 242
school to prison pipeline, x, 80, 236–37. *See also* discipline
Schwartz, Bernard, 125
Scovronick, Nathan, 251–52
Seeley, David, 85
segregation: effects of, 11–12, 26–29, 31–32, 38, 41, 43, 46–48, 96, 114, 124, 132–33, 135, 174, 186; evidence of, 17, 35, 45, 73, 128–30, 133–35, 145, 148, 151, 154, 165, 190; as a "group phenomenon," 96; maintenance of, 35–36; measurement of, 199–201, 204, 207; remedy-shaping, 18; and residential patterns, 134–37; sources of, 40; vestiges of, 77, 169, 185, 191. *See also* de jure/de facto distinction; desegregation; discrimination; Jim Crow; resegregation; tracking
separate but equal, 27, 66, 228. See also *Plessy v. Ferguson*
Siegel, Reva, 38–39
Singleton v. Jackson Municipal School District, 92, 94
"1619 Project" (Hannah-Jones), xi, 3–4
Skrentny, John, 40, 93
Sobeloff, Simon, 267–68
social-science evidence, 26–29, 34–49, 54–60, 115, 239–40, 257, 262, 278n76. *See also specific decisions*
socioeconomic status (SES): and academic performance, 48–49, 172, 213, 248, 250; and dropout rates, 58; and education spending levels, 80; as factor for school assignment, 7–8; and student

assignment, 263; and white flight, 152. *See also* poverty
Souter, David, 184, 188, 191
"Southern Manifesto," 13–14
southern strategy, 108, 117
special education programs, 21, 43, 173
Stancil, Will, 4
standards and accountability regime, 78–80, 207–8, 213, 229, 246
Steinberg, Matthew, 243
Stevens, John Paul, 30, 108, 111, 139, 187, 223
Stewart, Potter, 108, 121, 125, 133, 136, 140–41, 143, 184
stigmatization, 46–48, 77, 115, 186, 211
St. John, Nancy, 50–51
Stroub, Kori, 199
structural injunctions: embrace by school districts, 157–59; flexibility of, 17–18, 186–87, 260; frequency of, 167–68; goals of, 147; invention of, ix, 17, 146, 179; length of, 65, 181–82, 185, 206; and school funding, 86; scope of, 102, 149–50, 160–61, 163, 190; termination of, 76–78, 162, 169, 171, 174, 183, 188, 192–98. *See also* desegregation
Supreme Court: absence and silence of, x, 14, 65, 72, 82, 102, 141, 172; ambiguity of rulings, 9–13, 23–24, 26–29, 59, 62, 66, 115, 122, 125–27, 134, 142, 163, 179, 184, 224, 259–60; defining "unitary" status, 76, 181–83; division of, 7, 29, 64, 72, 107–8, 125, 135–36, 143, 188; and the Fifth Circuit, 94, 104–5, 119, 121; limiting available remedies, 137–38, 148, 190, 263; and private right of action, 222, 247; review of desegregation orders, 119–20, 128, 139, 168, 178; role of, 17, 142–44, 259; voting patterns, 109–11, 183. *See also* federal courts; *and specific cases and justices*
Swann v. Charlotte-Mecklenburg Board of Education, 12, 64–66, 73–75, 107–9, 123–36, 157–58, 184–85, 203–6, 218, 260–61

Tatel, David, 221
Taylor, William, 162
teachers: assignment of, 14, 42, 91, 102, 119, 175, 187, 235; diversity of, 269; effectiveness of, 254; licensure and certification, 230, 235; responsibility for implementing policy, 16, 80; salaries, 191. *See also* schools
teachers' unions, 213, 235
testing, 15, 43, 57–58, 75, 203–4, 213, 248–49, 251. *See also* tracking
Thomas, Clarence, 29–31, 34, 184, 188, 268, 276n21
Thompson, Myron, 197, 206
Thompson, Owen, 55–56
Thornberry, Homer, 94
Thurmond, Strom, 117

Title VI: and affirmative action, 65; as controversial, 85; and disparate impact, 228; drafting of, 84; enforcement mechanisms, 69, 87, 92, 103, 117, 215–18, 247, 257–58; guidelines of, 20, 79, 209–10, 216–17; and intentional discrimination, 240; interpretation of, x, 23, 233; and school discipline, 237; scope of, 261. *See also* Civil Rights Act of 1964
Title IX, 20–21, 209, 217, 234, 236, 248–49
Tocqueville, Alexis de, 252
tracking, 14, 21, 43, 75, 81, 102, 157, 173, 197, 249, 267. *See also* testing
Truman, Harry, 62
Trump, Donald, 8, 62, 65, 80, 225, 227, 236, 244–45
Tuttle, Elbert, 94

unitary status: beyond student body demographics, 42–43; indicators of, 10–11, 23, 65, 152, 169, 171, 178; as legal abstraction, 60, 260; opposition to, 195; and racial balance, 40, 73, 105, 266; uncertainty of, 70, 76, 96, 113, 119, 122, 134, 145–46, 164, 181–82, 185, 189, 198. *See also* desegregation
United States: compared to European nations, 19–20, 252; decentralized education system, 15, 252–53; legacies of racial oppression, x; systemic racism in, 4. *See also* civil rights state
United States Commission on Civil Rights, 11–12, 40–41, 73, 114, 128, 193
United States Commission on Equity and Excellence in Education, 228
U.S. v. Jefferson County Board of Education, 22, 64, 69–71, 82, 93–103, 112, 116, 256
U.S. v. Montgomery County Board of Education, 119
U.S. v. Scotland Neck City Board of Education, 123, 132, 134

Vigdor, Jacob, 195–96, 199–201, 205–6
Vinson, Fred, 66
voting rights, 67, 93
Voting Rights Act of 1965, 67

Wallace, George, 2, 118, 135, 253
Warren, Earl, 10, 27–29, 37, 46–48, 66, 72, 74, 108–16, 124, 150, 202, 232, 249, 257
Washington v. Davis, 138
Washington v. Seattle School District #1, 109
Weber, Max, 25
Weigel, Stanley, 159, 162, 169, 290n12
Weinstein, Jack, 159–60, 173
"We-Stink Defense," 158
Whipple, Dean, 162, 178
White, Byron, 108, 115, 121, 125, 138–39
white flight, xi, 6, 16, 33, 42, 48, 56, 134, 151–52, 167, 172, 177, 256. *See also* demographic changes; racial isolation
white supremacy, xi, 3, 253, 269. *See also* racism

Wilkinson, J. Harvie, 101
Wilson, James Q., 15, 254
Wisdom, John Minor, 69–70, 82–83, 92, 94–105, 113, 116
Wolf, Eleanor, 42, 160
Wolk, Allan, 85
Women's Equality Action League (WEAL), 220
Woodward, Bob, 120, 125

Wright, J. Skelly, 93, 159, 173
Wright v. Council of City of Emporia, 123, 132–33

Yale Law Journal, 103, 184
Yarborough, Ralph, 212
Young, Coleman, 153–54

Zippel, Kathrin, 20

The Chicago Series in Law and Society
Edited by John M. Conley, Charles Epp, and Lynn Mather

Series titles, continued from front matter

This Is Not Civil Rights: Discovering Rights Talk in 1939 America
by George I. Lovell

Failing Law Schools
by Brian Z. Tamanaha

Everyday Law on the Street: City Governance in an Age of Diversity
by Mariana Valverde

Lawyers in Practice: Ethical Decision Making in Context
edited by Leslie C. Levin and Lynn Mather

Collateral Knowledge: Legal Reasoning in the Global Financial Markets
by Annelise Riles

Specializing the Courts
by Lawrence Baum

Asian Legal Revivals: Lawyers in the Shadow of Empire
by Yves Dezalay and Bryant G. Garth

The Language of Statutes: Laws and Their Interpretation
by Lawrence M. Solan

Belonging in an Adopted World: Race, Identity, and Transnational Adoption
by Barbara Yngvesson

Making Rights Real: Activists, Bureaucrats, and the Creation of the Legalistic State
by Charles R. Epp

Lawyers of the Right: Professionalizing the Conservative Coalition
by Ann Southworth

Arguing with Tradition: The Language of Law in Hopi Tribal Court
by Justin B. Richland

Speaking of Crime: The Language of Criminal Justice
by Lawrence M. Solan and Peter M. Tiersma

Human Rights and Gender Violence: Translating International Law into Local Justice
by Sally Engle Merry

Just Words, Second Edition: Law, Language, and Power
by John M. Conley and William M. O'Barr

Distorting the Law: Politics, Media, and the Litigation Crisis
by William Haltom and Michael McCann

Justice in the Balkans: Prosecuting War Crimes in the Hague Tribunal
by John Hagan

Rights of Inclusion: Law and Identity in the Life Stories of Americans with Disabilities
by David M. Engel and Frank W. Munger

The Internationalization of Palace Wars: Lawyers, Economists, and the Contest to Transform Latin American States
by Yves Dezalay and Bryant G. Garth

Free to Die for Their Country: The Story of the Japanese American Draft Resisters in World War II
by Eric L. Muller

Overseers of the Poor: Surveillance, Resistance, and the Limits of Privacy
by John Gilliom

Pronouncing and Persevering: Gender and the Discourses of Disputing in an African Islamic Court
by Susan F. Hirsch

The Common Place of Law: Stories from Everyday Life
by Patricia Ewick and Susan S. Silbey

The Struggle for Water: Politics, Rationality, and Identity in the American Southwest
by Wendy Nelson Espeland

Dealing in Virtue: International Commercial Arbitration and the Construction of a Transnational Legal Order
by Yves Dezalay and Bryant G. Garth

Rights at Work: Pay Equity Reform and the Politics of Legal Mobilization
by Michael W. McCann

The Language of Judges
by Lawrence M. Solan

Reproducing Rape: Domination through Talk in the Courtroom
by Gregory M. Matoesian

Getting Justice and Getting Even: Legal Consciousness among Working-Class Americans
by Sally Engle Merry

Rules versus Relationships: The Ethnography of Legal Discourse
by John M. Conley and William M. O'Barr

Printed and bound by CPI Group (UK) Ltd, Croydon, CR0 4YY
02/02/2025

14636546-0004